LORENZO DI FILIPPO STROZZI AND NICCOLÒ MACHIAVELLI

Patron, Client, and the *Pistola fatta per la peste*

Lorenzo di Filippo Strozzi and Niccolò Machiavelli

Patron, Client, and the *Pistola fatta per la peste* / *An Epistle Written Concerning the Plague*

WILLIAM J. LANDON

UNIVERSITY OF TORONTO PRESS
Toronto Buffalo London

Toronto Buffalo London
www.utppublishing.com

ISBN 978-1-4426-4424-3

Library and Archives Canada Cataloguing in Publication

Landon, William J., 1974–, author
Lorenzo di Filippo Strozzi and Niccolò Machiavelli: patron, client, and the Pistola fatta per la peste / an epistle written concerning the plague / William J. Landon.

(Toronto Italian studies)
Includes the Italian text of Pistola fatta per la peste with English translation.
Includes bibliographical references and index.
ISBN 978-1-4426-4424-3 (bound)

1. Strozzi, Lorenzo di Filippo, 1482–1547. 2. Strozzi, Lorenzo di Filippo, 1482–1547 – Influence. 3. Strozzi, Lorenzo di Filippo, 1482–1547. Pistola fatta per la peste – Criticism, Textual. 4. Machiavelli, Niccolò, 1469–1527. 5. Plague in literature. 6. Authors, Italian – 16th century – Biography. I. Title II. Series: Toronto Italian studies

PQ4634.S825Z75 2013 853'.3 C2013-904361-6

This book has been published with the assistance of a grant from the Dean of the College of Arts and Sciences, Professor Samuel Zachary, at Northern Kentucky University.

University of Toronto Press acknowledges the financial assistance to its publishing program of the Canada Council for the Arts and the Ontario Arts Council.

University of Toronto Press acknowledges the financial support of the Government of Canada through the Canada Book Fund for its publishing activities.

For my wife, Carla,
and
my daughters, Florence and Beatrice,
and the late Ron Schoeffel,
without whom this book would not have been possible

Contents

Acknowledgments

Researching and writing this book often took me away from my family for extended periods of time. Whether I was away in Italy or locked in my office, my wife, Carla, and my daughters, Florence and Beatrice, were loving, patient, and supportive of me, though I infrequently deserved it. For their constancy, their kindness, their long-suffering, and their matchless grace, I dedicate this book without reservation to the loves of my life. Though Carla, Florence, and Beatrice are the recipients of my greatest esteem and affection, many others without whom this book would never have been realized also deserve special mention.

My parents, Dr George and Mrs Kathleen Landon, who raised me in a home where courtesy and politeness were revered, trained me for the rigours of academic life in the very best way possible. Professor Massimo Ciavolella initially suggested that I send my manuscript on Lorenzo Strozzi and Niccolò Machiavelli to Ron Schoeffel at the University of Toronto Press. Without Massimo's guidance and interest in my research, I would never have had the pleasure of working with Ron, who over many months patiently coaxed this book out of me, encouraging me and pushing me in the right direction. Both Massimo and Ron are gentleman of the sort who remind me why I became an academic in the first place. On the topic of gentlemen, Professor Richard Mackenney, my PhD supervisor and dear friend, provided me with the erudite advice that only he can muster. We spent many hours in conversation, working through problematic areas in our research and sharing breakthroughs. Richard's wife, Margaret, was likewise a source of friendship and encouragement. Professor Robert Davis's finely crafted comments and criticism, especially on my biography of Strozzi, undoubtedly made it better; I am indebted to him. Dr Simone Testa, my old friend from our days at Edinburgh, provided me with a number of important suggestions and insights. His knowledge of the early sixteenth-century Florentine dialect was invaluable. Similarly, Professor William J. Connell has been a source of tremendous insight and stimulation. Professor Brian Richardson deserves special mention, as he provided me with excellent comments on my edition of the *Pistola*, saving me from a number of errors. My colleague Dr Hilary Landwehr's expertise was appreciated more than she knew. I am also grateful to Professor Stephen Greenblatt for chairing a panel that I organized entitled "Renaissance Self-Fashioning Reconsidered." Professor Greenblatt's research continues to influence my own. I might also say the same of Professor Lauro Martines, whose scholarship, in many ways, proved foundational to this book.

The advice provided by the anonymous external readers, and by Toronto's internal Manuscript Review Committee, was as helpful as it was thorough. I thank each and every one of the scholars who read my book. My friends Michael Vaughn, Terry Fleming, and Dr Michael Templeton all made helpful comments on drafts of my manuscript. Professor Owen Dudley Edwards, via Richard Mackenney, suggested some very helpful readings that shaped the final version of this book. Beatrice Paolozzi Strozzi, director of the Bargello Museum in Florence, was especially kind to me. My former students Bernard Harpe, Leah Presser, Ryanne Schroder, and Glenn Bramble all endured numerous lectures on Lorenzo Strozzi and Niccolò Machiavelli. Their good-natured and intelligent reactions to my research were useful on many levels. I also thank the directors of the Biblioteca Medicea Laurenziana, the Biblioteca Nazionale Centrale di Firenze, and the Museo del Bargello for allowing me to reproduce manuscript pages and artwork held in their collections. The Interlibrary Loan librarians Cristen Ross, John Schlipp, Erin Smith, and Danny Lovell at the W. Frank Steely Library, Northern Kentucky University, worked tirelessly on my behalf and managed to track down texts that were essential to my research. My copy editor, Terry Teskey, was as ruthless as she was excellent; and my indexer, Alexander Trotter, produced an index that I am sure the reader will find helpful. Additionally, I wish to thank Louise D'Amboise, who was responsible for typesetting my book. Dealing with the presentational complexities of the *Pistola*'s edition was no small task, and she handled it with great skill. By the same token, Anne Laughlin, managing editor, patiently dealt with many messages and queries from me, and deftly handled the highly challenging production of these pages: thank you, Anne. I am also indebted to Samuel Zachary, dean of the College of Arts and Sciences, and to Professors Paul Tenkotte and Jeffrey Williams (who were successive chairs of my department as I wrote this book) at Northern Kentucky University for making the publication of this book possible.

Finally, Paul Oskar Kristeller's words concerning the necessity of editing works by lesser-known Renaissance scholars, Lorenzo di Filippo Strozzi in this case, became my motto. While it might be a stretch to consider the astronomically wealthy Strozzi as a representative of "the average mentality" of his age, all of the other prerequisites outlined by Kristeller are met by the *Pistola*, Strozzi, and his relationship with Niccolò Machiavelli:

> Scholars, especially younger ones, should be encouraged to edit as well as to study anything that interests them. In a time that professes to be against elitism (a prejudice which I do not share) and that on these grounds favours social history, a case may be made for the lesser authors as representatives of the average mentality of their age. Minor texts can be of great interest for the relations of their authors with greater contemporaries or with famous circles, for literary genres (*sit venia verbo*), themes, style and language of the texts themselves, and for a variety of other reasons.[1]

Earlier in the same lecture, Kristeller wrote that the "labour and expenses of [producing] critical editions especially at a time when public interest and support for these studies has been shrinking" is made all the more problematic when "this kind of work is held in less esteem than it was some time ago."[2] While I would never dare to suggest that Kristeller would have found my work on the *Pistola* to possess any merit, I am grateful that my editor, Ron Schoeffel, did. Furthermore, I am grateful that the University of Toronto Press, through editors like Ron, continues to encourage the publication of all sorts of texts, canonical and unknown. Ron is referred to as the "Erasmus of Toronto" for a reason. While this book is dedicated first and foremost to my wife and daughters, it is also dedicated to Ron Schoeffel, whose willingness to support young scholars and commitment to the dissemination of knowledge through print is unparalleled.

1 Paul Oskar Kristeller, *Studies in Renaissance Thought and Letters*, vol. 4 (Rome: Edizioni di Storia e Letteratura, 1996), 458.

2 Kristeller, *Studies in Renaissance Thought*, 457–8.

In Memoriam

Ronald Martin Schoeffel

I wrote the acknowledgments above on 24 May 2013. I have chosen to leave them as originally written as a testament to and celebration of Ron's life and friendship.

After hearing that Ron's beloved wife Jone had passed away, my spirit was stirred to share my acknowledgments with him in advance of this book's publication, and I am so glad that I did. In our correspondence that followed, Ron, in his usual kind and gentle fashion, invited me and my family to his home for dinner. In a better world, we would have met on 2 August, but here we are. On 9 July 2013 I received the news that Ron had gone on to join his wife. I never had the pleasure of meeting Ron in person and I regret that tremendously. But I count myself very lucky to have worked closely with him for nearly four years. Turning to Ron's family, and especially to his sons and grandchildren, I send my thanks for sharing such a wonderful man with the world, and I send you my heartfelt condolences and sincerest prayers for healing.

POSTQUAM [RONALDUS] E VITA MIGRAVIT
HISTORIA LUGET ELOQUENTIA MUTA EST
FERTURQUE MUSAS TUM GRAECAS TUM
LATINAS LACRIMAS TENERE NON POTUISSE

Upon Ronald's departure from this life
History is in mourning, eloquence struck dumb
The Muses, Greek and Latin alike,
Are unable to hold back their tears.[1]

1 This Latin inscription is found on the tomb of Florence's greatest republican chancellor, Leonardo Bruni, who was also one of the most brilliant and humane thinkers in the city's long history. Ron Schoeffel was a man after Bruni's own heart. I made one small change to the original, replacing "Leonardus" with "Ronaldus."

Notes on Translations and Editions Used

Except where otherwise noted, the translations in the text that follows are mine. For Italian editions of works by Lorenzo di Filippo Strozzi, I used the "standard" texts, nearly all of which were published in the nineteenth century. Those works are: *La Vita di Filippo Strozzi* [Il Giovane], edited by G.B. Niccolini (1847); *La Vita di Filippo Strozzi il Vecchio*, edited by Giuseppe Bini and Pietro Bigazzi (1851); *Le Vite degli Uomini Illustri della Casa Strozzi*, edited by Pietro Stromboli (1892); and the much more recent *Commedie: Commedia in versi, La Pisana, La Violante*, edited by Andrea Gareffi (1980). At times, Strozzi's original manuscripts provided better readings than the print editions listed above. In those instances, I refer the reader to the manuscripts themselves.

The two surviving manuscripts that I used to produce my edition and translation of Strozzi's *Pistola* are located in Florence's Biblioteca Medicea Laurenziana, Ashburnham 606 (Manuscript A in the study that follows) and in the Florentine Biblioteca Nazionale Centrale, Banco Rari 29 (Manuscript B). Unless otherwise noted, all quotations from the *Pistola* are from my Italian edition and English translation of the text, both of which are located below, following the concluding chapter of this study. Similarly, all references to Francesco Zeffi's *Vita* of Lorenzo Strozzi are from the new edition of his work that is found in appendix 2 of this study.

As for Machiavelli's works, which are cited with some frequency, I used Corrado Vivanti's three-volume *Opere* of Machiavelli published by Einaudi (1997–2005); the critical edition of Machiavelli's *Mandragola* edited by Pasquale Stoppelli (2005); and Machiavelli's *Lettere,* edited by Franco Gaeta. Many other editions are cited in this study, but the volumes produced by these Italian editors are most prominent.

LORENZO DI FILIPPO STROZZI AND NICCOLÒ MACHIAVELLI

Patron, Client, and the *Pistola fatta per la peste*

Introduction: An Interpretive Essay

Part 1: Foundations

There are those Florentines who, in the course of their lives, were far more influential than their inauspicious legacies suggest. While one is not working entirely in the dark in researching such Florentines, investigation is carried out in peripheral Renaissance shadows.[1] In those twilight studies, buried in footnotes and phrases dropped in passing, one might come across Lorenzo di Filippo Strozzi.[2] Traced back to their original sources, those notes and references reveal histories written by an excellent, detail-minded, humane, and often tender man;[3] and they also shed light on a poet and

1 "The biographer of Machiavelli cannot complain that he is working in the dark, for his hero lived in a generation that observed itself with more energy and objectivity than any since classical times" (John Rigby Hale, *Machiavelli and Renaissance Italy* [London: English University Press, 1966], 1).

2 One exception to this can be found in the work of Virgil Milani, who edited two of Strozzi's plays when he was a graduate student at the Catholic University of America in Washington, DC, and whose findings were never published. I am indebted to the librarians and interlibrary loan specialists at the W. Frank Steely Library at Northern Kentucky University for diligently helping to obtain copies of Milani's theses. Milani also wrote two brief articles on Strozzi's plays, published in 1965 and 1966. These are: Virgil I. Milani, "The Origins of the Spanish Braggart in Strozzi's *Commedia Erudita*," *Italica* 42, no. 3 (1965): 224–30; and Milani, "Boccaccio in Strozzi's *Commedia Erudita*," *Italica* 43, no. 4 (1966): 369–74.

3 Indicative of this, see the opening lines of Lorenzo Strozzi's biography of his father, Filippo: "Tanti e così grandi sono gli obblighi che hanno i figliuoli co' padri, che se la vita umana avesse più lungo corso di quello che la natura concede, niuno potrebbe mai esserne conoscitore non che remuneratore. Però non doverrà parere isconvenevole se io, che tra tutti gli altri sono al Padre mio obbligatissimo, col descrivere quali siano stati i

playwright of some talent. Strozzi's histories, plays, and poems are complemented by brief though splendid perversities written with the knowing and mischievous smile of a profane schoolboy.[4] Given that the city into which Lorenzo was born prided itself on its history, its economy, and its "appalling practical jokes," it is no surprise that Strozzi's historical and literary works reflect the temperament of Florence.[5]

Outside of his writing, in the tempest of late fifteenth- and early sixteenth-century Florentine politics, Strozzi proved himself to be able in every respect. Fabulously wealthy, he fluttered in and out of Medici Florence,

---

costumi, i modi, l'ottima e imitabil vita di quello, mi sforzerò mostrate qualche gratitudine de'suoi meriti verso di me" (*La Vita di Filippo Strozzi il Vecchio*, ed. Giuseppe Bini e Pietro Bigazzi [Florence: Tip. Della Casa Correzione, 1851], 5).

4 While Strozzi's works are covered in more detail in subsequent notes, it is worth listing his most important literary contributions to the Renaissance here. Strozzi wrote three plays: *La Commedia in versi*, *La Pisana*, and *La Violante*. More importantly, he wrote a number of important historical works detailing the history of his own family from its foundation to the death of his brother Filippo in 1537: *Le Vite degli Uomini Illustri della Casa Strozzi*, *La Vita di Filippo Strozzi* [Il Vecchio], and *La Vita di Filippo Strozzi* [Il Giovane]. He also wrote a number of burlesque and religious poems, some of which remain unpublished in the Ashburnham Codex 606 of the Biblioteca Medicea Laurenziana. After over one hundred years, the best general summary of Strozzi's literary output remains Pio Ferrieri's "Lorenzo di Filippo Strozzi e un codice Ashburnhamiano" in *Studi di storia e critica letteraria* (Milan: E. Trevisini, 1892): 221-332. In addition, Ferrieri published a handful of Strozzi's poems in his *Rime inedite di Lorenzo Strozzi* (Pavia, 1885). The University of Rome, La Sapienza has also made three of Strozzi's Carnival songs available online: http://www.bibliotecaitaliana.it/xtf/view?docId=bibit000704/bibit000704.xml&chunk.id=d4759e6817&toc.depth=1&toc.id=d4759e6817&brand=default.

5 "The Florentines were chiefly interested in making money and playing appalling practical jokes on stupid men" (Kenneth Clark, *Civilisation* [London: Folio Society, 1999], 76). For specific examples of this type of humour, see Lauro Martines, "The Fat Woodcarver," in *An Italian Sextet*, ed. Martines and Murtha Baca (New York: Marsilio, 1994), 171–213, and esp. 173. In that famous story, Antonio Manetti recounted a joke that Filippo Brunelleschi played on a friend of his known as Grasso, "the fat man." Grasso, a woodcarver, failed to turn up to a gathering of friends that included Brunelleschi and a number of wealthy individuals; the group was offended that a "simpleton" from a lower socio-economic background had snubbed them, so Brunelleschi hatched a plot to get even. "I would like to play an amusing joke on him of the sort which, in revenge for his not coming this evening, would bring us great pleasure and entertainment. If you play along with me, I'd love to do it. And I've just thought of the way: we'll make him believe that he has become someone else and that he's no longer Grasso the woodcarver" (173). This joke nearly drove Grasso mad. Such practical jokes rarely seem funny to the modern observer, but the Florentines found that type of vindictive humour delectable.

Savonarolan Florence, D'Este Ferrara, Venice, papal Rome, republican Florence, and Medici Florence with a natural grace befitting a socially nimble gentleman.[6] His biographer, Francesco Zeffi, summed up Strozzi's "ease" with the following words to his son Palla: "This is [true] as attested, that your [father] Lorenzo embodied [lit. "was"] the urbanity and the delights of his age, and [was] in all of his enterprises, honorable and grand."[7] In fact, Strozzi's impeccable manners, mild temperament and appearance of general ease personified that gentlemanly ideal famously called *sprezzatura*.[8] This quality was fundamental to Strozzi's uncanny ability not only to survive but also to thrive in any court, city, or country villa, and perhaps

6 "Selvaggia [Lorenzo's mother], however, had less interest in giving [Lorenzo and his older brother Filippo] the erudition of scholars than in rearing them as gentleman who would be able to move easily in the fashionable society of their time; and she certainly had no interest in preparing them for business" (Richard Goldthwaite, *Private Wealth in Renaissance Florence: A Study of Four Families* [Princeton: Princeton University Press, 1968], 80–1).

7 Francesco d'Antonio Zeffi da Empoli, "Un Ragionamento inedito di Francesco Zeffi sopra la Vita dell' Autore (Lorenzo di Filippo Strozzi)," in Lorenzo di Filippo Strozzi, *Le Vite degli Uomini Illustri della Casa Strozzi*, ed. Pietro Stromboli (Florence: Pei Tipi Salvadore Landi, 1892), ix. All quotations from Zeffi's *Vita* are drawn from appendix 2 of this study, which contains a new edition of Zeffi's work. See appendix 2, 15r 18–20. "Quésto è per confesso, che il uostro Lorenzo fù la gentilezza, e le delizie de suoi tempi, et in tutte le sue imprese honoreuole, e grandé."

8 By "gentleman," I mean a well-born, educated, often politically powerful man who moved in the highest circles of Renaissance society. A Renaissance gentleman such as Strozzi was as comfortable at court as he was writing poetry. In these pages I follow Castiglione's frequently quoted definition of *sprezzatura*: "I have discovered a universal rule which seems to apply more than any other in all human actions or words: namely, to steer away from affectation at all costs, as if it were a rough and dangerous reef, and (to use perhaps a novel word for it) to practice in all things a certain nonchalance [*sprezzatura*] which conceals all artistry and makes whatever one says or does seem uncontrived and effortless" (*Book of the Courtier*, trans. George Bull [New York: Penguin, 1976], 66–7). The original Italian is "Trovo una regula universalissima, la qual mi par valer circa questo in tutte le cose umane che si facciano o dicano più che alcuna altra, e ciò è fuggir quanto più si po, e come un asperissimo e pericoloso scoglio, la affettazione; e, per dir forse una nova parola, usar in ogni cosa una certa sprezzatura, che nasconda l'arte e dimostri ciò che si fa e dice venir fatto senza fatica e quasi sense pensarvi" (Baldassarre Castiglione, *Il libro del cortegiano*, ed. Walter Barberis [Turin: Einaudi, 1998], 128, I. 26). I would add that *sprezzatura,* though commonly translated as "nonchalance," involves making even the most difficult task appear to be effortless, and so is much more than nonchalance: following a theatrical motif, it signified the courtier's ability to perform without letting on that he was performing. This is how he "sold" himself to his prince. As

set him apart from his brother Filippo and from his friends and clients.[9] Certainly, that ability is amply demonstrated by the number of influential elected offices Strozzi held in Florence both under the Medici regime and under republican rule.[10] Only a society gadfly, an agreeable gentleman, and a serious politician rolled into one could pull off such a feat with so little apparent effort.[11] Lorenzo di Filippo Strozzi was, therefore, a fascinating man who deserves to be examined in detail, and so it is surprising to note that very little has been written about him. In fact, there has been no book-length study of either Strozzi or his literary works published in English. This is not to say that scholars have entirely neglected Strozzi, but rather that further research into his life (and especially into a little-known plague tract that was transcribed for Strozzi by Niccolò Machiavelli) might prove helpful in understanding some of the complexities of "gentlemanly" life in High Renaissance Florence and of manuscript production, and might even yield something new about Machiavelli himself.[12]

Harry Berger put it, a courtier utilizing *sprezzatura* acted as "if always under surveillance" (*The Absence of Grace:* Sprezzatura *and Suspicion in Two Renaissance Courtesy Books* [Stanford: Stanford University Press, 2000], 12).

9 The best and most recent study of Filippo Strozzi's life is Melissa Meriam Bullard, *Filippo Strozzi and the Medici: Favor and Finance in Sixteenth-Century Florence and Rome* (Cambridge: Cambridge University Press, 1980). It is well worth noting that Lorenzo and Filippo apparently shared the ability to succeed in republican and Medicean Florence, but Filippo, as has been well documented by Bullard, eventually rebelled against Medici rule, ending his life as a patriotic, romantic suicide. The classic English work on the life of Filippo Strozzi was written by T. Adolphus Trolloppe: *Filippo Strozzi: A History of the Last Days of Italian Liberty* (London: Chapman and Hall, 1860).

10 It is important to note that he did not hold public office in Florence until 1512, after the Medici restoration. Much more will be said on this in due course.

11 Bullard, *Filippo Strozzi*, 3. Bullard noted that Lorenzo (along with his younger brother Filippo) possessed the characteristics attributed to the former above.

12 In undertaking such a work, I am indebted to those scholars who have already contributed to our understanding of Strozzi's life and accomplishments. Prominent among these is Richard Goldthwaite, whose *Private Wealth in Renaissance Florence* contains a brief but elegantly written account of Lorenzo di Filippo Strozzi's life. Also prominent is Virgil Milani, whose unpublished theses on Strozzi's plays have been almost completely neglected, and Andrea Gareffi for notable critical, philological, and historical work on Strozzi's plays. Gareffi's contributions, in Italian, to the very small niche of Lorenzo di Filippo Strozzi studies are fundamental to any subsequent investigation. There are many others, to be sure, whose work will be noted reader in due course; here I will mention a further two, both much earlier works that make mention of Strozzi's contributions to literature in the Renaissance: Michaele Pocciantio Florentino, *Catalogus scriptorum florentinorum omnis generis* (Florence:

This study contains the first lengthy English biography of Lorenzo di Filippo Strozzi. The methodology employed to construct Strozzi's biography is firmly rooted in established Italian historiographical traditions, and it is especially indebted to the scholarship of Andrea Gareffi.[13] Gareffi's Italian biography of Strozzi is based upon a very close reading of Francesco Zeffi's *Vita* of Lorenzo Strozzi (c. 1529), and is supplemented with many other sources written during Strozzi's life.[14] For example, Gareffi's analysis of Zeffi's biography is complemented by other primary source materials from Strozzi's own historical works, Luca Landucci, Marino Sanuto, Jacopo Nardi, Paolo Giovio, and Giorgio Vasari to name a few; and he also relies on important secondary scholarship to tease out additional historical implications. My hope is that this new biography of Strozzi, being the first available in English, will be viewed as a small but important contribution to Anglophone Renaissance historiography and an essential step towards establishing Anglophone scholarship on the life of Lorenzo di Filippo Strozzi.

The first chapter's biography of Strozzi is followed by an examination of another neglected aspect of Lorenzo di Filippo Strozzi's life – his relationship with Niccolò Machiavelli. There is scholarly consensus on the facts

---

Apud Iunctum, 1589), 107; and P. Giulio Negri Ferrarese, *Istoria degli scrittori fiorentini* (Ferrara, 1727), 81. Both of those works were cited by Gareffi, *Commedie*, 35. Where Lorenzo's appearances in Anglophone, and even in Italian, historical works have been meagre, the Strozzi family, including Lorenzo's grandmother Alessandra Macinghi Strozzi, his father Filippo, and his brother Filippo "the younger," have been the subject of numerous admirable studies; those by Lorenzo Fabbri, Heather Gregory, Richard Goldthwaite, and Melissa Meriam Bullard are perhaps the best. See Fabbri, *Alleanza matrimoniale e patriziato nella Firenze del '400* (Florence: Leo S. Olschki, 1991); Strozzi, *Selected Letters of Alessandra Strozzi*, bilingual ed., trans. Heather Gregory (Berkeley: University of California Press, 1997); Goldthwaite, *The Building of Renaissance Florence: An Economic and Social History* (Baltimore: Johns Hopkins University Press, 1980); and Bullard, *Filippo Strozzi*. The reader should note that a great deal of the published scholarship dedicated to other members of the Strozzi family is in fact based upon the family histories written by Lorenzo di Filippo Strozzi, which are fundamental to any Strozzi-centric investigation based in the late fifteenth or early sixteenth centuries.

13 *La scrittura e la festa: Teatro, festa e letteratura nella Firenze del Rinascimento* (Bologna: Il Mulino, 1991), 107–22 contains Gareffi's biography of Strozzi.

14 There are, as Bullard noted (*Filippo Strozzi*, 3), letters written by Strozzi scattered throughout the Carte Strozziane of the Archivio di Stato, some of which might provide more detail about his "gentlemanly" behaviour, which is so frequently mentioned by Zeffi. These letters are rich potential fodder for future projects dedicated to Lorenzo Strozzi. However, Zeffi's biography has been fundamental, thus far, to Italian scholarship on Strozzi, and so it seems appropriate to make it the foundation for similar works in English, including this one.

that both men moved in the same intellectual circles at the Rucellai family's famous humanist haunt and orchard, the Orti Oricellari; that Machiavelli dedicated his *Arte della guerra* to Strozzi; and that Niccolò even copied two of Lorenzo's literary works. However, it has proven difficult to say more about their involvement with one another using "traditional" sources such as letters, as there is not a single surviving letter from Strozzi to Machiavelli or vice versa.[15] Pasquale Villari and Oreste Tommasini, to name only two of the most important contributors to nineteenth-century Renaissance studies, scoured the Strozzi archives, hoping to find some connection between Lorenzo and Niccolò – a connection that might explain why Machiavelli dedicated his *Arte* to Strozzi and why two of Strozzi's literary works survive as Machiavelli autographs.[16] Their investigations proved almost entirely unfruitful, with one notable exception. Tommasini edited and published *one* letter that shed a small ray of light on the Strozzi-Machiavelli relationship. That important letter was written by neither Lorenzo nor Niccolò, but by Filippo Strozzi to his older brother, Lorenzo.

In a letter dated 17 March 1520, Filippo expressed how pleased he was that Lorenzo had ushered Machiavelli into the good graces of Giulio de' Medici. From this, we might conclude that Filippo Strozzi and Machiavelli were on friendly terms. The fact that the two men also corresponded with one another on a number of occasions supports this conclusion.[17] However, there is no hard evidence to suggest that Lorenzo Strozzi was "friendly" with Machiavelli. By "conducting" Machiavelli into the circle of the Medici

---

15 Lorenzo Strozzi is mentioned in several of Machiavelli's letters, which are discussed in detail in chapter 2.

16 Oreste Tommasini, *La vita e gli scritti di Niccolò Machiavelli nella loro relazione col Machiavellismo: Storia ed esame critico di Oreste Tommasini*, 2 vols. (Turin: Ermano Loescher, 1883); Pasquale Villari, *Niccolò Machiavelli e i suoi tempi*, 3 vols. (Florence: Le Monnier, 1882). For an English translation of Villari's work, see *The Life and Times of Niccolò Machiavelli*, trans. Linda Villari, 3 vols. (London: Kegan Paul, Trench and Co., 1883).

17 There is only one extant letter from Filippo Strozzi to Machiavelli, dated 31 March 1526. Strozzi began the letter "a suo carissimo amico Niccolò di M. Bernardo Machiavelli," and he referred to Machiavelli as "Niccolò mio." In that letter, Filippo refers to other letters that Machiavelli wrote to him and also to his own, which were frequently late (Niccolò Machiavelli, *Opere, Volume Terzo: Lettere,* ed. Franco Gaeta [Turin: Unione Tipografico-Editrice Torinese, 1984], 582, letter 306). Filippo Strozzi also followed up with Machiavelli after Lorenzo "conducted" Machiavelli back into the Medici's good graces. For example, when Machiavelli was given his stipend for the *Istorie fiorentine*, Filippo Strozzi arranged for Machiavelli's salary to be increased (*Opere, Volume Terzo: Lettere*, 545–6 [letter from Francesco del Nero to Machiavelli, dated 27 July 1525]).

cardinal, Lorenzo might well simply have been doing his brother's friend a favour. Importantly, though, Lorenzo by this action became personally responsible for Machiavelli's partial rehabilitation in Medici-controlled Florence.[18] Furthermore, when Lorenzo arranged the meeting between Giulio de' Medici and Machiavelli, he also ushered Niccolò into the Medici client network. As a result of Lorenzo's assistance, Machiavelli also entered into Lorenzo's own client system.[19]

Contrary to the widely accepted view that Strozzi and Machiavelli were friends, the available evidence indicates that Strozzi was Machiavelli's patron rather than his confidant.[20] Not long after Machiavelli's reintroduction to the Medici family, he was awarded, with Cardinal Giulio de' Medici's approval, a contract for the *Istorie fiorentine* and in the following year, he dedicated his *Arte* to Lorenzo for "the favours I have received from you" – surely Machiavelli was referring to Lorenzo's assistance with the

18 "Piacemi assai habbiate condotto el Machiavello in casa e' Medici, che, ogni poco di fede aqquisti co' padroni, è persona per surgere." Lines contained in a letter from Filippo Strozzi to Lorenzo di Filippo Strozzi, 17 March, 1519 (1520 using modernized dating) (Tommasini, *La vita*, vol. 2, appendices, 1082).

19 With these facts, and with Tommasini's and Villari's authoritative scholarship in mind, I am hard pressed to suggest, as many contemporary scholars have, that Lorenzo Strozzi and Niccolò Machiavelli were friends. Strozzi's relationship with Machiavelli was nothing like Machiavelli's long and well-documented friendships with Francesco Vettori or Francesco Guicciardini (and to a lesser degree Filippo Strozzi). One is still left with the problem of interpreting the extant literary artifacts, noted above, which seem to indicate that some type of relationship existed between the two Florentines. For the best recent work on the Machiavelli-Vettori friendship, see John Najemy, *Between Friends: Discourses of Power and Desire in the Machiavelli-Vettori Letters of 1513–1515* (Princeton: Princeton University Press, 1993); for the best, and classic, examination of Machiavelli's relationship with Guicciardini, see Felix Gilbert, *Machiavelli and Guicciardini: Politics and History in Sixteenth-Century Florence* (New York: Norton, 1984). For a nicely edited Italian compilation of the letters shared by Machiavelli, Guicciardini, and Vettori, see Niccolò Machiavelli, *Lettere a Francesco Vettori e a Francesco Guicciardini*, ed. Giorgio Inglese (Milan: Libri e Grandi Opere S.p.A., 1996). Inglese's introductory essay (5–55) provides a fine synthesis of Machiavelli's political thought and also suggests a number of areas where Vettori and Guicciardini might have influenced that thought.

20 Quentin Skinner refers to Strozzi as one of Machiavelli's "closest friends" (*Machiavelli* [Oxford: Oxford University Press, 1981], 80). For a good examination of "patronage" and "friendship," see Guy Fitch Lytle's "Friendship and Patronage in Renaissance Florence," in *Patronage, Art and Society in Renaissance Florence*, ed. F.W. Kent and Patricia Simons (Oxford: Oxford University Press, 2002), 47, where Lytle wrote that "'friendship' could be both the synonym and the antithesis of 'patronage.'"

Medici family.[21] Machiavelli was, then, in 1520–21, and probably until 1524, indebted to Lorenzo Strozzi for his help.[22] When Machiavelli dedicated the *Arte* to Lorenzo, he acknowledged Lorenzo's patronage, but Lorenzo had further uses for his client. Discovering those requires, in the absence of any surviving letters between the two, an examination of two literary sources, Lorenzo Strozzi's *Commedia in versi* and his *Pistola fatta per la peste*, both of which are extant as Machiavelli autographs.

Why should Machiavelli autographs of these works exist? Some have suggested that Machiavelli might have made copies of Strozzi's works for his own library. This seems unlikely: while the *Commedia*, and the *Pistola* more especially, might have appealed to Machiavelli's literary tastes, it is difficult to imagine that he would have copied two mediocre works for later consultation.[23] This brings the argument back to the patron-client relationship between Strozzi and Machiavelli. Once Machiavelli became Strozzi's client, perhaps Lorenzo urged, or even required, Machiavelli to transcribe his *Commedia in versi* and his *Pistola fatta per la peste*. This helps to explain why two solid but far from brilliant works by Strozzi ended up as Machiavelli autographs. Both of those autograph texts are located in Florence, Biblioteca Nazionale Centrale, MS Banco Rari 29.[24] The Banco Rari 29 also contains the most famous and most complete autograph of Machiavelli's *Arte della guerra* and an autograph of his *Capitoli per una compagnia di piacere*. The presence of the *Pistola* and the *Commedia* autographs in that collection led to both works being incorrectly attributed to Machiavelli until the late nineteenth century. While the problems of attribution are discussed at length in Chapter 3, it is useful to make a few comments about the manuscripts themselves to illustrate just how important the *Pistola* in particular is to any discussion of a relationship between Strozzi and Machiavelli.

In one key respect, the *Pistola* manuscript differs from that of the *Commedia* – the *Pistola* survives in Machiavelli's hand, like the *Commedia*, but importantly, it contains corrections and additions in Lorenzo di

21 "De' beneficii ho ricevuto da voi" (*L'Arte della Guerra*, "Proemio di Niccolò Machiavegli Cittadino e Segretario Fiorentino Sopr'al Libro *Dell'Arte della guerra* a Lorenzo di Filippo Strozzi Patrizio Fiorentino," in Niccolò Machiavelli, *Opere*, vol. 1, ed. Corrado Vivanti [Turin: Einaudi-Gallimard, 1997], 530).

22 I suggest 1526 as the closing year of the "patron-client" relationship because Machiavelli's attempts in that year to arrange a marriage for Strozzi's son failed miserably. See the conclusion of this study for more on this topic.

23 Villari, *Life and Times of Machiavelli*, vol. 3, 373. There, Villari also argued that Machiavelli copied Strozzi's *Commedia* for the same reason.

24 Magl. VIII 1451 bis; B.R. A V 1. 14. Lorenzo di Filippo Strozzi, "Epistola fatta per la peste," Biblioteca Nazionale di Firenze.

Filippo Strozzi's hand. Due to that interesting fact, and because Andrea Gareffi has already examined the literary merits and the manuscript history of the *Commedia*,[25] this study focuses on the almost unknown *Pistola*. The *Pistola* is a concoction of grim comedy and sensuality, and it also possesses the hallmarks of, and illustrates, the Strozzi-Machiavelli patron-client relationship. While it purports to be a plague tract, the *Pistola* might also be read as an exercise in literary self-fashioning or, more basely, as a piece of "learned pornography."[26]

However one chooses to read it, the *Pistola*, if it is interpreted as a product of the Strozzi-Machiavelli relationship, is far more important for what it might tell us about Machiavelli than for its literary merits, and even for what it might tell us about Strozzi. I do not want to overstate this point, for Lorenzo Strozzi's contributions to Renaissance Florence cannot be discounted, but they are minute in comparison to Machiavelli's. Paul Oskar Kristeller's comments on minor Renaissance texts drives this point home. He once wrote that texts like the *Pistola* can "be of great interest for the relations of their authors with greater contemporaries."[27] Bearing all of this in mind, the third chapter of this study contains an examination of the *Pistola*'s manuscripts and a narrative exposition of the *Pistola*'s text. The final chapter of this study offers conclusions, following which the reader will find a new Italian edition and English translation of the *Pistola*. The Italian edition of the text provides a critical reading and critical apparatus, comparing both surviving manuscripts (Banco Rari 29, Manuscript B, and Ashburnham 606, Manuscript A)[28] of the *Pistola*; the English translation, located on the facing pages of the Italian edition, contains intertextual commentary on the text.

25 Lorenzo di Filippo Strozzi, *Commedie: Commedia in versi, La Pisana, La Violante*, ed. Andrea Gareffi (Ravenna: Longo, 1980), 36–40.

26 I use the term "learned pornography" because Strozzi's language, while sometimes overtly sexual in nature, is more closely related to Petrarch's descriptions of Laura than Pietro Aretino's vulgar personifications of prostitutes and courtesans. "Learned pornography" is discussed in detail by David O. Frantz in "'Leud Priapians' and Renaissance Pornography," *Studies in English Literature 1500–1900* 12, no. 1 (1972): 157–72. Also see Laura Macy, "Speaking of Sex: Metaphor and Performance in the Italian Madrigal," *Journal of Musicology* 14, no. 1 (1996): 1–34; Lynn Hunt, ed., *The Invention of Pornography: Obscenity and the Origins of Modernity* (Cambridge, MA: MIT Press, 1993); and David O. Frantz, "Festum Voluptatis": *A Study of Renaissance Erotica* (Columbus: Ohio State University Press, 1989).

27 Paul Oskar Kristeller, *Studies in Renaissance Thought and Letters*, vol. 4 (Rome: Edizioni di Storia e Letteratura, 1996), 458.

28 These are discussed in detail below.

An examination of the manuscripts revealed that Manuscript B (Banco Rari 29), which is largely in Machiavelli's hand, was written first, though it was heavily edited by Lorenzo Strozzi, in his own hand. Based on this evidence, it is probable that Machiavelli, as a part of his client obligations to Strozzi, acted as Lorenzo's scribe during Manuscript B's production. Manuscript A (Ashburnham 606), which survives entirely in Strozzi's hand and clearly descended from Manuscript B, incorporates many of the changes Strozzi made to the Machiavelli autograph portion of Manuscript B. While I will write much more about the *Pistola*'s manuscripts below, it is helpful to point out here that in Manuscript B, Machiavelli's precision and intellectual seriousness seem to have affected Lorenzo Strozzi. In fact, Strozzi's autograph portion of Manuscript B, and his emendations to the Machiavelli autograph, are not only written in a clearer, more elegant hand than is found in Lorenzo's own copy (Manuscript A), but they are also frequently better witnesses to the intended text of the *Pistola* than Manuscript A. The same thing might be said of Machiavelli's autograph portion of the B Manuscript. This suggests that while Machiavelli was involved in the project Lorenzo rose to the occasion, but when Machiavelli's abilities were no longer necessary (once their patron-client relationship dissolved), Lorenzo's interest in the project waned, producing a less accurate copy. When all of these details are taken into consideration, the special though strained nature of the Strozzi-Machiavelli relationship is brought to the fore. And the relationship between the manuscripts, and their authors, underscores Kristeller's rationale for studying minor texts. Moreover, the concrete historical and philological treatment given to the *Pistola* in chapter 3, and throughout the edition of the text, balances out and helps to substantiate some of my more tentative suggestions in chapter 2.

The *Pistola* itself claims to be a description of a plague[29] outbreak that struck Florence, Roberto Ridolfi argued, in May 1523.[30] It is roughly forty-seven hundred words in length. If we are to believe Strozzi's text, it was

29 This study is neither concerned with the epidemiology nor with the identity of the disease that is known as the plague or, more famously, the Black Death. Readers who are interested in those topics should consult Samuel K. Cohn's "The Black Death: The End of a Paradigm," *The American Historical Review* 107, no. 3 (2002): 703–38. For an extended treatment of the topics addressed in Cohn's article, reference his *The Black Death Transformed: Disease and Culture in Early Renaissance Europe* (New York: Arnold, 2002).

30 Ridolfi argued that the *Pistola* was written "in uno stuccoso stile boccaccevole, fu scritta in forma epistolare da Lorenzo Strozzi al Machiavelli durante la moria, e precisamente nel maggio del 1523" (in a saccharine Boccacciesque style in epistolary form by Lorenzo Strozzi to Machiavelli during a plague outbreak, and precisely in May of 1523) (Ridolfi, *Vita di Niccolò Machiavelli*, 2 vols. [Florence: Sansoni, 1969], vol. 2, 560–61n25).

written in May, but there is nothing further therein to indicate the year in which it was written.[31] Some external evidence, considered below, indicates that it could have been written in 1522.[32]

Authorship of Manuscript B (Banco Rari 29) is spelled out clearly by a third, heretofore unknown, hand that contributed a bizarre Latinate epigraph beginning "hanc epistolam agit Laurentius Philippi Stroci ciues florentinus ..."[33] Despite this clear indication that Strozzi, not Machiavelli, authored the text, eighteenth-century Italian editors and publishers passed off the *Pistola* as Machiavelli's simply because the only known manuscript of the text was in his hand. They ignored the explicit references to Strozzi's authorship, perhaps in their zeal to print a newly discovered work by Machiavelli.[34] However, by the middle of the nineteenth-century, Italian philologists began to recognize that the *Pistola* was stylistically different from Machiavelli's other works, and some began to re-examine the Nazionale manuscript (Manuscript B).

As a result, they correctly concluded that Strozzi authored the text. However, none of those great Italian *literati* examined the relationship that actually produced the *Pistola*. They seem to have been more concerned with

31 "la mattina del lieto principio di maggio." See the Italian edition, below, of the *Pistola*, 85v 10–11.

32 For example, in 1522 young Florentine republicans who had been influenced by Machiavelli's lectures at the Orti plotted to assassinate Cardinal Giulio de' Medici. As their instructor in republicanism, Machiavelli was surely on the Medici family's "watch list." (For more on Machiavelli's republicanism and the plot to assassinate Giulio de' Medici, see John R. Hale, *Florence and the Medici* [London: Phoenix, 2001],107.) At the same time that the conspiracy was being planned, Machiavelli himself took a tremendous risk. In a political treatise on the proposed reform of the Florentine government, he assumed the identity of Cardinal Giulio de' Medici and proposed that Florence be moulded into a republican oligarchy. Lorenzo Strozzi was similarly inclined. I will argue in chapter 2 that Lorenzo influenced, though briefly, Niccolò's political thought. And I will suggest that Lorenzo also might have sheltered his client, Machiavelli, from the Medicean fury that followed discovery of the conspiracy to murder Giulio de' Medici. A quick perusal of Machiavelli's personal letters from 1522 reveals only a handful: in 1522 Machiavelli's correspondence went nearly silent. Perhaps he spent part of that very difficult year transcribing Strozzi's *Pistola*. Though there is a great deal of very interesting circumstantial evidence that points to 1522 as the year in which the *Pistola* was written by Strozzi and transcribed by Machiavelli, I cannot prove that the work originated in 1522.

33 Appendix 1, 2r 5–6, below. Manuscript A, the Strozzi autograph, is signed by Lorenzo himself.

34 See Polidori's comments in Niccolò Machiavelli, *Opere minori di Niccolò Machiavelli: Rivedute sulle migliori edizioni, con note filologiche e critiche di F-L Polidori* (Florence: Le Monnier, 1852), 415–17.

disproving Machiavelli's authorship of the text. Much of the motivation to disassociate Machiavelli from the *Pistola* can be traced to its macabre and perverse content, which scholars such as Lord Macaulay viewed as beneath the famous Florentine.[35] One wonders why Macaulay and others did not reference some of Machiavelli's own scandalous personal letters, which provide their readers with stories of prostitutes and privy humour.[36] Despite proofs of Strozzi's authorship, the *Pistola* nevertheless remained associated with Machiavelli's *opere* until 1892.[37]

In that year Pio Ferrieri published a thorough investigation of Ashburnham 606. He found that the codex contained a Strozzi autograph of the *Pistola* (Manuscript A). That discovery allowed Ferrieri definitively to attribute the plague tract to Strozzi. When carried further, Ferrieri's discovery actually

---

35 Lord Macaulay, *The Works of Lord Macaulay, Complete, Edited by His Sister, Lady Trevelyan*, 8 vols. (London: Longman, Green, 1875). His essay "Machiavelli" is contained in vol. 5. For his particular criticism of the *Pistola*, see esp. 68. Macaulay's comments are dealt with at length in chapter 3. Also see Polidori, *Opere minori*, "Descrizione della peste," 415–17 for his conclusions regarding the *Pistola*. It is interesting that while Macaulay rejected Machiavelli's authorship of the *Pistola*, Polidori published the *Pistola* as a work by Machiavelli.

36 There are several notorious letters that one could mention here, but perhaps the best examples are the "Prostitute Letter" (Letter 178: 8 December 1509) and the "Toilet Letter" (Letter 270: 17 May 1521). Both of these are discussed in detail by Arlene W. Saxonhouse in her chapter titled "Comedy, Letters and Imaginary Republics," in *The Comedy and Tragedy of Machiavelli: Essays on the Literary Works*, ed. Vickie B. Sullivan (Newhaven: Yale University Press, 2000). In Saxonhouse's chapter, Letter 178 is discussed in all of its pornographic detail on 65–8, Letter 270 on 63 and 205 n17. Raymond Crawfurd, wrote: "Villari, Macaulay, and others have declined to accept the *Descrizione* as an authentic product of Machiavelli's pen. They cannot reconcile its garrulous obscenity with the stern cold-blooded restraint of the author of the *Principe* – the frivolity of the one with the sinewy manhood of the other. They seem to forget that, so far back as 1502, amid the stirring life of the camp of Caesar Borgia, he found leisure to write similar puerilities to his friends in Florence. Political rectitude, or if we may not ascribe this to Machiavelli, political sagacity is no guarantee of moral righteousness, and sensuality is not the exclusive property of the young" (*Plague and Pestilence in Literature and Art* [Oxford: Clarendon, 1914], 154). Crawfurd incorrectly attributed the *Pistola* to Machiavelli, but he certainly nailed Machiavelli's character and the flavour of the *Pistola*.

37 Pio Ferrieri's examination of the Biblioteca Medicea Laurenziana's Ashburnham 606 brought a Strozzi autograph manuscript of the *Pistola* to light, formally placing that work in Strozzi's official works. "Sull'autorità dello stesso [codice 606] manoscritto, restituti a Lorenzo Strozzi la nota epistola descrittiva della peste del 1527, stampata sempre fino ad oggi fra le opere del Machiavelli" ("Lorenzo di Filippo Strozzi e un codice Ashburnhamiano," in *Studi di storia e critica letteraria* [Milan: E. Trevisini, 1892], 224).

allows one to argue, with some conviction, that Manuscript B (Banco Rari 29) preceded its Ashburnham counterpart (A). As noted above, this conclusion is based upon the fact that the majority of the emendations Strozzi made throughout Manuscript B were incorporated in Manuscript A. Perhaps more important to the theme at hand, there are multiple examples where Strozzi transferred the emendations present in Manuscript B into Manuscript A. But thereafter Strozzi emended A again, producing new readings that illustrate more forcefully that Manuscript B was produced before Manuscript A. These occurrences are discussed in detail in the edition of the *Pistola,* but it is worth highlighting here the definitive proofs that Manuscript B preceded Manuscript A. These are revealed when one examines how Strozzi emended the text of Manuscript A, text that was recorded verbatim from unemended portions of Manuscript B.

On multiple occasions, for example, Manuscript B includes the informal possessive pronouns *tua* and *tuoi.* These informal pronouns were originally recorded by Strozzi in Manuscript A, but he proceeded to emend them to the formal *uostra* and *uostri.* These small changes necessitated other changes to Manuscript A that are not present in Manuscript B. For instance, in order to harmonize the relationship between the emended personal pronoun *uostri* (formerly *tuoi*) and the verb, originally rendered in both manuscripts as *dimori* in Manuscript A Strozzi changed the latter to *dimorite.* These emendations affected the tone of Manuscript A, differentiating it from Manuscript B, and illustrating that A followed B in the text's development. (For particular details on these emendations, see the edition of the *Pistola,* 87r 5, ff.)

After Ferrieri's research was published, investigations into the *Pistola* suddenly ended, apart from an incomplete English translation that appeared in 1926, still incorrectly attributed to Machiavelli.[38] Since 1926, and only sporadically, Italian journal articles on the *Pistola* have appeared, but there have been no lengthy investigations into the Strozzi plague tract.[39] In large part this might be because so few scholars, with the notable exception of Andrea Gareffi, have spent any sustained effort examining the life and

38 Johannes Nohl, *The Black Death: A Chronicle of the Plague*, trans. C.H. Clarke (Yardley, PA: Westholme, 2006; repr. of 1926 Unwin ed.), 216–26.

39 Roberto Ridolfi, "Schede per l'Epistolario del Machiavelli etc.," in *G.S.L.I.*, 138 (1961): 232–8; see esp. 237 for reference to the *Pistola.* Interestingly, Sam Cohn recently referred to the *Pistola* as a work by Machiavelli; see his *Cultures of Plague: Medical Thinking at the End of the Renaissance* (Oxford: Oxford University Press, 2010), 96. Cohn based his attribution of the *Pistola* on an article by Rino Radicchi ("Descrizione della peste dell' anno 1527 di Niccolò Machiavelli," *Lanternino* 12 [1989]: 11–16).

works of Lorenzo di Filippo Strozzi. The *Pistola*, therefore, might be used as a focal point from which one might learn more about Strozzi, and more about Machiavelli, through an investigation of the text itself.

This brings the argument full circle, back to the proposed patron-client relationship between Strozzi and Machiavelli, and more broadly back to their respective legacies. When we weave all these arguments and suggestions together, we are left with two impressionistic, though still vivid, portraits of Lorenzo di Filippo Strozzi and Niccolò Machiavelli: of Strozzi as a master political survivor – the Renaissance gentleman – who was able to dominate the brilliant though sometimes too outspoken Machiavelli, and of a Machiavelli who appears in a sadder than usual light.

Traditionally, Machiavelli's public career throughout the 1520s has been viewed as partly rehabilitated. After all, he was awarded the contract for the *Istorie*, he published the *Arte,* and he was able to use his former title – *segretario fiorentino* – in print at least. Tellingly, Machiavelli owed each of those successes, in some fashion or other, to Strozzi.[40] Therefore, privately, Machiavelli might have been reduced to copying Strozzi's whimsical, sometimes "pornographic" literary works to repay his patron for the "favours" that Strozzi bestowed upon him.

These conclusions may seem speculative, particularly in the field of Florentine Studies where scholars are used to dealing with the detailed observations recorded by Florence's self-aware citizens. However, such arguments do help to explain more thoroughly how and why Machiavelli transcribed two of Strozzi's literary works. And, they also yield plausible explanations based upon the available evidence, as to why Strozzi and Machiavelli worked together, or rather, perhaps why Machiavelli worked for Strozzi. Of equal importance, this study, while it is primarily concerned with the relationship between Strozzi and Machiavelli, also accords Strozzi greater significance in the history of High Renaissance Florence. It will do so through a blend of biography and a textual analysis of his *Pistola fatta per la peste*.

40 I am aware of Machiavelli's successful Florentine (c. 1520) and Venetian productions of the *Mandragola* (c. 1526). They were triumphs. Tommasini, and more recently Gareffi, have noted that Strozzi's *Commedia in versi* seems to have been written as a moralizing counterpoint to Machiavelli's *Mandragola*. Both works seem to have been written in the late 1510s. See Gareffi's *La Scrittura*, 123, and Tommasini, *La vita e gli scritti di Niccolò Machiavelli nella loro relazione col Machiavellismo: Storia ed esame critic di Oreste Tommasini*, vol. 2, pt. 2 (Rome: 1911), 409. For more detail on the relationship between Strozzi's *Commedia* and Machiavelli's *Mandragola*, see chapter 1.

Part 2: Gentleman, Exile, and *Pistola*

When one examines the *Pistola*'s surviving manuscripts, what comes to the fore is that the writing process Strozzi and Machiavelli shared in producing such a work was complex and maybe even collaborative. But more than that, the *Pistola* represents, one could argue, Strozzi's desire to flee the formalities of gentlemanly culture. In other words, in the literary world that he created, Strozzi was able to remove his "masks" and let slip the constraints of *sprezzatura*.[41] In fact, he might have been suffering from the feelings of alienation and loneliness that, Lauro Martines has argued, the gentlemanly life bred. Perhaps he used literature as a means of escaping the rigidity of his status-based obligations to his family, his city, and his friends. Digging a bit deeper in Martines' scholarship, we might be able to gain insight not only into Strozzi's proposed sense of alienation, but also into Machiavelli's.

Martines contends that the seemingly well-adjusted Renaissance gentleman and his exiled counterpart, the loudmouthed outcast, might have shared a sense of loneliness. In order to survive, the gentleman had to sacrifice his real identity, and the exile suffered for not being able to conceal his true identity: the gentleman had to conform and the exile was forced to leave. Surely Strozzi fits into the former category and Machiavelli into the latter. Here, the *Pistola* is essential. A close reading of Strozzi's plague tract uncovers what appears to be an attempt to escape the bonds of gentlemanly duty for Strozzi and the weariness of fringe living for Machiavelli. One might be led to conclude that this brief literary treatise represents attempts by both men to overcome the "strains of isolation in the body politic."[42]

A very brief overview of the action and setting of the *Pistola* will make this point more forcefully. While the *Pistola* appears to have been inspired by a real plague outbreak in Florence, its content appears to be completely fictitious. Strozzi, in the work's introductory letter, tempts one to believe that he actually experienced everything he claims to have experienced, but

41 Wayne A. Rebhorn, *Courtly Performances: Masking and Festivity in Castiglione's* Book of the Courtier (Detroit: Wayne State University Press, 1978). This is a study of the *Courtier* that pays special attention to social interaction and the wearing of "masks" in Renaissance courts.

42 See Lauro Martines, "The Gentleman in Renaissance Italy: Strains of Isolation in the Body Politic," in *The Darker Vision of the Renaissance*, ed. Robert S. Kinsman (Los Angeles: University of California at Los Angeles Press, 1974), 77-93.

this is improbable. For example, Strozzi included this serious reason why he had written to his friend[43] about the plague:

> Therefore I am stirred (knowing how much one who is away from the fatherland [*patria*] is grateful to receive even the smallest piece of news) to write about all that I have seen in our distinguished city, with my wet yet unhappy [infelicitous] eyes; and even though the matter will bring you little pleasure, hearing that you are out of so perilous a place should make you grateful.[44]

Grave enough; but Strozzi followed those lines with a hint of the material to come:

> Furthermore, while it proves to you that I (of whose death perhaps you have pondered) might yet live, it also will oblige you to make less grave every melancholy or other painful nuisance.[45]

The *Pistola* was intended to lighten the spirits of the recipient; and it allowed Lorenzo Strozzi, for a brief moment, to show his true self to his friend. From this perspective, the *Pistola* begs to be read as a novella, after the style of Boccaccio's bawdy tales, but it does not invite the reader to take it too seriously. This of course led some of the work's critics (Macaulay for example) to condemn it as trivial. That view, certainly a product of its time, deserves revision. The *Pistola*, following Stephen Greenblatt's research on "self-fashioning," allows the reader to use literature in order to see through the many layers of Strozzi's fashioned public image. This sets up a fascinating paradox: through literature, one is able to get at the "real" Lorenzo Strozzi, or at least the Lorenzo Strozzi that he wished he could be in the "real" world. In fact, it might be helpful to think of self-fashioning, at least as it appears in the *Pistola*, as a type of corrupt counterpart to Castiglione's supposedly genteel *sprezzatura,* which was meant to be used in the "real" world, not one conjured in literature.[46]

---

43 The man to whom Strozzi addressed the *Pistola* – Girolamo di Maestro Luca – is named only in Manuscript A. For more on Maestro Luca, see chapter 3.

44 See the Italian edition of the *Pistola*, 84r 29–34, and English translation.

45 Ibid., 84r 34–6, and English translation.

46 I follow Stephen Greenblatt's method of reading the text as the primary means of interpreting the *Pistola.* This reading is central to my discussion in chapter 3. I realize that more traditional methods are also useful and have therefore included a discussion of the plague tract genre and important source materials in chapter 3. Stephen Greenblatt, *Renaissance Self-Fashioning: From More to Shakespeare*

In the pages of *Pistola*, Strozzi wanders through the streets of Florence meeting and speaking with a number of Florentines from different social backgrounds. The majority of his journey throughout the city was conducted entirely alone. However, by the end of the *Pistola*, Strozzi appeared to have overcome such detachment – one might suggest, gentlemanly isolation – by finding a young and beautiful wife. For him, such a marriage could only happen in a concocted literary world. In reality, in the harsh milieu of Florentine politics, he, like all gentleman of his rank, entered into an arranged marriage – and his bride was said to have been "deformed."[47] Such were the sacrifices required of a gentleman.[48] Strozzi's carefully constructed façade of ease and tranquility probably masked his loneliness; and it seems that the only place he was able to find true solace was in fanciful writing with an equally lonely, equally detached former exile. One could argue that Strozzi would have been free to be "himself" at the Orti Oricellari, but even there he would have been conscious of his family name and the need to maintain his own position in Florence.[49] At the Orti Machiavelli could have been less restrained, but the relationship that he developed with Strozzi gave him insights into a world that was inaccessible to him.

Machiavelli was able to spend time in fictional fantasies with Strozzi, basking in the glow of aristocratic privilege. In Strozzi's *Pistola*, Machiavelli, as its transcriber, was able to stroll through the streets as only

---

(Chicago: University of Chicago Press, 1980). Greenblatt defined "self-fashioning" as "the practice of parents and teachers; it is linked to manners or demeanor, particularly that of the elite; it may suggest hypocrisy or deception, an adherence to mere outward ceremony; it suggests representations of one's nature or intention in speech or actions. And with representation we return to literature, or rather we may grasp that self-fashioning derives its interest precisely from the fact that it functions without regard for a sharp distinction between literature and social life" (3).

47 "Si sposò nel 1503 per volere della madre, che badava a motivi d'interesse, con la deforme Lucrezia Rucellai figlia di Bernardo, dalla quale ebbe Palla e Giovan Battista" (Gareffi, *Commedie*, 31). For further details on marriage in the Renaissance, see F.W. Kent, *Household and Lineage in Renaissance Florence* (Princeton: Princeton University Press, 1977).

48 For a study of marriage alliances in the Strozzi family and more generally in Florence, see Lorenzo Fabbri, *Alleanza matrimoniale e patriziato nella Firenze del '400* (Florence: Leo S. Olschki, 1991). For other examples, this time from Venice, see Marino Sanuto, Patricia H. Labalme, Laura Sanguineti White, and Linda Carroll, "How to (and How Not to) Get Married in Sixteenth-Century Venice (Selections from the Diaries of Marino Sanuto)," *Renaissance Quarterly* 52, no. 1 (1999): 43–72.

49 Felix Gilbert, "Bernardo Rucellai and the *Orti Oricellari*: A Study on the Origin of Modern Political Thought," *Journal of the Warburg and Courtauld Institutes* 12 (1949): 101–31.

an "unrestrained" aristocrat of rank could do, flirting with beautiful women, escaping the plague, and taking an elegant and attractive young wife. This latter point is a poignant one, especially when one remembers that Machiavelli's marriage had become strained by the 1520s.[50] Here was one of life's bitter pills that the two men had in common.

Despite all of this, as noted previously, one should not be tempted to conclude that Strozzi and Machiavelli were "friends." There is nothing anywhere in either man's work to indicate that their connection was anything other than professional. In fact, it exhibits features of a relationship between patron and client. That type of formal relationship resonates in the language that Machiavelli adopted in the dedication to the *Arte della Guerra*, wherein he referred to Strozzi as "Lorenzo di Filippo Strozzi Patrizio Fiorentino."[51] That choice of words is significant. For when Niccolò sought patronage, or when he was responding to the help given to him by a patron, as in the dedication to the *Arte*, one finds him to be almost fawning.[52] The dedications of *Il Principe* (1513–1515) and the *Istorie fiorentine* (1521–1525) strengthen this conclusion.

In *Il Principe*, Machiavelli referred to Lorenzo de' Medici as "vostra Magnificenzia" (your Magnificence) among other appellations. One might easily imagine that if Machiavelli had referred to Lorenzo de' Medici in familiar tones, his book would have been rejected out of hand. But though Machiavelli followed all of the proper conventions, particularly in regard to the formalities of language and rhetoric, his search for a patron in Lorenzo de' Medici, which is so clearly exemplified in *Il Principe*'s dedication, bore

50 Maurizio Viroli, *Niccolò's Smile*, trans. Antony Shugaar (New York: Farrar, Straus and Giroux, 2000), 48–51. Their marriage, Viroli concluded, was shaky from the start. Guido Ruggiero has also argued that while Machiavelli may have "claimed an affectionate relationship with his wife, Marietta ... that was a separate world – a separate consensus reality of family and clan – which simply did not intersect on the level of sex with their [Machiavelli's and Francesco Vettori's] friendship and self-portrayal as lovers in an illicit world that was particularly important for their self-portrayals and concepts of self" (*Machiavelli in Love: Sex, Self and Society in the Italian Renaissance* [Baltimore: Johns Hopkins University Press, 2007], 114).

51 *L'Arte della guerra*: "Proemio di Niccolò Machiavegli Cittadino e Segretario Fiorentino Sopr'al Libro *Dell'Arte della guerra* a Lorenzo di Filippo Strozzi Patrizio Fiorentino," in Niccolò Machiavelli, *Opere*, vol. 1, ed. Corrado Vivanti (Turin: Einaudi-Gallimard, 1997), 529.

52 One of the best studies of this type of formal language, particularly as it related to patrons and their clients, is Guy Fitch Lytle, "Friendship and Patronage in Renaissance Florence."

Machiavelli no fruit.[53] It took Lorenzo Strozzi's patronage for Machiavelli to make any headway with the Medici clan. Once Strozzi shepherded Machiavelli into the Medici client network, Machiavelli was bound to respond formally to the Medici, as he did to Lorenzo Strozzi. In the dedication of the *Istorie*, for example, one will find that Machiavelli addressed Giulio de' Medici (Pope Clement VII) as "Vostra Santità, Beatissimo et Santissimo Padre."[54] This form of address is only proper considering that Giulio was the pontiff when Machiavelli delivered the *Istorie* to him. And if Machiavelli wanted further patronage from the pontiff he was required to maintain a certain decorum when he addressed him. So, in *Il Principe*, the *Arte*, and the *Istorie* one will find three examples of works that Machiavelli dedicated to his social superiors, not his friends, and the language that he adopted in their respective dedications underscores this point. Machiavelli's *Discorsi* contains a completely different type of dedication.

His language in the dedication to the *Discorsi* (1515–1517) is self-deprecating, playful, and yet tinged with sadness, for Machiavelli admitted that his attempts to find a patron in the Medici family had failed (he needed Strozzi to direct him through those difficult avenues). In the *Discorsi*, Machiavelli reserved the following words for his real friends Zanobi Buondelmonti and Cosimo Rucellai:

> Take this, however, in the spirit in which all that comes from a friend should be taken, in respect whereof we always look more to the intention of the giver than to the quality of the gift. And, believe me, that in one thing only I find satisfaction, namely, in knowing that while in many matters I may have made mistakes, at least I have not been mistaken in choosing you before all others as the persons to whom I dedicate these *Discourses*; both because I seem to myself, in doing so, to have shown a little gratitude for kindness received, and at the same time to have departed from the hackneyed custom which leads many authors to inscribe their works to some Prince, and, blinded by hopes of favour or reward, to praise him as possessed of every virtue; whereas with more reason they might reproach him as contaminated with every shameful vice. To avoid which error I have chosen, not those who are, but those who from their infinite merits deserve to be Princes; not such persons as have it in their power to load me with honours, wealth, and preferment, but such as, though they

53 For a lengthy study of Machiavelli's rhetoric, see Victoria Kahn, *Machiavellian Rhetoric: From the Counter-Reformation to Milton* (Princeton: Princeton University Press, 2004). For a specific a specific example from *Il Principe*, see *Opere*, vol. 1, 117.

54 *Istorie fiorentine*, in *Opere*, vol. 3, ed. Corrado Vivanti (Turin: Einaudi, 2005), 305.

lack the power, have all the will to do so. For men, if they would judge justly, should esteem those who are, and not those whose means enable them to be generous; and in like manner those who know how to govern kingdoms, rather than those who possess the government without such knowledge.[55]

In the dedication of the *Discorsi*, Machiavelli showed true affection for his friends. In his other book-length historical works, he sought patrons and he wrote to them as such. With this distinction in mind, it is clear that Machiavelli dedicated the *Arte* to Lorenzo as his social superior, his patron, not his friend.

Of equal importance, in the *Arte*'s dedication, Machiavelli was able to refer to himself as "cittadino e segretario fiorentino," a title that he could not have adopted safely without Lorenzo's patronage and protection.[56] Recapping, it is quite likely that Lorenzo's patronage not only helped Machiavelli to regain some standing with the Medici, but also produced a proper commission: Giulio de' Medici, the future Pope Clement VII (and close friend of the Strozzi brothers), commissioned Machiavelli to write the *Istorie fiorentine*.[57] None of this would have been possible without Lorenzo di Filippo Strozzi's guidance and patronage. It is therefore no

55 Niccolò Machiavelli, *Discourses on the First Decade of Titus Livius*, trans. Ninian Hill Thomson (London: Kegan Paul, Trench and Co., 1883), 1–2. The Italian original is "Pigliate adunque questo in quello modo che si pigliano tutte le cose degli amici; dove si considera più sempre l'intenzione di chi manda che la qualità della cosa che è mandata. E crediate che in questo io ho una sola sodisfazione, quando io penso che, sebbene io mi fussi ingannato in molte sue circunstanzie, in questa sola so ch'io non ho preso errore, d'avere eletti voi, ai quali sopra ogni altri questi mia *Discorsi* indirizzi: sì perché faccendo questo, mi pare aver mostro qualche gratitudine de' beneficii ricevuti: sì perché e' mi pare essere uscito fuora dell'uso comune di coloro che scrivono, i quali sogliono sempre le loro opere a qualche principe indirizzare; e, accecati dall'ambizione e dall'avarizia, laudano quello di tutte le virtuose qualitadi, quando da ogni vituperevole parte doverrebbono biasimarlo. Onde io, per non incorrere in questo errore, ho eletti non quelli che sono principi, ma quelli che, per le infinite buone parti loro, meriterebbono di essere; non quelli che potrebbero di gradi, di onori e di ricchezze riempiermi, ma quelli che, non potendo, vorrebbono farlo. Perché gli uomini, volendo giudicare dirittamente, hanno a stimare quelli che sono, non quelli che possono essere liberali, e così quelli che sanno, non quelli che, sanza sapere, possono governare uno regno" (*Discorsi*, in *Opere*, vol. 1, 195–6).

56 Bonfantini called Lorenzo di Filippo Strozzi Machiavelli's "protettore nelgi anni difficili dopo 1512" [Machiavelli's "protector in the difficult years following 1512"] (Niccolò Machiavelli, *Opere*, ed. Mario Bonfantini [Milan: R. Ricciardi, n.d.], 495).

57 Peter Godman, *From Poliziano to Machiavelli: Florentine Humanism in the High Renaissance* (Princeton: Princeton University Press, 1998), 237–8.

wonder that Machiavelli spent so much time, quite likely transcribing Strozzi's dictation, in producing such works as the *Pistola*.

The *Pistola*'s literary merits were misunderstood and unfairly judged by nineteenth-century commentators. A simple, surface reading of the work might tempt the reader to toss it aside as a profane adaptation of Boccaccio's *Decameron*, just as Lord Macaulay did.[58] However, a closer reading opens a small crack through which one might peer into a Renaissance gentleman's private thoughts. Indicative of the *Pistola*'s overlooked complexity, it also, somewhat paradoxically, reveals for its reader Strozzi's subtle and somewhat disturbing use of self-fashioning.

Here, as one wanders into the labyrinth of Renaissance identities, *sprezzatura* and literary self-fashioning can be unnerving, because the hidden and the surface can be so widely divergent. Strozzi's public and private personalities, at least as they are displayed in the *Pistola*, differed tremendously. The public, courtly conventions of politeness that defined good manners and social interactions in the Renaissance are displayed by Strozzi throughout the *Pistola*; yet his private character in the work is crude and ill-mannered.

More specifically, in the *Pistola*, when Strozzi included dialogue between himself and the people whom he met in plague-ridden Florence, his words reflected that decorous cultivation which only a gentleman could muster. Encountering a beautiful young widow, he poses the following questions: "Gracious Lady, if a courteous question is not noisome to you, might it please you to tell me for what reason you stay here for so long? And may I offer some aid to you?"[59] He seems kind and sensitive, like a gentleman. However, this is how Strozzi described the young woman to the *Pistola*'s reader:

> Her envious clothes did not give me leave to gaze on the creamy, beautiful and finely sculpted chest, adorned with two little fresh and sweet smelling apples, which I believe were grown in the famous orchards of the Hesperides. But, by the manner in which they refused to yield to her dress, they demonstrated their beauty and firmness; and between them flashes a way, at the end of which, the wanderer might reach the ultimate bliss.[60]

Perhaps Strozzi's persona in the *Pistola* foreshadows the "honest" Shakespearean scoundrel. While the other, the moral and good, characters in Shakespeare's plays remain unaware of the villain's machinations, the

58 See above and esp. chapter 3 for more detail.

59 See the Italian edition of the *Pistola*, 89r 5–7, and English translation.

60 Ibid., 88v 22–8, and English translation.

villain frequently lets the audience in on his/her plans.[61] Similarly, the *Pistola*'s reader knows that Strozzi hoped to "reach the ultimate bliss," but his female counterpart in the text, though shrewd herself, remains unaware that the apparently caring gentleman with whom she spoke wished to undo her dress and caress her with "carnal affection."[62]

Lorenzo Strozzi might have allowed his reader to steal a glimpse behind the façade of his carefully constructed public image, but that personal view was only meant for his reader, his audience. Apparently, he even felt the need to hide his "real" personality/identity from the fictitious persons he created to populate his plague tract.

To put this another way, even in a fashioned literary world where he might have considered himself free, habitually, he utilized *sprezzatura* – or self-fashioning. This lack of distinction between the "real" and the "literary" is indicative of the tightrope that Strozzi walked: he simultaneously cultivated his gentlemanly public image and his private sexual fantasies and gallows humour.[63] Given this, surely Strozzi's *Pistola* exhibits the characteristics that Martines so eloquently defined in its gentleman author – Strozzi – and his exiled client – Machiavelli. Both men, and the archetypes they represent, were disturbed and alienated, even amidst the bustling streets of High Renaissance Florence. They used literature as a means to escape the confines and harsh realities of their respective lives. When one adds together the important role the *Pistola* plays in helping one to understand how Lorenzo, the Renaissance gentleman, operated, with the realization that Machiavelli acted as Strozzi's scribe/client when Strozzi first wrote

---

61 Falstaff, "Honest Iago," Aaron the Moor, and Richard III fit this mould. For more on similar themes, see Stephen Greenblatt, *Will in the World: How Shakespeare Became Shakespeare* (New York: W.W. Norton, 2004), 33–4

62 See the Italian edition of the *Pistola*, 88v 27, and English translation. Also 86v 27–8, and English translation. These portions of the text are integral to chapter 3.

63 For an essay on *sprezzatura*, see Eduardo Saccone's "Grazia, Sprezzatura, Affettazione," in *Castiglione: The Ideal and the Real in Renaissance Culture,* ed. Robert W. Hanning and David Rosand (New Haven: Yale University Press, 1983), 59, for a very nice discussion of irony and *sprezzatura* as dissimulation. Also, Strozzi's rather strange gentlemanly perversion led Raymond Crawfurd to conclude about the *Pistola* that "the *liaisons* of licentious monks, the vile ribaldry of infamous buriers, the vain recourse to preservatives against the plague, these are the things that are uppermost in his mind, as he depicts his own amorous intrigues against the dark background of the place, with the fidelity of a Pepys and the light-hearted insouciance of Guy de Maupassant" (*Plague and Pestilence in Literature and Art* [Oxford: Clarendon, 1914], 154). Crawfurd incorrectly attributed the *Pistola* to Machiavelli, but even given this mistake, his summary is an interesting and poignant one.

the work, the *Pistola* becomes a much more important and thoroughly interesting piece of Renaissance literature.[64]

Lorenzo di Filippo Strozzi's contributions to the political, literary and, of course, musical elements of Renaissance Florence were numerous and colourful.[65] Yet he has remained elusive, appearing very infrequently in studies outside of Italy and only infrequently there. Perhaps this is due to the fact that Lorenzo lived in a time and in a city that was filled with so many titanic intellects and notable scoundrels that he has, for the most part, escaped history's spotlight. Perhaps, but it is equally likely that since Lorenzo was one of the members of the delegation who handed over Florence's last humiliated republic to the Medici family in 1530, he has been overshadowed by his brother Filippo, who committed suicide in 1537 as a patriotic, republican martyr. Or, and this is the most likely, maybe Lorenzo was simply so adept at using *sprezzatura* that his ability to blend in cost him his legacy. Whatever the case, the time is right to give Lorenzo his due.

In Lorenzo, we find a man who was able to mingle at court, to advise princes and republics, and to wrangle Niccolò Machiavelli into a patron-client relationship that produced a dark though comedic exercise in "humanist pornography" and escapist self-fashioning – the *Pistola fatta per la peste*.

64 The *Pistola*, its genre, and its content are discussed at length in chapter 3.

65 For Lorenzo's musical accomplishments see Frank A. D'Accone, "Transitional Text Settings in an Early Sixteenth-Century Florentine Manuscript," in *Words and Music – The Scholar's View: A Medley of Problems and Solutions Compiled in Honor of A. Tillman Merritt by Sundry Hands*, ed. Laurence Berman (Cambridge, MA: Harvard University Press, 1972), 29–58. For further details on Lorenzo and music, see Richard J. Agee, "Filippo Strozzi and the Early Madrigal," *Journal of American Musicological Society* 38, no. 2 (1985): 227n2. Strozzi's musical and singing abilities are discussed in Anthony M. Cummings, *Maecenas and the Madrigalist: Patrons, Patronage, and the Origins of the Italian Madrigal* (Philadelphia: American Philosophical Society, 2004), 23, 27–31, 36, 38–9, 53–5. Cummings' text contains further references to Strozzi's contributions to Renaissance music; I have listed only the most relevant to the discussion at hand.

1 The Life of Lorenzo di Filippo Strozzi: An Overview

This account of Lorenzo Strozzi's life is based, in part, upon the *Vita* of Strozzi that was written by his childhood tutor, Francesco di Antonio Zeffi da Empoli. Zeffi's *Vita* is the only document that covers Lorenzo's youth, chronicling his life from roughly 1489 until the end of the summer of 1529 – the final months of the last Florentine republic. Unfortunately, in 1546 Zeffi died before he was able to complete his biography of Strozzi.[1] What we are left with, according to Zeffi's account, is a biography of Lorenzo di Filippo Strozzi that covers the formative and most active years of his life. However, a close reading of Strozzi's own works (some of which are unpublished), other seminal *cinquecento* sources, and important secondary scholarship allows a reconstruction of the entirety of Lorenzo di Filippo Strozzi's life.

---

1 Francesco Zeffi da Empoli, "Un Ragionamento inedito di Francesco Zeffi sopra la Vita dell' Autore (Lorenzo di Filippo Strozzi)," in Lorenzo di Filippo Strozzi, *Le Vite degli Uomini della Casa Strozzi*, ed. Pietro Stromboli (Florence: Pei Tipi Salvadore Landi, 1892), xxvi, where the text itself seems to indicate this; it ends abruptly with the words "la capitolazione trattatasi in prima, ebbe effetto: che se altrimenti avveniva, male per la città nostra" (before the surrender of the city took effect: otherwise [futher] misfortunes would have come to our city). Zeffi died in 1546, and Lorenzo lived until 1549. Zeffi wrote his biography of Strozzi, and addressed it to Lorenzo's son, Palla, while Lorenzo was still alive. Why would Zeffi have chosen to end his biography of Lorenzo on such a sad note, particularly as he was trying to highlight the greatness of the Strozzi house and Lorenzo's contributions to it? Also see xxvi, n.1, where the editor of the text, commenting on the strange ending of the *Vita*, wrote, "forse l' autore lasciò l' opera sua così imperfetta per morte o per altra cagione" (perhaps the author left his works so imperfect due to his death or another reason). Unless otherwise noted, all references to Zeffi's *Vita* are drawn from appendix 2 of this book. For another of Zeffi's works, see *Epistole di S. Girolamo, volgarizzate nel secolo XVI da Giovan Francesco Zeffi* (Florence: Manuelli, 1861).

Francesco Zeffi's *Vita* of Lorenzo Strozzi was published only once, in 1892. The editor of that edition claimed that the manuscript from which he transcribed the *Vita* was "mutilated," implying that further investigations into the manuscript were pointless if not impossible. After an extensive period of research, and a bit of good luck, I was able to locate Zeffi's manuscript in the Florentine Archivio di Stato, where I discovered that, contrary to the original editor's suggestion, the manuscript is wonderfully preserved.[2] As well, Zeffi's hand is elegant and precise. I have accordingly prepared a new transcription based on the manuscript of Zeffi's *Vita*, which can be found in appendix 2. (All quotations and references to the *Vita* are drawn from this new edition.)

From Zeffi's *Vita* of Lorenzo, it is possible to gain insight into the type of man Lorenzo was and also to recreate, in part at least, the context in which he lived. It is also possible to gather from Zeffi's narrative and the accompanying exposition of his text that there are tangible connections between elements of Strozzi's personality, his actions, and the proposed patron-client relationship between him and Machiavelli – and the *Pistola* that probably resulted from that relationship. There are no references to Machiavelli in Zeffi's *Vita*. There are, however, two events in Strozzi's life – the "death float" he and Piero di Cosimo produced for the Florentine Carnival season, described by Zeffi; and a dinner he gave that was so appalling guests left his villa covered in their own vomit, the incident described in a letter written by Marino Sanuto – that foreshadow the *Pistola*'s perverse storyline. If Machiavelli acted as Strozzi's scribe, then he was brought, perhaps unwittingly, into the strangely warped plot of Strozzi's own life through the pages of the *Pistola*. These two events, discussed below, are used as interpretive "touchstones" within chapters 2 and 3. And when the *Pistola* is placed into the broader context of Strozzi's life, it becomes all the more peculiar. The vast majority of his historical and literary works are distinctly "moral" in content. Even his amorous love sonnets are really not that amorous: they are somewhat dry though occasionally moving poems that were clearly influenced by Petrarch.[3] Lorenzo's plays are interesting contributions to Renaissance theatre, though more for their

2 I am indebted to Hamilton R. Mathes, who documented the location of Zeffi's *Vita* in the Archivio di Stato. See Mathes' "On the Date of Lorenzo's *Sacra Rappresentazione di S. Giovanni e Paolo*, Febr. 17, 1491," in *Aevum* 25 (1951): 324–8. The ms is found in the Carte Strozziane, Terza Serie, n. 92, 14r–28r.

3 For examples of Strozzi's poetry, see Pio Ferrieri, ed., *Per le nozze: Vigo-Magenta: Rime Inedite di un Cinquecentista (da un codice Ashburnhamiano)* (Pavia, 1885).

classical verse style than their comedic or dramatic content – which has recently been characterized as "monotone."[4] His biographical histories, on the other hand, are excellent and sometimes touching contributions to Renaissance literature. His Strozzi family biographies are like his poetic and theatrical works in that they are "moral": they air none of his family's indiscretions, and deal delicately with politically dangerous moments in his famous ancestors' lives. For example, Lorenzo's *Vita* of Filippo the younger, who famously rebelled against the Medici at Montemurlo (1537) before committing suicide (1538), is carefully crafted so that Lorenzo could memorialize Filippo but also remain a friend to and client of Duke Cosimo de' Medici. These subtleties were revealed by examining the autograph manuscript of the *Vita*, rather than relying solely on the published nineteenth-century editions.

Furthermore, an investigation of unpublished Strozzi manuscripts, especially the two manuscripts catalogued as *Trattato della patienza*, demonstrates that after 1530 and especially after 1537/38, Lorenzo became increasingly religious. An examination of these works and others, along with Zeffi's *Vita*, highlights just how anomalous the *Pistola* is in the context of Strozzi's literary output. With its perverse setting and humanistic lewdness, the *Pistola* is a one-off. Its atypical nature, especially when it is read as an exercise in literary self-fashioning, suggests that Strozzi used the brief work as an escape not only from his usual literary style but also from the confines of an otherwise "gentlemanly" life defined by the use of *sprezzatura*.

The *Pistola* also reflects the strangeness of Strozzi's brief relationship with Machiavelli, the nature of which is brought into starker relief when contrasted with Strozzi's friendship and literary collaborations with Donato Giannotti. Strozzi and Giannotti exchanged numerous letters with one another in the early 1530s, many of which are quoted at length below.[5] They collaborated on at least two plays – *La tragedia di Bruto* and *La tragedia della passione* (of Christ) – though neither was ever finished.[6] Giannotti even asked Strozzi to "versify" one of his plays, *Il vecchio amoroso*, and to "touch

4 Giovanni da Pozzo, *Storia letteraria d'Italia: Il Cinquecento, Tomo 1, 1494–1533* (Padua: PICCIN, 2007), 520, esp. n. 26, which includes a brief plot outline of each of Strozzi's plays.

5 Strozzi was a prolific writer. His personal letters, and there are hundreds of them, are scattered throughout the *Carte Strozziane* in Florence's Archivio di Stato. See Melissa Meriam Bullard, *Filippo Strozzi and the Medici: Favor and Finance in Sixteenth-Century Florence and Rome* (Cambridge: Cambridge University Press, 1980), 3.

6 See letters from Donato Giannotti to Lorenzo Strozzi in *Giornale Storico degli Archivi Toscani*, vol. 7 (Florence: G.P. Vieusseux, 1863), 156–7.

up" his *Milesia.*[7] Given that Strozzi so frequently corresponded and collaborated with Giannotti, and numerous other friends and colleagues,[8] it is useful to juxtapose this mountain of literary evidence suggesting friendship and mutual respect with the fact that no letters between Strozzi and Machiavelli survive. It is possible that their letters were lost, but it is more likely that the absence of correspondence between the two men reflects a relationship grounded in business rather than pleasure.

In many respects, Strozzi's importance is derived from his connections with Machiavelli. But to understand how and why this strange bond developed, we must delve more deeply into Strozzi's life. Considering these points, this biography will trace the development of Lorenzo Strozzi's personal and political associations. These were linked, perhaps inextricably, with his obligations to his family name, and therefore to its posterity. Lorenzo was forced on numerous occasions to sublimate his personal desires and to suppress his republican sentiments. This conclusion emphasizes how resilient he was, but it also emphatically underscores how painful his worldly position could be.

Before travelling back to 1482, the year of Lorenzo's birth, it is helpful to jump back a bit further in time, to 1466, the year in which Lorenzo's father, Filippo di Matteo Strozzi, returned from exile to Florence. Even a brief examination of Filippo's life shows that Lorenzo emulated his illustrious father, and so studying the father provides insight into the son's development as a fine example of Renaissance courtliness, one who became adept at utilizing dissimulation and even *sprezzatura.*[9] Filippo was himself

---

7 Pio Ferrieri, "Lorenzo di Filippo Strozzi e un codice Ashburnhamiano," in *Studi di storia e critica letteraria* (Milan: E. Trevisini, 1892), 221–332; see p. 305.

8 Many of these other friends include individuals who were also friends of Machiavelli. Francesco Vettori certainly comes to mind here. Vettori, to whom Machiavelli sent some of his most famous letters, also corresponded at length with Lorenzo and Filippo Strozzi. See Rosemary Devonshire Jones, *Francesco Vettori, Florentine Citizen and Medici Servant* (London: Althone Press, 1972), 148, 188.

9 For my definitions of "simulation" and "dissimulation," I have borrowed the succinct definitions provided by Sir Richard Steele, who wrote, "simulation is a pretense of what is not, and dissimulation a concealment of what is" (*The Tatler*, ed. George A. Aitken, vol. 4 [London: Duckworth, 1899], 97). There is a famous passage in Machiavelli's *Il Principe* dealing with simulation and dissimulation: "But it is necessary to know well how to color this nature [the nature of the fox], and to be a great simulator and dissimulator" (*The Prince*, ed. and trans. Angelo M. Codevilla [New Haven: Yale University Press, 1997], 66). The Italian original is "Ma è necessario questa natura saperla bene colorire, et essere gran simulatore e dissimulatore" (*Il Principe*, in *Opere*, vol. 1, ed. Corrado Vivanti [Turin: Einaudi-Gallimard, 1997], 166).

encouraged by his mother, Alessandra Macinghi Strozzi, to hone the art of *sprezzatura*,[10] in almost exactly the same fashion that Lorenzo was urged to do so by his own mother, Selvaggia.[11] But the relationship between Filippo the Elder and his son Lorenzo has not been examined in any detail.[12] An analysis of a few crucial moments in Filippo's life, then, will provide greater insight into Lorenzo's own biography.

An Example for Lorenzo: Filippo di Matteo Strozzi

In 1433 the Strozzi family, together with several other old Florentine families, forced the Medici into exile. When Florence's economy quickly ground to a halt in the absence of Medici patronage, the Medici were recalled by the Florentine government and in 1434, in the tit-for-tat politics made famous by the Florentines, they exiled the Strozzi and their anti-Medicean allies. Thirty-two years later Filippo di Matteo Strozzi, after years of moving about Europe from one branch of the Strozzi family (and their banks) to another, insinuating himself deeply into the Neapolitan court, and cultivating a close working relationship with Piero de' Medici,

10 For Castiglione's definition of *sprezzatura*, see Foreword.

11 Alessandra's influence on her son has been thoroughly documented by Heather Gregory. For a translation of her letters, and a fine historical analysis of her life and context, see Alessandra Strozzi, *Selected Letters of Alessandra Strozzi*, bilingual ed., trans. Heather Gregory (Berkeley: University of California Press, 1997), 1–25. Briefly, Alessandra Macinghi was born in 1408 and died in 1471. In the early fifteenth-century, the Macinghi were gaining wealth and prominence in Florence, and Alessandra's father Filippo, following traditional practice, sought a good marriage for his daughter, into a family of greater wealth and lineage, in this case the Strozzi family. Alessandra and Matteo Strozzi were married in 1422 and had eight children, including Filippo Strozzi, Lorenzo's father. In 1434, the Strozzi family in general, and Matteo's in particular, were exiled from Florence by the resurgent Medici family. Alessandra, Matteo, and their children fled to Pesaro, where Matteo promptly died of plague, leaving Alessandra to fend for herself and her children. Her private letters show her to be concerned for her sons. Alessandra, though not educated, had a keen and shrewd mind. She arranged for her sons to study banking; Filippo, her second son, flourished as a banker; when he returned to Florence, he returned a wealthy and important man.

12 Filippo Strozzi's life has been the subject of much research. See Richard Goldthwaite's *Private Wealth in Renaissance Florence: A Study of Four Families* (Princeton: Princeton University Press, 1968); and Goldthwaite, *The Building of Renaissance Florence: An Economic and Social History* (Baltimore: Johns Hopkins University Press, 1980). The latter study examines Filippo's grand and successful scheme for building the Palazzo Strozzi.

was in 1466 officially allowed to return to Florence.[13] Naturally, a great deal of political intrigue in Florence and Naples was involved in Filippo's safe return to Florence, from which we are able to glean just how cleverly Filippo laid the groundwork for his homecoming.[14]

In the months preceding Filippo's restoration, Piero de' Medici's position in Florence was precarious due to the death of his father Cosimo. When he assumed the mantle of Medici leadership, Piero inherited all of the prerequisites for political disaster. After nearly thirty-two years of Medici rule, Florentine republican sentiment and "constitutional crisis" boiled over into the streets, threatening Medici dominance.[15] Piero realized that he needed weighty foreign allies to substantiate his claims. Thus, like Lorenzo the Magnificent a few years later, Piero looked to the Neapolitan court.[16] Filippo Strozzi was there, and he was strategically placed to broker, or at least to facilitate, tacit Neapolitan support for the Medici regime. Ultimately, Piero received the backing that he so desperately needed, and Filippo, following a time-honoured Florentine tradition, had his banishment rescinded, allowing him to return to Florence.[17]

Filippo returned to Florence already engaged to Fiametta di Donato Adimari.[18] In the following years the couple had seven children, including a male heir, Alfonso (1467–1534). Fiametta passed away, and in 1477 Filippo took a second wife. The sons that Filippo had with his new wife, Selvaggia di Bartolommeo Gianfigliazzi, proved to be more adept than their elder half-brother at navigating Florentine politics. The eldest, Lorenzo di Filippo Strozzi (1482–1549), shunned his brother Filippo the

---

13 Christine Shaw, *The Politics of Exile in Renaissance Italy* (Cambridge: Cambridge University Press, 2000), 206–7. Shaw covers more of the negotiations that led to Filippo's repatriation.

14 Heather Gregory, "The Return of the Native: Filippo Strozzi and Medicean Politics," *Renaissance Quarterly* 38, no. 1 (1985): 1–21. Gregory's article remains one of the best and most concise treatments of this period in Florence as it pertained to the life of Filippo Strozzi.

15 John R. Hale, *Florence and the Medici: The Pattern of Control* (London: Phoenix, 2001), 43. Hale's concise treatment of the Medici family and its relationship with Florence is unsurpassed. His coverage of Piero di Cosimo de' Medici is particularly useful here; see 43–8.

16 Later, after the Pazzi Conspiracy, Lorenzo de' Medici too looked to Naples for external support for his regime. That topic is covered in vivid detail by Lauro Martines in *April Blood: Florence and the Plot against the Medici* (New York: Oxford University Press, 2004).

17 Shaw, *Politics of Exile*, 203–33.

18 Gregory, "The Return," 11.

younger's (1488/9–1538) brand of sometimes public political showmanship, "preferr[ing] always to remain in discreet rapport with the Medici."[19] This approach makes Lorenzo neither boring nor unprincipled, but rather just like his father, from whom he learned not only how to survive in Medici-controlled Florence but also how to thrive in any circumstance.

Reading Lorenzo's *Vita di Filippo di Matteo Strozzi*, one is often struck by the fondness with which Lorenzo recalled his father, particularly when one realizes that Filippo died in 1491 when Lorenzo was nine years old. Yet this premature loss does not seem to have lessened the impact Filippo had on the young Lorenzo, as the pages of the biography attest. Lorenzo informed readers that he spoke with many people in order to reconstruct his father's life; but he also relied on his own memories and experiences, both of which shaped him as politician, gentleman, and outstanding representative of the Strozzi family.[20]

Lorenzo recalled one episode in his father's life in such detail that it assumes greater significance within the rest of his father's biography. It deals with Filippo's political astuteness in the building of the family home, the Palazzo Strozzi,[21] and recounts his careful management of his

19 "Lorenzo si mantenne alieno dalle eroiche inquietudine di Filippo preferendo rimanere sempre in discreti rapporti con i Medici" (Lorenzo di Filippo Strozzi, *Lorenzo di Filippo Strozzi: Commedie, Commedia in versi, La Pisana La Violante*, ed. Andrea Gareffi [Ravenna: Longo Editore, 1980], 31). At the time of his father's death in 1491 "Lorenzo was 9 years old" ("Lorenzo d'età d'anni 9") (*Ricordo* of Filippo Strozzi, in Lorenzo di Filippo Strozzi, *Filippo Strozzi: Tragedia,* ed. G.-B. Niccolini [Florence: Le Monnier, 1847], 339).

20 "Tanti e così grandi sono gli obblighi che hanno i figliuoli co'padri, che se la vita umana avesse più lungo corso di quello che la natura concede, niuno potrebbe mai esserne conoscitore non che remuneratore. Però non doverrà parere isconvenevole se io, che tra tutti gli altri sono al Padre mio obbligatissimo, col descrivere quali siano stati i costumi, i modi, l'ottima e imitabil vita di quella, mi sforzerò mostrare qualche gratitudine de' suoi meriti verso di me. E se bene le lodi sue sariano nell'altrui bocche di maggiore autorità e fede, non tacerò io solo quello che hanno tutti gli altri di lui veduto e parlato; penando in quel modo ch'io posso a mio Padre satisfare, se la vita e virtù sue semplicemente, per non li torre quella reputazione che egli stesso si ha procacciata, sarrano da me narrate" (Lorenzo di Filippo Strozzi, *La Vita di Filippo Strozzi il Vecchio*, ed. Giuseppe Bini and Pietro Bigazzi [Florence: Tip. Della Casa Correzione, 1851] 5).

21 See Goldthwaite, "The Building of the Strozzi Palace: The Construction Industry in Renaissance Florence," *Studies in Medieval and Renaissance History* 10 (1973): 97–194. For additional works on the Strozzi palace and piazza, see F.W. Kent, "Palaces, Politics and Society in Fifteenth-Century Florence," *I Tatti Studies* 2 (1987): 41–70; and, by the same author, "'Più superba de' quella de' Lorenzo': Courtly and Family Interest in the Building of Filippo Strozzi's Palace," *Renaissance Quarterly* 30 (1977): 311–23. Also see Caroline Elam, "Piazza Strozzi: Two Drawings by Baccio

public persona, a lesson obviously not lost on Lorenzo, who learned a great deal about survival in Florence from his father.

> Filippo, having already provided sumptuously for his descendants, desired fame more than riches, and not having any surer way to leave a memorial of himself, and being inclined by nature to architecture (and having not a little knowledge of it), conceived in his spirit to construct a building which should bring honor to himself and all (who shared) his name in Italy and abroad. But this was attended with no little difficulty, because, the one who was supremely powerful [Lorenzo de' Medici] might imagine that such glory might obscure his own; [Filippo] feared therefore to awaken his envy.
>
> From whence (or out of such fear) [Filippo] began to spread rumors that one who had fathered so many children and had so small a house, should also provide a suitable place for them to live; and that this could be done much better by him while he lived than by them after his death. He began, therefore, to consult at length first with masons and then with architects, pointing out his need for a home; and sometimes he would seem about ready to begin to build; and at other times, he would seem irresolute, and pained to spend in a short time that which he earned, over so many years with such toil and industry; dissimulating his intentions astutely to everyone in order to attain his end more easily; saying always that all he wanted was a large yet useful house befitting a citizen, but not pompous.
>
> But the masons and architects, following their customs, surpassed all his designs, for which Filippo was grateful; even though he might feign completely to the contrary saying that they forced him to do that which he could neither want nor afford. On top of this, he who ruled [over Florence] desired that the city should be exalted with every type of decoration and so for those reasons he began to involve himself in (and wanted to see) the designs; which, when he had seen and considered them, besides many other expenses, added a façade of unhewn stones.
>
> Filippo, the more he was seen to be encouraged, the more he seemed to resist; he said that nothing could make him want such a façade, for it would not be civil and it would be too expensive for a house that he was constructing for utility, and not for bragging rights; additionally designing the street level to be used for

---

d'Agnolo and the Problems of a Private Renaissance Square," *I Tatti Studies* 1 (1985): 105–35, 274–86. For more general works on Florentine palace building and architecture, see Nicolai Rubinstein, "Palazzi Pubblici e palazzi privati al tempo del Brunelleschi," in *Filippo Brunelleschi: La sua opera e il suo tempo*, vol. 1, ed. Franco Borsi et al. (Florence: Centro Di, 1980), 27–36.

> shops, to bring income to his children. This was adamantly opposed, by pointing out how ugly, servile and incongruous it would be to the inhabitants.
>
> Filippo still seemed in some respects against the idea, sometimes sharing his sadness with his friends that he entered into an undertaking which only God could tell whether the end result would be satisfactory, and that he wished he had never thought of it rather than finding himself in such a labyrinth.[22]

Even as Filippo feigned regret and sadness, and shared worries with his friends and by extension with Lorenzo the Magnificent, he was literally laying the foundations of a colossal achievement.

On the morning of 16 August 1489, Filippo di Matteo Strozzi laid the first stone of his family home, the Palazzo Strozzi. As construction began, Filippo finally allowed himself to enjoy his feat, celebrating with masses,

22 "Filippo adunque avendo provveduto copiosamente alla sua successione, cupido più di fama che di roba, non avendo altro maggiore né più securo modo a lasciare di sé memoria, essendo per natura inclinato all'edificare ed avendone non poca intelligenza, si messe in animo di fare uno edifizio che a sé e a tutti suoi in Italia e fuori desse nome. Ma li restava di ciò una difficultà non piccola, perché, potendo chi reggeva dubitare che l'altrui gloria non oscurasse la sua, temeva di non far cosa che li generasse invidia. La onde cominciò a spargere voce, che aveva tanti figliuoli e sì piccola abitazione, che gli bisognava, così come egli generati gli aveva, pensare anche dove potessino abitare; e che molto meglio ciò potrebbe egli e saprebbe fare in vita, che loro dopo la morte sua. Cominciò adunque dalla lunga, prima co'muratori, poi con architettori a ragionare, mostrando la necessità sua dell'abitare, e qualche volta fingeva voler dar tosto principio, e qualche volta non esser risoluto, e dolergli lo spendere in breve tempo quello che in tanti anni e con tanta fatica e industria avea guadagnato; dissimulando a ciascuno astutamente l'animo e fine suo, non per altro se non per poterlo meglio conseguire; dicendo sempre che li bastava una abitazione agiata e cittadinesca, utile e non pomposa. Ma muratori ed architettori, secondo il costume loro, augumentavano ogni suo disegno; il che a Filippo era grato, quantunque egli dimostrasse tutto il contrario, dicendo che lo sforzavano a quello che non voleva né poteva fare. Aggiungevasi a questo, che chi reggeva desiderava che la città fosse con ogni specie d'ornamento esaltata ... e per così fatte cagioni cominciò ad ingerirsi e voler vedere i disegni; allí quali, poiché gli ebbe veduti e considerati, oltra molt' altre spese, v' aggiunse ancora quella dei bozzi di fuori. Filippo quanto più si vedeva incitare, tanto maggior sembiante faceva di ritrarsi; e per niente diceva di voler fare i bozzi, per non esser cosa civile e di troppa spesa; e che murava per utile e non per pompa, disegnando di fare sotto la casa molte botteghe per entrate dei suoi figliuoli: il che arditamente gli era contradetto, mostrando di quanta bruttezza, servitù e incommodo saria alii abitatori. Filippo si contrapponeva pure con qualche rispetto; dolendosi talvolta con gli amici che entrava in una impresa che Dio volesse che il fine fosse buono, e che vorria piuttosto non ne aver mai ragionato, che trovarsi in tal laberinto" (*Vita di Filippo il Vecchio*, 22–5).

dinners, and fine wine.[23] Subtlety, cleverness, tenacity, and patience were all central traits of Filippo's character, and his son Lorenzo carried those qualities to new heights as he grew into maturity.

Given the powers of dissimulation that Lorenzo ascribed to his father ("dissimulando a ciascuno astutamente l' animo e fine suo"), and the clear admiration that he had for Filippo, it is not surprising to discover that he followed in his father's footsteps. Such political acumen places Lorenzo in distinguished company: Francesco Vettori, Francesco Guicciardini, and even Marcello Virgilio Adriani all survived the vacillations of Florence's political leadership. One could argue that such men (perhaps excepting Adriani, who survived by careful posturing and intellectual prowess) were able to sustain their reputations in Florence due to their family connections.[24] But reputation and connections were not enough to thrive in republican and then in Medicean Florence; to flourish, one also needed to possess skill. Lorenzo possessed the latter in abundance; and it is most likely that he learned some early lessons from a master of the art of survival: his father.

As Lorenzo recalled his father's life and studied the manner in which Filippo the Elder managed to succeed in Medicean Florence, he probably felt a connection with his father that allowed him to mimic Filippo's survival strategies. This connection with, and emulation of, his father can be glimpsed in the fact that Lorenzo was writing his biography of Filippo the Elder in 1537, the year in which Filippo the younger was preparing his final rebellion against Duke Cosimo de' Medici. Although Lorenzo was a republican, he wanted nothing to do with his brother's revolutionary republicanism. In fact, after 1530, and more emphatically after 1537, Lorenzo turned nearly all of his attention to scholarly pursuits. He knew which way

23 "A dì 16 d' Agosto, appunto su l' uscire del Sole da' monti, in nome di Dio, e di buon principio per me e mia discendenti, e di qualunque se ne travaglierà, gettai la prima pietra ne' fondamenti. E a questa medesima ora feci cantare una Messa dello Spirito Santo da' frati di S. Marco, e una dalle Donne delle Murate, e una alla mia S. Maria di Licceto, e una da' frati di S. Maria di Licceto, tutti mia divoti, con pregare Iddio, che sia in buon principio per me, e per mia discendenti, e per tutti quelli, che in detta muraglia daranno favore. Ebbi tal punto dal soprannominato Benedetto Biliotti, e Maestro Niccolò, e Maestro Antonio Benivioni medici, el Vescovo de' Pagagnotti, e M. Marsilio; tutti lo approvorono per buono" (*Vita di Filippo il Vecchio*, 70).

24 For a book-length study that considers the machinations and intellectual gymnastics of Marcello Virgilio Adriani, see Peter Godman, *From Poliziano to Machiavelli: Florentine Humanism in the High Renaissance* (Princeton: Princeton University Press, 1998). Additionally, see my *Politics, Patriotism and Language: Niccolò Machiavelli's* "Secular Patria" *and the Creation of an Italian National Identity* (Peter Lang: New York, 2005), 51–68.

the wind was blowing, and chose to preserve his family and his fortune rather than sacrifice them on the altar of the "Brutus cult."[25] In this we can see his father's instinct for survival.

The Life of Lorenzo di Filippo Strozzi according to Francesco Zeffi, 1489–1526[26]

Very little is known about Lorenzo's early childhood. Without doubt, he would have been enthralled by the continuous activity within his father's household attendant on the construction of the family's palazzo. The young Lorenzo would have been surrounded by designers, masons, and architects, and such an atmosphere would have been stimulating, to say the least. But of this and such matters we can only surmise. In other areas, however, we are on surer footing; in particular, there is one event that his biographer, Francesco Zeffi, felt compelled to mention because of its importance to Strozzi's later life.

When Lorenzo was only seven years old (1489/90), he was selected by Lorenzo the Magnificent to act as the young Giuliano de' Medici's *consigliere* at one of the celebrations for the festival of saints John and Paul.[27] The term *consigliere* itself resonates interestingly with Lorenzo's own life. The *consigliere* was a character in Italian theater, and public performances more generally, who was responsible for delivering speeches containing advice, genuine or fraudulent, to the main characters;[28] in the festivities of 1489, the young Lorenzo acted as advisor to a future prince, Giuliano de' Medici. This must have delighted his father, who, one imagines, would have relished the bittersweet irony of his son's part in the festivities: Filippo, who had spent a large part of his life in exile due to Medici decree, now had

25 See D.J. Gordon, "Giannotti, Michelangelo and the Cult of Brutus," in *Fritz Saxl, 1890–1948: A Volume of Memorial Essays from his Friends in England*, ed. D.J. Gordon (London: Thomas, Nelson, 1957): 281–96.

26 Zeffi's biography does not divide Lorenzo's life into periods; this span of years is imposed by me, to mark what I see as two distinct periods in his life: the period of Medici support (1526 and before) and that of open republicanism (1527 and after).

27 "A'pena era nel settimo anno, ché recitando il Mag(nifi)co Lorenzo de Medici nel Uangelista una sua festa di San Giouanni, e Paulo, della quale il Messere, ò il sig(no)re che dir uogliamo, era Giuliano figlio del detto Mag(nifi)co Lorenzo, elesse uostro padre per Consigliere, doue non tanto per essere riccam(en)te adornato" (Appendix 2, 15r 20–15v 3).

28 Wolfgang Clemen, *English Tragedy before Shakespeare: The Development of Dramatic Speech* (New York: Routledge, 1980), 52–3.

a son acting as advisor to the same family. Sadly, Filippo did not have long to savour his son's emerging courtliness and erudition, for he passed away in 1491.

Thereafter, Lorenzo's mother Selvaggia assumed full control over his education. Richard Goldthwaite has shown that she wanted Lorenzo to become a comfortable gentleman like his father but did not want him to waste too much of his time on business or the *studia humanitatis*.[29] Francesco Zeffi makes this point even more forcefully. Writing to Lorenzo's son Palla, Zeffi concluded that "in his tender years, your father did not attend much to letters, [his] mother furnishing them [Lorenzo and Filippo] tutors more for manners than for elaborate letters."[30] In other words, she pushed Lorenzo and his younger brother Filippo to focus on proper courtly behavior, not on languages, classical eloquence, and rhetoric – the fundamental elements of what Castiglione would later call *sprezzatura*. One might infer from the "curriculum" that Selvaggia felt financially comfortable enough to steer her sons away from business training. However, her insistence that her sons avoid a classical education proved galling to Lorenzo and Filippo. As they matured, both young men seem to have insisted on a proper humanist education. Lorenzo, for example, might have had a hand in seeing to it that Filippo studied with Marcello Virgilio Adriani, the head of the Florentine Academy and the professor who assumed Poliziano's chair upon the latter's death.[31] Lorenzo himself went on to study with a number of other influential Latinists and Greek experts while he was still quite young.[32]

While bothersome to Lorenzo, his mother's stubborn anti-intellectualism and insistence on courtly training did in fact benefit him, as attested by one

---

29 "Selvaggia, however, had less interest in giving them the erudition of scholars than in rearing them as gentleman who would be able to move easily in the fashionable society of their time; and she certainly had no interest in preparing them for business careers" (Goldthwaite, *Private Wealth*, 80–1). In the same work, see p. 81, n. 13, where Goldthwaite references another of Strozzi's biographies: Lorenzo di Filippo Strozzi, "La Vita di Filippo Strozzi [Il Giovane]," in *Filippo Strozzi: Tragedia,* ed. G.-B. Niccolini (Florence: Le Monnier, 1847), x–xi.

30 "Uostro padre nelli suoi teneri anni non attendesse molto à lettere, prouedendoli la madre i precettori più di costumi che di lettere ornati" (Appendix 2, 18v 7–9).

31 "La Vita di Filippo Strozzi [Il Giovane]," xi. For more details on Filippo's education and on his tutors, see Luigi Limongelli, *Filippo Strozzi, Primo Cittadino d'Italia* (Milan: Casa Editrice Ceschina, 1963), 21. Limongelli writes that Filippo studied Latin with Adriani and Greek with Fra Zanobi Acciaiuoli.

32 Richard Goldthwaite, citing Pio Ferrieri's research, noted that "their tutors included Messer Antonio da Milano, Messer Niccolò da Bucine, and Bartolomeo Fonzio" (*Private Wealth*, 80n1).

incident in particular from his youth. On 17 November 1494 the Florentine republican government (which had only very recently been reinstituted after ousting Piero de' Medici) selected forty of the city's brightest youths to meet the invading French monarch, Charles VIII, just outside of the San Frediano Gate.[33] Lorenzo led that group of young people – he was twelve years old.[34] He must have been an elegant, well-mannered boy: why else would they send him to greet one of the most powerful men in Europe at the head of a sizeable army (roughly 18,000: 9,000 infantry and an equal number of horse) waiting for the command to put Florence to the sack?[35]

In the following years, Lorenzo grew accustomed to a life of travel, luxury, and leisure. In fact, the Strozzi brothers, and Lorenzo in particular, represented that formidable type of Florentine elite that emerged in Medici-controlled Florence – an elite that was able to live off its accumulated wealth and investments. However, with the fall of the Medici in 1494, Florence's wealthy families, who once orbited as satellites in and around the Medici court, were struggling to find their place in the new, perhaps too "popular," republic. Selvaggia Strozzi, for example, was inclined to side with the conservative wing of the Florentine patricians, who had once sided with the Medici but had also nursed republican leanings. After her husband's death, she turned to the *de facto* leader of that wealthy and influential group, Bernardo Rucellai, who provided her with advice on her affairs and on those of her sons.[36]

---

33 Lauro Martines, *Fire in the City: Savonarola and the Struggle for the Soul of Renaissance Florence* (New York: Oxford University Press, 2006), 44: "The Signoria, its two advisory councils, and all the city's outstanding citizens were at the gate to meet him [Charles VIII], and including forty youths, selected from the richest and most eminent Florentine families, each on horseback and expensively dressed in 'the French fashions.'"

34 "... quanto per l'attitudine, e prontezza d'ingegno in simili honorati piaceri s'acquistò àpò tutto il popolo fior(enti)no sì fatta grazia, che di poi nel 1494, entrando Carlo Re di Francia in Fior(en)za, Lorenzo, benche di tenera età, fù tra li primi Cittadini comandato dalla Signoria à riscontrare il Cristianiss(im)o un miglio fuor della Porta. La oue essendo con due familiari di uelluto tanè à librea vestito, tanto destramente il suo giannetto atteggiaua, che ancor uiue ne cuori di molti cittadini la marauiglia: i quali al costume de uecchi raccontando tale honoreuole entrata, sempre d'auanti a'gl'occhi loro si rappresenta questo grazioso giouinetto" (Appendix 2, 15v 3–16).

35 Richard Mackenney, *Sixteenth-Century Europe: Expansion and Conflict* (London: Macmillan, 1993), 71.

36 Bullard, *Filippo Strozzi*, 4. For a lengthier study of Bernardo Rucellai, see Felix Gilbert, "Bernardo Rucellai and the *Orti Oricellari*: A Study on the Origin of Modern Political Thought," *Journal of the Warburg and Courtauld Institutes* 12 (1949): 101–31.

From around 1501 until 1503, Lorenzo followed his emerging literary and political interests to courts and cities around Italy. His biographer, Zeffi, highlighted Lorenzo's trips to Ferrara, where he provided entertainment at the marriage of Alfonso D'Este and Lucrezia Borgia. Evidently, there Lorenzo recited original poetry and showcased his musical talents. This was likely a special occasion for Lorenzo, particularly as he was able to spend time with other members of the Strozzi family who had relocated to Ferrara after their 1434 exile from Florence. Zeffi noted that, at the court of Ferrera "where all of the princes, and nobles of Italy competed," Lorenzo apparently charmed everyone he met.[37] The young boy who acted as *consigliere* to Giuliano de' Medici and who was sent to greet the king of France in 1494 was obviously becoming a gentleman of some considerable talent. His accomplishments are all the more impressive when one considers that at this point he was still a teenager, only about eighteen years old. His abilities were augmented by his good looks: he was tall and slender with an aristocratic visage, dark eyes, long elegant hands, and an impressive physique.[38] He was, in short, the embodiment of courtly manners and appearance.

Eventually, quite likely in 1503, Lorenzo travelled to Venice, where the Venetian citizens welcomed him warmly. He made such an impression on the young Venetian noblemen that he was offered a special honour – he was invited to join one of the *Compagnie delle Calze* (Stocking Groups: so called because of the multicoloured hose they wore).[39] The *Compagnie* were a long-standing and very Venetian tradition, involving young Venetian nobility.[40] That the young Florentine Lorenzo was invited to take part in a very Venetian tradition attests to the esteem and affection he aroused in noble circles.

37 "Doue concorsero tutti li principi, e li nobili d'Italia" (Appendix 2, 15v 22–3).

38 See plate XCII in Guido Pampaloni, *Palazzo Strozzi: Il restauro dell'edificio di Gino Cipriani* (Rome: Instituto Nazionale delle Assicurazioni, 1982), for a portrait of Lorenzo when he was an older man. All of the characteristics listed above are still evident. This portrait of Lorenzo di Filippo Strozzi, attributed in the text above to the collection of Count Paolozzi, was sold to a private collector when the Paolozzi family palace and its contents were sold in 1968–69. Its whereabouts are presently unknown. I am grateful to the director of the Bargello Museum in Florence, Beatrice Paolozzi Strozzi, for providing me with this information.

39 Appendix 2, 16r 9ff.

40 These groups of young Venetian noblemen came together sometimes only for the Carnival season, but other Compagnie stayed together for much longer periods of time: Edward Muir, *Civic Ritual in Renaissance Venice* (Princeton: Princeton University Press, 1986), 167–8. Also see Juergen Schulz, "Vasari at Venice," *The Burlington Magazine* 103, no. 705 (1961): 500–11.

Going back to Lorenzo's formative years, roughly 1494–98, the same years that overlap with regime change in Florence and Savonarola's rise to power, the initial struggle to form the new republic centred on a fundamental question: what type of republic ought it to be? Lauro Martines has pointed out the enormous influence the Venetian form of government exerted on Savonarola's own republican vision.[41] Savonarola wanted a grand council, after the Venetian style. However, the Venetian Grand Council consisted of a closed group of ruling elites. Bernardo Rucellai and his followers, including Lorenzo di Filippo Strozzi, may have represented a very similar, though of course Florentine, group of elites. That group was the most familiar with how politics in Italy worked; and they knew the ins-and-outs of court intrigue. Martines concluded that they were the natural group of leaders for the new Florentine republic. However, Savonarola deviated from the Venetian example by arguing that the old Florentine elites who had been sympathetic to the Medici should be forced to sit alongside the "masses" in Florence's ruling body. Savonarola's preaching and Florentine republican zeal, combined with a hearty and justified distrust of the Medici court and its attendants, dragged Florence's republic into a revolutionary form of populism, one where even shopkeepers, tanners, and merchants could sit in the government. To the contemporary eye, Savonarola's populist republicanism seems almost "modern." However, it was too revolutionary for late *quattrocento* Florence.

Savonarola's populist passion kept the old elites, even those sympathetic to republican causes, at the periphery of Florentine power. The Strozzi family and the Rucellai were sidelined. It is no wonder that Lorenzo spent a great deal of time outside of Florence, nor is it surprising that he was well received in Venice. He probably felt at home in Venice's strong, noble-citizen-dominated republican tradition. But it is important to note that before he left Florence for Venice, Lorenzo was briefly infatuated with Savonarolan politics and religion. Raul Mordenti has contended that even later in life, Lorenzo tried to balance the secular republicanism espoused by the members of the Orti Oricellari group and his own religious sentiments.[42] Mordenti's scholarship sheds new light on the dual nature of Lorenzo's literary output and on the difficulties attendant on his habitual use of *sprezzatura*. In order to maintain his family's position in Florence,

41 Martines, *Fire*, 63.

42 Bartolomeo Cerretani, *Dialogo della mutazione di Firenze*, ed. Raul Mordenti (Rome: Edizioni di Storia e Letteratura, 1990), p. XLVIff. This reference is drawn from Mordenti's historiographical essay that prefaces his edition of Cerretani's *Dialogo.*

Strozzi had to be all things to all people. His true political and religious affiliations are therefore hard to ascertain, though evidence suggests he was a republican and a Catholic whose devotion fluctuated. The full implications of Mordenti's scholarship explain how and why Strozzi could write the *Tragedia di Bruto* (co-authored with Giannotti in the lead-up to the assassination of Alessandro de' Medici) and the religious/philosophical *Trattato della patienza* (which he dedicated to Duke Cosimo de' Medici in the aftermath of Filippo Strozzi's failure at Montemurlo in 1537). But in this context what might one say about the *Pistola*?

It is not hard to imagine a "fervent Savonarolan,"[43] as Mordenti referred to Strozzi, writing the *Pistola*, which contains both anti-clericalism and a critique of Florence's "little-loving" citizenry.[44] Savonarola preached on similar themes.[45] But how do the *Pistola's* lusty descriptions of women fit into his supposed Savonarolan mindset? This is more difficult to answer; it is probable that the strains of gentlemanly life led Strozzi to create a fictional world where he could escape the constraints of real life, religious and otherwise, without damaging his reputation. The *Pistola* may have provided a safe environment for Lorenzo to act as he wished to within the rigidly defined society of Renaissance Florence. This supposition casts doubt on the nature of Strozzi's loyalty to Savonarola, and on Mordenti's characterization of Strozzi as a life-long follower of the Dominican friar.

In 1497/98, Strozzi was certainly more interested in Savonarola's musings than was Machiavelli.[46] But in the context of a long and shifting

43 Cerretani, *Dialogo*, p. XLVI.

44 One of the protagonists in the *Pistola* refers to the Florentines as "poco amoreuoli cittadini." See the Italian edition of the *Pistola*, 87v 5, and English translation.

45 These themes are addressed in detail throughout Donald Weinstein's *Savonarola and Florence: Prophecy and Patriotism in the Renaissance* (Princeton: Princeton University Press, 1970). Weinstein's recent biography of Savonarola sheds new light on the prophet's relationship with Florence: *Savonarola: The Rise and Fall of a Renaissance Prophet* (New Haven: Yale University Press, 2011).

46 Simone del Pollaiolo, called "il Cronaca," *Tre Lettere*, ed. Jodoco del Badia (Florence: Tipografia all'Insegna di S. Antonio, 1869). See letter dated 24 April 1497, 9–10, where Il Cronaca wrote to Lorenzo about Savonarola. From letters of this type, scholars suggest that Lorenzo was a follower of Savonarola. Machiavelli concluded that the friar "coloured his lies to suit the times." The lengthier Italian original is "E così, secondo el mio iudicio, viene secondando e tempi, e le sue bugie colorendo" (Machiavelli, *Opere, Volume Terzo: Lettere*, ed. Franco Gaeta [Turin: Unione Tipografico-Editrice Torinese, 1984], 70, letter 3 dated 9 March 1498). For more on Machiavelli's distaste for Savonarola and priests in general, see Lorenzo Polizzotto, *The Elect Nation: the Savonarolan Movement in Florence, 1494–1545* (Oxford: Clarendon, 1994), 270n136, 311n319.

political life, how seriously should we take the religious affiliations of a fifteen-year-old who had yet to take the helm of his family's *casa*? It cannot easily be extrapolated from Lorenzo's teenage religiosity that he remained a devout Savonarolan in his later years. Granted, he experienced a slow return to religion after 1527 and especially after 1530; but in his youth, and particularly in the early 1500s, when faced with the harsh realities of Savonarolans' anti-oligarchic republicanism and the difficulties of the secular republic that followed, Lorenzo left Florence for Venice.[47] Read in this light, his youthful activities do not reflect serious devotion to anything other than his own family.

In 1503,[48] Lorenzo di Filippo Strozzi, always the gentleman, "honourably refused" the invitation to join the ranks of the Venetian Compagnie because his mother had arranged his marriage.[49] This marriage was designed to cement the good terms between the Rucellai and Strozzi families. Lorenzo married Bernardo's daughter, Lucrezia Rucellai. She was not a beauty. In fact, as noted above, she was said to be "deformed."[50] Lorenzo's mother Selvaggia provided the stern encouragement that her son needed to go through with the marriage because the family needed a sound alliance to preserve its place in Florence.[51] Given that Bernardo Rucellai had been Selvaggia's closest advisor since Filippo's death in 1491, the union of their families was almost to be expected. The Strozzi-Rucellai marriage of 1503 was not viewed favourably by the exiled Piero de' Medici (though his opinion counted but little, for he died not long after the wedding), as the union of two of Florence's great, old families could have created a significant obstacle to a Medici return to Florence. This had been a long-standing objection on the part of Piero, made even more urgent by the expulsion of the Medici family in 1494.[52] In fact, his worries proved to be unfounded,

47 Savonarola was burned at the stake, along with two of his followers on 23 May 1498, but his supporters, though temporarily silenced, regained their voice in the years following his death. See Polizzotto, *The Elect Nation;* he covers this theme throughout.

48 There is some disagreement over the date of the marriage. Luca Landucci, for example, placed it in 1504, but Richard Goldthwaite and Andrea Gareffi both traced it to 1503. See Goldthwaite, *Private Wealth*, 82, and Gareffi, *Commedie*, 31. On this matter I choose to follow Goldthwaite and Gareffi.

49 "Lorénzo honoreuolm(ent)e rifiutato" (Appendix 2, 16r 20).

50 This theme is discussed in the Foreword.

51 "Il uedeua pupillo, e ricco, senza protettore, e difensoré rimasto, gl'haueua sposata auanti al témpo maturo" (Appendix 2, 16v 4–6).

52 Lorenzo married Lucrezia Rucellai, daughter of Bernardo di Giovanni Rucellai, despite the Medici family's long-standing objections (Appendix 2, 16v 18 and ff).

for a reason he could not have foreseen: the distaste the Rucellai and Strozzi families developed for Piero Soderini.

Evidently, rumours of the marriage at least initially caused something of a stir in the city, particularly amongst supporters of its *Gonfaloniere* for life, Piero Soderini.[53] It was well known that there were tensions between Soderini and Lorenzo Strozzi (and there had been long-standing troubles between Bernardo Rucellai, Lorenzo's long-time supporter, and Piero Soderini), as for several years before and after the 1503 wedding Soderini had backed Alfonso Strozzi, Lorenzo's and Filippo's much older half-brother, in a legal dispute.[54] Alfonso was Filippo the Elder's oldest son from his first marriage and therefore ought to have been the heir to most or all of his father's wealth, but Filippo's second wife Selvaggia persuaded her husband to favour her sons' rights over those of Alfonso, thereby diluting the eldest brother's claims.

In reality, however, Alfonso's grievances were at least partially of his own making. When he realized that his stepmother was attempting to undermine his hereditary rights, he took legal action, emancipating himself in 1489. Not long thereafter he divested his "own financial interests from [Selvaggia's]."[55] This meant that Filippo's estate was effectively divided into thirds, shared out equally between Alfonso, Lorenzo, and Filippo; and his perception of favouritism and of his stepmother's greed left Alfonso bitter, more than a little jealous, and apt to act on his grievances. For example, he liquidated some family business holdings in Naples that were supposed to remain in the family. He also refused to pay for his portion of the Palazzo

53 Piero Soderini was made *Gonfaloniere a vita* in 1502. Although the title *Gonfalioniere* indicated that Soderini was the head of the state for life, his actions were constrained by the Florentine constitution and balanced by the other branches of the Florentine government. His regime only lasted until 1512, when he fled Florence in the face of a church (and Medici) funded Spanish mercenary army. For what is still one of the finest discussions, in English as least, of the politics of Florence during the time of Soderini, see H.C. Butters, *Governors and Governments in Early Sixteenth-Century Florence, 1502–1519* (Oxford: Clarendon, 1985). For another classic article on Machiavelli and his relationship with Soderini, see Sergio Bertelli, "Machiavelli and Soderini," *Renaissance Quarterly* 28, no. 1 (1975): 1–16.

54 In fact, part of the dispute between Alfonso and Lorenzo and Filippo reached a head in August 1503 just two months after Lorenzo's wedding. Goldthwaite, *Private Wealth*, 75n2. Sadly, Alfonso died in self-imposed exile in Naples in 1534, still unwilling to pay his brothers, who were forced to continue the litigation, as it pertained to the unfinished palazzo, against Alfonso's heirs. The dispute was not resolved until 1540, six years after Alfonso's death.

55 Goldthwaite, *Private Wealth*, 75.

Strozzi. He was entitled to half of the structure, but because he would not fund his part of the construction it remained unfinished and an eyesore. Lorenzo and Filippo were forced to seek restitution for those and other losses in the Florentine court system, and in this dispute Piero Soderini took Alfonso's side. Soderini's intervention in what was essentially a family affair earned him the scorn of Lorenzo di Filippo Strozzi. Following his usual methods, Strozzi was subtle enough to keep his complaints to himself. And with all of this happening in the background, Lorenzo and Lucrezia were married. The wedding celebrations were joyous,[56] and the family home was sufficiently far along in construction that it could not only host the celebrations but was also ready for the newlyweds to inhabit.[57]

Lorenzo and Lucrezia had their first son soon after their marriage. Giovan Battista was born on 3 October 1504 (d. 1571). With an heir produced so early in his marriage, Lorenzo turned to flirtations and affairs outside of the matrimonial bedchamber. Even as he captivated a number of women in Florence, he still remained a gentleman, though an unfaithful one. According to Virgil Milani, Lorenzo was not frequently rejected, but when he was he gave the woman who refused his advances gifts, together with apologies for offending her sensibilities.[58] Lorenzo did not make enemies, with the exception of Piero Soderini. The anomalous nature of their strained relationship invites consideration of Lorenzo's "political" character in greater detail.

It seems clear that Lorenzo did not let his dislike of the unscrupulous *Gonfaloniere*'s actions colour his own republican sentiment. Illustrating this, Lorenzo's biographer Zeffi wrote that he "was naturally inclined to the liberty of his native city (*patria*)" and especially toward republican government.[59] But Zeffi also concluded that if the political winds changed, then Lorenzo was prepared to do what was necessary to survive.

---

56 "Le nozze di poi ché la città fù quiétata nel 1503 si celebrarono nel palazzo grandé con tal pompa, ché per ancora à ogn'un priuato cedono" (Appendix 2, 16v 18–20).

57 "E al dì 16 di giugno fu finito questo palagio degli Strozzi, questa mezza parte; e menovvi moglie dentro Lorenzo di Filippo Strozzi, e fece molto belle nozze e begli apparati" (Luca Landucci, *Diario Fiorentino dal 1450 al 1516 di Luca Landucci: Continuato da un anonimo fino al 1542*, ed. Iodoco del Badia [Florence: Sansoni, 1883], 269). Landucci's text was cited by Beatrice Paolozzi Strozzi in "La Nostra Casa Grande," in *Palazzo Strozzi: Cinque Secoli di Arte e Cultura*, ed. Giorgio Bonsanti (Florence: Nardi Editore, 2005), 66.

58 Virgil I. Milani, "An Edition of Lorenzo di Filippo Strozzi's Comedy, *'La Violante,'* with an Introduction to the *Commedia Erudita* of the Cinquecento," master's thesis, Catholic University of America, 1960; see p. x.

59 "Egli naturalm(ent)e era inclinato alla libertà della patria sua" (Appendix 2, 20r 22–3).

> From whence, he knew how to steady his boat in the tempestuous times of the Florentine Republic [1494–1512]; so that no change kept him out of a safe port, living agreeably with princes and most acceptable to the people.[60]

The subtlety that Zeffi ascribed to Lorenzo was partly derived from his mother's insistence that he learn the gentlemanly arts, a parental directive compelled through blunt force, and his father's tutelage in the art of dissimulation. The ease with which Lorenzo ingratiated himself with Lucrezia Borgia and the Venetian nobility demonstrates that he carried on his father's legacy, but with some careful guidance from his mother.

In the years following his marriage, Lorenzo returned to the arts and particularly to the street theatre of Florentine civic processions.[61] Here, we have come to one of the bizarre moments in Lorenzo Strozzi's life, mentioned at the outset of this chapter, which coincides with the *Pistola*'s fictional plot. In 1506,[62] Lorenzo was selected by Piero di Cosimo to orchestrate a macabre float for the Florentine Carnival. Lorenzo's biographer, Zeffi, described the ensuing spectacle in some detail:

> In the year 1506, I believe, [Lorenzo] was made designer and conductor of Death's parade float; of all of the *mascherete* which had ever been performed in Florence, this was perhaps the most marvelous, and the material both so novel and horrendous that preparations for it had to be prudently conducted, not only regarding the costumes which were required for it, but also to keep it a secret.[63]

---

60 "Onde seppe la sua barca nelli tempestosi tempi della Rep(ubblica) Fior(entin)a tranquillare; siche per nissuna mutazione gli mancò il sicuro porto, uiuendo à principi accetto, et accettissimo al popolo" (Appendix 2, 20v 12–15).

61 Still the best general survey of public spectacle and civic processions in Renaissance Florence is Richard Trexler's *Public Life in Renaissance Florence* (New York: Academic Press, 1980). For ritual and procession associated with death and with funerals, see Sharon T. Strocchia's *Death and Ritual in Renaissance Florence* (Baltimore: Johns Hopkins University Press, 1992).

62 Interestingly, Machiavelli's newly constituted "Florentine" militia also made its debut during this same Carnival. Neither man commented on the other's contributions to the Carnival. For more on Machiavelli's 1506 militia, see Mikael Hörnqvist, "Perché non si usa allegare i Romani: Machiavelli and the Florentine Militia of 1506," *Renaissance Quarterly* 55, no. 1 (2002): 148–91.

63 "L'anno credo 1506 fù inuentore, e conduttore del carro della Morte, che delle mascherate, che mai si fecero in Fior(enz)a, fù forse la più merauigliosa, e per la materia pér sé stessa nuoua, et orrenda, e per essersi prudentem(ent)e condotta, non tanto con l'abbigliature che à ciò si ricercauano, q(ua)nto col tenerla segreta" (Appendix 2, 17v 5–11).

Under Lorenzo's careful supervision, and with Piero di Cosimo's usual strangeness and attention to detail, the parade float was turned into a mobile cemetery, complete with tombs from which citizens dressed like rotting skeletons would leap at the appointed stops. The dead then sang a song while some three hundred participants on foot and horseback filtered through the surrounding crowd reminding the onlookers that they too would die at the appointed hour.[64]

The song of the dead was written by Castellano Castellani.[65] Its title hints at its intended effect: *Dolor, pianto e penitenza*. Piero di Cosimo's brilliant designs, combined with Lorenzo Strozzi's natural gifts as a showman, produced one of the most memorable Carnivals in early sixteenth-century Florence.[66] It was remarkable enough for Giorgio Vasari to comment on it almost fifty years later, in a lengthy but evocative passage:

> Among these spectacles, which were numerous as well as ingeniously arranged, I am inclined briefly to describe one, which was, for the most part, invented by Piero, when he had already attained to mature age; this show was not of a pleasing or attractive character, but, on the contrary, was altogether strange, terrible, and unexpected: it gave no small pleasure to the people nevertheless, for as in their food they sometimes prefer the sharp and bitter savours, so in their pastimes are they attracted by things horrible; and these, provided they be presented to us with art and judgment, do indeed most wonderfully delight the human heart, a truth which is made apparent from the pleasure with which we listen to the recitation of tragedy. The spectacle here alluded to was the Triumph of Death; the car was prepared in the Hall of the Pope by Piero himself, and with so much secrecy, that no breath or suspicion of his purpose got abroad, and the completed work was made known and given to view at one and the same moment. The Triumphal Car was covered with black cloth, and was of vast size, it had skeletons and white crosses painted upon its surface, and was drawn by buffaloes, all of which were totally black: within the Car stood the colossal figure of Death, bearing the scythe in his hand, which around him were covered tombs, which opened at all the places where the procession halted, while those who formed it chanted

64 Appendix 2, 17v.11ff.

65 Until the turn of the twentieth century, scholars thought that the Carnival song that accompanied the float was written by Antonio Alamanni. For details on the problems of attribution, see William F. Prizer, "Creation of a Carnival Song," in *Early Music History: Studies in Medieval and Early Modern Music*, vol. 23, ed. Iain Fenlon (Cambridge: Cambridge, University Press): 185–252.

66 See the note in the published edition of Zeffi's *Vita* on p. xi.

lugubrious songs, when certain figures stole forth, clothed in black cloth; on these vestments the bones of a skeleton were depicted in white; the arms, breasts, ribs, and legs, namely, all which gleamed horribly forth on the black beneath. At a certain distance appeared figures bearing torches, and wearing masks, presenting the face of death, as well as the skeleton neck beneath them, also exhibited to view, were not only painted with the utmost fidelity to nature, but had besides a frightful expression which was horrible to behold. At the sound of a wailing summons, sent forth with a hollow moan from trumpets of muffled yet inexorable tones, the figures of the dead raised themselves half out of their tombs, and seating their skeleton forms thereon, they sang the following words, now so much extolled and admired, to music of the most plaintive and melancholy character: *Dolor, pianto, e penetenzia.* Before and after the car rode a train of the dead on horses, carefully selected from the most wretched and meager animals that could be found, the caparison of these worn, half-dying creatures were black, covered with white crosses; each was conducted by four attendants, clothed in the vestments of the grave; these last-mentioned figures, bearing black torches and a large black standard, covered with crosses, bones and death's heads.[67]

---

67 Giorgio Vasari, *Lives of the Most Eminent Painters, Sculptors and Architects*, vol. 2, trans. Mrs. Jonathan Foster (London: Bell and Daldy, 1871), 417–18. The Italian original is: "Fra questi, che assai furono ingegnosi, mi piace toccare brevemente d'uno che fu principale d'invenzione di Piero già maturo d'anni, e non come molti piacevole per la sua vaghezza, ma per il contrario per una strana e orrible ed inaspettata invenzione di non piccola satisfazione a'popoli; che come ne'cibi talvolta le cose agre, così in quelli passatempi le cose orribili, purchè siano fatte con giudizio e arte, dilettano maravigliosamente il gusto umano: cosa che apparisce nel recitare le tragedie. Questo fu il carro della Morte da lui segretissimamente lavorato alla sala del Papa, che mai se ne potette spiare cosa alcuna, ma fu, veduto e saputo in un medesimo punto.

Era il trionfo un carro grandissimo tirato da bufoli tutto nero e dipinto d'ossa di morti e di croci bianche, e sopra il carro una Morte grandissima in cima con la falce in mano, ed aveva in giro al carro molti sepolcri col coperchio; ed in tutti que'luoghi che il trionfo si fermava a cantare, s'aprivano e uscivano alcuni vestiti di tele nera, sopra la quale erano dipinte tutte le ossature di morto nelle braccia, petto, rene, e gambe, che il bianco spiccava sopra quel nero, ed apparendo di lontano alcune di quelle torce con maschere che pigliavano col teschio di morto il dinanzi e'l di dietro e parimente la gola, oltre al parere cosa naturalissima, era orribile e spaventosa a vedere; e questi morti al suono di certe trombe sorde e con suon roco e morto uscivano mezzi di que'sepolcri, e sedendovi sopra, cantavano in musica piena di malinconia quella oggi nobilissima canzone: *Dolor, pianto, e penitenza, ec.* Era innanzi e dietro al carro gran numero di morti a cavallo sopra certi cavalli con somma diligenza scelti de'più secchi e più strutti che si potessero trovare, con covertine nere piene di croci bianche e ciascuno aveva quattro staffieri vestiti da

Although Vasari makes no mention of Lorenzo Strozzi here, the Strozzi account books detail the event and corroborate not only Lorenzo's involvement in the Carnival but also Zeffi's date of 1506.[68]

Vasari also speculated that the resurrected dead were to be interpreted allegorically, as a wish on the part of Piero di Cosimo and the Carnival organizers for the return of the Medici "from the dead."[69] This seems preposterous, for Lorenzo had only recently had rough dealings with Piero de' Medici over the former's marriage to Lucrezia Rucellai. That Lorenzo craved a Medici restoration seems misguided at best. As Andrea Gareffi has noted, the float, the songs, and the symbolism of the *memento mori* were far more likely to be related to the recent prophecies and millenarianism associated with the late Savonarola than to any desire to see the Medici restored.[70] Whatever the motivation behind the float, there remains at least one important link between the Carnival of 1506 and Strozzi's later literary life, which Zeffi's and Vasari's descriptions of the Carnival suggest: its relationship to Lorenzo di Filippo Strozzi's *Pistola*.

The way in which Lorenzo, his brother Filippo, and Piero di Cosimo designed their float, and especially the way in which the float's attendants interacted with the audience, is reflected almost exactly in Lorenzo's *Pistola*. The float was designed to terrify, but it also provided shock value and gruesome entertainment. The *Pistola* used very similar imagery to provoke the same reactions from its readers. Its subject matter was horrible, but the manner in which Strozzi dealt with it was humourous and even lewd. I will have more to say on this below, where I show that Lorenzo's evidently rather large part in the Carnival of 1506 helped to shape his

---

morti con torce nere ed uno stendardo grande nero con croci ed ossa e teste di morto. (Giorgio Vasari, *Vite de' più eccellenti pittori, scultori e architetti*, vol. 7 [Milan: Della Società Tipografica de' Classici Italiani, 1809], 191–3).

68 Stephen J. Craven, "Three Dates for Piero di Cosimo," *The Burlington Magazine* 117, no. 870 (1975): 572, 574–6. For the details of the Strozzi *giornale*, see 575 and notes 15–17. For a recent book on the life and works of Piero di Cosimo, see Dennis Geronimus, *Piero di Cosimo: Visions Beautiful and Strange* (New Haven: Yale University Press, 2006).

69 Vasari, *Le Vite*, 193–4.

70 Andrea Gareffi, *La scrittura e la festa: Teatro, festa e letteratura nella Firenze del Rinascimento* (Bologna: Il Mulino, 1991), 114. Gareffi noted that one of Lorenzo's early childhood tutors, Fonzio, was a supporter of Savonarola. For more information on Fonzio's humanist studies, see F. Saxl, "The Classical Inscription in Renaissance Art and Politics: Bartholomaeus Fontius: Liber monumentorum Romanae urbis et aliorum locorum," *Journal of the Warburg and Courtauld Institutes* 4, no. 1–2 (1940–1941): 19–46.

literary vision of Florence during a plague outbreak.[71] It is also possible that the spectacles of 1506 not only informed Lorenzo's literary tastes, but also heightened his fondness for the grotesque in general.[72]

Vasari's erroneous attempt to connect the Carnival float of 1506 with the Medici family in 1506 set a precedent. In 1588, for example, Fra Serafino Razzi wrote that the *carro* had been designed by Lorenzo de' Medici, the Magnificent. Within the space of roughly eighty-two years, then, the macabre float entered into Florentine legend and in that legend Lorenzo Strozzi had become Lorenzo the Magnificent.[73] What might we make of this? Perhaps Lorenzo Strozzi's actions were so memorable, so brilliant, that the Florentines could only associate them with the "Magnificent" Lorenzo. Or perhaps Strozzi's legacy had faded so extensively that by 1588 the Florentines had forgotten who he was; perhaps he was so adept in his

---

71 For more on the Carnival of 1506, see Richard Trexler, *Public Life in Renaissance Florence* (Ithaca: Cornell University Press, 1991), 511ff.

72 As a case in point, in March 1519 Lorenzo put on a dinner party for Carnival in Rome that was so vile and so macabre his guests vomited in horror before fleeing his home. This incident is discussed below.

73 "They recount that the preceding *lauda* ['Dolor pianto e penitenza'] was composed for a *canto* [*carnascialesco*] that the Magnificent Lorenzo de' Medici had done [and that] he secretly guided the evening of carnival, having knocked down a portion of the walls of the Medici gardens on the Piazza S. Marco. There came forth a *carro* full of tombs, from which skeletons emerged and returned, and on this *carro* were the singers, also dressed as skeletons. Behind the *carro* followed, four in a row, a good number of youths, they and their horses nude and dressed only in costumes with the signs of death. And they recall that the frightening sound of the music, and the sight of so many seeming dead, and the splendour of innumerable torches with those nocturnal shadows moved the whole city of Florence to understanding, and the following morning began a holy Lent" (Prizer, "Carnival Song," 195). The Italian original is: "Narrano come la precedente lauda fu composta per un canto fatto fare dal Magnifico Lorenzo de' Medici, il quale condotto segretamente, la sera del carnevale, gittata in terra una parte del muro del giardino de' Medici su la piazza di San Marco. Usci fuori con un carro pieno di sepolture, donde uscivano et entravano morti, e sopra detto carro erano i cantori, essi ancora in sembianza di morti; e dietro al carro seguitavano a coppia, o vero a 4 per fila, buon numero di giovani, eglino et i cavalli loro nudi e con sole sopravesti dipinte con insegne pure di morti; e riferiscono, come al canto della musica che atteriva, et alla vista di tante sembianze di morti, la città di Firenze, et allo splendore di torcie innumerabili, con quelle notturne tenebre, tutta si commosse a comprenzione; e la mattina seguente si principio una santa quaresima" (Prizer, "Carnival Song," 248, document 3). The ms cited by Prizer is located in the Biblioteca Nazionale Centrale (Florence) MS Pal. 173, fol. 156v. *S. Razzi, Libri Quattro di laudis critti e composti da Fra Serafino Razzi dell'ordine Predicatori e Provincia Romana.*

use of *sprezzatura* that he blended into, and was eventually lost in, the vivid tapestry of *cinquecento* Florence. In either case, Lorenzo Strozzi's identity became obscured less than forty years after his death.

Zeffi misattributed another event in Strozzi's life, transplanting it to the Medici palace in 1506. In that year, along with cultivating a sense of theatrical style, Lorenzo also busied himself with perfecting his poetry, singing, and musical abilities. Zeffi wrote that in the same period as the Carnival of 1506 Lorenzo was invited by Lorenzo de' Medici, Duke of Urbino, to recite a number of original poems and to conduct performances of two of his plays. The plays that Lorenzo directed were most likely his *Commedia in versi* and *La Pisana*.[74] Though generally reliable, Zeffi's chronology is incorrect here. Sorting out the error in Zeffi's *Vita* of Strozzi requires a detour to the late 1510s (and an examination of the relationship between Strozzi's plays and Machiavelli's *Mandragola*).

There are three details in particular that must be addressed to situate this event in Strozzi's life properly. First, Strozzi's plays could not have been performed in 1506, as neither was written until several years, perhaps even a decade, later. Second, the Medici were still in exile in 1506, so his plays could not have been staged in the Medici palace in that year.[75] Third, the Ashburnham 579 autograph of Strozzi's *Commedia in versi* contains further proofs of Zeffi's error. At the outset of that manuscript, on the recto of folio two, there is an interesting note concerning Strozzi's eldest son Giambattista: "Commedia del S. Giambattista Strozzi / recitata in Casa i Medici circa il 1506" (Comedy by S. Giambattista Strozzi/ recited [or performed] in the Medici house circa 1506). Zeffi also mentioned that Giambattista had a speaking role in the play's first production.[76] But Giambattista was only two years old in 1506; clearly a two year old could neither write nor take part in a play. An unknown hand later corrected the manuscript's attribution, striking through "Giambattista" and replacing it

74 Gareffi, *Commedie*: 37–42. The *Commedia* was published for the first time in the 1769 Cosmopoli edition of Machiavelli's *Opere*. However, it was then only tentatively attributed to Machiavelli. In 1797 it was published as a work *by* Machiavelli. See vol. 7 of Machiavelli's *Opere di Niccolò Machiavelli: Segretario e cittadino fiorentino*, ed. Gaetano Poggiali and Giovanni Battista Baldelli Boni (Livorno, 1797), 287–368.

75 "Onde accompagnata l'arte con l'ingegno naturale, si messe à comporre trà gl'altri Poemati più Comedie, delle quali la prima si recitò nel Palazzo de Medici ad intanza del Mag(nifi)co Lorenzo Duca d'Vrbino" (Appendix 2, 18v 14–17).

76 "Doue uoi, et il maggior' uostro fratello ui portaste nel recitare la parte uostra in tal maniera, che trà li istrioni, che per tutto il dominio si erano procacciati, si conobbe euidente la prontezza della pronunzia uostra" (Appendix 2, 18v 18–22).

with "Lorenzo." On the recto of folio three, one finds a Lorenzo Strozzi autograph addition that states explicitly, "La prima commedia ch'io facessi/mai recitata in casa e Medici" (The first comedy that I wrote/ever recited [or performed] in the Medici's home).[77] So then, based upon Andrea Gareffi's scholarship and on Strozzi's own testimony, we must conclude that the *Commedia* was performed in the Medici palace.[78] But, if we accept that the remainder of the details provided by Zeffi are correct, the *Commedia* could only have been performed there after Lorenzo became Duke of Urbino in 1516 and before 4 May 1519, when he died.

Within this relatively narrow range, Roberto Ridolfi and Alessandro Parronchi[79] both concluded that 1518 was the most likely year of first production of the *Commedia in versi* (and *La Pisana*).[80] There is, however, a great deal of debate on the specific dates of their productions. For example,

---

77 See Gareffi, *La Scrittura*, 120–1, for more background and detail.

78 Gareffi, *Commedie*, 37. There Gareffi pointed out that there are two ways to read "mai" in Strozzi's testimony, presenting a *lectio difficilior*, or harder reading. "Mai" as Gareffi read it, a reading that I have followed, should be translated as "ever." However, depending upon the placement of punctuation, which is absent in the original, "mai" might also be translated as "never." Gareffi concluded that this second reading is doubtful, as it cancels the note on 2r.

79 Alessondro Parronchi, "La prima rappresentazione della *Mandragola*," *La Bibliofilia* 64 (1962): 80–1 where Parronchi argued for September 1518. Roberto Ridolfi suggested February of the same year; see his *Composizione, rappresentazaione e prima edizione della Mandragola*, in *Studi sulle commedie del Machiavelli* (Pisa: Nistri-Lischi, 1968), cited in Giovanni da Pozzo, *Storia letteraria d'Italia: Il Cinquecento, Tomo 1, 1494–1533* (Padua: PICCIN, 2007), 30n26.

80 Gareffi, *La Scrittura*, 122–7. For debates on the dates of Machiavelli's and Strozzi's plays see *La Mandragola*: *Storia e filologia, con l'edizione critica del testo secondo il Laurenziano Redi 129*, ed. Pasquale Stoppelli (Rome: Bulzoni, 2005), 69–89. For an older though still helpful contribution to the debate on the date of the *Mandragola*, see Sergio Bertelli, "When Did Machiavelli Write *Mandragola*?" *Renaissance Quarterly* 24, no. 3 (1971): 317–26. Gareffi's scholarship on Strozzi's plays is the most comprehensive and most accurate. For his coverage of Lorenzo's three plays see *Commedie*, 36–42. Gareffi, for the first time, traced all of Strozzi's plays to their manuscript sources, all of which are located in Florence. The manuscripts of the *Commedia in versi* are found in Biblioteca Nazionale Centrale, Banco Rari 29, 118r–171r (this is the Machiavelli autograph of the *Commedia*); Biblioteca Medicea Laurenziana, Ashburnham 579, 4r–56r, contains the Strozzi autograph of the *Commedia*. The Prologue is found on 58v (in the hand of a copyist with revisions in Strozzi's hand); and in the same library the "mutilated" Ashburnham 578 is found. *La Pisana*, also in the Medicea Laurenziana, is located in the Ashburnham 606, 3r–38r in a copyist's hand with autograph corrections by Strozzi. *La Violante* is also found in the Ashburnham 606, 47r–74r. It too survives in a copyist's hand.

Ridolfi concluded that Strozzi's plays were staged in February 1518 and Parronchi opted for September 1518, as both months witnessed celebrations of Lorenzo de' Medici's marriage to Madeleine de la Tour d'Auvergne at the Medici palace.[81] Moreover, in 1518 Giambattista Strozzi was fourteen years old, certainly old enough to take part in the productions, as Zeffi intimated. These are cogent reasons for supposing that Strozzi's plays were, as Parronchi and Ridolfi argued, produced in 1518.

Ridolfi and Parronchi also proposed that Machiavelli's *Mandragola* was presented at the same wedding festivities as Strozzi's plays. Ridolfi based his conclusion on the fact that the *Mandragola*'s prologue contains the lines "Quest'è Firenze vostra, / Un'altra volta sarà Roma o Pisa" (This is our Florence / [On] another occasion it will be Rome or Pisa). Strozzi's *Commedia* is set in Rome and his *La Pisana*, as its title indicates, is set in Pisa. Relying on this textual and contextual evidence, Ridolfi suggested that the *Mandragola* refers directly to the settings of Strozzi's plays.[82] If Ridolfi is correct, then Machiavelli's and Strozzi's plays were produced in very close proximity to one another, and we might also gather from Ridolfi's scholarship that in September 1518 Machiavelli was at least superficially familiar with Strozzi's work. Ridolfi's conclusions have, however, come under sustained attack by Sergio Bertelli and Carlo Dionisotti.[83]

The *Mandragola* is not referred to in Machiavelli's personal letters, or anywhere else for that matter, until 26 April 1520 and following. Contrary to Ridolfi's and Parronchi's dating of the *Mandragola*'s first production as 1518, Bertelli and Dionisotti suggest a date of 1519 or later.[84] If this is accurate, then the *Mandragola*'s references to Rome and Pisa seem less likely to refer to Strozzi's plays. Furthermore, there is no concrete evidence to

81 Parronchi, "La prima rappresentazione," 80–1, where Parronchi argued for September 1518. Roberto Ridolfi suggested February of the same year; see his *Composizione*: 11–35. Andrea Gareffi rejected Parronchi's and Ridolfi's conclusions, though he did not provide definitive dates for the productions of either of Strozzi's plays; see his *La scrittura*, 120–2.

82 Roberto Ridolfi, *Composizione*, 11–35, cited in da Pozzo, *Storia letteraria d'Italia*, 30n26.

83 Bertelli, "When Did Machiavelli Write *Mandragola*?" 321; Carlo Dionisotti, "Appunti sulla Mandragola," *Belfagor* 39 (1984): 621–44.

84 The "Mandragola" in Florence, Biblioteca Medicea Laurenziana, Rediano 129, 110r–131r is dated 1519. For more on this ms, see Bertelli, "When Did Machiavelli Write *Mandragola*?" 321. For more on the probable 1520 productions (Florence and Rome) of Machiavelli's play, see Paolo Giovio, *Gli elogi degli uomini illustri (Letterati, Artisti, Uomini d'arme)*, ed. Renzo Meregazzi, *Opere*, vol. 8 (Rome: Instituto Poligrafico dello Stato, 1972), 111–12, cited in Franco Fido, *Machiavelli,*

suggest that the three plays were staged back to back in 1518. For example, Andrea Gareffi and Sergio Bertelli both demonstrated that the letter on which Parronchi based his claim that Strozzi's plays were staged, along with Machiavelli's, in 1518 in fact refers to just one play by name, *Il Farlagho*.[85] Parronchi suggested, without any evidence, that *Il Farlagho*, must in fact have been Strozzi's *Commedia in versi*. The letter cited by Parronchi also mentions that two other plays were produced, one before and one after *Il Farlagho*. Parronchi, again without evidence, insisted that the unnamed plays were Strozzi's *La Pisana* and Machiavelli's *Mandragola*. Here Gareffi's scholarship is decisive.

Gareffi pointed out that even though Francesco Zeffi's *Vita* of Strozzi incorrectly traces the production of Strozzi's plays to 1506, his comments on the staging of the plays contain important, unnoticed evidence. In Zeffi's account, there is no mention of a wedding celebration, though one would think that having one's plays staged for the Duke of Urbino's wedding would be worth mentioning. Zeffi wrote only that Strozzi's plays were performed at the insistence of Lorenzo de' Medici, Duke of Urbino. This still leaves the dates of 1516 to 1519, the years that Lorenzo held the title Duke of Urbino, as the only years that Strozzi's plays could have been produced in the Medici palace. Internally, Strozzi's plays narrow the date to one specific year: in act 3, scene 1, verses 4–6 of *Commedia in versi*, the "parasite" refers to the "bisesto"; and in *La Pisana*, act 4, scene 2, verse 195, one of the players refers to "l'anno del bisesto" (leap year). The year 1516[86] was the only "anno del bisesto" during the Duke of Urbino's tenure, so the *Commedia* and *La Pisana* could certainly have been produced in that year.[87]

Gareffi admits that 1516 was the most likely year for the production of Strozzi's plays, but he also concedes that there is not enough evidence to assign their staging to particular days in that year.[88] Using internal, textual

---

Guicciardini e storici minori del primo Cinquecento (Padua: Piccin Nuova Libraria, 1994), 28. Carlo Dionisotti suggested 1520 as the year of the *Mandragola*'s first production; see his "Appunti".

85 Bertelli, "When Did Machiavelli Write *Mandragola*?" 319–20; Gareffi, *La scrittura*, 122.

86 In Gareffi's *Commedia*, he concluded that 1518 was an "*anno bisestile*." He was incorrect. The year 1516, however, was. Gareffi's error was corrected by Alberto Asor Rosa, *Letteratura italiana: Storia e geografia*, vol. 2 (Einaudi, 1989). Gareffi's *La Scrittura*, 123, reflects the correct date, but it makes no mention of Asor Rosa's research.

87 Gareffi, *Commedie*, 38–9, 41–2.

88 Ibid., 39.

evidence, Gareffi corrected Zeffi's chronological error. In addition, his research, combined with Bertelli's, proves that Strozzi's and Machiavelli's plays could not have been produced during the same period. In fact, their productions were probably several years apart. But how might we explain the existence of Machiavelli's autograph copy of Lorenzo di Filippo Strozzi's *Commedia in versi* located, together with the *Pistola*, in the Banco Rari 29 manuscript?

Machiavelli signed his autograph of the *Commedia* with the strange "ego Barlachia recensui" (I, Barlachia, have examined and corrected this).[89] There are a number of ways that Machiavelli's pseudonym might be interpreted. Domenico Barlacchi was a well-known Florentine actor and town crier. Lorenzo Strozzi even dedicated four poems to him.[90] In an effort to disprove Machiavelli's authorship of the *Commedia*, while simultaneously attempting to prove who did author it (and how a copy of it ended up as a Machiavelli autograph), Angelo Solerti suggested that Barlacchi prepared a redaction of the *Commedia in versi*, which he also might have authored, and that Machiavelli based his autograph of the *Commedia* on Barlacchi's redaction.[91] This theory certainly explains why Machiavelli signed his copy of the *Commedia* with "Ego Barlachia," but there is simply no proof that Machiavelli had access to Barlacchi's redaction (if there ever was one). When Pio Ferrieri published his research on the Ashburnham 606 codex, the *Commedia* was definitively attributed to Strozzi. Simultaneously, the links between Machiavelli's "ego Barlachia," the real Domenico Barlacchi, and

89 Translated by Ronald L. Martinez. He argued that Machiavelli took the name of the "Florentine herald and jokester Barlachia while aping the formula at the end of ancient copies of Terence ('Calliopius recensui'), long thought to be a reference to the producer of Terence's plays." See Martinez's essay, "Comedian, Tragedian: Machiavelli and Traditions of Renaissance Theater," in *The Cambridge Companion to Machiavelli*, ed. John M. Najemy (Cambridge: Cambridge University Press, 2010), 206–22 (p. 207 for quotation). For the first serious investigation into Machiavelli's use of "Barlachia" see Fortunato Pintor, "Ego Barlachia recensui," *Giornale Storico della Letteratura Italiana* 39 (1902): 103–9.

90 Ferrieri, "Lorenzo di Filippo Strozzi," 226ff, esp. notes on 226–2.

91 Angelo Solerti, "La rappresentazione della Calandria a Lione nel 1548," in *Raccolta di studii critici dedicate ad Alessandro D'Ancona, festeggiandosi il XL anno del suo insegnamento* (Florence: Barbèra, 1901): 693–9; Abd-el-kader Salza, "Domenico Barlacchi: Araldo, attore e scapigliato fiorentino del secolo XVI," in *Rassenga Bibliografica della Letteratura Italiana*, vol. 8, ed. E. Spoerri (Pisa: Mariotti, 1901): 27–33

the text of Strozzi's play disintegrated.[92] Therefore, it is improbable at best that Machiavelli would have seriously styled himself after Barlacchi. So why might he have adopted the town crier's name?

The most widely accepted explanation for Machiavelli's "Ego Barlachia recensui" is that Machiavelli was aping "Calliopius recensui," which is found at the end of several ancient manuscripts of Terrence's plays.[93] Machiavelli surely had Terrence on his mind, as evidenced by his Florentine translation of Terrence's *Andria,* which is also located, along with the *Commedia* and the *Pistola*, in the Banco Rari 29 codex.[94] Understood in this light, Machiavelli's use of "Barlachia" may be read as an exercise in histrionics, or as a tongue-in-cheek, inside joke. If he was making a joke, it remains unclear whether he made it at his own expense ("Barlacchio" might also be translated as "simpleton") or at the expense of the real Domenico Barlacchi. In some respects, though, "simpleton" resonates with how Machiavelli probably felt as he copied Strozzi's inferior play. If he did act as Strozzi's client and copyist, then he might have thought the tasks required of him as beneath him, though crushingly necessary.[95]

Andrea Gareffi noted that everything about Strozzi's moralizing play was "alien to the spirit of Machiavelli."[96] Even more importantly, he concluded that the Machiavelli autograph of Strozzi's *Commedia* resulted

92 Salza's famous essay was published in 1900, eight years after Ferrieri published his research on the Ashburnham codex. Even though Fortunato Pintor, relying on Ferrieri's research, systematically disproved Salza's (and Angelo Solerti's) theory, it continues to have its supporters, including Alessandro Parronchi, who insists that Machiavelli's "Ego Barlacchi" is a reference to Machiavelli's supposed redaction of the *Commedia in versi* prepared by Domenico Barlacchi. Alessandro Parronchi, "La prima rappresentazione della Mandragola: Il modello per l'apparato-L'allegoria," *La Bibliofilia* 64 (1962).

93 Martinez, "Comedian, Tragedian," 207.

94 Machiavelli's Florentine translation of *Andria* is found on 173r–208v in the Banco Rari 29 codex. For more on the language used in that play see Brian Richardson, "Evoluzione stilistica e fortuna della traduzione machiavelliana dell'Andria,'" *Lettere Italiane* 25 (1973).

95 "Car Barlachia n'est probablement qu'un nom de guerre pris par Machiavelli lui-meme (*Barlacchio* veut dire *imbecile*) ..." (K. Hillebrand, *Études historiques et litteraires, Tome 1, Études Italiennes* [Paris: Librairie A. Franck, 1868], 352n1). Hillebrand's conclusion was transmitted by Pasquale Villari in *The Life and Times of Niccolò Machiavelli*, trans. Linda Villari, vol. 4. (London: Kegan Paul, Trench and Co., 1883), 202, note. Villari added that "Barlachia" or "simpleton" is "in fact a colloquial meaning of the term *barlacchio* or *barbalucchio*."

96 "Aliena dallo spirito di Machiavelli" (Gareffi, *Commedie*, 15).

from Machiavelli offering "his client's attention to Strozzi."[97] This rings true. The *Commedia*, like the *Pistola*, is a product of a lesser talent, but Lorenzo Strozzi was a powerful political survivor, plus he had been the agent of Machiavelli's reintegration within Medici circles in March 1520. With this fact in mind, it seems that Machiavelli's genius was reduced, sometime after the spring of 1520 (most likely in 1522), to copying the inferior literary works of Lorenzo di Filippo Strozzi, to whose early life we now return.

In 1508, Lorenzo's earlier problems with Piero Soderini resurfaced when it was made public that Filippo Strozzi, Lorenzo's younger brother, intended to marry Clarice de' Medici. Soderini opposed this powerful union on the grounds that it was unconstitutional, and in this he was right.[98] In fact, in 1506 Soderini had quashed the Medici's attempt to arrange a marriage between Clarice and a member of the Pitti family by appealing to his constitutional obligations to obstruct the marriage. Soderini had the "prospective groom's father summoned before judicial council and forced him to deny the arrangement." Shortly thereafter, Soderini attempted to arrange a marriage between one of his *own* nephews and Clarice, which also met with failure (which act exposed him as a hypocrite and sullied the reputation of the Republic more broadly). Filippo Strozzi was, therefore, the third Florentine man whom the Medici considered as husband to Clarice, and this time they succeeded.[99]

The driving force behind the betrothal was none other than Bernardo Rucellai, who convinced Selvaggia Strozzi that the best way to protect her family's patrimony (and to guard against an unjust exile for them all) was to marry Filippo to Clarice. Selvaggia was open to his advice, particularly when she considered the sizable dowry, roughly six thousand florins, that Clarice would contribute to the depleted Strozzi accounts.[100]

Evidently, Filippo refused to confide in Lorenzo about his marriage until after the contract was drawn up. Lorenzo did his best to disrupt the nuptials, but he was too late. His desire to derail the marriage of Filippo and Clarice may have indicated his distrust of the Medici, and perhaps it

97 "Sua attenzione di cliente allo Strozzi" (Gareffi, *Commedie*, 15).

98 The Florentine constitution forbid Florentine citizens from marrying into the Medici family on the grounds that, through marriage, the Medici would regain a foothold in the city. This matter is discussed below.

99 Melissa Meriam Bullard, "Marriage Politics and the Family in Florence: The Strozzi-Medici Alliance of 1508," *American Historical Review* 84, no. 3 (1979), 672.

100 Bullard, "Alliance," 673–4.

also highlights his fear that a resurgent Medici might bring down the Florentine republic – even though he disliked Soderini personally.

> Although Filippo, his brother, was already practically married to his wife Clarice di Piero de' Medici, [Filippo] did not discuss the marriage agreement with Lorenzo until after it was concluded (even though they lived together in harmony); for no other reason than he [Filippo] knew that he [Lorenzo] was completely foreign to such extraordinary affairs. So Lorenzo skillfully decided to disrupt and impede the marriage in every way possible. But Madonna Selvaggia, their mother, and Bernardo Rucellai, and Filippo Buondelmonti, conspired together ... And so the marriage followed.[101]

This episode proved instructive for Lorenzo. While he failed to halt his brother's marriage to a Medici, primarily due to his youth and political inexperience, in time he seems to have realized that Bernardo's motives were for the good of the Rucellai and Strozzi families. This alliance with the Medici family provided both the Strozzi and the Rucellai with protection. In due course, Lorenzo decided on a similar course of action: he sought out the Medici in preparation for a possible Medici restoration. Over the following years he spent a great deal of time outside of Florence, testing political waters and cultivating relationships with important members of the Medici family. It is likely that Lorenzo, who continued to nurse a hearty dislike for the *Gonfaloniere*, was encouraged in this course as he sensed Piero Soderini's weakness and therefore the inherent weakness of the "Soderini republic."

One must view Strozzi's actions within the broader context of his life and through the much wider lens of Renaissance Italy. He was a gentleman and a noble; the survival of his family and his own standing were of the utmost importance to him. This enabled him to remain sympathetic to the ideals of Florentine republicanism even as he positioned himself to survive the political transition should the Medici be restored to Florence. Lorenzo sacrificed some of his own republican ideals for the long-term good of his

101 "Quando adunque Filippo suo fratello hebbe in pratica di sposare per sua moglie la Clarice di Piero de Medici ribello, non conferì altrimenti à Lor(enz)o tal parentado, se no(n) concluso, benche insieme unitamente uiuessero, non per altro, se non che lo conosceua del tutto alieno dalle cose straordinarie: pure cosi Lor(enzo) s'ingegnò di turbare, et impedire tale coniugio per tutte quelle uie, che gli furono possibili; mà essendo Mad(on)na Seluaggia lor madre, e Bernardo Rucellai, e Filippo Buondelmenti à tal fatto congiuratisi, gli bisognò torsi dall'impresa, et cosi segui il parentado" (Appendix 2, 20v 16–26).

"house." Or, as his biographer Zeffi put it, Lorenzo did what was necessary "to maintain the rank of his noble family."[102] But it is doubtful that doing what was necessary made Strozzi's actions any easier.

Against what was likely a time of internal struggle for Lorenzo, his brother's marriage plans went forward, but a number of legal issues had to be sorted out before it could become official. Most of these were put in place by Piero Soderini, whose meddling here generated a great deal of animosity from not only Florence's aristocrats but also the common people. Lorenzo Strozzi also believed that Machiavelli was behind at least one of Soderini's attempts to thwart the marriage by accusing Filippo of violating the republican constitution, and thereby supporting a potential insurrection.[103] In an overlooked passage in Strozzi's *Vita di Filippo Strozzi* [Il Giovane], one comes across this:

> So an accusation against Filippo, following the style of our laws, was secretly presented to the Eight. It was composed with such artfulness and its arguments arranged so well that it was believed that Niccolò Machiavelli (secretary to the Signoria and intrinsically bound to the *Gonfaloniere*, i.e. Soderini, who later wrote our *Histories*) was, at the insistence of the said [*Gonfaloniere*], the author of it.[104]

The gist of the accusation turned on what Soderini, probably through Machiavelli's pen, argued was Filippo's implied support for a Medici *coup d'état*. It had no basis in fact, but it nevertheless made matters difficult for Filippo and therefore also for Lorenzo. That Machiavelli was suspected of involvement makes the patron-client relationship that later developed between him and Lorenzo that much more striking, and the later friendship between him and Filippo all the more remarkable. In the interim, however, the 1508 marriage alliance between the Strozzi and Medici families, and the "autocratic" means Soderini utilized to attempt to thwart it, led to Soderini's fall from favour in Florence. Yet Soderini's protests, though

102 "Mantenere il grado della sua nobile famiglia" (Appendix 2, 20v 11–12).

103 See Limongelli, *Filippo Strozzi*, 29ff., for a discussion of "Il tranello di Piero Strozzi."

104 "Così fu presentato agli Otto segretamente secondo lo stile degli ordini nostri, una accusa di Filippo, con molto arte et con molto ordine composta, sì che per certo si credette che Niccolo Machiauegli che fu di poi scrittore delle nostre hystorie, segretario all'hora della Signoria et molto intrinseco al Gonfaloniere, ne fusse ad istantia del detto autore" (Florence, Biblioteca Nazionale Centrale, Gino Capponi 94 *Vite di personaggi di casa Strozzi*, 112v).

hypocritical, were prophetic: the Strozzi-Medici alliance of 1508 once again gave the Medici a foothold in their native city.[105]

Sensing the fragility of the republic, and refusing to work with Soderini, Lorenzo never held an office during Soderini's republic. In fact, in 1511, he was elected to serve as an official of the Florentine Monte, but he refused, paying the resulting fine – a steep one of three hundred scudi – without complaint.[106] Lorenzo, as mentioned above, was not anti-republican, but he did have a long and problematic history with Piero Soderini, and that history was enough to keep him out of public service until after Soderini's fall. Lorenzo seems eventually to have smoothed over his disagreements with Rucellai, becoming a regular at the Rucellai gardens, the Orti Oricellari. In the years between 1508 and 1512, Lorenzo's life might be summed up by the word "patience": he waited and, with the exception of Soderini, offended no one. He did, however, remain informed about the Medici-sponsored sack of Prato in 1512.[107] While he was most likely shocked at the Medici's and Spaniards' ruthlessness, this did not stop Lorenzo from aligning himself with Florence's former masters.

Once the Medici returned to Florence in 1512, Strozzi entered into public service with gusto, holding several important positions in their government.[108] However, after the death of Lorenzo de' Medici, who became

105 For a summary of these intrigues, see Bullard, "Alliance."

106 See Appendix 2, 22r 12, for details concerning Lorenzo's fine, and Goldthwaite, *Private Wealth*, 83n17 for additional information.

107 Antonio Strozzi wrote to Alfonso and Lorenzo di Filippo Strozzi "in Lucca, o dove fussino" about the horrors of the sack and the miracles that happened in the city, exposing the Spaniards' hypocrisy. The letter is dated 3 September 1512. (Cesare Guasti, ed., *Il sacco di Prato e il ritorno de' Medici in Firenze nel MDXII: Narrazioni in versi e in prosa* [Romagnoli, 1880], 174–5).

108 For example, under the restored Medici Regime, Lorenzo held the following offices: Official of the Rivers (1513, for five years), Official of the Monte (1514), Otto di Custodia (1515), prison official (1516), prison official (1520), prior (1521), Official of the Monte; prison official and *Balia* (1522), ambassador to Clement VII (1523), prison official (1524), prison official, Conservator of the Law, *Onestatis Officiale* (1525), and prison official (1526) (Goldthwaite, *Private Wealth*, 83n19). Goldthwaite gleaned this information from the *Tratte*, 84 passim. However, this extensive service to the Medici should be balanced against the fact that when the Medici were once again expelled from Florence in 1527, Lorenzo played an integral part in the administration and defense of the republic. One therefore cannot call him a whole-hearted supporter of the *Palleschi* faction (intense Medici supporters) in Florence, or a republican after Soderini's fashion. Rather, following the strain of republicanism that was channeled through Bernardo Rucellai, he seems to have been an oligarchic republican; willing to serve whatever regime was in power,

Duke of Urbino, in 1519, he felt he could begin to oppose the Medici more publicly, though not stridently, and it is to that crucial year that my focus now turns.[109] The duke was the last of the direct descendants of Lorenzo the Magnificent. Strozzi, out of consideration for his father and his father's tense, though cordial, relationship with the Medici prince, restrained himself. Strozzi was, of course, a friend of Giulio de' Medici, the future Pope Clement VII, but he also opposed the illegitimate Medici princes whom Giulio installed in Florence when he had to vacate the city for the Vatican.[110] As a result of his opposition to Medici power in Florence, Lorenzo, though he did hold some important offices in the city, was not elected to any position that would allow him to direct the affairs of the Florentine state. In 1523, as stated above, he was selected to be Clement VII's ambassador at Rome; perhaps Giulio wanted to keep an eye on the powerful Strozzi. Lorenzo's activities stand in stark contrast to Filippo Strozzi's numerous roles in Florence and Rome during the same period.[111] Lorenzo was accommodating of the Medici in nearly every way. He had always maintained republican sympathies, but it took what he perceived to be a real abuse of power after 1519 to turn him towards a more solid, though admittedly oligarchic, republicanism.

One particular event, a dinner party he gave in 1519, might indicate Lorenzo's emerging dislike for the Medici family. Alternatively, its roots might lie much more deeply within the man's character: perhaps the *Pistola* and the much earlier Carnival float of 1506 were the products of a rather warped personality usually kept from the public eye, but on this occasion

---

waiting for the opportunity to exert some real influence. Lorenzo was consistently involved in public service from the return of the Medici until their expulsion in 1527. For further details on the *Palleschi* see Machiavelli's text of "Ai Palleschi" in *Opere*, vol. 1, ed. Corrado Vivanti (Turin: Einaudi-Gallimard, 1997), 87–9. Also, J.N. Stephens and H.C. Butters noted that "Ai Palleschi" is not written to Medici followers, but actually to the Medici themselves ("New Light on Machiavelli," *English Historical Review* 97, no. 382 [1982]: 59n3). For further materials on the same work, see Alfredo Bonadeo, "The Role of the 'Grandi' in the Political World of Machiavelli," *Studies in the Renaissance* 16 (1969): 9–30; for particular references to "Ai Palleschi" see 29–30.

109 It is quite likely that Lorenzo waited to "rebel" against the Medici until after Lorenzo de' Medici's death because his wife's mother was the sister of Lorenzo Il Magnifico. See Anthony M. Cummings, *Maecenas and the Madrigalist* (Philadelphia: American Philosophical Society, 2004), 169.

110 Goldthwaite, *Private Wealth*, 105–6.

111 Filippo's life and his roles in Medici government are covered in Bullard, *Filippo Strozzi.*

unleashed on a number of Rome's elites. If this dinner in 1519 showcased the "real" Lorenzo, that Lorenzo mirrors the persona he fashioned in the pages of the *Pistola*, suggesting that the *Pistola*'s perverse and strange fictional content converged, though briefly, with actual events in his life.

The dinner party is described in detail in an entertaining letter written by Tomà Lipomano to Bortolomio dal Banco, dated 13 March 1519 and transmitted by Marino Sanuto:

> I can't refrain from telling you about a banquet that was put on by Lorenzo Strozzi from "The Bank," brother of the brother in law of Lorenzo Duke of Urbino, for four Most Reverend Cardinals, Rossi, Cibo, Salviati and Ridolfi, all nephews and sons in law of the Pope, and certain other Florentine buffoons [jesters] and three courtesans. It was one of handsomest banquets thrown in Rome, but a dreadful thing and one not pleasing to the Cardinals. When they entered the house of the said Strozzi, it was lit by [only] one penny candle, they went up a set of stairs and then down, then they traversed an abyss, and came back to a black door where the said door opened. They found themselves in a room completely immersed in black, shadowed and the walls roundabout, full with death's heads [human skulls]. And in the four corners of the said room were hung four dead extremely grotesque and terrifying corpses, with one little candle behind each which induced a tremendous fearfulness. In the middle of the room was a table covered in black with a wooden plate in the middle, and on it was a death's head with four bones from a dead man and four wooden goblets filled with wine. The patron [Lorenzo] said: "Gentleman, eat lunch, for then we will go to supper." No one wanted to eat, because it was such a terrifying scene, and then those skulls rotated, producing cooked pheasants, and from the bones [came] sausages. And one who is called Fra Mariano, the Pope's jester, said to Brandino (the one who is at Venice frequently with Marietta Tressa who came to be called by everyone here, *Cordiale*), Fra Mariano asked of them, "My Cordiale, where have they brought us? I do not want us to lose everything," and they commenced to eat a mouthful and to drink a glass of wine. Then, they left that place, and entered into a grand hall which was like unto a very beautiful starry world, with so many lights, and in that room was a table with thick coverings, and they sat at the table. There were 14 [of them] in all. Straight away they heard a noise from the floor around them and 14 bowls of salad appeared in the midst of them, one for each. Then they were asked to drink and 14 glasses of wine were delivered, but it was not known from whence they came, but probably from under the floor [as well]. Then came pheasants and partridges in large quantities, and just as they were about to eat, they heard a tremendous crash, and

the world commenced to turn around. And just as the pheasants had, other things which were worthless arrived before them, and the lights dimmed. In that moment, two men, one dressed like Fra Mariano and the other like Brandino, appeared and said: "I am Fra Mariano and I want more to eat," and Brandino said something similar. The real Fra Mariano, who was seated at the table, seeing them, said, "My Cordiale, we are still here. I don't know who they are." After a while, the world calmed, and the two men who were dressed like Fra Mariano and Brandino went away, and the cardinals began to vomit,[112] along with some of the others, three or four of them, maybe more, including one of the foremost whores in Rome, who is called *Madre mia non vole.* Almost immediately there came other provender of diverse sorts, but the cardinals did not want to stay at the table any longer and they got up and went their way, even though the supper wasn't finished, not even the third course. Nevertheless, it is said that such a wonderful supper had never been given in Rome and that it surely cost a great deal of money. But, everyone was terrified tremendously. I wish that I had seen it myself, even if it might have cost me a few ducats. But, I knew nothing of it, save that it was over.[113]

---

112 Perhaps Strozzi added a purgative to the meal.

113 The Italian original is in Marino Sanuto's *Diarii,* Tomo 27, ed. Federico Stefani et al. (Venice, 1890), cols. 74–5: "Non voglio restar de avisarvi de uno convito fece Lorenzo Strozi *dal Bancho,* fratello dil cugnato dil ducha Lorenzo di Urbino, a quarto reverendissimi cardinali, zoè Rossi, Cibo, Salviati, et Redolfi tutti nepoti et zermani dil Papa, et certi altri fiorentini bufoni et tre putane; qual fu de li belli conviti sia stà fati in Roma; ma cosa spaurosa et che non piacete a li cardinali. Quando introrono in casa del dito Strozi, fu acesa una candeleta da uno quatrino, et furno menati per certe scalete che andavano suso et in zoso et per traverso a modo in bissa, e tanto andono che i zonzeno a una porta nera, dove alzata dita porta, introrno in una sala tuta coperta di negro, scura, et atorno de li ori pieno di teste di morto, et ne li quarto cantoni di dita salota erano dipente quarto morte molto brute et spaurose, con una candeleta picola da drieto che faceva grandissima paura. In mezo di la salota era una tavola coperta pur di negro, con un piato di legno in mezo, et era dentro do teste de morto con quarto ossi da morto et quarto taze di legno piene di vino. El patrone disse: 'Signori fate colazione, che poi anderemo a cena.' Niun non volse mangiare, perchè era una cosa spaurosa; et rote quelle teste, insì fora fasani coti, e de li ossi salzizoni; et uno chiamato fra Mariano, che è buffone dil Papa, disse a Brandino, che quello è stato molto a Venecia con Marietta Tressa et vien chiamato di qui da tutti *Cordiale,* fra Mariano li disse: 'Cordial mio, dove siamo conduti? Non voglio perdiamo in tutto' et scomenzono a manzar uno boccone et bever una taza del vino. Da poi i se partino di quello loco, et introrono in una sala grande che pareva uno mondo stellato molto bello, con assaissime luce, et in questo locho era se non una tavola con li mantili fitti, et sentorno a tavola. Erano in tutto 14. Subito sentati intorno la salla, saltò suso 14 taze de insalata, et fu messa una per cadauno; poi fu dimandato da bere, altri 14 bichieri di vino fu portati, che non si sapeva dove i

Mandell Creighton has suggested that Strozzi's ghastly dinner party was an exercise in one-upmanship, as he was locked in a contest to outspend a fellow banker, Agostino Chigi, in Rome.[114] Perhaps it was. However, when one recalls Strozzi's hand in Piero di Cosimo's Carnival float of 1506, and then considers the morbid, comedic, and "pornographic" style of the *Pistola*, one begins to discern a common element among these and Strozzi's extravagantly grotesque supper. The macabre dinner of 1519 and the Carnival of 1506, like the *Pistola*, open a window into Lorenzo Strozzi's usually veiled, twisted sense of humour.

The rest of his life, as Zeffi confirms, was one of courtesy and good manners. The *Pistola*, the dinner, and the *Carnivale* of 1506 might of course be aberrations in an otherwise typical aristocratic life. But they can also be seen as a rare few moments when Strozzi broke free of the constraints of his status and the rigidity of social and political expectations. The bizarre dinner might also be viewed as a not-so-subtle jab at the Medici family: his antics did after all cause the Medici cardinal nephews to leave the contents of their stomachs in his Roman palazzo. It is probable, therefore that this event was indicative of Strozzi's own strange personality and of his emerging distaste for the Medici. But, even as Strozzi was beginning to test anti-Medicean waters in 1519, he remained an active member of the Medicean Sacred Academy and a signatory of the Academy's request to Leo X to bring Dante's body back to Florence for proper,

---

venivano se non de soto la salla; poi vene fasani et starne in copia; et in quello che erano sul bello di manzare, se sentì uno schiopo grandissimo, et el mondo comenzò andar atorno, et cussì come i haveano i fasani dinanti, veniva altre cosse che non valevano nulla, et si smorzò le luze. E in questo venevo do, vestili uno da fra Mariano e l'altro da Brandino et disseno: 'Io son fra Mariano che voglio ancor io mangiare,' el simile disse il Brandino. Et fra Mariano vero, che era li a tavola, vedendo costoro, disse: 'Cordial mio, nui siamo pur qui; non so che cosa costoro sia.' Hor *tandem* il mondo si aquietò; et quelli due da fra Mariano et Brandino vestiti andorno via, et li cardinali comenzorno a vomitar, et cussi li altri, da tre in quarto in fora, et una di quelle putane de le prime di Roma chiamata *Madre mia non vole*. Et subito vene altre vivande di diverse cose; ma li cardinali non volseno star più a tavola et se levorno suso et andorno via, che la cena non era finita nè fata il terzo. Sichè si tien questa è stata di le belle cena sia stà fatte mai in Roma, et habi speso assai danari; ma tutti avèno grandissima paura, Io voria esser stato a vederla e che mi havesse costato uno paro di ducati; ma non si sape nulla, salvo da poi la fu fata." I am indebted to Professor Richard Mackenney, who assisted me with the Venetian dialect, and to Georgina Masson, who provided a good translation upon which I based my own. See Masson's *Courtesans of the Italian Renaissance* (New York: St. Martins, 1976), 72ff.

114 Mandell Creighton, *A History of the Papacy from the Great Schism to the Sack of Rome*, vol. 6 (London: Longmans, Green and Co., 1919), 197.

patriotic burial.[115] While the effort to restore Dante to Florence failed, Lorenzo did not let this setback deter his other literary or political ambitions. Where Lorenzo's political ambitions are concerned, his career under the Medici continued to blossom, and soon thereafter, he was selected to be ambassador to Pope Clement VII. As for his literary ambitions, Strozzi developed a close working relationship with the musician and composer Bernardo Pisano. Of the thirty-five secular compositions written by Pisano, twelve were written as settings for Strozzi's poetry.[116] This probably indicates that, when Strozzi found the political world too unrewarding, he retreated to his literary and musical studies to pursue personal gratification: a pattern that is replicated throughout his life. However, until the collapse of the last Florentine republic in 1530, Lorenzo always rebounded into political service. After 1530, by contrast, he focused almost exclusively on literary and academic pursuits.

1527 to 1549: Republic and Retirement

The year 1527 was simultaneously difficult and exhilarating for Lorenzo Strozzi. His probable client, Niccolò Machiavelli, died, and so did his wife, Lucrezia. As noted above, Lorenzo as a young man frequently enjoyed the pleasures of other women. As he grew older, and as the pressures of state

115 See Anthony M. Cummings, *MS Florence, Biblioteca Nazionale Centrale, Magl. 164–167* (Aldershot: Ashgate, 2006), 62n18. Cummings pointed out that Strozzi signed his name to the petition as "Laurentius Stroza." For the text of the petition, see Ludovico Frati and Corrado Ricci, eds., *Il Sepolcro di Dante* (Bologna: Premiato Stab. Tip. Succ. Monti, 1889), 55–7. For a lengthy treatment of Platonism in Renaissance Italy, see James Hankins, *Plato in the Italian Renaissance*, 2 vols. (Leiden: Brill, 1990). Additionally, it is worth noting that Machiavelli was, as recently as 1515, strongly opposed to regarding Dante with anything other than suspicion. This fact is another reason to consider the relationship that developed between Strozzi and Machiavelli as unlikely. For coverage of Machiavelli's treatment of Dante in the former's *Discorso o dialogo intorno alla nostra lingua*, see "Machiavelli and Dante" in William J. Landon, *Politics, Patriotism and Language: Niccolò Machiavelli's Secular Patria and the Creation of an Italian National Identity* (New York: Lang, 2005), 73ff.

116 Frank A. D'Accone, "Bernardo Pisano: An Introduction to His Life and Works," *Musica Disciplina* 17 (1963): 115–35. For details on Strozzi poems that were set to music by Pisano, see 124ff. For the locations of particular manuscripts, see 126ff. It is worth noting some of D'Accone's sources here. Florence, Conservatorio Musicale, Basevi 2440 contains three Strozzi/Pisano collaborations: 20v–22r, 24v–26r, 41v–43r, and 50v–52r. For a lengthier list of similar Strozzi/Pisano mss, see p. 129.

mounted on him, he seems to have settled down, growing comfortable with his wife and family: after the 1510s I have been unable to find references to any extra-marital escapades in his life. In fact, out of respect for his wife, Lorenzo chose not to re-marry, focusing his energies instead on the needs of Florence.[117] In fact, with all of the tumults that 1527 ushered into his personal and political life and into the Italian political landscape generally, Lorenzo grew into a serious and mature man – and he became more devout, especially after the sack of Rome. These biographic and contextual points of reference help to explain why Lorenzo dove headlong into republican service after the expulsion of the Medici, another key event in 1527.

As Felix Gilbert noted, service in the last republic was easier for men such as Strozzi, because the last republic "came into the hands of the aristocrats," or adherents to the *governo stretto* – the oligarchs.[118] The head of the last republic, Niccolò Capponi, was in fact related to Strozzi by marriage.[119] However, by 1528 Capponi, as a result of his back-door negotiations with the Medici family, had lost the support of many in the republic.[120] Lorenzo by contrast thrived. A more favourable political climate and familial bonds, then, only go so far towards explaining why, in the last full year of the republic's existence, Lorenzo held several key offices. His belief in the republic, apart from personal considerations, provides the rest of the story. He served the last republic with care and with little attention to his own safety.

For example, in 1529 Lorenzo was elected *Commissario del Dominio* for munitions and the fortifications of the cities of Prato, Pistoia, Empoli, and Colle.[121] In the same year he, together with Giovanni Borgherini, was elected

---

117 Ferrieri, "Lorenzo di Filippo Strozzi," 289.

118 Felix Gilbert, "Florentine Political Assumptions in the Period of Savonarola and Soderini," *Journal of the Warburg and Courtauld Institutes* 20, no. 3 (1957): 188.

119 Lorenzo di Filippo Strozzi's sister, Alessandra, was married to Niccolò Capponi in 1497. See Bullard, *Filippo Strozzi*, 3–4.

120 Gilbert, "Political Assumptions," 189. One of Capponi's "staunchest supporters" was Donato Giannotti. See Giannotti's *Republica Fiorentina*, ed. Giovanni Silvano (Geneva: Librairie Droz, 1990), 16, for more background. Giannotti's work, particularly book 2, covers the failed Florentine republics of Soderini and Capponi. Silvano cited the work of Rudolph von Albertini to support his suggestions about the relationship between Capponi and Giannotti. See R. von Albertini, *Das Florentinische Staatsbewusstsein im Übergang von der Republik zum Prinzipat* (Bern, 1955): 146–66.

121 "Li Signori Dieci fecéro Lor(enz)o Commessario del Dominio à munire, e fortificare Prato, Pistoia, Empoli e Colle, hauendo in sua compagnia Iacomo Corso, e M(esser) Giovanb(attist)a da Messina, huomini esperti et intelligenti del mestiero della guerra" (Appendix 2, 24v 16–20).

"oratore," to represent the Florentine cause before Pope Clement VII's Legate, "the most reverend Farnese" who not long after was elevated to the papacy as Pope Paul III.[122] Again in 1529 Lorenzo was selected to organize the importation of grain from the Florentine dominions into Florence itself. And finally, in the same year he was elected ambassador to the Prince of Orange (Captain General of the Emperor and Viceroy of Naples) as he approached Valdarno. In reality, Lorenzo was probably sent to gather intelligence concerning the size of the prince's army and to ascertain his disposition. That same army eventually laid siege to Florence. The grain supplies dwindled rapidly, and once again the Florentine Republic called on Lorenzo for help: he was sent to broker a treaty and favourable terms of surrender for the Florentines.[123] Not long thereafter, the Medici returned, this time for good.[124] Foreshadowing the likes of Francis Bacon, in 1530 Lorenzo Strozzi, frustrated and depressed, gave up politics and the active life for literary pursuits.[125]

After the collapse of the last republic in 1530, Lorenzo spent most of his time at his villa, Santuccio, there turning to writing and commentary on events outside of Florence.[126] In one newly attributed autograph, dated 15 August 1531, for example, Strozzi briefly described strange apparitions that appeared in the sky over Puglia, and provided a fine drawing of these apparitions (see figure 1).[127] The date of that description and drawing coincides with the 1531 appearance of Halley's Comet. Strozzi makes no mention of the comet, and it is doubtful that he was in Puglia to document the comet's appearance first hand, but there are other extant drawings, preserved

122 Appendix 2, 24v 20–4.

123 Appendix 2, 27v 1–5.

124 Readers interested in discovering the details of the "last republic" should consult John M. Stephens, *The Fall of the Florentine Republic: 1512–1530* (Oxford: Clarendon, 1983).

125 Bacon famously wrote that he chose "to retire from the stage of civil action and to betake myself to letters." Quoted in James Shapiro, *Contested Will: Who Wrote Shakespeare?* (New York: Simon and Schuster, 2010), 90.

126 Ferrieri, "Lorenzo di Filippo Strozzi," 277.

127 I came upon this Strozzi autograph while examining other letters to and from him located in Florence's Biblioteca Nazionale Centrale. Strozzi's handwriting was immediately recognizable to me. After I compared the handwriting in the Fondo Nazionale ms with other examples of Strozzi's handwriting, my initial suspicions were confirmed. See "Iris," Florence, Biblioteca Nazionale Centrale, Fondo Nazionale II IV (Magl. VIII 1409), 19r for Strozzi's drawing and brief description of the sky over Puglia. Further research on Strozzi's drawing, and how it relates to similar contemporary documents concerning Halley's Comet, is necessary.

by Marino Sanuto,[128] that are nearly identical to his. Strozzi noted that two suns, in addition to the "normal" sun, appeared over "Troya in Puglia," and that two rainbows appeared in the sky at the same time. The account preserved by Sanuto, dated 17 August 1531, includes three suns, three moons, and thirteen stars that appeared in "Troia" near "Napoli." On the folio (18v) preceding Strozzi's drawing (19r), there is a cryptic note in Strozzi's hand that reads "La inondatione di Fiorenza" (the deluge of Florence).

The appearance of a comet was frequently considered as a sign of imminent divine judgment.[129] The arrival of the comet in 1531 did not bring any natural calamities to Florence, but it did coincide with the Medici family's tightening grip on Strozzi's native city.[130] By the following year, 1532, the Florentine constitution and the last vestiges of its republican heritage had been gutted by a council formed by Pope Clement VII. On 27 April, with the full blessing of Clement, the Signoria was abolished along with the office of *Gonfaloniere*, replaced with a hereditary Medici principate that was required to work in cooperation with two newly established legislative bodies (four supreme magistrates and a forty-eight-seat senate elected by the magistrates). In theory, this restrained the power of the new Medici duke, Alessandro. In practice, Alessandro's first act as duke was to remove the bell from the Palazzo Vecchio to underscore the fact that the republican Signoria would never meet there again.[131]

A few months later, in August 1532, Strozzi began corresponding with republican historian and playwright Donato Giannotti, who had been

128 Marino Sanuto, *Diarii*, Tomo 54, ed. Federico Stefani et al. (Venice, 1899); see drawing located below cols. 551/552. The drawing is accompanied by the following text: "Questi sono li tre Soli & tre Luni con tredici stele aparsi nel reame de Napoli sopra una terra chiamata troia ..."

129 For more on Renaissance "occult dispositions," see Antony Parel, *The Machiavellian Cosmos* (New Haven: Yale University Press, 1992), 17.

130 For an introduction to representations of Halley's Comet (and others) in Renaissance art, see Robert J. M. Olson, "And They Saw Stars: Renaissance Representations of Comets and Pretelescopic Astronomy," *Art Journal* 44, no. 3 (1984): 216–24.

131 John R. Hale, *Florence and the Medici: A Pattern of Control* (London: Phoenix, 2001), 120ff. By selecting Alessandro (who was quite likely his son), Clement infuriated Ippolito de' Medici who wanted, perhaps more than anything, to make up for his earlier failed attempt to lead Florence. Ippolito was already a cardinal and therefore could not produce any legitimate heirs. This left Alessandro as the obvious choice to head the new Medici government at Florence. Ippolito was so stung by Clement's supposed favouritism that, in 1535, he plotted to assassinate Alessandro. His plan was discovered before it could be carried out; he died so suddenly thereafter that the Florentine exiles spread rumours that Alessandro poisoned him.

permanently exiled from Florence.[132] The two men exchanged a number of letters, but two in particular resonate with events in Florence, and they indicate that both men were contemplating the rigours of classical and contemporary republicanism. By the very same token, these letters indicate that there is reason to believe Lorenzo had a hand in disseminating Machiavelli's *Discorsi*, his treatise on republicanism, in Venice.[133]

In a letter dated 19 August 1532, Giannotti wrote that he would be asking Lorenzo for his copy of Machiavelli's *Discorsi*: "Li Discorsi del Machiavello

---

132 Strozzi's and Giannotti's collaborations and correspondence span the breadth of many themes that are fundamental to our understanding of the Renaissance. They moved with ease from discussions of Brutus and Roman republicanism to the death and resurrection of Christ. Giannotti even asked Lorenzo Strozzi to "versify" the former's *Vecchio amoroso* and to "touch up" his *Milesia*. See Ferrieri, "Lorenzo di Filippo Strozzi," 305. For an edition of the *Vecchio amoroso*, see Giannotti, *Opere*, 193–290. For an edition of *Milesia,* see 291–369 in the same volume. Strozzi's later correspondence with Giannotti includes a reference to a passion play that Lorenzo was composing. Giannotti hoped to meet Lorenzo at the latter's retirement villa, Santuccio, and there to read Strozzi's outline for the *Tragedia della passione*. Probably using Strozzi's sketch as a starting point, Giannotti went on to write an outline of his own with a similar title. "Tanto che io spero, non so se in vano, di trovarmi con voi al Santuccio a leggere la tragedia della Passione, la quale penso che a questa ora abbiate fatta; o qualche altra poetica composizione." (Donato Giannotti, *Opere politiche e letterarie*: *Collazionate sui manoscritti da F.L. Polidori*, vol. 2 [Florence: Le Monnier, 1850], 409–10, for letter dated 22 May 1534). For Giannotti's outline of the unfinished play, see *Passione*, 371–9. Perhaps Strozzi's religious interests, as previously noted, were affected by his early flirtations with Savonarolan millenarianism; but they are also plausibly viewed as exemplary fissures that were opened in Renaissance society after the rediscovery of classical antiquity. Moreover, Strozzi's exchanges with Giannotti highlight just how strange the content of the *Pistola* is when compared with the remainder of Lorenzo's literary and historical output. The *Pistola* does not fit neatly into either a "pagan" or "Christian" category. It is also clear from Strozzi's correspondence that he wrote to his collaborators, and Giannotti in particular, at length. In the light of this, the absence of any letters between him and Machiavelli buttresses the suggestion that Strozzi and Machiavelli were not friends, but patron and client.

133 Thomas Mayer, *Thomas Starkey and the Commonwealth: Humanist Politics and Religion in the Reign of Henry VIII* (Cambridge: Cambridge University Press, 2002), 56–7. Mayer illustrated that Strozzi helped Antonio Brucioli to introduce the *Discorsi* to Venice. Randolph Starn also pointed out that Brucioli was, later, also one of Duke Cosimo de' Medici's informers. Brucioli kept the duke well informed of the exiles' activities in Venice. See Starn, *Donato Giannotti and His 'Epistolae,'* Biblioteca Universitaria Alessandrina, Rome, Ms 107 (Geneva: Droz, 1968), 46. For more on how manuscripts of Machiavelli's works were transmitted in manuscript form, see Brian Richardson, *Manuscript Culture in Renaissance Italy* (Cambridge: Cambridge University Press, 2009), 18–19, 49, 78, 165, 167.

vi manderò fra vj giorni."[134] In a second letter dated 29 March 1533, Giannotti wrote to Lorenzo in some detail about a play that they seem to have been co-authoring. Giannotti referred to it as the *Tragedia di Bruto.*[135] The fact that Giannotti and Strozzi, among others, were discussing Brutus in 1533 strongly indicates that Florentine exiles and oligarchic republicans like Strozzi (and shortly his younger brother Filippo) were at least beginning to consider the historical and theoretical costs of tyrannicide.[136]

---

134 "Mag.co Lorenzo. Io mi ero imaginato che voi non mi havessi a rispondere altro che quello che havete fatto per la vostra de' xviij, perché sapevo bene quale era la vostra liberalità naturale verso ciascuno, et quale ella dovesse essere verso me: molte vostre cortesie, oltre alle offerte fattemi, facilmente me lo dimonstravano. Io vi ringratio quanto posso di questo servigio che mi fate, il quale io reputo grande, sì per le qualità d'esso, sì et perché nasce da voi, et sanza havere causa alcuna di cosi bene operare verso di me. Desidero extremamente havere facultà di mostrarvi quanto questo vostro buono animo mi sia grato. Resta che io solleciti li miei procuratori che riscuotino, acciò vi satisfaccia; uno de'quali è se Baccio di Ruffino apportatore di questa, al quale darete li ducati ventisette. Et mi vi raccomando quanto posso. Di Comiano, alli xviiij di agosto 1532. Li Discorsi del Machiavello vi manderò fra vj giorni. Servitor Donato Giannotti" (Letter from Donato Giannotti to Lorenzo Strozzi in *Giornale Storico degli Archivi Toscani,* vol. 7 [Florence: G.P. Vieusseux, 1863], 156–7).

135 "Mag.co Lorenzo. Io vi mando la dispositione della tragedia di Bruto, fatta in quel modo che a me è parso che stia bene. Bisogna che la consideriate diligentemente et rassettiate quello vi pare stia male. Io ho lasciato la consideratione di quello che ha a dire il Choro; et non porta, perchè potrà essere l'ultima cosa che si farà: hanno ad essere iiij canzone in materia grave et civile, et non mancherà tempo a pensare il particulare subiecto loro. Sommi partito dalla historia in qualche luogo, perchè io fu che Portia et Iunia siano in campo con Bruto; il che non è vero; che Iunia s'ammazza come Portia; il che non si truova: che Bruto s'ammazza in campo; che non è vero; perchè havendo egli nel fatto d'arme perso gli alloggiamenti, non vi potette entrare. Ho fatto questa variatione dalla verità della historia, perchè altrimenti non la potevo condurre: ma questo è cosa consueta a' poeti. Il subiecto mi piace più l'uno di che l'altro: et s'ella vi riuscirà come io mi persuado, sanza dubio ne troverremo poche simili appresso i Greci. Prima che ci mettiate mano, sarebbe necessario che ci parlassimo, perchè vi advertirei di qualche cosa observata da'Greci; che saria molto a proposito: et anco rivedendo insieme la dispositione, sono certo che la miglioreremo in qualcho loco. Et perchè io giudico che sia bene nel comporre questa opera possedere bene la historia, vi rimando Appiano. Possovi anchora mandare il Plutarcho; et volendolo al Santuccio, lo faro posare quivi. Altro non ho che dirvi, se non che io mi raccomando quanto posso. Di Comiano, all xxviiij di marzo 1533" (Letter from Giannotti to Strozzi in *Giornale Storico degli Archivi Toscani*, 1570).

136 As a further indication of their interest in Caesar's republican assassin, both Strozzi and Giannotti had recently been reading Machiavelli's *Discorsi*, which contains six references to Marcus Brutus (Machiavelli, *Discourses on Livy*, trans. Harvey C.

Strozzi and Giannotti, despite their republican sympathies, had by 1533 broadly transitioned from the arena of political action to the world of intellectualism, academics, and speculation. It is impossible to imagine either man actually putting his republicanism into action by mimicking Marcus Brutus and assassinating Alessandro de' Medici: they were not murderers. Lorenzino de' Medici, in contrast, was less scrupulous. On 5 January 1537, when Lorenzino took up the tyrannicide's dagger to murder his cousin, Alessandro, the results were at first anticlimactic. Medici partisans who supported hereditary rule kept the assassination quiet, thereby limiting its political ramifications and forcing Lorenzino to flee Florence. Once news of the assassination trickled out, the republican exiles sat on their hands, the old families in Florence, including the Strozzi, kept silent, and the people of Florence were stupefied. Machiavelli's comments on the reasons that Marcus Brutus failed to restore the Roman Republic after Caesar's assassination ring true here:

> In other times the authority and severity of Brutus, together with all the eastern legions, were not enough to hold it [Rome] so disposed as to wish to maintain that freedom that he, in likeness of the first Brutus, had restored to it. This arose from the corruption that the Marian parties had put in the people; Caesar, as their head, could so blind the multitude that it did not recognize the yoke that it was putting on its own neck.[137]

Despite the fact that Lorenzino killed Alessandro in order to liberate Florence, he found himself isolated and unable to believe that his heroic republican statement had fallen so flat. Lorenzino also underestimated the strength of the Medici's grasp on Florence, its links with Charles V, and the wishes of the Florentine majority. In much the same way that Republican Rome after decades of civil war welcomed Augustus's perpetual monarchy,

---

Mansfield and Nathan Tarcov [Chicago: University of Chicago Press, 1996], 352). Mansfield's and Tarcov's translation of the *Discourses* contains a useful glossary and index of proper names; see 311–67.

137 *Discourses*, I.17.1., 48. The Italian original is "E negli altri tempi non bastò l'autorità severità di Bruto, con tutte le legioni orientali, a tenerlo disposto a volere mantenersi quella libertà che esso a similitudine del primo Bruto gli aveva renduta. Il che nacque da quella coruzzione che le parti mariane avevano messo nel popolo; delle quali sendo capo, Cesare potette accecare quella moltitudine, che ella non conobbe il giogo che da se medesima si metteva in sul collo" (Niccolò Machiavelli, *Edizione Nazionale delle opere di Niccolò Machiavelli: Discorsi sopra le prima deca di Tito Livio*, ed. Francesco Bausi, vol. 1 [Rome: Salerno Editrice, 2001], 109).

Florence likewise opened its arms to Alessandro's successor, the eighteen-year-old Cosimo de' Medici.[138] Lorenzino de' Medici was eventually hunted down in Venice and killed by bounty hunters sent out by his own family.[139]

In 1537 Lorenzo Strozzi wrote to his brother Filippo, who had fled into exile in 1536,[140] that Florence's governing body, the Forty-Eight, had decreed that Filippo and many of his fellow exiles could return to Florence.[141] Clearly Lorenzo, although he was living at Santuccio, was forced to return his attention to the goings-on in Florence. Lorenzo realized that Filippo's exile was harmful to their *casa* and therefore, as the head of the Strozzi family, he diligently tried to restore his brother to Florence. Filippo, however, could not be convinced and chose to remain in exile. Almost simultaneously, the Florentine exiles were organizing themselves. They hoped to convince Cosimo de' Medici to restore some semblance of republicanism to Florence. If they could achieve that fundamental goal, the exiles believed they could broker a return to Florence on their own terms. Donato Giannotti, acting as spokesman for the exiles,[142] met with Cosimo on 31 May 1537 and found Cosimo completely unwilling to negotiate. Duke Cosimo knew well in advance of the meeting what Donato hoped to gain for the Florentine

---

138 For broader background on Cosimo de' Medici and his wife Elenora, see Konrad Eisenbichler, ed., *The Cultural World of Elenora di Toledo Duchess of Florence* (Aldershot: Ashgate, 2004).

139 "Dico dunque che il fine mio era di liberare Firenze, e l'ammazzare Alessandro era il mezzo" (*Apologia*, 221 in Lorenzino de' Medici, *Aridosia, Apologia, Rime e Lettere*, ed. Federico Ravello [Turin: Unione tipografico-editrice torinese, 1921]). Cited in Kate Lowe, "Conspiracy and its Prosecution in Italy, 1500–1550: Violence Responses to Violent Solutions," in *Conspiracies and Conspiracy Theory in Early Modern Europe: From the Waldensians to the French Revolution* (Aldershot: Ashgate, 2004): 45n51.

140 Feared and distrusted by his new masters, in 1536 Filippo went into self-imposed exile in Venice, where he was greeted warmly and given protection by the Doge. For more background on Filippo's exile see Melissa Meriam Bullard, *Filippo Strozzi and the Medici: Favor and Finance in Sixteenth-Century Florence and Rome* (Cambridge: Cambridge University Press, 1980), 1.

141 Lorenzo di Filippo Strozzi, *Filippo Strozzi: Tragedia*, ed. G.-B. Niccolini (Florence: Le Monnier, 1847), 231, letter dated 30 January 1537.

142 Randolph Starn, *Donato Giannotti and his 'Epistolae':* Biblioteca Universitaria Alessandrina, Rome, Ms 107 (Geneva: Droz, 1968), 44. The Florentine exiles formed a government in exile that was given a hearing by Charles V and Cosimo de' Medici, but Starn concluded that Charles could hardly have been expected to side with the exiles against Cosimo, his own son-in-law. Charles had too much invested in Florence to turn its government over to the republicans, no matter how convincing their arguments were.

exiles. Several years earlier Antonio Brucioli, a supposed fellow republican and friend of the exiles, began sending messages to Cosimo about the exiles' activities in Venice. Giannotti's name first appeared in Brucioli's dispatches to Cosimo on 21 March 1537.[143] The exiles were outwitted every step of the way. The date of the failed meeting, 31 May 1537, marked the last time Giannotti would set foot in Florence.[144]

Meanwhile, Lorenzo Strozzi continued to shun talk of republican revolution, busying himself with writing because, as Pio Ferrieri put it, the thought of Florentine civil war was "repugnant to his [Lorenzo's] upright spirit."[145] Though he must have known the seriousness of the situation in Florence, the first weeks of May found him writing to Filippo Strozzi about the *Vita* of their father that he was composing, going so far as to ask Filippo to read and edit the work if he could find the time.[146] Perhaps he was attempting to calm his brother and instill patience in him by reminding him of their father's many accomplishments.

Here again, Lorenzo seems to have modelled his interactions with the Medici dukes on his father's careful dealings with the Medici. He realized that rebellion on the part of both brothers would bring about his family's certain ruin. As a pragmatic and intelligent man in the mould of Filippo the Elder, then, Lorenzo acted to preserve his family and its wealth even if that meant forgiving the Medici for their ongoing campaign against republican freedoms and ambitions.

Filippo the Younger would have none of it. He was uninterested in living harmoniously with the Medici, and his emerging hatred for Cosimo de' Medici intensified as word of Giannotti's failure spread. The exiled republicans were, for all practical purposes, leaderless. They needed a person of substance to guide their cause. The yoke of revolution fell, then, on Filippo's shoulders.[147] Any comfort that Lorenzo's conciliatory letter offered his

143 Starn, *Donato Giannotti*, 46.

144 Ibid., 47.

145 "La guerra civile ripugnava al suo animo retto" (Ferrieri, "Lorenzo di Filippo Strozzi," 286).

146 *La Vita di Filippo Strozzi il Vecchio*, ed. Giuseppe Bini and Pietro Bigazzi (Florence: Tip. Della Casa Correzione, 1851), 3–4, letter dated 12 May 1537.

147 It is not exactly clear why Filippo, who for the majority of his life had been an ardent Medici supporter, turned so decisively on his patrons. However, Bullard claims that after the death in 1534 of Clement VII, Filippo's greatest patron, his successors Alessandro and later Cosimo de' Medici found Filippo to be too powerful. According to Bullard, he was "forced into his celebrated role as leader of the Florentine exiles, defiant captive, and heroic suicide." See Bullard, *Filippo Strozzi*, 1.

younger brother must have been short lived as Filippo cast patience aside and prepared for war. But Lorenzo did not give up hope. Later in June 1537, he gently suggested to his brother, using himself as example, that it was still possible to retire to a quiet life in the country.[148] Filippo rejected his older brother's advice.

Realizing that collective military action was their last hope, the Florentine republicans and exiles rallied behind Filippo Strozzi.[149] In Florence itself, Alessandro seized Filippo's half of the Strozzi palace (leaving Lorenzo's untouched). When Lorenzino de' Medici assassinated Alessandro, he went straight to Filippo's home in Venice. The assassination, and subsequent military action, failed to restore republicanism to Florence. Famously, and almost pathetically, the republicans were routed at Montemurlo by Cosimo's Florentine forces, which were strengthened by imperial Spanish mercenaries; Filippo Strozzi was taken captive. While Filippo was being transferred to the Fortezza da Basso in Florence, Lorenzo was held for four days as surety, though he was freed once his brother was imprisoned.[150]

It is quite likely that these experiences informed Lorenzo Strozzi's next piece of writing, his *Trattato della patienza,* and his decision to dedicate that work to Duke Cosimo de' Medici.[151] In much the same way that Seneca admonished the youthful Nero to cultivate the virtue of clemency, Strozzi urged the youthful (he was just eighteen years of age) Cosimo to cultivate both religious and philosophical patience, perhaps hoping that he would spare Filippo Strozzi's life.[152] The *Trattato* is undated, but given its religious and philosophical themes, and Filippo's imprisonment following the

148 See letter dated 9 June 1537 from Lorenzo to Filippo Strozzi. See also *Vita di Filippo il Vecchio,* p. 51, where Lorenzo wrote: "Ho caro commendi la vita mia del starmi alla Villa e godermi la quiete, unico refugio della mia indisposizione, e quello che io stimo non manco, senza offensione di niuno. Doveresti bene ancora tu pensare a potere un dì, se di presente non puoi, fare il medesimo senza aggirarti tanto, e più per l'utile e comodo altrui che per il tuo; che nulla è difficile a chi vuole."

149 Bullard, *Filippo Strozzi,* 1.

150 Gareffi, *La scrittura,* 116.

151 Lorenzo wrote a companion work to the *Trattato della patienza* that is referred to as *Sopra la limosina* and was, evidently, published in 1573. See Christian Bec, *Les Livres des Florentins: 1413–1608* (Florence: Leo S. Olschki, 1984), 80. More work needs to be done on the manuscript(s) of Strozzi's work in order to understand how it relates to Strozzi's unpublished *Trattato della patienza.*

152 For an edition, commentary, and historiography of Seneca's work, see Lucius Annaeus Seneca, *De Clementia,* ed. and trans. Susanna Morton Braund (Oxford: Oxford University Press, 2009). For a brief examination of Seneca's medieval and Renaissance reception, see 77–9.

disastrous republican defeat at Montemurlo, it likely dates from 1537 or 1538. In the latter year, the concept of patience was clearly on Lorenzo's mind. In a letter to his friend Benvenuto Ulivieri in Venice dated 25 June, Lorenzo, still hoping that Filippo might be freed from prison, wrote succinctly: "God knows how great the goal is, patience!"[153] Lorenzo's lengthy treatise on patience begins (see figure 2):

To the Most Excellent Lord Cosimo
De' Medici Duke of Florence
Lorenzo Strozzi

> When I consider, Illustrious Duke, how nearly all the writers direct their works to those persons, who by virtue, nobility, glory or friendship, are more worthy than themselves; or truly to those, from whom they have received, or hoped to receive, honor or usefulness; and I, wishing to do the same, certainly cannot find one with whom these writings of mine on Patience more assuredly agree (neither to whom I might have greater obligation, or who might benefit me more), than your Excellency.[154]

At the moment, it is not possible to prove that Cosimo received Strozzi's *Trattato.* It is tempting to speculate that its passionate refrains summoning the examples of Socrates, Philip of Macedon, and Christ caused Cosimo de' Medici to withhold judgment on Filippo Strozzi (who was imprisoned for seventeen months before committing suicide).[155] Lorenzo's treatise is certainly

153 "Dio sa quanto sia a proposito, pazienza!" (*Vita di Filippo* [Il Giovane], 311).

154 This quotation is from the "presentation copy" of the *Trattato*; Florence, Biblioteca Nazionale Centrale, Magl. Cl. XXXV, MS. 32 (hereafter BNCF, Magl. XXXV, 32): Lorenzo di Filippo Strozzi, *Trattato della Patienza*, 1r–61r. For quotation, see 1r: "Allo Eccellentissimo Sig(no)re Cosimo De Medici Duca Di Firenze. Lorenzo Strozzi, Considerando io Ill(ustrissi)mo Duca, come quasi tutti gli scrittori indirizano l'opere loro à quelle persone, che per uertu, nobilità, gloria, ò amicitia, piu degne ne paiono loro; ò ueramente à quelle, da cui ha(n)no, riceuto, ò sperano di riceuere, honore ò utile; et uolendo fare io il medesimo, certo no(n) uedeua à chi questi miei scritti della Patienza piu meritame(n)te si conuenissero, ne co(n) chi io hauessi maggiore obligo, ò chi mi potesse piu benificare, che la Ecc(elen)za u(ost)ra." The "draft" version of the *Trattato* is located in Florence, Biblioteca Nazionale Centrale, Magl. Cl. XXXV, MS 106. Lorenzo di Filippo Strozzi, *Trattato della Patienza*, 1r–70r.

155 BNCF, Magl. XXXV, 32. Christ is mentioned throughout the *Trattato*, but see 55r and following for typical examples. See 29v for references to Socrates and 13v for references to Philip of Macedon.

a heartfelt exhortation to patience, but it is also a painful and distressing confession. The real irony of this introductory passage is that its author, fifty-five years old in 1537, alienated from Florentine politics as result of his own actions in the last republic and more emphatically by those of his brother, was forced to seek a patron in the eighteen-year-old Medici duke.

After Filippo's suicide in 1538, Lorenzo remained almost exclusively at his country villa. There he turned his energies to writing some of the finest biographies produced in the Renaissance, his *Vite di personaggi di casa Strozzi*.[156] The *Vite*, thirty-four[157] in all, trace the Strozzi family's lineage from late medieval Florence through the end of his brother Filippo's life, "essendo egli in carcere dove fini miseramente la vita sua" (where he, being incarcerated, miserably [or pathetically] ended his life).[158] This is the reading provided by the frequently cited 1892 (and the earlier 1847) edition of Strozzi's *Vita di Filippo* [Il Giovane].[159] The editors of those editions, like so many nineteenth-century editors, silently accepted manuscript changes without noting variants or, as in this case, retained words in their edited volumes that were meant to be deleted from the original manuscript. The autograph provides a subtler approach to the text just cited, and it also provides evidence that Lorenzo Strozzi was struggling with how he ought to document his brother's suicide.

156 Florence, Biblioteca Nazionale Centrale, Gino Capponi 94 *Vite di personaggi di casa Strozzi*, 1r–279v (hereafter BNCF, Capponi 94).

157 There is discrepancy over the total number of lives about which Lorenzo wrote. The Florentine Gino Capponi ms contains thirty-four autograph lives. The other manuscript of the *Vite* (see below) contains thirty-nine lives. The Biblioteca Marucelliana (Florence) recently made their manuscript catalog available online. The indices for Strozzi's *Vite* contain the following details: "copiate dagli scritti di sua propria mano." I have yet to examine this second ms of Strozzi's *Vite*. The published edition of the *Vite*, based on the Gino Capponi ms contains only twenty-five lives. Five more lives from the Gino Capponi ms were transcribed by Pietro Stromboli for the Strozzi-Corzine wedding of 1890. See Lorenzo di Filippo Strozzi, *Vite di Alcuin Familiar Strozzi despite da Lorenzo nel secolo XVI* (Florence: Pei Tipi di Salvatore Landi, 1890).

158 As stated, I have not yet examined the Marucelliana ms of Strozzi's *Vite*. It will be interesting to find out how, if at all, the reading contained in the Marucelliana ms of Strozzi's *Vite* differs from that of the Gino Capponi ms.

159 Lorenzo di Filippo Strozzi, *Le Vite degli Uomini Illustri della Casa Strozzi*, ed. Pietro Stromboli (Florence: Pei Tipi Salvadore Landi, 1892), 185; Filippo Strozzi, *Tragedia*, CV.

The text in the manuscript does read "essendo egli in carcere dove fini miseramente la sua vita" (see figure 3).[160] But Strozzi emended the text using standard (for the period) editorial practices. For example, when he placed dots under words, as he did in the passage just quoted, Lorenzo meant for the word(s) to be deleted; if he provided an alternate reading in the margin or interlineally, he intended the alternate to replace the underscored text. There is no alternate reading provided for "miseramente," so he meant for the word to be expurgated. The line should read: "essendo egli in carcere dove fini la vita sua" (where he, being incarcerated, ended his life). This reading is less emotional, and was probably less liable to provoke a response from the Medici should Lorenzo elect to publish the work. Given that his life of Filippo the Younger was not published until 1725, one must assume that Lorenzo was still in the process of revising it at the time of his death.[161]

In the period between Filippo Strozzi's suicide and his own death, Lorenzo Strozzi lived peacefully, spending most of his time at his country villa but venturing into Florence on occasion. As he aged, Lorenzo also took it upon himself to advise Duke Cosimo de' Medici, especially on domestic matters, and in return Cosimo provided his personal blessing to the marriage of Lorenzo's youngest son Palla and Nannina Antinori in 1547.[162] Lorenzo's impact was such that the ruptured relationship between the Strozzi and Medici families was bridged, bringing the Strozzi of Florence, and the Strozzi family more generally, solidly back into Duke Cosimo's good graces and therefore back into his patronage network. Like another great survivor, Francesco Guicciardini, who frequently hid his personal

160 BNCF, Capponi 94, f. 253r. The vast majority of the manuscript is a Lorenzo Strozzi autograph. Folio pages 255r–279r, a later addition to the life of Filippo Strozzi the Younger, is in a different, unknown hand. It is quite unlikely that Lorenzo authored this text. There is another manuscript of the *Vite* located "presso i duchi di Forano e nella Marucelliana, *Scaff.* C. Cod. 132." This manuscript contains thirty-nine lives of famous Strozzi family members, including Filippo the Elder and Younger. For a description of this ms, see Domenico Moreni, *Bibliografia storico-ragionata della Toscana; a sia Catalogo degli scrittori che hanno illustrate la storia delle città, luoghi, e persone delle medesima*, vol. 2 (Florence: Accademia delle belle arti, 1805), 369. Moreni mistakenly counted thirty-seven lives in this ms.

161 Lorenzo di Filippo Strozzi, *Vita di Filippo Strozzi* [Il Giovane], in Benedetto Varchi, *Storia fiorentina* (Venice, 1725).

162 Ferrieri, "Lorenzo di Filippo Strozzi," 289ff.

beliefs in order to preserve his status, Lorenzo Strozzi cared more for the future of his "house" than his present happiness.[163]

Lorenzo di Filippo Strozzi died in 1549, aged sixty-seven. Although a poet, playwright, musician, and an excellent historian, he did not until the end of his public life dare to allow his political beliefs to guide his public actions. Even then, when it became clear that the last Florentine republic could not withstand the force of the Medici, Lorenzo quickly donned the courtier's mask, disassociating himself from the actions of Florence's radical republicans, including his own brother, and electing to retire to a life of letters.[164] With the exception of his service to the last Florentine republic, the Carnival of 1506, and the *cena* of 1519, one must turn to Strozzi's literary works to see behind his mask. One work and one relationship in particular allow us to do this in a new way – the work is the *Pistola fatta per la peste* and the relationship was with Niccolò Machiavelli.

163 "I know no man who dislikes more than I do the ambition, the avarice, and the lasciviousness of the priesthood: not only because each of these vices is odious of itself, but also because each of them separately, and of them together, are quite unsuitable in men who make profession of a life dedicated to God … And yet the position I have served under several popes has obliged me to desire their greatness for my own self-interest; and were it not for this, I would have loved Martin Luther as myself" (Francesco Guicciardini, *The History of Italy*, trans. Sidney Alexander [Princeton: Princeton University Press, 1984], xvi).

164 Wayne A. Rebhorn, *Courtly Performances: Masking and Festivity in Castiglione's* Book of the Courtier (Detroit: Wayne State University Press, 1978).

2 Lorenzo di Filippo Strozzi and Niccolò Machiavelli

The chief questions I address in this chapter are: when did Niccolò and Lorenzo become familiar with one another? Why did Niccolò dedicate his *Arte* to Lorenzo? And why did they enter into what appears to have been a patron-client relationship that eventually produced the *Pistola*?

An Overview of the Evidence

As discussed above, there are no surviving letters between Strozzi and Machiavelli, though Lorenzo is referred to several times in Niccolò's private letters. Lorenzo first appears in Machiavelli's private correspondence in 1509, but there is nothing in that letter to suggest that the two Florentines were in any way friendly with one another; they did, however, move in the same circles. Later, in 1514, when Machiavelli teetered on the edge of bankruptcy, Francesco Vettori encouraged him to appeal to the Florentine *Monte* for aid.[1] This was an appalling moment in Machiavelli's life: even though he had just finished one of the most brilliant contributions to Renaissance political thought, *Il Principe*; he was drinking and gambling too much, with money that he did not have; and he was forced to petition the *Monte* for financial assistance.

Lorenzo Strozzi was a member of the *Monte* at the time of Machiavelli's request. Since the *Monte* refused to extend Machiavelli a loan or aid of any kind, it is doubtful that Strozzi and Machiavelli were at all friendly in 1514; had they been so, Strozzi probably would have used his position to help a

1 For the best examination of Machiavelli's personal letters during this period, see John Najemy, *Between Friends: Discourses of Power and Desire in the Machiavelli-Vettori Letters of 1513–1515* (Princeton: Princeton University Press, 1993).

friend. Adding insult to injury, in the winter of 1514–1515, "Giulio [de' Medici] ... decided that the Medici had no use for Machiavelli, either in Rome or in Florence." But in 1520 and following years, "Cardinal Giulio's opinion of Machiavelli softened; he secured for him the commission from the Studio for the composition of the *Istorie fiorentine* and, as Pope Clement VII, formally accepted the book, which Machiavelli even dedicated to him, in 1525."[2] What happened in the interim to change Cardinal Giulio's mind?

An extant letter dated 17 March 1520 provides a forceful answer. In that letter, Filippo Strozzi wrote to his older brother Lorenzo thanking the latter for conducting Machiavelli back into the Medici court and therefore back into the "patrons'" good graces.[3] In so doing, Lorenzo bestowed on Machiavelli a substantial benefit, and by dedicating the *Arte della guerra* to Lorenzo, Machiavelli acknowledged that benefit. Soon after Lorenzo reintroduced Machiavelli to the Medici, Machiavelli found them suddenly open to his ideas. "At the urging of Cardinal Giulio," Machiavelli wrote a discourse on the reform of the Florentine government, which he dedicated to Pope Leo X.[4] Then, as Najemy noted, Cardinal Giulio arranged for Machiavelli's commission of the *Istorie fiorentine*. All of Machiavelli's successes in the early 1520s can be traced to Lorenzo di Filippo Strozzi's patronage and the access he provided to the Medici family. But when he accepted Lorenzo Strozzi's help with the Medici family, Machiavelli became not only a Medici client but also a client of Strozzi's.

These events led up to 1522, which, evidence indicates, was a pivotal year for Machiavelli and his relationship with Strozzi. In the spring of 1522, Giulio de' Medici issued a general call to Florence's political elite for suggestions on how he ought to reform the Florentine government. Machiavelli

---

2 Najemy, *Between Friends*, 312.

3 Letter from Filippo Strozzi to Lorenzo di Filippo Strozzi dated 17 March 1519 (1520 using modern dating). This letter appears in Oreste Tommasini, *La vita e gli scritti di Niccolò Machiavelli nella loro relazione col Machiavellismo: Storia ed esame critico di Oreste Tommasini* (Turin: Ermano Loescher, 1883), vol. 2, appendices, 1082. The pertinent portion of the letter is cited below.

4 Patricia J. Osmond, "Conspiracy of 1522 against Cardinal Giulio de Medici: Machiavelli and *"gli esempli delli antiqui,"* in *The Pontificate of Clement VII: History, Politics, Culture*, ed. Kenneth Gouwens and Sheryl E Reiss (Aldershot: Ashgate, 2005), 60. In 1520, Machiavelli's "Discourse" on reform was too radical to be taken seriously by the Medici family. For the "Discourse," see "Discursus Florentinarum Rerum Post Mortem Iunioris Laurentii Medices," in *Opere*, vol. 1, ed. Corrado Vivanti (Rome: Einaudi, 1997), 733–45. The manuscript of the *Discursus*, an apograph, survives in the Biblioteca Nazionale Centrale di Firenze, *Strozziane*, 1060.

jumped at the chance to "advise" Cardinal Giulio. He framed his reform document as a decree written by Giulio himself and proposed that his suggestions (and elections/appointments) be made effective before or at the start of May ("*calendi maggio proxime futuro*" and alternately as "*dì primo dì maggio proxime futuro*").[5] Machiavelli's choice of words here might link his *Minuta di provvisione* chronologically with the *Pistola fatta per la peste,* which describes the *calendimaggio* alternatively as the "lieto principio di Maggio,"[6] "maggio le calendi,"[7] and "el primo di di maggio."[8]

Machiavelli uses another term to describe Florence's citizens in the *Minuta* that resonates wonderfully with the *Pistola*: he refers to Florence's "amorevoli cittadini." (He referred to "cittadini amorevoli" in his *Istorie fiorentine*, and that is the only other time that one finds those words linked in his *opere*.)[9] Compare the *Pistola*, in which one of Strozzi's characters refers to the Florentines as "poco amorevoli cittadini."[10] One wonders if Strozzi's choice of words in the *Pistola* affected Machiavelli's in the *Minuta*. These similarities in vocabulary, referencing a particular time of year and Florence's citizens, have gone completely unnoticed until now, and lead me to conclude that both works can probably be traced to the same year and roughly to the same period – late spring, 1522.[11] This link between the two

5 See appendix 4, Machiavelli's *Minuta di provvisione*, etc., 22.11–12, 15–16; 27.18–19; 28.21 for particular references to "*maggio*." For studies of more recent and contemporary "May" rituals, theatrical productions, and song, see Marcello Conati, "Il Maggio drammatico nel parmense," 309–50, in *Il Maggio Drammatico: Una tradizione di teatro in musica*, ed. Tullia Magrini (Bologna: Poligrafici L. Parma, 1992), esp. 310n5. I am grateful to the Bayerische Staatsbibliothek München for sending this book to me via interlibrary loan. For more background on the linking of theater and the "*calendimaggio*" see Paolo Toschi, *Le origini del teatro italiano*, vol. 1 (Turin: Bollati Boringhieri, 1999).

6 See the Italian edition of the *Pistola*, 85v 11.

7 Ibid., 87v 33.

8 Ibid., 89v 26.

9 See appendix 4, *Minuta*, 26.24–5. I used the vocabulary and word usage search functions at "Intratext.com" to gather this information.

10 See the Italian edition of the *Pistola*, 87v 5.

11 The chronology of Machiavelli's works fits this scenario. "Nella cronologia delle opere politiche di messer Niccolò, la *minuta di provvisione*, segue il *Discursus* e l'*Arte della guerra*, mantra è contemporanea primi brani delle *Istorie fiorentine*." See p. 257 in Guidubaldo Guidi, "Machiavelli e i progetti di riforme costituzionali a Firenze nel 1522," in *Machiavellismo e Antimachiavellismo nel Cinquecento: Atti del Convegno di Perugia 30.IX–1.X. 1969* (Florence: Leo S. Olschki, 1970). There is a critical edition of the *Provvisione* found on 263–8. On the specific date of the *Provvisione*, Guidi suggested, following Jacopo Pitti's *cinquecento* commentary on the period, that

works, and between Strozzi and Machiavelli, in turn supports some provisional conclusions. If the two men were "patron and client" during the spring of 1522, then that would help to explain why Machiavelli's *Minuta di provvisione* embodies an oligarchic form of republicanism. Given that Strozzi played such a central part in the final Florentine republic, which was certainly oligarchic in nature,[12] and that later Strozzi collaborated extensively with Donato Giannotti whose own republicanism was "oligarchic,"[13] it is probable that Machiavelli's political thought, under Strozzi's patronage, was similarly affected in the spring of 1522.

There are still more connections to be made here. In early 1522 Giulio de' Medici's calls for documents that might aid the reform of the Florentine constitution were apparently issued in good faith. However, as the year unfolded his motivations changed. What Machiavelli did not know (but Strozzi might have) was that there was a conspiracy afoot in Florence and abroad to murder Giulio de' Medici.[14] The conspirators, including the Soderini family

---

Machiavelli probably wrote it in early April 1522 (255). To substantiate his argument, Guidi cited Jacopo Pitti's *Istoria fiorentina*, in *Archivio storico Italiano*, vol. 1 (Florence: Vieusseux, 1842), esp. 124 for a quotation that indicates April as the time of year in question.

12 Felix Gilbert, "Florentine Political Assumptions in the Period of Savonarola and Soderini," *Journal of the Warburg and Courtauld Institutes* 20, nos. 3–4 (1957), 188 where Gilbert discussed in detail the Florentine "*governo stretto*" or "oligarchic government" of the last Florentine republic.

13 For more on Giannotti's "oligarchic republicanism," see Randolph Starn, *Donato Giannotti and his 'Epistolae'*: Biblioteca Universitaria Alessandrina, Rome, Ms 107 (Geneva: Droz, 1968), 15, 19–21, and Quentin Skinner, *Foundations of Modern Political Thought,* vol. 1, *The Renaissance* (Cambridge: Cambridge University Press, 2002), 160–1. These are cited in Thomas Mayer, *Thomas Starkey and the Commonwealth: Humanist Politics and Religion in the Reign of Henry VIII* (Cambridge: Cambridge University Press, 2002), 56, notes 98 and 101.

14 The reason that Lorenzo might have known about the conspiracy is related to the Strozzi brothers, Filippo and Lorenzo, and their knowledge of the 1510 conspiracy of Prinzivalle di Luigi della Stufa. Prinzivalle tried to enlist the Strozzi family in a conspiracy against Piero Soderini, c. 1510, but they refused after initially finding the idea worth serious consideration. For more on the conspiracy, see John Najemy, *A History of Florence: 1250–1575* (Malden, MA: Blackwell, 2006), 424ff. Also see Melissa Meriam Bullard, *Filippo Strozzi and the Medici: Favor and Finance in Sixteenth-Century Florence and Rome* (Cambridge: Cambridge University Press, 1980), 61. Della Stufa, with his plan to overthrow Florence fully formed, went straight to the Strozzi palace in December 1510 to inform Filippo of his intentions. Filippo listened intently. The next morning, he went directly to Soderini and informed him of the plot. Filippo was kind, however, forcing della Stufa to flee Florence before he informed the government of the plot against Soderini.

and a number of other young republicans, believed that if they could decapitate the Medici family, they might restore a popular republic at Florence. As 1522 wore on, and as information concerning the threats to Giulio became more immediate, Giulio continued to ask for recommendations on the future of the Florentine political system, gambling that the conspirators might show their cards with "suggestions" of their own.[15] By a stroke of luck and with ruthless planning, the conspiracy was uncovered; and two of the men who were involved were tried and executed.[16]

Troublingly for Machiavelli, the central conspirators – Zanobi Buondelmonti, Luigi Alamanni, and Battista della Palla – were former "students" of his at the Orti Oricellari.[17] They were particularly influenced by his lectures (which eventually became chapters in the *Discorsi*) on conspiracies and the murder of tyrants. Machiavelli was, therefore, directly linked with the conspirators who planned to assassinate Cardinal Giulio.

While Machiavelli was never charged in connection with the conspiracy, in 1522 his personal correspondence went almost completely silent. Tantalizingly, we are left wondering just what Machiavelli did to occupy his time during that troubled year. While it is likely that he began at least some work on the *Istorie* in the spring and summer of 1522, it is also possible, though not provable, that Lorenzo Strozzi shielded Machiavelli from the Medici family's campaign of retribution in that year. Here, we are confronted with the Machiavelli autographs of Strozzi's *Pistola* and *Commedia in versi*. With little to occupy him, Machiavelli could easily have spent time with Lorenzo Strozzi, copying the latter's literary works. This scenario sheds different and multifaceted light on Machiavelli's tragic fall. The "ferocious genius" of Machiavelli was reduced to transcribing Lorenzo di Filippo Strozzi's inferior literary works, while he was simultaneously bound to write the *Istorie* for Giulio de' Medici, the architect of the Florentine republic's destruction. Machiavelli was caught in an inescapable

15 For more context see John R. Hale, *Florence and the Medici: A Pattern of Control* (London: Phoenix, 2001), 107. The primary historical documents that detail this period in Florentine history are discussed below.

16 Patricia J. Osmond's "Conspiracy of 1522 against Cardinal Giulio de Medici: Machiavelli and '*gli esempli delli antiqui*,'" in *The Pontificate of Clement VII: History Politics Culture*, ed. Kenneth Gouwens and Sheryl E Reiss (Aldershot: Ashgate, 2005), 57. Jacopo da Diacceto and Luigi Alamanni (not Machiavelli's friend, but another man of the same name) were both executed on 7 June 1522.

17 Machiavelli dedicated his *Discorsi* to Cosimo Rucellai, the host of the Orti gatherings, and Luigi Alamanni. Buondelmonti, Alamanni, and della Palla even appeared as characters in Machiavelli's very recently completed *Arte della guerra*.

web of patronage and obligation, torn between his own republican sentiments, Strozzi's literary and theatrical mediocrity, and Giulio de' Medici's ruthlessness. When the contextual details of Machiavelli's life in this period are analysed and compared to the textual references to the "calendimaggio" in both Machiavelli's *Minuta* and Strozzi's *Pistola*, both events and texts appear to coincide in 1522, making that year the most likely for the formalization of the Strozzi-Machiavelli patron-client relationship.[18] There is not much additional evidence to work with; however, there are a few important letters between Machiavelli and Francesco Guicciardini that included references to Lorenzo Strozzi. Those letters, written in 1526, detail Machiavelli's attempts to arrange a marriage between Lorenzo Strozzi's son and Guicciardini's daughter.

The exchanges between Guicciardini and Machiavelli are significant here. Clearly, Machiavelli knew Strozzi well enough to meddle in Strozzi family affairs, but Lorenzo toyed with him, led him on, and ultimately stymied his attempts to arrange the marriage. Are Strozzi's actions those of a good friend? Probably not; but they do smack of the sometimes dismissive manner with which a patron might treat his client. The details of that botched marriage negotiation are discussed much more extensively below, in the conclusion of this study.

I stress that such arguments cannot be presented as definitive proofs. However, when we weave together the various threads of the arguments contained in this chapter (arguments grounded firmly in the available evidence) we might begin to think we have arrived at a plausible and even likely reconstruction of the relationship that existed between Strozzi and Machiavelli. At the heart of that relationship, in my view, stands the *Pistola fatta per la peste*.

Strozzi and Machiavelli: The Gentleman and the "Puppet"

In the previous chapter I argued that Lorenzo Strozzi was a republican, but likely of that strain of Florentine republican thought that reflected support

18 By "formalization" I mean that in 1522 Machiavelli began to act as Strozzi's scribe. Roberto Ridolfi suggested 1523 as the year that Strozzi wrote the *Pistola* "to" Machiavelli. He produced no evidence for that claim. The date that I ascribe to the *Pistola* is close to Ridolfi's, but I provide evidence to support my claim. See the foreword of this study for more detail.

for oligarchic rather than popular rule.[19] Arguably, Niccolò Machiavelli was more inclined to the populist approach espoused by Piero Soderini.[20] In fact, Machiavelli's almost slavish support of Soderini led some members of the Florentine government to refer to him as Soderini's "*mannerino*" or puppet.[21] Strozzi, on the other hand, maintained a tense relationship with the *Gonfaloniere*. In other words, there was nothing, at least on the surface of their political persuasions, that ought to have brought Lorenzo and Niccolò together. And when one considers their respective characters, one sees why Lorenzo was able to shift from one delicate political situation to the next with his reputation and wealth intact, while Machiavelli, at least during the fall of the republic in 1512 and the subsequent Medici restoration, paid a price for his failure to mask his republican zeal. Strozzi was willing to sacrifice his public identity for the safety of his family, while Machiavelli could do nothing but be Niccolò. This, of course, earned him exile.

Strozzi might be viewed as a graceful tightrope walker, while Machiavelli, in this context, ought to be viewed as a linguistic pugilist. Consider Machiavelli's own advice to princes concerning flatterers, and then compare his forthright commentary with Francesco Guicciardini's more tactful approach.[22] While Machiavelli advised unwise princes to avoid able and overly ambitious advisors, Guicciardini argued to the contrary. Here is Machiavelli:

> Because this is a general rule which is never false – a prince, who is himself unwise, cannot be well advised, unless he places his trust in a most prudent person who governs everything. In this case, a prince may be able to abide well, but to endure for only a short time, because his governor would soon usurp his state.[23]

---

19 See chapter 1 for a discussion of Bernardo Rucellai's influence on Selvaggia Gianfigliazzi Strozzi, Lorenzo's mother. Rucellai's strain of republicanism certainly leaned toward the oligarchic.

20 Machiavelli's "true" republican beliefs remain contested; this matter is discussed below.

21 John Hale, *Florence and the Medici: A Pattern of Control* (London: Phoenix, 2001), 92.

22 The classic text on the context and the relationship between Machiavelli and Guicciardini remains Felix Gilbert, *Machiavelli and Guicciardini: Politics and History in Sixteenth-Century Florence* (New York: Norton, 1984).

23 "Perché questa è una regola generale che non falla mai: che uno principe, il quale non sia savio per sé stesso, non può essere consigliato bene, se già a sorte non si rimettessi in uno solo che al tutto lo governassi, che fussi uomo prudentissimo. In questo caso, potria bene essere, ma durerebbe poco, perché quello governatore in breve tempo li torrebbe lo stato" (Niccolò Machiavelli, "Il Principe" in *Opere*, vol. 1, ed. Corrado Vivanti [Rome: Einaudi, 1997], 184).

Having read this, one is left with the question *Quis custodiet ipsos custodes*?[24] Guicciardini answered that question by counselling the prince's "advisors" on how to survive in a troubling court environment that might operate in a fashion directly opposed to their political inclinations:

> I say that a good citizen and lover of the fatherland (*patria*) should seek to stand well with a tyrant, not only for his own security – for he is in danger when he is suspected – but also for the benefit of the fatherland (*patria*). For by conducting oneself thus, one comes to the occasion with counsels and with works which favour the implementation of many useful measures and disfavouring many which are harmful; and those who blame him are fools, because they and their city would be miserable if the tyrant had none but wretches around him.[25]

The contrast set up between Machiavelli's and Guicciardini's political advice is *à propos* because it acts as a mirror of sorts for the lives of Lorenzo Strozzi and Niccolò Machiavelli himself. Like Guicciardini's astute citizen advisor, Strozzi knew how to please everyone, especially at the Medici court, and Machiavelli could please no one, least of all himself. In fact, the advice that he gave to the Medici princes turns on the phrase "a prince who is himself unwise." Giuliano (and later Lorenzo de' Medici) were not "unwise" princes. Rather, Machiavelli hoped that they were intelligent enough to recognize a good advisor when he presented them with an advice book.

---

24 "Who will guard the guards themselves?" For this translation and an interesting discussion of Juvenal's *sententiae* see Maria Plaza, *Persius and Juvenal* (Oxford: Oxford University Press, 2009), 461ff.

25 The translation is mine. The Italian original reads; "Dico che uno buono cittadino ed amatore della patria non solo debbe intrattenersi col tiranno per sua sicurtá, perché è in pericolo quando è avuto a sospetto, ma ancora per beneficio della patria, perché governandosi così gli viene occasione co' consigli e con le opere di favorire molti beni e disfavorire molti mali. E questi che gli biasimano sono pazzi, perché sarebbe fresca la cittá e loro se el tiranno non avessi intorno altro che tristi!" (Francesco Guicciardini, *Ricordi*, *Edizione critica*, ed. Raffaele Spongano [Florence: Sansoni, 1951], 232). This *ricordo* was apparently important to Guicciardini. It appeared first in the A *ricordi* (84), then in the B *ricordi* (108), and then, with some revisions, in the C *ricordi* (220). The text of the C version reads, "Credo sia uficio di buoni cittadini, quando la patria viene in mano di tiranni, cercare d'avere luogo con loro per potere persuadere el bene e detestare el male; e certo è interesse della città che in qualunque tempo gli uomini da bene abbino autorità. E ancora che gli ignoranti e passionati di Firenze l'abbino sempre intesa altrimenti, si accorgerebbono quanto pestifero sarebbe el governo de' Medici se non avessi intorno altri che pazzi e cattivi." I thank one of the very careful anonymous external readers at the University of Toronto Press for this information and clarification.

This failed attempt at flattery, and at getting his job back, leads to the conclusion that the Medici princes would have been unwise if they had offered Machiavelli a post in their court. Giuliano and Lorenzo de' Medici knew that a relentless republican (even one who provided advice to princes) like Machiavelli could not be trusted in their regime, and Machiavelli's links with the conspirators of 1522 proved them correct. Strozzi was infinitely more cautious. His devotion to the Strozzi *casa*, under the guise of patriotism, would never have allowed him to have been caught out in this way.

Lorenzo could play the pragmatic chameleon; he contended that one had to temper one's public actions for the long-term good of the *patria*, even if that required acting in a manner that caused one, publicly at least, to abandon some deep-seated political beliefs. Moreover, Strozzi's actions are those of a man for whom exile would have meant the destruction of the Strozzi's family influence, which he had worked decades to restore fully. This is certainly the implication of the *Pistola*. Strozzi, perhaps through Machiavelli his scribe, wrote:

> He errs much less who seeks to preserve himself for his native city (*patria*) so that he might be able to serve it at a later time than those who, feigning to serve it, exposed themselves to the danger of leaving it forever.[26]

This passage from the *Pistola* could be taken at face value. Perhaps Strozzi cared for his *patria* (his native city). But it also could be read as an excuse for his refusal to take a stand on anything of real political importance – until 1527, the year that the last republic began at Florence and the year that Machiavelli died. Strozzi's conclusions resonate with Guicciardini's approach to political service, but they also imply criticism of his client. After all, the inability to hide his integrity and his devotion to republicanism led Machiavelli to an unjust exile. It is an extreme irony that Strozzi wrote that those whose "feigned" service to the *patria* were exiled when Machiavelli's service to Florence was unmatched in its intensity and sincerity. One can only imagine how painful it must have been for Machiavelli as he transcribed this passage in Strozzi's text. In the end, Lorenzo's approach guaranteed seamless transitions from one regime to the next, where Machiavelli's promised eternal fame.[27]

---

26 See the Italian edition of the *Pistola*, 87v 5–8, and English translation.

27 There is a letter written by Lorenzo Strozzi to his younger brother Filippo, dated 1537, that echoes the sentiment shown in the *Pistola*. "In his correspondence with Filippo, Lorenzo continually invokes the obligations of a citizen to furnish the 'security and

However one chooses to read Strozzi's commentary on service to the *patria*, one is left to draw two important conclusions. The first is that Strozzi's words laid bare the "strains of isolation." He admitted that he would "preserve himself" for the *patria*, even though so doing meant losing himself in whatever service the ruling regime required. Machiavelli, although he was exiled for his lack of flexibility, lived the authentic life that Lorenzo, the ideal gentleman and courtier, could only dream of living. The second point to be made is an ironic one, and it exemplifies the brand of self-fashioning that Castiglione was to make famous. *Sprezzatura* (nonchalance), simulation ("a pretence of what is not"), and dissimulation ("a concealment of what is") were fundamental to the courtier's (that is, Lorenzo's) success.[28] Therefore, every move that Lorenzo made had to involve a calculated and conscious effort to "fashion" his public image; he was an early

quiet' of one's *patria*, rhetorically opposing the menace of war and turmoil posed by the exiles with the ideal state of peace that a 'loving and good citizen ought to desire.'" (This quotation and the quotations from Lorenzo's letter are found in Nicholas Scott Baker, "For Reasons of State: Political Executions, Republicanism and the Medici in Florence, 1480–1560," *Renaissance Quarterly* 62 [2009]: 465 and n. 67). "ASF, Carte Strozziane, Serie 5, 1207, busta titled "Lettere a Filippo Strozzi numero 3," doc. 106: "sicurtà et quiete"; "debbe desiderare ogni amorevole et buono cittadino." See also similar language in docs. 105 and 159; and in Carte Strozziane, Serie 5, 1209, busta titled "Lettere di Diversi al Mag.co Filippo di Filippo Strozzi dal primo Gennaio al primo Giugno 1537, Numero 8," docs. 64 and 206.

28 For my definitions of "simulation" and "dissimulation," I have borrowed the succinct definitions provided by Sir Richard Steele. The bibliographical details for Steele's *Tatler* are noted in the Introduction of this book. Castiglione's multi-faceted definitions of these terms are useful to have to hand. In Castiglione's advice book for courtiers, simulation (*simulazione*) is only used one time (Book 2, 26) in reference to the impenetrable "pretenses" or "lies" that every human being hides in the recesses of their minds: "Però essendo a me intervenuto piú d'una volta l'esser ingannato da chi piú amava e da chi sopra ogni altra persona aveva confidenzia d'esser amato, ho pensato talor da me a me che sia ben non fidarsi mai di persona del mondo, né darsi cosí in preda ad amico, per caro ed amato che sia, che senza riserva l'omo gli comunichi tutti i suoi pensieri come farebbe a se stesso; perché negli animi nostri sono tante latebre e tanti recessi, che impossibil è che prudenzia umana possa conoscer quelle *simulazioni*, che dentro nascose vi sono." Simulation is therefore not something that can be "practised" because it is internal, psychological. However, knowledge of one's own hidden agendas and motives, Castiglione argued through the voice of Pietro Bembo, ought to cause one to be weary of even a close friend's motives.

Dissimulation (*dissimulazione*), on the other hand, is used to define a necessary form of deception, the art of concealing the facets of one's physique or character that deserve "little praise" (Book 2, 40): "Non è ancor disconveniente che un omo che si senta valere in una cosa, cerchi destramente occasion di mostrarsi in quella, e medesimamente nasconda le parti che gli paian poco laudevoli, il tutto però con una certa avvertita *dissimulazione*."

Paolo Sarpi of sorts.[29] This type of self-fashioning, when taken to its logical conclusion, was even more effective – and perhaps more dangerous – than Machiavelli's concept of "appearances" and the *verità effettuale*.[30]

While Machiavelli's prince struggled to recognize the "effectual truth," or the "real truth," and then plotted his actions based upon probable outcomes and "appearances," he found himself surrounded by chameleons such as

---

Here, one is caught in Castiglione's semantic net. If one's internalized secrets and even moral defects are considered "simulation" or at least the byproducts of them, then the courtier is to use dissimulation to conceal his simulation. Every thought, every action, and every word that left the courtier's mouth would have to be carefully considered in the light of Castiglione's advice. Dissimulation is, then, part self-preservation and part self-promotion. Linked with both of those themes, Castiglione adds a third; the use of dissimulation in "humour" (Book 2, 72): "Assai gentil modo di facezie è ancor quello che consiste in una certa *dissimulazione*, quando si dice una cosa e tacitamente se ne intende un'altra; non dico già di quella manera totalmente contraria, come se ad un nano si dicesse gigante, e ad un negro, bianco; o vero, ad un bruttissimo, bellissimo, perché son troppo manifeste contrarietà, benché queste ancor alcuna volta fanno ridere; ma quando con un parlar severo e grave giocando si dice piacevolmente quello che non s'ha in animo." The third iteration of dissimulation is linked with searing wit and healthy doses of irony and sarcasm. In the court environment, one needed a sharp tongue and good timing. A courtier would never want to unleash a deadly one-liner on a fellow courtier (a competitor) at an inappropriate time. The courtier had to maintain his carefully constructed façade with the mortar of *sprezzatura* (Book 1, 26). This construct, articulated by JoAnn Cavallo ("Joking Matters: Politics and Dissimulation in Castiglione's *Book of the Courtier*," *Renaissance Quarterly* 53, no. 2 [2000]: 402–24), resonates wonderfully with one of Oscar Wilde's epigrams, "A gentleman is one who never hurts anyone's feelings unintentionally."

29 Paolo Sarpi (1552–1623) has become almost synonymous with Venetian politics and its protean character: "My character is such that, like the chameleon, I imitate the behaviour of those amongst whom I find myself. Thus, if I am amongst people who are reserved and gloomy I become, despite myself, unfriendly. I respond openly and freely to people who are cheerful and uninhibited. I am compelled to wear a mask. Perhaps there is nobody who can survive in Italy without one" (Richard Mackenney, *Renaissances: The Cultures of Italy, c. 1300–c.1600* [New York: Palgrave Macmillan, 2005], 201). For a book-length treatment of Sarpi, see David Wooton, *Paolo Sarpi: Between Renaissance and Enlightenment* (Cambridge: Cambridge University Press, 1983).

30 See Harry Berger's *The Absence of Grace:* Sprezzatura *and Suspicion in Two Renaissance Courtesy Books* (Stanford: Stanford University Press, 2000). This book, while controversial to some, contains research on the "dangerous" and "theatrical" qualities of Castiglione's gentleman courtier. When viewed as an essential part of courtly survival, and when used artfully, *sprezzatura* concealed everything; simulation and dissimulation were kept invisible. The courtier who practiced *sprezzatura* wore a literal and figurative costume, topped off with a handsome and impenetrable mask.

Strozzi who advised him and guided his actions.[31] The courtier's appearances and actions only infrequently correlated with his true motives, but even an astute prince would have a difficult time extrapolating a courtier's intentions from his actions. At this point, readers who are familiar with Castiglione's *Cortigiano* might be wondering about the conclusions just drawn. Was it not the courtier's job to advise the prince? Yes, certainly it was, but as Lauro Martines noted when contextualizing the courtier in the sixteenth-century, "personal integrity must have been doubly rare then."[32]

Is it any wonder that Renaissance courts were often places of treachery and deceit? With that picture firmly in mind, one can see those tensions in the patron-client relationship that seems to have existed between Strozzi and Machiavelli. The latter might have recognized the "real truths" of Florentine politics, but his commitment to republicanism would have made him an ineffective long-term advisor to a prince. The former "set the murderous Machiavel to school."[33] The courtier schooled the failed politician in the art of self-fashioning and the wiles of simulation and dissimulation, paradoxically, by cloaking all of those practices with the nonchalance of *sprezzatura*.

A closer look at the actions of both men will illustrate the above points. Niccolò could be no one but Niccolò – brilliant, though loudmouthed and opinionated. He certainly knew how to dispense advice that was often as shocking as it was useful; but Strozzi knew how to maintain his position in Florence without offending the Medici or his republican circle of friends. This contrast between Strozzi and Machiavelli is telling, for it helps to explain why, though their political paths often differed, both men ended up discontented at the end of their lives. What one must do is highlight the points where their paths intersected, and the best way to do that is to scour through Machiavelli's personal letters.

On 2 July 1509, Filippo Casavecchia sent a rather indignant letter to Machiavelli, railing against the latter's inability or perhaps refusal to write or keep in touch. Casavecchia wanted Niccolò to attend a dinner party and a trout-fishing expedition. He was careful to mention all of their mutual acquaintances, including Lorenzo Strozzi, who had recently visited to

31 For the famous "*verità effettuale*" passage see "Di quelle cose per le quali li uomini, e specialmente i principi sono laudati o vituperate" (chap. 15 of *Il Principe*, in *Opere*, vol. 1, 159).

32 Lauro Martines, "The Gentleman in Renaissance Italy: Strains of Isolation in the Body Politic," in *The Darker Vision of the Renaissance,* ed. Robert S. Kinsman (Los Angeles: University of California at Los Angeles Press, 1974), 77.

33 William Shakespeare, *Henry VI, Part III,* in *The Complete Signet Classic Shakespeare*, ed. Sylvan Barnet (New York: Harcourt Brace Jovanovich, 1972), 190–232. See III.ii.182–95, 215–16.

partake in extravagant parties and to enjoy, as Filippo bragged, "both the air and the wines, which are recognized to be the best in Tuscany."[34] This is the first time Strozzi's name is mentioned in Machiavelli's correspondence. From this reference to Strozzi, it is likely that Niccolò knew, or at least knew of, Lorenzo on some level, as both would have associated with those Florentines who influenced their government, but there is no evidence to suggest that a close friendship existed between the two men. There is, however, evidence to suggest that they were at odds with one another.

Machiavelli was closely associated with Piero Soderini, whom Lorenzo Strozzi neither liked nor trusted a result of the *Gonfaloniere*'s attempts in 1508 to derail Filippo Strozzi's marriage to Clarice de' Medici. As we saw earlier, Machiavelli was, or at least Strozzi believed that he was, the author of the state's complaint against Filippo Strozzi. Lorenzo himself was not in favour of the marriage, but he was indignant that Soderini (and Machiavelli) involved themselves in the marriage dispute after Soderini had failed to arrange a marriage between Clarice de' Medici and one of his own nephews. That Strozzi should have taken offence at Soderini's hypocrisy is ironic to say the least, but Strozzi's anger should also be understood within the context of the Florentine social hierarchy: it is probable that Lorenzo did not want Florentines of lesser stock than himself interfering with the Strozzi family's business.

The same analysis can be applied to the relationship between Lorenzo and Machiavelli: it seems certain that problems associated with rank and status were also elements of the Strozzi-Machiavelli relationship. Machiavelli was a member of an old Florentine family, but his was an illegitimate line; and Strozzi was a member of one of Florence's oldest and wealthiest aristocratic families.[35] In 1513, during the darkest period of Machiavelli's forced *otium*, he brooded over the differences between his own background and that of Giuliano de' Medici's. These ruminations, in part at least, caused him to set aside the republican *Discorsi,* which he probably began in 1513, in favour of

34 Filippo Casavecchia to Niccolò Machiavelli, letter dated 2 July 1509, in Niccolò Machiavelli, *Machiavelli and His Friends: Their Personal Correspondence*, trans. and ed. James B. Atkinson and David Sices (Dekalb: Northern Illinois University Press, 1996), 183. The Italian original is "Sì per l'aria quanto per'vini, che hanno capitolato esser e migliori che fieno in Toscano" (Niccolò Machiavelli, *Opere*, *Volume Terzo: Lettere,* ed. Franco Gaeta [Turin: Unione Tipografico-Editrice Torinese, 1984], 310).

35 For a breakdown of the wealth accumulated by the Strozzi family, particularly after Filippo the Elder returned to Florence, see Richard Goldthwaite, *Private Wealth in Renaissance Florence: A Study of Four Families* (Princeton: Princeton University Press, 1968): 74–107.

Il Principe.[36] The stark imagery of *Il Principe*'s dedication, which paints a picture of the princely mountain top and the lowly plain, brings into clearer focus Machiavelli's political relationship not only with Giuliano de' Medici but also with Lorenzo Strozzi.

> Nor I hope will it be reputed as presumptuous if a man of base and lowest status dares to discuss and reason about the governing of princes; because, just as some who draw the countryside place themselves low in the plain to consider the nature of mountains and the high places, and to consider that which is low place themselves high atop the mountains; similarly, to understand fully the nature of the people, one needs to be a prince, and to understand princes fully one must be of the people.[37]

The physical and metaphorical distance between Machiavelli and men like Giuliano de' Medici and Lorenzo di Filippo Strozzi was insurmountable. Despite the elegance and unparalleled genius of Machiavelli's *Il Principe*, it failed to gain him access to and patronage from the Medici court (it took Lorenzo Strozzi to do that). When this project failed, he returned to his true love, republicanism. However, Machiavelli always held out hope that the Medici would recognize his genius and his devotion to Florence. One might argue that they recognized both, bestowing on Machiavelli roughly seven years (1513–1520) in political limbo. During that period, Machiavelli received patronage from Francesco Vettori, eventually from Lorenzo di

---

36 For the classic debates on the composition of *Il Principe* and the *Discorsi*, see Genarro Sasso, "Intorno alla composizione dei *Discorsi* di Niccolò Machiavelli," in *Giornale storico della letteratura italiana* 134 (1957): 482–534 and 135 (1958): 215–59; Felix Gilbert, "The Composition and Structure of Machiavelli's *Discorsi*," *Journal of the History of Ideas* 14 (1953): 136–56; Hans Baron, "The *Principe* and the Puzzle of the Date of the *Discorsi*," *Bibliotheque d'humanisme et renaissance* 18 (1956): 405–28; J. H Whitfield, "*Discourses* on Machiavelli VII: Gilbert, Hexter, and Baron," *Italian Studies* 13 (1958); J.H. Hexter, "Seyssel, Machiavelli and Polybius VI: The Mystery of the Missing Translation," *Studies in the Renaissance* 3 (1956): 75–96.

37 My translation. The Italian original is "Né voglio sia imputata prosumptione, se uno uomo di basso et infimo stato ardiscie discorrere e regolare e governi de' principi. Perché, così come coloro che disegniano e paesi si pongano bassi nel piano a considerare la natura de' monti e de' luoghi alti, e per considerare quella de' luoghi bassi si pongano alti sopra e' monti; similmente, ad cognoscere bene la natura de' populi bisogna essere principe, et ad cognoscere bene quella de' principi conviene esser populare" (Niccolò Machiavelli, *Opere di Niccolò Machiavelli*, ed. Rinaldo Rinaldi, vol. 1, bk. 1, *De Principatibus, Discorsi sopra la prima deca di Tito Livio* [bks. 1–2] [Turin: Unione Tipografico-Editrice Torinese, 1999], 109–10).

Filippo Strozzi, and through Strozzi from Giulio de' Medici. The long and winding road that led Machiavelli to the patronage of Giulio de' Medici is littered with irony and tragedy. For even though his writings demonstrate keen insights into the workings of princes, the machinations of Florentine nobility, profound knowledge of constitutional republicanism, and a healthy distrust of human nature, in real life it seems that Machiavelli failed to understand the complexities of his own personal relationships with the Florentine nobility who dominated his existence.

Lorenzo and Niccolò: Under the Restored Medici Regime

In 1512, Niccolò Machiavelli lost his post when the restored Medici fired the vast majority of Soderini's republican sympathizers. In the following year he was sent into rural exile, where he whiled away time at his family home in San Casciano.[38] As noted above, the *otium* of his exile concentrated his genius. During 1513, Machiavelli probably completed most of *Il Principe* and likely began his *Discorsi*. However, by 1514 he was nearing bankruptcy – a fact that brought him into Strozzi's sphere of influence.

As Machiavelli languished on the outskirts of Florentine life, Strozzi transitioned into Medici-controlled Florence with ease, taking a position as an official of the Florentine *Monte* (a position he had refused to accept in Soderini's republic). The *Monte* was an important Florentine institution, for it was the state-run bank and public finance office that made loans to private citizens, where interest rates varied according to the amount of money that an individual borrower contributed via taxes and the like to the *monte* or "mountain" of Florentine governmental funds.[39] Machiavelli, in financial

38 Peter Godman, *From Poliziano to Machiavelli: Florentine Humanism in the High Renaissance* (Princeton: Princeton University Press, 1998) is one of the best recent Anglophone works on these themes. There are the standard Italian classics by Villari and Ridolfi and more recently by Maurizio Viroli, which are cited frequently in this book, but there is a more recent Italian study: Francesco Bausi, *Machiavelli* (Rome: Salerno, 2005). Bausi daringly chose to re-evaluate and revise the "myth" of Machiavelli. Maurizio Viroli's most recent monograph on Machiavelli's "religion" is almost as adventuresome as Bausi's. Therein, Viroli tries to illustrate that while Machiavelli might not have subscribed fully to the Catholic Church's version of Christianity, he was nevertheless Christian in his outlook. See Viroli, *Il Dio di Machiavelli e il problema morale dell' Italia* (Rome: Laterza, 2005).

39 Machiavelli, *Personal Correspondence*, 521n11: "Monte: the officials of the Florentine system for public financing of the town's debt, the 'mountain.'" The *Monte redivisible* (redeemable) would issue to private citizens credits, which drew interest and were

straits, hoped that the *Monte* would lend him money or at least provide some assistance so that he could meet his steep obligations.

We find details about this in a letter that Machiavelli wrote to Francesco Vettori dated 16 April 1514, and, by extension, we also find a reference to Strozzi – an official of the *Monte*.

> I do the best I can to make ends meet. If you could see your way clear to write to one of these officials [i.e., Strozzi] attesting to my impossible state, I would put myself in your hands. There is no need to write the Magnificent because he does not attend to these matters – writing to one or two of the others would suffice.[40]

Vettori did not respond to this portion of Machiavelli's letter, but he did write to the officials of the *Monte* on Machiavelli's behalf. In Vettori, we see a splendid example of patronage in action. He confided in the officials (including Lorenzo) that Niccolò "is poor and worthy, and whatever may be said to the contrary, is really so, I can confirm he finds himself with heavy liabilities, with a scanty income, is now penniless and burdened with children."[41]

In the ensuing correspondence between Machiavelli and Vettori, the latter carried on as if Machiavelli had not even mentioned his financial situation, and nothing seems to have come of Vettori's minimal intervention. In response to Vettori's silence on the matter, and, with his usual dramatic flair, Machiavelli wrote to Vettori on 10 June 1514:

> I am going to stay just as I am amid my lice, unable to find any man who recalls my service or believes I might be good for anything. But I cannot possibly go on like this for long, because I am rotting away and I can see that if

---

negotiable, in amounts equal to their contributions to the "mountain" of public debt. Thus a public bank was created in Florence with an accumulation, a "mountain," of money and assets. The *Monte comune* ought not to be confused with the *Monte di Pietà*. For details of the latter, see Carol Bresnahan Menning, "The Monte's 'Monte': The Early Supporters of Florence's Monte di Pietà," *Sixteenth-Century Journal* 23, no. 4 (1992).

40 Letter from Machiavelli to Vettori, dated 16 April 1514, in Machiavelli, *Personal Correspondence*, 285. The Italian original is "Io mi arrabatto qua il meglio che posso. Se a voi paresse di scrivere una lettera ad alcuno di questi ufiziali, e fare loro fede della mia impossibilità, me ne rimetto a voi. Al magnifico non bisogna scrivere, perché non vi si raguna; basta a uno o dua di quelli altri" (*Lettere*, 454).

41 Villari, Pasquale. *The Life and Times of Niccolò Machiavelli*, trans. Linda Villari, vol. 3 (London: Kegan Paul, Trench and Co., 1883), 200. For Italian original see Pasquale Villari, *Machiavelli e i suoi tempi*, vol. 2 (Milan: Editore-Libraio,1895), 223.

God does not show a more favorable face to me, one day I shall be forced to leave home and to place myself as tutor or secretary to a governor, if I cannot do otherwise, or to stick myself in some deserted spot to teach reading to children and leave my family here to count me dead; they will do much better without me because I am causing them expenses, since I am used to spending and cannot do without spending.[42]

From the rather pathetic tone taken here, one can easily gather that neither Vettori nor Strozzi was willing to risk his position in the fickle Medici regime by speaking out publicly in Machiavelli's support. We hear nothing of Strozzi in Machiavelli's letters until much later in the 1520s, when Machiavelli tried to arrange a marriage for one of Lorenzo's sons. Of course, this attempt failed, but the significant point is that Machiavelli felt comfortable enough to advise Lorenzo on the marriage of his son; this suggests that the two became much more familiar with one another in the years following the 1514 *Monte* debacle.[43]

It is likely that Strozzi and Machiavelli came into more frequent contact with one another at the Orti Oricellari (the Rucellai Gardens). Beginning in late 1514, both men attended the Orti with some frequency.[44] It was only natural for Strozzi to attend as he was related by marriage to Cosimo Rucellai (who inherited the family gardens from his father Cosimo, c. 1514) and to Bernardo Rucellai, who was responsible for founding the gardens and turning them into a gathering point for Florence's and Italy's great

42 Letter from Machiavelli to Vettori dated 10 June 1514, in Machiavelli, *Personal Correspondence*, 290. The Italian original is "Starommi dunque così tra' miei pidocchi, senza trovare uomo che della servitù mia ricordi, o che creda che io possa essere buono a nulla. Ma egli è impossibile che io possa stare molto così, perché io mi logoro, e veggo, quando Iddio non mi si mostri più favorevole, che io sarò un dì forzato ad uscirmi di casa, e pormi per ripetitore a cancelliere di un connestabile, quando io non possa altro, a ficcarmo in qualche terra deserta ad insegnare leggere a' fanciulli, e lasciare qua la mia brigata, che facci conto che io sia morto, la quale farà molto meglio senza me, perché io le sono di spesa, sendo avvezzo a spendere, e non potendo fare senza spendere" (*Lettere*, 461–2).

43 For the letters concerning Machiavelli's "marriage-making" skills, see Machiavelli, *Personal Correspondence*, letter 296 (17 August 1525, Machiavelli to Guicciardini), 363–4 and letter 311 (2 June 1526, Machiavelli to Guicciardini), 389. Machiavelli was trying to arrange a marriage between one of Guicciardini's daughters and Lorenzo Strozzi's son Giambattista.

44 For further details of Lorenzo di Filippo Strozzi's involvement in the Orti, see Anthony M. Cummings, *Maecenas and the Madrigalist: Patrons, Patronage, and the Origins of the Italian Madrigal* (Philadelphia: American Philosophical Society, 2004), 172–173, table 6.

literary and political minds.[45] An important thing to note here about the Orti is that the Rucellai family, which by the time of Cosimo had come to support the Medici, was open to those of opposing points of view and especially open to republican theorists. Machiavelli gave some of his most important lectures, foretastes of his *Discorsi*, at the Orti. The Rucellai Gardens also provided a place for those who were publicly sympathetic to the Medici family but who may have had private republican leanings. The open intellectual atmosphere of the Rucellai Gardens allows us to reflect on the experiences of Machiavelli and Strozzi in the broader context of Florence.

In 1514 and the following years, Strozzi in his public persona could have been considered a Medici supporter, particularly when one considers how many important public offices he held between 1514 and 1520. One must consider Strozzi's public Medici support in light of the fact that he served the restored Florentine republic between 1527 and 1530, and also remember that Lorenzo's taste for the Medici soured after the death of Lorenzo, Duke of Urbino, the last of the Magnificent's direct heirs. After 1521, he held no offices that guided state policy in Medici-controlled Florence. All of this, in tandem with his giving up of public life not long after the Medici restoration of 1530, suggest that Lorenzo's republican sentiments were stronger than his love for the Medici family.[46]

From 1513 onward, Machiavelli struggled at the fringes of Florentine society, attempting to regain his office while writing some of the Renaissance's most memorable political and literary treatises. Strozzi and Machiavelli make an awkward pair, to say the least, but somehow they appear to have entered into a patron-client relationship that bore fruit, apparently, as Machiavelli put the finishing touches on the *Arte della guerra* – which he dedicated to Strozzi in 1521. Might Machiavelli's dedication of the *Arte* to Strozzi be viewed as a sign of his appreciation and his desperation?

Between 1515 and 1519, as stated above, Machiavelli gave lectures on the *Discorsi* at the Orti. The exact size of his audiences is not known, but is it quite likely that his lectures were attended by Lorenzo Strozzi and his brother Filippo. Additionally, Machiavelli wrote the *Mandragola*, *L'Asino*,

45 Felix Gilbert, "Bernardo Rucellai and the *Orti Oricellari*: A Study on the Origin of Modern Political Thought," *Journal of the Warburg and Courtauld Institutes* 12 (1949): 101–31.

46 For more on this as it pertains to Lorenzo's biography, see chapter 1, particularly the portion of the chapter that covers the dates 1482–1526.

and a number of other minor works during those years.[47] His writings, and the mind and striking personality that produced them, probably attracted a number of admirers and supporters at the Rucellai gardens. Perhaps those lectures he delivered led the Strozzi brothers to help Machiavelli in his quest to regain his former office. Certainly they did come to his assistance, as an extant letter from the period indicates.

In a letter dated 17 March 1519 (1520 following the contemporary calendar) Filippo wrote to Lorenzo concerning Machiavelli: "I am quite pleased that you have conducted Machiavello into the Medici house, for if he should obtain a little faith [*fede*] from the patrons [*padroni*] he is a person who will rise in the world."[48] Strozzi likely arranged the personal audience that Machiavelli had with Cardinal Giulio de' Medici on 17 March 1520. Lorenzo Strozzi was quite the gadly and also quite the diplomat; he could easily run with anti-Medicean radicals at the *Orti* and then arrange meetings between one such radical and the Medici prince. Very few Florentines were capable of balancing interactions between such divergent groups. Strozzi's aristocratic background opened doors that never would have opened to Machiavelli of their own accord. Lorenzo used his connections with the Medici family to ease Machiavelli, eventually, into a patron-client relationship with the Florentine overlords. But in so doing, he also brought Machiavelli into his own sphere of influence – he became Machiavelli's patron. While Machiavelli showed his indebtedness to Strozzi by dedicating the *Arte* to him, their relationship probably did not produce the *Pistola* until 1522. Interestingly, while Machiavelli clearly developed a friendship with Lorenzo's brother Filippo, he did not develop a friendship with Lorenzo.[49] This is quite likely because by 1519 Lorenzo had become

47 Still one of the classic works that places Machiavelli, throughout this period, at the Orti, is Hans Baron's "Machiavelli on the Eve of the *Discourses*: The Date and Place of the *Dialogo intorno alla nostra lingua*," *Bibliothèque d'Humanisme et Renaissance* 23 (1961): 449–76.

48 "Piacemi assai habbiate condotto el Machiavello in casa e' Medici, che, ogni poco di fede aqquisti co' padroni, è persona per surgere" (Letter from Filippo Strozzi to Lorenzo di Filippo Strozzi dated 17 March 1519 (1520), in Tommasini, *La vita*, vol. 2, appendices, 1082). The original letter is located in the Archivio di Stato di Firenze, Strozzi-Uguccioni, 108, c. 40.

49 Machiavelli was definitely one of Filippo Strozzi's friends. There is a letter from Filippo to Niccolò dated 31 March 1526 that includes the following, and other statements, about their friendship: "Those who, in addition to bearing more than usual love and affection for you, have such character and qualities that everyone ought to make them better and closer friends, among which number you hold the principal place for me" (Machiavelli, *Personal Correspondence*, 383). The Italian

the head of the Strozzi family, a position that not only granted significant status but also required careful management of a large patronage network. Even though he and Machiavelli moved in the same Orti circle, Lorenzo's noble rank set him apart from Machiavelli. While many of the men who frequented the Rucellai Gardens were fast friends, and these friendships sometimes bridged divides in rank, Strozzi was more aloof. However, Machiavelli's brilliance probably encouraged Lorenzo to take him under his wing and help him regain a position in Medici Florence; but fraternization beyond that could hardly be expected.

This is one of the great ironies of the period: that Machiavelli, author of *Il Principe*, the most brilliant example within the genre of such advice books, had to turn to a much younger and savvier politician, Lorenzo Strozzi, for direction in dealing with the Medici. Irony aside, Machiavelli was so moved by his help that, as we have seen, he decided to dedicate his *Arte della guerra* (published in 1521) to Lorenzo, "Patrizio fiorentino" (Florentine patrician or gentleman):

> You, Lorenzo, ought therefore to consider the qualities of these efforts of mine and give them, with your judgment, the censure or the praise which they will seem to have merited. These I present to you (being customary to honor with similar works those who shine in their nobility, wealth, ingenuity and liberality,) to demonstrate my gratefulness for the favours ["*benefizi*"] that I have received from you, even though my ability does not measure up; I know that where wealth and nobility are concerned you do not have many equals, few in genius and none in liberality.[50]

The "favours" to which Machiavelli referred were linked to the aid that Lorenzo gave him with the Medici family. Lorenzo's support, guidance, and

---

original is "E quelli ancora meritano sia tenuto più conto di loro, quali oltre al portarti non mediocre amore e affezione, hanno in loro tale parte e virtù, che ciascuno debbe di amici cercare di farseli amicissimi, nel qual numero voi appresso di me tenete il principal luogo" (*Lettere*, 582).

50 The translation is mine. The Italian original is "Voi pertanto, Lorenzo, considererete le qualità di queste mie fatiche e darete loro, con il vostro giudicio, quel biasimo o quella lode la quale vi parrà ch' elle abbiano meritato. Le quali a voi mando sì per dimostrarmi grato, ancora che la mia possibilità non vi aggiunga, de' benefizi ho ricevuto da voi, sì ancora, perché, essendo consuetudine onorare di simili opere coloro i quali per nobiltà, ricchezze, ingegno e liberalità risplendono, conosco voi di ricchezze e nobiltà non avere molti pari, d'ingegno pochi e di liberalità niuno" (Niccolò Machiavelli, *L'Arte della Guerra,* in *Opere*, vol. 1, ed. Corrado Vivanti [Rome: Einaudi, 1997], 530–1).

patronage eventually led Cardinal Giulio de' Medici to hire Machiavelli to write a history of Florence.[51] Machiavelli was then contracted by the Studio for two years, the first definite and the second at their whim. He was paid fairly well, one hundred florins per year, with the understanding that the Studio could require him to undertake additional works if they saw fit.[52] That salary provided Niccolò with a modicum of wealth and stabilized his life. He showed his gratitude by dedicating his *Histories* to Giulio de' Medici, who was elevated to the throne of St Peter in 1523 as Pope Clement VII.

One small and easily overlooked detail – an offer to Machiavelli of alternative employment – brings into sharper focus Strozzi's emerging influence on Machiavelli. Piero Soderini, Machiavelli's old boss at the Chancellery and Strozzi's long-time enemy, wrote to Niccolò as soon as he got wind of his new commission, evidently urging him to reject the Studio's offer in favour of one he had arranged, which paid more and would allow Machiavelli to leave Florence. Here is the text of that letter, dated 13 April 1521:

> My very dear Niccolò. Because the affair of Ragusa was not satisfactory to you, Lord Prospero has asked me to recommend a man capable of managing his affairs and I know your trustworthiness and your ability, I proposed you to him. You are very satisfactory to him because he has information about you. He has authorized me to ask you about it. The stipend will be two hundred gold ducats and expenses. Think it over, and if it be satisfactory to you I would urge you, without discussing it, to get here before your departure is known about there. I know of no better prospect at present, and I judge it much better than to stay there and write histories for sealed florins [*fiorini di suggello*].[53]

51 "On 8 November, the Florentine Studio, headed by Giulio de' Medici, entrusted him with a task customarily assigned to Chancery officials: the writing ('in Latin or in Tuscan, as he pleased') of what was envisaged as the 'annals or chronicles' which became the *Istorie Fiorentine*" (Godman, *Poliziano to Machiavelli*, 237–8).

52 Villari also included a transcription of the contract: "Die viij. mensis novembrio M.D.XX. Conduxerunt Niccholaum de Machiavellis civem florentinum ad serviendum dicto eorum officio, et inter alia ad componendum annalia et cronacas florent. Et alia faciendum, que et prout dictis dominis officialibus fuerit expediens pro tempore et termino duorum annorum initiatorum die prima presentis mensis novembris, uno scilicet firmo, altero verum ad beneplacitum dictorum dominorum officialium cum salario quolibet anno florenorum centum, ad rationem librorum quatuor pro quolibet floreno solvendorum de quatuor mensibus in quatuor menses cum taxis obligationibus et aliis conseutis" (Villari, *Life and Time*, vol. 3, 321).

53 Machiavelli, *Personal Correspondence*, 334. The Italian original is "Nicolò carissimo. Da poi non vi satisfece il partito di Ragugia, ricercandomi el signore Prospero d'uno uomo sufficiente da maneggiare le cose sue, conoscendo la fede vostra e suficienzia,

Either Machiavelli did not answer Soderini's letter or his response did not survive; at any rate, he took up the commission from the Studio. Might Lorenzo Strozzi have had something to do with his decision to remain in Florence? Given that Lorenzo's patronage of Machiavelli was beginning to bear fruit, and given his long-standing aversion to Soderini, it seems very likely that he would have encouraged Machiavelli to remain in Florence. One might of course argue that Machiavelli, of his own initiative, never would have left his native Florence for a permanent job elsewhere. So, which is it? Did Strozzi's influence tether Machiavelli to Florence, or did Machiavelli's patriotism compel him to stay? As much as one might like to think that Machiavelli's patriotic sentiments kept him in the city, it seems more likely that Strozzi's influence and protection caused Machiavelli to reject Soderini's offer. To this end, let us consider a work that Machiavelli wrote in 1522, in which we might see Lorenzo di Filippo Strozzi's sway writ large.

The text in question is a response to a general request by Cardinal Giulio de' Medici for suggestions for reorganization of the Florentine government. It was a short treatise providing a detailed blueprint for a new Florentine republic. Earlier, of course, Machiavelli had written a similar document for Leo X, but it had been too radical to be taken seriously, calling for a speedy return to popular – though still Medici-influenced – republican rule.[54] Machiavelli's suggestions to Cardinal Giulio embody a more nuanced and carefully considered approach to Medici rule and republican politics. One could argue that this approach reflects Lorenzo Strozzi's political persuasions, and the work's decorous and genteel style his gentlemanly influence. However, the vehicle that Machiavelli adopted to present the document was typically brash. He cast his suggestions for reform as a decree written by Giulio de' Medici himself, putting uncharacteristic words in the mouth of the future pope. While Machiavelli's republican treatise is concise and mercurial, it is also supremely reckless. That a disgraced republican, who had only recently been set on the road to rehabilitation,

---

ve li proposi. Sodifateli assai perché ha notizia di voi: hammi commesso ve ne ricerchi. La provisione sarà 200 ducati d'oro e le spese: pensatela, e satisfacendovi, vi conforterei, senza conferirlo, a essere prima là, che di costà si sapessi la partita; né altro migliore partito mi occorre al presente, il quale giudico molto meglio che stare costì a scrivere storie a fiorni di suggello" (*Lettere*, 516).

54 "Discorso delle cose fiorentine dopo la morte di Lorenzo." For more detail see Roberto Ridolfi, *Vita di Niccolò Machiavelli*, 2 vols. (Florence: Sansoni, 1972), esp. vol. 1, 286, and vol. 2, 547n28. For a recent Italian edition of Machiavelli's work, see "Discursus Florentinarum Rerum Post Mortem Iunioris Laurentii Medices," in *Opere*, vol. 1, ed. Corrado Vivanti (Rome: Einaudi, 1997).

would impersonate the Medici cardinal illustrates that Machiavelli failed to recognize the precariousness of his situation. Machiavelli could only be reined in so far.

Summarizing the decree, John Hale wrote that Machiavelli argued "it would be wise to re-institute the Great Council but control appointments to it … This proposal enabled Machiavelli to legislate for a republic while providing means to preserve Medici domination during the lifetime of his patrons."[55] Hale concluded that the Medici, and concerns over their influence in his life, drove Machiavelli to formulate his suggestions in such a fashion. This is part of the story. The Grand Council that Machiavelli wanted restored would resemble the last Grand Council of 1512, and he also concluded that the office of *Gonfaloniere* ought to be restored as well, though it would not be "for life" but rather open to elections every three years. Here, one begins to find some subtle oligarchic influences creeping into Machiavelli's republican vision.[56]

For example, he suggested that the Grand Council and the *Gonfaloniere* be restrained by a new "senate" of one hundred *Signori* who would in turn elect a special council of twelve *Signori*. (However, while Cardinal Giulio remained in Florence he would oversee all elections and appointments.) Machiavelli argued that membership of the Twelve ought to be restricted to Florentine citizens over the age of forty-five.[57] Additionally, he contended that its members ought to be given extraordinary powers to create "laws and statutes" that would govern the future of the republic. This power would be conferred on the Twelve for a single year – but what an important

---

55 John R. Hale, *Florence and the Medici* (London: Phoenix, 2001),107. For much greater detail see Ridolfi, *Vita*, vol. 1, 315 and vol. 2, 557n10. The "*bozza autografa*" of Machiavelli's suggestions to Giulio de' Medici may be found in the Biblioteca Nazionale Centrale di Firenze, *Carte Machiavelli*, I, 79. The ms begins with "Considerando i nostri magnifici et excelsi, etc." For a recent print edition, see Machiavelli, *Opere*, vol. 1, ed. Corrado Vivanti (Rome: Eniaudi, 1997). For the full text of the *Minuta*, see appendix 4 of this study.

56 Machiavelli's republicanism, as I have noted elsewhere, is a touchy subject in Machiavelli studies. For a good survey of some of the most salient elements of his republican vision, see Gisela Bock, Quentin Skinner, and Maurizio Viroli, eds., *Machiavelli and Republicanism* (Cambridge: Cambridge University Press, 1990).

57 Interestingly, in the *Minuta* ms, Machiavelli originally suggested that members should be forty years of age; Lorenzo Strozzi was forty years old in 1522. Niccolò cancelled that suggestion, raising the age restriction to forty-five. One wonders if this was a jab at Strozzi. "Et ciascuno di detti (elezionari) nomini uno cittadini di 40 anni forniti, habile al Consiglio, et netto di spechio … i quali così nominati vadino ad partito" (Appendix 4, n. 7).

year that would be.[58] Since Giulio de' Medici would oversee the selection of the Twelve, its members would likely be drawn from Florence's old families, many of whom were on very good terms with the cardinal. In 1522, Lorenzo Strozzi had not yet reached forty-five, but it is entirely possible that his professional relationship with Machiavelli helped to shape at least this part of Machiavelli's proposal. For even as Lorenzo seems to have advised Machiavelli, it is important not to forget that he was selected to be the Florentine Ambassador to Giulio de' Medici after he was elected Pope Clement VII. In that role, Lorenzo suggested to the pope some of the very same ideas contained in Machiavelli's treatise.[59] This appears to be much more than a coincidence.

If Lorenzo Strozzi did guide Machiavelli as he wrote his "decree" of 1522, then it is possible that Strozzi's influence and ideas, contained in Machiavelli's brash treatise, enmeshed Machiavelli in a very dangerous Medici plot. Recall that Machiavelli's lectures at the Orti had inflamed a group of young republicans to take action against the Medici.[60] Later in the same year, 1522, the politically astute Cardinal de'Medici, along with mercenary armies that he dispatched, dealt with an attempt to take Siena.

58 Villari, *Life and Times*, vol. 3, 329–30.

59 Appendix 2, 24r 4–9 where Zeffi, Lorenzo's biographer, wrote that Lorenzo suggested the Florentine republic be restored and governed by a Gonfaloniere who would be elected every three years. See below for more detail.

60 The best recent work on Machiavelli's influence on the 1522 conspirators is Patricia J. Osmond's "Conspiracy of 1522 against Cardinal Giulio de Medici: Machiavelli and '*gli esempli delli antiqui*,' in *The Pontificate of Clement VII: History, Politics, Culture*, ed. Kenneth Gouwens and Sheryl E Reiss (Aldershot: Ashgate, 2005), 55–6n3. There Osmond references the "principal published editions for the conspiracy of 1522," most of which were cited earlier by Pasquale Villari, who was mentioned above. The sources Osmond noted are: Filippo de' Nerli, *Commentari de' fatti civili occorsi dentro la città di Firenze dall'anno 1512 al 1537,* vol. 2 (Trieste: Colombo Coen Tip. Editore, 1859), 10–23; Jacopo Nardi, *Istorie della città di Firenze*, vol. 2, ed. L. Arbib (Florence: Società editrice delle Storie del Nardi e del Varchi, 1838–41), 74–81; Scipione Ammirato, *Istorie fiorentine*, vol. 6, ed. L. Scarabelli (Turin: Cugini Pomba e Comp. Editori, 1853), 344–6; G. Capponi, *Storia della Repubblica di Firenze,* vol. 1 (Florence: g. Barbèra, 1930), 335–58 (bk. 6, chap. 6); C. Guasti, "Documenti della congiura fatta il cardinale Giulio de' Medici nel 1522," *GSAT* 3 (1859): 121–50, 185–213, 239–67. There is another helpful article on Italian Renaissance conspiracies that includes the 1522 republican conspiracy at Florence: Kate Lowe, "Conspiracy and Its Prosecution in Italy, 1500–1550: Violent Responses to Violent Solutions," in *Conspiracy and Conspiracy Theory in Early Modern Europe: From the Waldensians to the French Revolution*, ed. Barry Coward and Julian Swann (Aldershot: Ashgate, 2004), 35-53.

He was also able to expose a much larger plot on his own life in Florence which had tentacles extending all the way to Rome. This was troubling for Giulio, as he did not know who his enemies in Florence were – but he knew they were republicans. In a very shrewd move, he continued to encourage Florentine republicans to provide further suggestions for reforms in the city. He suspected, rightly, that the most radical republicans, those who wanted to assassinate him, would continue to provide suggestions on reform so as to appear blameless. He was correct. Republican reformers Luigi Alamanni, Zanobi Buondelmonti, and a number of others authored a steady stream of "suggestions." Vigilance, police-state tactics, and good luck turned up the evidence that the cardinal needed to begin a bloody cleansing. One of Battista della Palla's couriers who brought messages from the conspirators in Florence to him in Rome was captured in Florence, interrogated, and tortured. He gave up the names of the Florentine conspirators, most of whom immediately scattered, some to as far away as France. But several were caught unaware in Florence and summarily tried and beheaded. All of the Florentine Soderini family, members of the conspiracy from the start, were condemned in absentia, and the promise of Florentine liberty and the tantalizing vision of a new republic were snuffed out.[61]

Machiavelli was supremely fortunate not to have been drawn completely into the conspirators' circle. Pasquale Villari noted with some surprise that "by great good luck, no suspicion fell on Machiavelli."[62] Jacopo Nardi, who wrote about the conspiracy in 1553, provided a very different picture: suspicion did fall on Machiavelli due to his close associations with the chief conspirators.[63] Paolo Giovio went even further, suggesting that Machiavelli,

61 For more details of the conspirators and the aftermath of their failed attempt to restore the republic, see Delio Cantimori and Frances A. Yates, "Rhetoric and Politics in Italian Humanism," *Journal of the Warburg Institute* 1, no. 2 (1937): 91 and n. 1.

62 Villari, *Life and Times*, vol. 3, 333.

63 "Per il che detto Niccolò [Machiavelli] era amato grandemente da loro, e anche per cortesia sovvenuto, come seppi io, di qualche emolumento: e della sua conversazione si dilettavano maravigliosamente, tenendo in prezzo grandissimo tutte l'opere sue, in tanto che de' pensamenti e azioni di questi giovani anche Niccolò non fu senza imputazione" (Jacopo Nardi, *Istorie della città di Firenze*, vol. 2, ed. Agenore Gelli [Florence: Le Monnier, 1888], 77). Another useful source is Filippo de' Nerli. He wrote that the conspirators, who might have relied on Machiavelli's *Discorsi* as a blueprint for a properly ordered conspiracy, missed the point of Niccolò's text: "che se bene lo avessero considerato, o non l' avrebbero fatto, o se pure fatto l' avessero, almeno più proceduti sarebbono" (*Commentari de' fatti civili occorsi dentro la città di Firenze dall'anno 1512 al 1537,* vol. 2 [Trieste: Colombo Coen Tip Editore, 1859], 12, quoted in Patricia J. Osmond, "Conspiracy of 1522," 57n8).

though employed by the Medici, was viewed as the central architect of the plot to kill Cardinal Giulio.[64] There are no records indicating that formal charges were ever pressed against Machiavelli; although Nardi's comments illustrate that people in Florence were talking about his connection with the conspirators, in the end he once again escaped the executioner's blade. He may have survived not by his own abilities, but as a result of the intervention of Lorenzo di Filippo Strozzi.

There are concrete connections between Machiavelli's "suggestions" to Giulio de' Medici and Strozzi's *Pistola*. Those connections centre on the use of the term "*calendimaggio*," or very closely related derivatives, in both texts. Machiavelli's *Minuta* refers to the upcoming "*calendimaggio*" and Strozzi's *Pistola* claims to describe a walking tour of Florence on the same day. From this, we may reasonably infer that the *Minuta* was written earlier in the spring of 1522 and the *Pistola* probably not long after the start of May. If the *Minuta* and its oligarchic tendencies were influenced by Strozzi, then it is entirely possible that Strozzi, having brought Machiavelli into the Medici's crosshairs, shielded him from their vengeance. Thereafter, with suspicion still hanging over him, Machiavelli would have found great relief in the relative peace of transcribing Strozzi's literary works, as his former students were scattered by the Medici and as others were beheaded. Strozzi probably saved Machiavelli's life with literature and a good dose of the courtier's survival techniques.

Conclusions and Comments on the Sources

Lorenzo must have known how passionately republican Machiavelli was; it is a testament to his courtly abilities that he as patron was able to maintain his client in the good graces of the Cardinal de' Medici. In fact, he quite likely helped Niccolò to receive the commission for the *Istorie*, and he seems to have guided Niccolò's own contributions to Giulio's "invitation" for republican reforms. Had Machiavelli been left to his own devices, things

64 Osmond, "Conspiracy of 1522," 66n42, also quoted Paolo Giovio, who was even more specific regarding Machiavelli's role in the conspiracy: "Tuttavia, poichè nei suoi scritti egli aveva continuato a esaltare Bruto e Cassio, si era sospettato che egli fosse stato architetto della congiura antimedicea in cui avevano trovato la morte Alammani e il Diacceto." Giovio was cited by G. Procacci's *Studi sulla fortuna del Machiavelli* (Rome: Instituto storico italiano per l'età moderna e contemporanea, 1965), 266.

would have ended rather differently for him, particularly when one remembers that some of his protégés at the Orti lost their lives as a result of their intense republicanism – a republicanism inspired by Machiavelli. From this we can draw an important conclusion, not about Machiavelli, but about Strozzi: in public Lorenzo always appeared (at least before 1521–22) to be sympathetic to the Medici family, but even as he worked closely with them, he remained even more sympathetic to Florentine republicanism.[65] One might be led to this conclusion by considering the company he kept outside of his public service. He frequented the Orti but did not harbour any nostalgia for the days of the "popular" republican period under Savonarola's and Soderini's regimes. Rather, representative of his social background, Lorenzo was much more willing to support a republican oligarchy very close to the Twelve that Machiavelli suggested to Giulio de' Medici in 1522.[66] Moreover, as discussed above, the references to the "*calendimaggio*" in the *Minuta* and the *Pistola* not only link both works to a similar period, but also strongly indicate that Lorenzo in fact guided Machiavelli as he wrote his suggestions to Giulio.

Lorenzo di Filippo Strozzi's influence over his client was thoroughgoing and cut much deeper than has been previously recognized. Perhaps, through backdoor dealing, Strozzi even had a hand in shielding Niccolò from the maelstrom that swallowed some of Florence's best and brightest young republicans in the Medici-sponsored annihilation of 1522. These conclusions help to answer some difficult questions about this period in the lives of Machiavelli and of Strozzi.[67]

---

65 I use the phrase "in public" intentionally, because we know that Lorenzo privately tried to disrupt his brother Filippo's marriage to Clarici de' Medici. See chapter 1.

66 Machiavelli's evolving republican views are not my focus here, but his republicanism, particularly in light of his *Istorie fiorentine* and his "suggestions" to the Medici princes of 1520 and 1522, is a fascinating and contentious issue. One of the briefest and best considerations of that theme is found in John Najemy's reflections on the late Hans Baron's "republican" Machiavelli: "Baron's Machiavelli and Renaissance Republicanism," *American Historical Review* 101, no. 1. (1996): 119–29. For a more extensive analysis of Machiavelli's *History of Florence* and his *Discourse of the Affairs of Florence after the Death of Lorenzo de' Medici*, see Najemy's "Machiavelli and the Medici: The Lessons of Florentine History," *Renaissance Quarterly* 35, no. 4 (1982): 551–76. Also see Maurizio Viroli, *Il Dio di Machiavelli e il problema morale dell' Italia* (Rome: Laterza, 2005), 143–202, for an interesting discussion of Machiavelli's view of republicanism and its relationship with religion.

67 In 1522, Machiavelli wrote only two letters that we know of, and neither of those contain any pertinent information.

For example, in 1523, while Lorenzo was acting as the Florentine representative to Pope Clement VII, the pontiff chose to revisit the debate concerning the nature and type of the Florentine government. While the majority of those whom the pope queried agreed that Ippolito de' Medici ought to rule the city in the pontiff's absence, Lorenzo, who was opposed to such an arrangement, proposed that the pope should reinstitute the Florentine republic, with a *Gonfaloniere* either for life or for three years, and a *Signoria* of elected officials.[68] This resolves any possible debate about Lorenzo's true political leanings. Given that Lorenzo was still pushing for an oligarchic republican arrangement in 1523, Machiavelli's oligarchic *Minuta* of 1522 was probably more "Strozzian" than "Machiavellian." In other words, Machiavelli's suggestions of 1522 were not so much his own as they were Lorenzo Strozzi's. This helps to explain why Machiavelli's republicanism veered toward the oligarchic so swiftly and so briefly. The "founder of modern political science," the shrewdest mind in Renaissance politics, might also be viewed as a rather sad though brilliant man who sought patronage first from Piero Soderini and eventually from Lorenzo Strozzi and the Medici family. After 1520, Machiavelli unwittingly became Strozzi's "*mannerino*."[69]

In 1522 Lorenzo used Machiavelli to forward his own political agenda, which simultaneously brought Machiavelli's past republicanism and anti-Medicean politics into sharp focus for Giulio de' Medici. It is almost miraculous that Niccolò was not rounded up with the other anti-Medicean radicals and executed. He could easily have been blamed for instructing Alamanni and Buondelmonti on necessary conspiracies; he had frequently lectured on that topic at the Orti and had included chapters on such conspiracies in his *Discorsi*.[70] And, according to Jacopo Nardi, there were allegations floating about Florence of Machiavelli's involvement in the conspiracy. Yet even with these serious allegations arrayed against him, he emerged unscathed, which helps to render plausible the suggestion that Lorenzo again intervened on Machiavelli's behalf to deflect Giulio de' Medici's vengeance against those who plotted his assassination. The gentlemanly façade that Lorenzo di Filippo Strozzi constructed in fact masked a very shrewd character, for he kept his personal and familial goals central to his actions. If one of his clients was endangered by the political necessities required to achieve those goals, Lorenzo might have been willing to sacrifice them. But Strozzi's shrewdness probably had its limits. It seems

68 Appendix 2, 24r 4–9.

69 Hale, *Florence and the Medici*, 92.

70 Osmond, "Conspiracy of 1522," 55–72.

that he had other plans for Machiavelli; in 1522, when he could have allowed Machiavelli to be either assassinated or executed along with the other republicans, Strozzi protected him from Giulio de' Medici's fury and brought him firmly into his own patronage network.

There are many references to Niccolò Machiavelli and to Lorenzo Strozzi in contemporary histories and personal letters, but none of those links either directly to the other.[71] We have Machiavelli's personal letters, which mention Strozzi, and the famous letter between the Strozzi brothers, which sets out their plan to restore Niccolò; but we have nothing more from these men. There is also the conspicuous dedication to the *Arte della guerra*, probably the best piece of evidence to suggest the nature of the Strozzi-Machiavelli patron-client relationship. Then of course we have the *Pistola* manuscript itself – Strozzi's work in Niccolò's hand – and the *Commedia in versi*, one of Strozzi's plays also transcribed by Machiavelli. Finally, there is Machiavelli's *Minuta,* which is arguably far more oligarchic in its republicanism than anything else written by the famous Florentine. All of these works were published, written, or transcribed during the years 1521–1522. The patron's influence over his client was concentrated and substantial.

In conclusion, one might suggest that 1522 was a pivotal year in the Strozzi-Machiavelli relationship for two central reasons. First, it seems that Strozzi's influence swayed Niccolò's usually "popular" republican tendencies towards the oligarchic, and second, if we may date the *Pistola* to that troubled year, then its serious content and debauched and humorous style reflect the nature of the Strozzi-Machiavelli relationship. Perhaps the *Pistola* brought patron and client together, allowing them to escape, though briefly, the constraints and troubles of daily life in Medici-controlled Florence.

---

71 Bartolomeo Cerretani, *Ricordi*, ed. Giuliana Berti (Florence: Leo S. Olschi, 1993). Also by Cerretani, see *Dialogo della mutatione di Firenze*, ed. Raul Mordenti (Rome: Edizioni di storia e letteratura, 1990); in the *Dialogo* one of the characters is named "Lorenzo," and it has been argued that that character, a republican, was based on Strozzi. See also Jacopo Nardi, *Istorie della città di Firenze*, vol. 2, ed. Agenore Gelli (Florence: Le Monnier, 1888), 70, 73; Filippo de' Nerli, *Commentari de' fatti civili occorsi dentro la città di Firenze dall'anno 1512 al 1537,* vol. 2 (Trieste: Colombo Coen Tip. Editore, 1859), 10–23; Jacopo Nardi, *Istorie della città di Firenze*, vol. 2, ed. L. Arbib (Florence: Società editrice delle Storie del Nardi e del Varchi, 1838–41), 74–81; Scipione Ammirato, *Istorie fiorentine*, vol. 6, ed. L. Scarabelli (Turin: Cugini Pomba e Comp. Editori, 1853), 344–6; G. Capponi, *Storia della Repubblica di Firenze*, vol. 1 (Florence: g. Barbèra, 1930), 335–58 (bk. 6, chap. 6); C. Guasti, "Documenti delle congiure fatta contro il cardinale Giulio de' Medici nel 1522," *GSAT* 3 (1859): 121–50, 185–213, 239–67.

3 A History of the *Pistola fatta per la peste*: Its Manuscripts and Publication History, and a Close Reading of the Text

Lorenzo di Filippo Strozzi's *Pistola* is a dark and perversely comedic literary exercise in self-fashioning with an equally interesting history in manuscript and in print form. If the patron-client relationship between Strozzi and Machiavelli produced the *Pistola*, then it is essential to examine Strozzi's plague tract from several angles. This chapter will touch upon, in turn, the manuscripts of the *Pistola*, its print history, and the contents of Strozzi's treatise. The task is a difficult one, but the *Pistola*'s history, first in manuscript form and much later as a printed work, is fascinating. And while its content is often distasteful and even lewd, it is no more so than that of its famous antecedent *The Decameron*.[1] Between the two, however, there is an important distinction: Boccaccio might be seen as using the comedic elements of his stories as distractions from the plague; Strozzi by contrast sometimes turned the devastation of the plague itself into a joke. Nineteenth-century critics therefore condemned the *Pistola* as a degenerate mockery of

1 I thank Professor Massimo Ciavolella for his historiographical and textual suggestions, which informed my research. For specific primary texts that might support an alternate reading to the one suggested here, see Giovanni Boccaccio, *The Decameron*, trans. Guido Waldman, ed. Jonathan Usher (Oxford: Oxford University Press, 1998); Boccaccio, *Decameron*, in *Tutte le opere di Giovanni Boccaccio*, vol. 4, ed. Vittore Branca (Milan: Mondadori, 1976); Thucydides, *A History of the Plague of Athens*, trans. Charles F. Collier (London, 1857); Lucretius, *De rerum natura libri sex* (Berolini: Impensis G. Reimeri, 1860); Marsilio Ficino, *Consiglio contro la pestilenza*, ed. Enrico Musacchio and Giampaolo Moraglia (Bologna: Cappelli, 1983). For relatively recent scholarship on the plague and literary genres associated with it, see Samuel K. Cohn, *The Black Death Transformed: Disease and Culture in Early Renaissance Europe* (New York: Arnold, 2002); Joseph P. Byrne, *The Black Death* (Westport, CT: Greenwood, 2004) and *Daily Life during the Black Death* (Westport, CT: Greenwood, 2006). Alternate readings of the *Pistola* are discussed below.

the *Decameron*. It could also be read as "humanist pornography."[2] Against these charges, however, one might just as easily view the *Pistola* as an attempt to escape formality, on which interpretation Strozzi the gentleman and his outcast client Machiavelli wrote the *Pistola* to overcome the "strains of isolation in the body politic." Before we delve further into the *Pistola*'s content, its reception, and its authors, however, it is useful to investigate its manuscript history.

There are two extant manuscripts of Strozzi's epistle, the first of which survives almost entirely in Niccolò Machiavelli's hand but with a number of Strozzi's additions and corrections in the margins and in interlinear notations. That manuscript is now in Florence, Biblioteca Nazionale Centrale, MS Banco Rari 29 (Manuscript B); that collection also contains what is perhaps the most important autograph copy of Machiavelli's *Arte della guerra*. There were no plague outbreaks in Florence in 1521, so 1522, a year that witnessed a massive outbreak, seems to be the most likely year that Strozzi, with Machiavelli's help, authored the *Pistola*. The very presence of the *Pistola* and the *L'Arte* in such close physical proximity links both works to a similar period: 1521–1522. References in Machiavelli's *Minuta di provvisione* to the upcoming "*calendimaggio*" season and references to the same season in the *Pistola* are further evidence to support 1522 as the year in which Machiavelli transcribed the *Pistola* for Strozzi. The Banco Rari 29 manuscript also contains a Machiavelli autograph of Strozzi's *Commedia in versi*. Given the fact that Machiavelli transcribed two of Strozzi's compositions (and dedicated his *Arte della guerra* to Strozzi in 1521), it is plausible that the two Florentines worked closely with one another, probably during the period 1521–1522.[3] Moreover, the Banco Rari manuscript of the *Pistola* is a complete, fair copy of the *Pistola*, upon which Strozzi's authorial copy of the *Pistola* was based (see the edition of the *Pistola* 87r 5, ff. for examples that illustrate this point).[4] This might be illustrated by examining the second manuscript of the *Pistola*. Strozzi's authorial copy of the *Pistola* (entirely in his hand) is located in Florence, Biblioteca Medicea Laurenziana, MS Ashburnham 606 (Manuscript A). Therein, Strozzi incorporated nearly all of the changes and emendments that he included in the margins of the Banco Rari manuscript. While the Banco Rari manuscript was discovered in

2 David O. Frantz, "*Festum Voluptatis*": *A Study of Renaissance Erotica* (Columbus: Ohio State University Press, 1989).

3 While evidence strongly supports 1522, there remains a possibility that the *Pistola* was written subsequent to that year.

4 Also see the Foreword of this study for particular examples.

the Strozzi Library during the mid-1790s, the Ashburnham *Pistola* was not discovered until the late nineteenth century and was not studied in any depth until 1892. Only then was the *Pistola* formally listed as a work by Lorenzo di Filippo Strozzi.

This manuscript history helps to explain why the *Pistola* was attributed to Niccolò Machiavelli until the 1850s in Italian editions of his work, and until the first quarter of the twentieth century in Anglophone scholarship. Here, my focus in describing the manuscripts is on their production, their content, and on the hands that contributed to Manuscript B (Banco Rari 29), both on the folios containing the *Pistola* and on other folios throughout the manuscript. The methods that I used to produce the Italian edition and English translation of the *Pistola*, together with detailed descriptions of both *Pistola* manuscripts, are outlined in the section below containing that edition and translation.

Manuscript B: The Banco Rari 29 Manuscript of the *Pistola*

The Banco Rari manuscript of the *Pistola* (3v–4v and 9r–17r) is written in two distinct hands, Lorenzo di Filippo Strozzi's and Niccolò Machiavelli's. I will consider each of their contributions in turn. First, however, I will discuss the text of the *Pistola* in order to establish authorship. That text is both prefaced by and interrupted by additional text that is essential to establish Strozzi as author. For example, on folio 2r (transcribed in full in appendix 1 below) one is confronted with a bizarre Latinate epigraph that clearly names Lorenzo di Filippo Strozzi – "hanc epistolam agit Laurentius Philppi Stroci ciues florentinus" – as the work's author. (The author of that text also provided the *Pistola* with a working title: "Epistola fatta per la peste." As Manuscript A, Strozzi's copy, refers to the *Pistola fatta per la peste*, I chose to follow his title.)

In his 1852 edition of the *Pistola*, based only upon the Banco Rari manuscript, Filippo Luigi Polidori observed that the Latinate epigraph that opens the *Pistola* appears to be "almost a first tentative attempt at writing" both in its form and content.[5] Though this is true, one is able to make sense of the epigraph and to identify its heretofore unknown hand by examining

5 "Quasi come un primo tentativo di scriverla" (Machiavelli, *Opere minori di Niccolò Machiavelli: Rivedute sulle migliori edizioni, con note filologiche e critiche di F-L Polidori* [Florence: Le Monnier, 1852], 415).

what appears to be a botched poem written by Lorenzo di Filippo Strozzi on 3r of the manuscript (2v is blank).

There, Strozzi referred to one "Palla," who by process of elimination and association we can deduce was probably his son Palla Strozzi (1514–1544).[6] If the *Pistola* was written in 1522, Palla would have been only eight years old at the time it was penned.[7] Furthermore, Palla added two more brief passages to the *Pistola,* both pointing to his father as the work's author.[8] More will be said of the work's attribution when I discuss its print history below. After Palla's dedicatory epigraph and Lorenzo's poem, one encounters the formal dedication of the *Pistola* (3v–4v), the start of the text proper. Until now, the hand that contributed this formal dedication has remained unknown. However, a close comparison of Strozzi's earlier contributions and the script used in the *Pistola*'s dedication proves Lorenzo Strozzi to be the author and writer of both (see figure 4). Folios 5r–5v are blank; on 6r Palla Strozzi added another Latinate passage, once again attributing the *Pistola* to Lorenzo Strozzi.[9]

Interestingly, the Banco Rari manuscript does not contain the name of its intended recipient, but it might offer a clue. Folio 7r of the manuscript contains a very strange contribution, in Lorenzo's hand. Strozzi wrote "al mo," but he wrote these words upside down and backwards.[10] Virgil Milani, discussing abbreviations frequently used by Strozzi, pointed out that "mo"

---

6 Goldthwaite, *Private Wealth*, 107n71. "Unfortunately, we know next to nothing about Palla." However, "in 1533 Lorenzo made over credits to Palla, who was with the company of Filippo Strozzi and Capponi in Lyons." See the following note for more details on Palla.

7 See appendix 1, 3r, for this text. Palla Strozzi eventually left Italy for France, where he took over his father's portion of one of the Strozzi family businesses. He was a poet and playwright of some talent, but also possessed an interesting sense of humour. For example, he wrote a *canzona* "To the Carrot," which begins: "'Dolce salubre et desiato et caro / Singular frutto et singular radice, / Tu beato fai l'uom, saggio et felice …' and concludes 'Maravaglia ho che si come del tondo / Non prese forma di carrota il mondo.' (Sweet, wholesome, desired and dear / Singular fruit and singular root / You make men blessed, wise and happy … I marvel that the world, instead of being round, / Did not take the form of a carrot.) (Original and translation from Judith Bryce "The Theatrical Activities of Palla di Lorenzo Strozzi in Lyon in the 1540's," in *The Theater of the English and Italian Renaissance*, ed. J.R. Mulryne and Margaret Shewring [New York: St. Martin's, 1991], 59.)

8 These are transcribed in appendix 1.

9 Transcribed in appendix 1.

10 I am indebted to Dr Simone Testa for suggesting that Strozzi's contribution on 7r might be written in a coded format.

is Strozzi's shorthand for "maestro."[11] Could Strozzi's strangely coded addition here be a reference to the work's intended recipient, Girolamo del Maestro Luca? I discuss this question in more detail below.

As late as the twentieth century, even after most recognized the work as Strozzi's, some scholars continued to perpetuate the mistaken claim that the *Pistola* was intended for Machiavelli, given the "affection" that Strozzi exhibited for his supposed recipient.[12] This is misguided, since there is no surviving evidence to suggest that the relationship between Strozzi and Machiavelli was particularly friendly or affectionate. Indeed, the view became untenable with the discovery of the Ashburnham 606 manuscript of the *Pistola,* which authoritatively settled all questions about the identity of the recipient.

Folio 7v of the Banco Rari manuscript contains four readable but unintelligible lines in Strozzi's hand.[13] Folios 8r–8v are blank. Then, on folio 9r, we arrive at Machiavelli's portion of the *Pistola* manuscript (see figure 5). The vast majority of the Banco Rari manuscript is in fact in his hand. However, as mentioned previously, there are Strozzi autograph emendations throughout the *Pistola* (Manuscript B), with only a few emendations contributed by Machiavelli. The Banco Rari manuscript of the *Pistola* presents a compelling picture of a group effort, with patron and client plus patron's son working to produce it. But Lorenzo Strozzi was clearly the principal force, bringing the circle of writers together and providing the vast majority of the content, as can be seen by examining the second, and only other, manuscript of the *Pistola*, located in the Ashburnham 606 manuscript.

Manuscript A: The Ashburnham 606 Text of the *Pistola*

In 1892, Pio Ferrieri examined the Biblioteca Medicea Laurenziana's Ashburnham 606.[14] That collection of Strozzi manuscripts, most of which are autographs, contained Strozzi's *Pistola fatta per la peste*. A comparison

11 Lorenzo di Filippo Strozzi, *La Nutrice: A Comedy in Hendecasyllabic Blank Verse*, ed. Virgil Milani, master's thesis, Catholic University of America, Washington, DC, 1960, xvi.

12 "In uno stuccoso stile boccaccevole, fu scritta in forma epistolare da Lorenzo Strozzi al Machiavelli durante la moria ..." (Roberto Ridolfi, *La vita*, 560–1n25).

13 See appendix 1, 7v, for a transcription of these lines.

14 Florence, Biblioteca Medicea Laurenziana, Lorenzo di Filippo Strozzi, "Pistola fatta per la peste," Ashburnhamiano 606, ff. 84r–89v.

of the Ashburnham manuscript with Strozzi's contributions to the Banco Rari manuscript (Manuscript B) proves, as Ferrieri concluded, that the Ashburnham manuscript is exclusively in Strozzi's hand. Interestingly, Strozzi included the name of the *Pistola*'s recipient in the Ashburnham manuscript, a name that might have been hinted at in the Banco Rari manuscript. He dedicated the *Pistola*, or perhaps intended to send it, to Girolamo di Maestro Luca (see figure 6), not to Machiavelli as Roberto Ridolfi concluded.[15] Maestro Luca was a grammarian, tutor, and politician; he would probably have enjoyed Strozzi's literary contortions, and his being the dedicatee may help to explain the *Pistola*'s exaggerated linguistic flourishes. There was another Girolamo del Maestro Luca who lived in *cinquecento* Florence, but he was a great deal younger than Lorenzo Strozzi, and it is safe to conclude that the Girolamo to whom the *Pistola* was dedicated was in fact the grammarian and politician.[16]

Beyond clearing up the problem of who the *Pistola* was intended for, the Ashburnham manuscript is also important because it incorporates nearly all of the interlinear and marginal emendations and additions that Strozzi included in the Banco Rari manuscript. This textual evidence suggests that the Banco Rari manuscript was written first and was followed by Strozzi's copy of the *Pistola* in the Ashburnham 606. Those manuscripts also illustrate just how closely Machiavelli and Strozzi worked with one another. The first manuscript is almost entirely in Machiavelli's hand (with additions by Strozzi), and the second manuscript is entirely in Strozzi's hand:

15 Ridolfi, *La vita,* 560–1n25.

16 There is a reference to the grammarian Girolamo del Maestro Luca in a letter written by Girolamo da Empoli to his nephew Giovanni di Lionardo di Giovanni di Niccolò da Empoli: "Erano in quel tempo maestri di scuola di grammatica, maestro Girolamo del Maestro Luca, nostro fiorentino, gentile maestro, etc." The letter is cited by Robert Black in *Education and Society in Florentine Tuscany: Teachers, Pupils, Schools, c. 1250–1500* (Leiden: Brill, 2007), 144n487. Del Maestro Luca also served in the Signoria as late as 1525. He was the last of that particular family line in Florence. See Roberto Ciabani, *Le Famiglie di Firenze*, vol. 3 (Florence: Casa Editrice Bonechi, 1992), 658. As for the other line and the younger "Girolamo," there is a letter written by Alessandro Ottaviano de' Medici (later Pope Leo XI) to Pietro Vasari in which Alessandro mentioned one "Girolamo di Maestro Luca." It must be noted, however, that the letter is dated 1577, twenty-eight years after Lorenzo's death. See *Lo Zibaldone di Giorgio Vasari*, ed. Alessandro del Vita (Rome: R. Instituto d'Archeologia e Storia dell'Arte, 1938), 281–3. The younger Girolamo was a well-respected "gold-beater" in Florence. For coverage of his artistic endeavours, see Heidi J. Hornik, *Michele Tosini and the Ghirlandaio Workship in Cinquecento Florence* (Portland: Sussex, 2009), 17, 20, 24–7, 29, 152n65, 154n108.

surely this is strong evidence of their patron-client relationship. At first, Strozzi utilized Machiavelli's chancery skills to transcribe the *Pistola*; he also, it seems, relied on Machiavelli's other works, particularly *Il Principe* and *L'Asino*, to inform the *Pistola*. Strozzi then corrected the first manuscript and produced the second and final edition of the *Pistola* that is contained in the Ashburnham 606 folio.

Manuscript A, Strozzi's copy of the *Pistola,* might also tell us more about how Strozzi viewed his working relationship with Machiavelli. It was written much more carelessly than Manuscript B; for example, the introductory epistle in Manuscript B is written in Strozzi's elegant chancelloresque hand. It is probable that the time Strozzi spent with the older, brilliant Machiavelli caused him to take the project seriously. Similarly, Strozzi's additions and emendations to Machiavelli's portion of Manuscript B are thoughtful and well organized. Manuscript A, by contrast, even though it transmits most of Strozzi's corrections to Manuscript B, contains multiple errors that produce inferior readings. So, while Strozzi worked with Machiavelli, he took on his client's seriousness, but when the two parted ways, the quality of Strozzi's work deteriorated considerably.[17]

The Print Tradition of the *Pistola*

The *Pistola* was first published in 1796.[18] Thereafter, it was printed numerous times throughout the first half of the nineteenth century as a work written by Machiavelli.[19] All of those editions were based only upon the

17 I write about the textual relationship between Manuscripts A and B in much greater detail in the preface to the edition that follows.

18 The 1796 edition (edited by Gaetano Poggiali) of Machiavelli's *Opere* was the first collection of his works that had access to the Strozzi Library and especially to its many Machiavelli autograph manuscripts. The *Pistola* was there. Pasquale Villari noted that the Strozzi family would not allow access to those manuscripts, but upon the death of the last of that part of the Strozzi line, the "Grand Duke purchased the most precious manuscripts of the family library." See Villari, *Life and Times*, 507–8n5.

19 Here are a few examples: "Descrizione della peste," in *Opere di Niccolò Machiavelli, Cittadino e Segretario Fiorentino*, vol. 1 (Milan: Dalla Società Tipografica de'Classici Italiani, contrada di S. Margherita, No. 1118, 1804), 222–39; "Descrizione della peste di Firenze dell'Anno 1527," in *Opere Complete di Niccolò Machiavelli con molte correzioni e giunte rivenute sui manoscritti originali*, ed. Alcide Parenti (Florence: Le Monnier, 1843), 589–94; "Descrizione delle peste di Firenze dell'Anno MDXXVII," in *Opere di Niccolò Machiavelli*, ed. Giuseppe Zirardini (Parigi: Baudry, Liberia Europa, 1851), 522–8.

Banco Rari manuscript, for the Ashburnham manuscript was not discovered until later in the same century and was not studied in detail until 1892.

Strangely, the *Pistola*'s first editors completely ignored the Latinate epigraph at the beginning of the Banco Rari manuscript explicitly stating that Lorenzo Strozzi had authored it, choosing instead to place the work within Machiavelli's *opere*. More subversively, the first published editions of the *Pistola* included only its dedication and the portion of the manuscript transcribed by Machiavelli.[20] It appears that those early editors wanted to find and to publish an undiscovered work by Machiavelli, and they edited their sources to make it appear that they had. Of course, this troubled later Italian and Anglophone scholars who were familiar with Machiavelli's output and his writing style. The *Pistola*, while some of its content seemed to have been directly influenced by Machiavelli, could not have been written by him: Strozzi's sentence construction and syntax are nothing like Niccolò's. More bizarrely, Gaetano Poggiali and other early editors went so far as to change the *Pistola*'s name, publishing the work under the title *Descrizione della peste*, sometimes adding "*dell'Anno 1527*."

Why the first editors, and Poggiali in particular, chose the year 1527 is still not known. Strozzi claimed that he wrote the *Pistola* on the first of May ("*la mattina del lieto principio di maggio*"), but he did not date his work.[21] There was an outbreak of plague in the summer of 1527, but Machiavelli died in June of that year, and it is most unlikely that he was transcribing the work of any other scholar as his health quickly deteriorated.[22] These facts, combined with the evidence discussed above concerning Strozzi's and Machiavelli's patron-client relationship, led me to consider the year 1522 as the most likely year in which the *Pistola* was written.

Some Italian scholars did question Machiavelli's authorship of the *Pistola*. In fact a small number, though they printed the *Pistola* as Machiavelli's, expressed reservations about the attribution. Those doubts were given substance in 1852 when Filippo Luigi Polidori first printed Palla Strozzi's bizarre dedicatory epistle to the *Pistola*. This was the best and most complete edition of the *Pistola* to be published to that point in its history, though Polidori only had recourse to the Banco Rari manuscript; the inclusion of Palla Strozzi's

---

20 The 1796 edition of the *Pistola* contains only the materials cited above.

21 See the Italian edition of the *Pistola*, 85v 10–11, and English translation.

22 Pasquale Villari argued that it seems implausible "that amid the many grave thoughts by which at that time (May 1527) he was overwhelmed, [Machiavelli] could have found leisure to employ himself upon a description of the plague." See *Life and Times*, vol. 3, 373.

contributions ended the debate on the *Pistola*'s authorship. Yet the work was published in *Opere minori di Niccolò Machiavelli*: Polidori still published the *Pistola* as a work by Machiavelli.[23] This is very strange indeed, particularly since this edition of Machiavelli's works contained a section titled "Operette attribuite a Niccolò Machiavelli."

Scholars continued to have reservations. One writer, Thomas Babington, Lord Macaulay, showed good instincts regarding the *Pistola*'s authorship. The style was not Machiavelli's and Macaulay knew it. He was one of the first scholars of the early nineteenth century to challenge Machiavelli's authorship. By mid-century, utilizing Polidori's 1852 edition as their guide, a number of scholars had re-examined the *Pistola*, and nearly all doubted Machiavelli's authorship of it. One of these, Pasquale Villari, wrote that the "*Descrizione* ... could never be imputed to Machiavelli by anyone acquainted with his works."[24]

Polidori gave scholars the tools needed to end debate over the *Pistola*'s authorship; but the text itself encountered heated opposition. The first zealous critic of the *Pistola* was not even Italian: the above-mentioned Thomas Babington, Lord Macaulay was a British gentleman, and in his essay titled "Machiavelli," originally published in 1827, he unleashed a torrent of criticism of the *Pistola,* which we can take as representative of reaction to it:

> Nothing was ever written more detestable in matter and manner. The narrations, the reflections, the jokes, the lamentations, are all the very worst of their respective kinds, at once trite and affected, threadbare tinsel from the Rag Fairs and Monmouth-streets of literature. A foolish schoolboy might write such a piece, and, after he had written it, think it much finer than the incomparable introduction of "The Decameron." But that a shrewd statesman, whose earliest works are characterized by manliness of thought and language, should, at near sixty years of age, descend to such puerility, is utterly inconceivable.[25]

Macaulay, one suspects, was disgusted with the lusty descriptions of women in the *Pistola* and with the gallows humour employed throughout it. Also, the *Pistola*'s author claimed to have found a wife by the time he reached the

23 Polidori, *Opere minori di Niccolò Machiavelli,* 415–17, notes only.

24 Villari, *Life and Times*, vol. 3, 373.

25 Lord Macaulay, *The Works of Lord Macaulay, Complete, Edited by His Sister, Lady Trevelyan* (London: Longman, Green and Co., 1875). See Macaulay's essay "Machiavelli," 68.

end of the treatise. Machiavelli remained married until his death, a fact Macaulay certainly would have known, and perhaps such "puerile" fantasies struck Macaulay as unseemly and unworthy of Machiavelli.

Macaulay's righteous indignation takes into account neither how frequently Machiavelli turned to women other than his wife for physical pleasure (he began a passionate affair with an actress in 1524)[26] nor how often he was involved in ridiculous practical jokes with men from much more distinguished families than his own. (Francesco Guicciardini comes to mind here.) But there is a much more fundamental problem with the sort of critique that Macaulay and others directed at the *Pistola:*[27] it takes Strozzi's text seriously. Through black humour and sexual innuendo, the *Pistola* was written to "lighten every tedious care," and Francesco de Sanctis recognized this fundamentally important interpretive point.[28]

De Sanctis approached the *Pistola* from a completely different perspective. He always believed the *Pistola* to be Machiavelli's, and in that he was wrong; but he was able to see through the *Pistola*'s debauchery and its dark humor, straight to its core. He realized that the *Pistola*'s language was so different, so varied and sometimes so vulgar because it was a product and a synthesis of its time.

> In prose Machiavelli exhibited literary pretensions, following the ideas which circulated during that age. At times he utilizes the expressions and language of Boccaccio, as in his sermon to the confraternity, in his *Descrizione della peste* and in his speeches which he put in the mouth of his historic personages. You see an example of this at his meeting with a lady in a Church at the time of the plague, where abound the ornaments of rhetoric and the artifices of style: what one might call "elegance."[29]

---

26 See letter 294, dated 7 August 1525, from Guicciardini to Machiavelli, in Niccolò Machiavelli, *Machiavelli and His Friends: Their Personal Correspondence,* trans. and ed. James B. Atkinson and David Sices (Dekalb: Northern Illinois University Press, 1996), 360–2.

27 Nor was Macaulay alone in his moralizing criticism. Carlo Gioda concluded that the *Pistola* contained "a varied style, sometimes awkward, connected to tremendously vulgar concepts and expressions." In general, the majority of the attention paid to the *Pistola* was negative, and the criticism, like Macaulay's critique, tended to be based on moral objections to the *Pistola*'s content. See Carlo Gioda, *Machiavelli e le sue opere* (Florence: G. Barbara, 1874), 214: "Lo stile vario, goffo talvolta, congiunti a una mirabile volgarità di concetto e d'espressione." For a similar argument, see Villari, *Life and Times*, vol. 3, 373.

28 See the Italian edition of the *Pistola*, 84r 27–28, and English translation.

29 The translation is mine. The Italian original is "In prosa Machiavelli ebbe pretensioni letterarie, secondo le idee che correvano in quella età. Talora si mette la giornea e boccacceggia, come nelle sue prediche alle confraternite, nella descrizione

That is exactly how the *Pistola* ought to be viewed, particularly since Strozzi intended the grammarian Girolamo del Maestro Luca to be its recipient. Strozzi and Machiavelli entered into a patron-client relationship that resulted in a bawdy, dark, and sometimes funny description of a plague outbreak in Florence. Their work included all of the artifices, all of the "elegance," of Renaissance literature. But it was never intended to be taken as a definitive description of the plague and how it ravaged Florence; rather, it was written as a flourish-filled piece of "escapist literature." Perhaps the fact that the *Pistola*'s style and content bridge so many different genres – from plague tract to love story to political advice pamphlet – make it difficult to categorize. However, if we allow those various genres and its equally varied content to represent, even symbolize, for us the layers of social life and experiences of its author and his client, then paradoxically the *Pistola* might be read not only as "escapist," but also as an exercise in "self-fashioning."[30]

The Pistola fatta per la peste

Strozzi's *Pistola* proper may be divided into three parts. The first comprises an introductory epistle dedicated to Girolamo del Maestro Luca. The second is a brief overview of the plague outbreak in Florence that is heavily indebted to Boccaccio. The final section, the lengthiest of the three, is Strozzi's supposedly autobiographical narrative of a day-long walk through Florence during the said plague outbreak. Each of these sections is unified by the plague itself, and one is confronted therein with a world that has been turned upside down: once bustling streets now empty and quiet; a wool industry and markets ground to a halt; familial relationships broken down and fresh graves in once beautiful cloisters. In this almost post-apocalyptic vision Strozzi went so far as to suggest that Florence looked like a city left in

---

della peste e ne' discorsi che mette in bocca a' suoi personagge storici. Vedi ad esempio il suo incontro con una donna in chiesa al tempo della peste, dove abbondano i lenocini della rettorica e gli artifici dello stile: ciò che si chiamava 'eleganza'" (Francesco de Sanctis, *Scrittori d'Italia: Storia della letteratura Italiana: nuove edizione a cura di Benedetto Croce*, vol. 2 [Bari: Laterza, 1912], 60).

30 Matteo Bandello's *novelle* are similar to Strozzi's *Pistola*, both in their indebtedness to Boccaccio and in their wide-ranging genres. For more on Bandello, see the recent article by Barbara Alfano, "Il narrator delle 'Novelle' del Bandello e la funzione mediatrice della scrittura," *Italica* 81, no. 1 (2004): 16–23; and the older though very insightful article by Salvatore Di Maria, "Fortune and the 'Beffa' in Bandello's Novelle," *Italica* 59, no. 4 (1982): 306–15.

shambles after being sacked by the Turks. But then, especially in the third part of the *Pistola*, one is yanked back from the precipice and confronted with beautiful and sensual young mourners, dancing grave diggers, and crippled and blind elderly people flirting with one another in the Duomo. So, the *Pistola* is "real" enough to be convincing, but just as one becomes fully immersed in Strozzi's vision of Florence as it suffers a plague outbreak, the jokes begin. In short, the effectiveness of the text turns on comic timing and shock value. And it is fast paced, in order to draw its reader into Strozzi's world. The *Pistola*'s opening "epistle" illustrates this point nicely, echoing strains of friendship and loss that rise to a fever pitch.

Reading the introduction, one quickly realizes that Strozzi's language is elevated, complex, and perhaps overly emotive; but it certainly did not deserve the derision that some later scholars heaped upon it.[31] Here is a brief quotation from Strozzi's introduction:

> To my most beloved and highly honoured friend: although your sweet companionship has always kept me truly happy, and I have always taken singular pleasure, not only from your honest and courteous manners, but also from your pleasant and exceptionally humane reasoning: I am not happy, however, when I am deprived of it for some time, as it often happens that you are absent, or i involved in graver activities. I have felt sorrow in part somewhat similar to that which I feel at present, due to the length of time that you remain far away from your city.[32]

This introduction, far from being trite, demonstrates real affection for the intended recipient, Girolamo del Maestro Luca. Near its end, one meets the first example of Strozzi's rather strange comic sensibility: his statement to Girolamo that the *Pistola* was intended "to lighten every tedious care." Strozzi decided to use the horrors of the plague and his own supposedly autobiographical experience of dodging the dreaded pestilence to make his friend laugh. While strange, this is nevertheless touching, in that Lorenzo wanted his friend to know he was alive and well and in fact having a rather good time in plague-ridden Florence.

Although Lorenzo claimed to have experienced everything that he included in the *Pistola* – from seeing candles that were lit not by torches but by the profanity of priests, to finding a beautiful young wife – in just one eventful day, here one ought not to take him at his word. On one level, the

31 Especially Macaulay, whose criticisms were discussed above.

32 See the Italian edition of the *Pistola*, 84r 3–9, and English translation.

Pistola ought to be read, as argued above, as escapist literary fun that allowed Machiavelli and Strozzi to live outside of the formality and drudgery of their daily lives.

On a deeper level, one has to remember that the threat of plague was a very real part of everyday life in Renaissance Italy; it, and the cityscape of Florence, provided the set and backdrop for Strozzi's scandalous commentary. However, the jokes themselves, like the emotions of a man who himself survived the plague but lost beloved family members to it, were bittersweet. In reality neither Strozzi nor Machiavelli possessed the existential freedom or nihilistic daring to live with the recklessness that Strozzi described in his *Pistola*. In the real world of Florentine politics, Lorenzo was married and bound by duty to protect the honour of his family; to act in an untoward fashion would have ruined his gentlemanly public image and damaged the reputation of his *casa*. Machiavelli, by the same token, had been sent into exile for acting and speaking out; he needed to remain in the good graces of the Medici, and for that he needed Lorenzo Strozzi, who would not have risked his own reputation to help restore Machiavelli's. The content and tone of the *Pistola* itself, from start to finish, ought to be read in light of its authors' social expectations and pragmatic concerns.[33] Such a reading surely silences those critics who condemned the *Pistola* for being purely frivolous. The obverse is true: when the text is read from a revised, "self-fashioning" perspective, it is precisely its bittersweet frivolity that makes it special.

There is an additional point to make about the *Pistola*'s introduction. Stephen Greenblatt's famous *Renaissance Self-Fashioning* includes a chapter

---

33 Here, I have followed Stephen Greenblatt's approach to "self-fashioning" particularly as it is related (or evidenced) in surviving literature from the Florentine Renaissance. Outlining his methods, Greenblatt wrote, "I do not shrink from these impurities – they are the price and perhaps among the virtues of this approach – but I have tried to compensate for the indeterminacy and incompleteness they generate by constantly returning to particular lives and particular situations, to the material necessities and social pressures that men and women daily confronted, and to a small number of resonant texts. Each of these texts is viewed as the focal point for converging lines of force in sixteenth-century culture; their significance for us is not that we may see *through* them to underlying and prior historical principles but rather that we may interpret the interplay of their symbolic structures with those perceivable in the careers of their authors and in the large social world as constituting a single, complex process of self-fashioning and, through this interpretation, come closer to understanding how literary and social identities were formed in this culture" (*Renaissance Self-Fashioning: From More to Shakespeare* [Chicago: University of Chicago Press, 1980], 5–6).

dedicated to Sir Thomas Wyatt's poetry wherein Greenblatt highlights a particular poem, probably by Wyatt, that resonates with Strozzi's *Pistola*, especially as the poem seems to be so sexually charged:

> To wet your eye withouten tear,
> And in good health to feign disease,
> That you thereby mine eye might blear,
> Therewith your friends to please[34]

The "self-fashioning" that is evident in that poem focuses on the "real" versus the "perceived" or what Machiavelli might have called the "imagined." While one might publicly shed a tear, or even weep a river of them, those outward signs do not necessarily correlate with the weeper's true emotions. The tears could arise out of genuine grief, but they could equally well be an attempt to manipulate a lover or other people. At its very heart, this type of Renaissance "self-fashioning" is, as Greenblatt noted, filled with potential "menace."[35] There is also the political side of self-fashioning to consider, and Strozzi's *Pistola* provides ample opportunity for that. For instance, near the end of the introductory letter, Strozzi wrote these words:

> Therefore I am stirred (knowing how much one who is away from the fatherland (*patria*) is grateful to receive even the smallest piece of news) to write about all that I have seen in our distinguished city, with my wet yet unhappy [infelicitous] eyes; and even though the matter will bring you little pleasure, hearing that you are out of so perilous a place should make you grateful.[36]

---

34 Greenblatt, *Self-Fashioning*, 137.

35 There are a number of additional sources that illustrate the dangerous side of self-fashioning – Shakespeare's Richard of Gloucester for example – but the poem highlighted by Greenblatt works well as an archetype in this instance. For one of the most famous examples of this type of self-fashioning menace, see "Why, I can smile, and murder whiles I smile, And cry, 'Content' to that which grieves my heart, And wet my cheeks with artificial tears, And frame my face to all occasions. I'll drown more sailors than the mermaid shall; I'll slay more gazers than the basilisk; I'll play the orator as well as Nestor, Deceive more slyly than Ulysses could, And, like a Sinon, take another Troy. I can add colors to the chameleon, Change shapes with Proteus for advantages, And set the murderous Machiavel to school. Can I do this, and cannot get a crown? Tut, were it farther off, I'll pluck it down" (William Shakespeare, *Henry VI, Part 3*, in *The Complete Signet Classic Shakespeare*, ed. Sylvan Barnet [New York: Harcourt Brace Jovanovich, 1972], III.ii.182–95, 215–16).

36 See the Italian edition of the *Pistola*, 84r 29–34, and English translation.

If the *Pistola* was written in 1522, then Strozzi's tears might be viewed as symptomatic of his displeasure with the Medici regime, which clamped down on Florence in that year. Furthermore, the almost alter-universe that Strozzi created in the *Pistola* might reflect his views on just how much the regime of Giulio de' Medici had warped Florentine republican traditions. After all, even though Strozzi was pragmatic and willing to serve the Medici, he was a republican. This facet of the *Pistola* illustrates one of the problems with Renaissance self-fashioning: the layers, the masks, and the "multiple personalities" of Renaissance writers and gentlemen can make interpretation of their work very difficult.[37] Trying to unearth an author's intent based solely upon literary evidence can be as dangerous as self-fashioning itself; interpretations can sometimes be boundless.

Yet the "menace" of self-fashioning is precisely what makes it so interesting to the historian. And however one interprets Strozzi's "wet yet unhappy eyes," it seems clear that harnessing the power of how others perceived one's emotions, and especially false ones, became an essential part of Renaissance self-fashioning in Italy and later in England. It also is clear that the *Pistola* is filled with further references to self-fashioning. First, however, Strozzi sets the stage by describing Florence during the plague outbreak, for example in the following, which obviously mimics Boccaccio:

> The neat and beautiful streets, which used to be bursting with rich and noble citizens, are now stinking, ugly and swarming with the poor. One passes by their impudent and fearful shrieks with difficulty and trepidation. The shops are locked, the businesses closed, the judges, the courts and the lawyers dragged away, prostrating the laws. Now one hears of this theft, now of that murder: the piazzas and markets, where the citizens used to be in the habit of gathering frequently, are now made into communal graves, and vile dens of thieves.[38] Men go about alone, and in exchange for friends, one meets

37 Harry Berger suggested that, utilizing *sprezzatura* (the real-world counterpart to literary self-fashioning), the gentleman acted as "if always under surveillance" (*The Absence of Grace:* Sprezzatura *and Suspicion in Two Renaissance Courtesy Books* [Stanford: Stanford University Press, 2000], 12).

38 "Now with our city in such a state, the laws of God and men had lost their authority and fallen into disrespect in the absence of magistrates to see them enforced, for they, like everyone else, had either succumbed to the plague or lay sick, or else had been deprived of their minions to the point where they were powerless" (*The Decameron* [1998], 9). The Italian original is "E in tanta afflizione e miseria della nostra città era la reverenda auttorità delle leggi, così divine come umane, quasi caduta e dissoluta tutta per li ministri e essecutori di quelle, li quali, sì come gli altri

> people infected with this deadly plague. Even if one parent finds the other, or a brother finds his brother, or a wife her husband, each one keeps a safe distance from their relations: and what is worse? Fathers and mothers spurn their own children, abandoning them.[39]

This is all standard plague-related fare: enough detail to provide some realism, but too general to be vivid. In other words, while Strozzi imitated Boccaccio in passages such as the above, he was not able to invoke the sense of dread and hopelessness that Boccaccio mustered. However, as the *Pistola* transitions to its final, lengthiest section, one comes across a very Machiavellian turn of phrase, where Strozzi moves from a general discussion of the effects of the plague in Florence to what can only be described as detailed autobiography.

> The thing imagined compared with the truth of that which one imagines never adds up.[40] Nor am I able, it seems to me, to illustrate this with a finer example

---

uomini, erano tutti o morti o infermi o sì di famiglie rimasi stremi, che uficio alcuno non potean fare; per la qual cosa era a ciascun licito quanto a grado gli era d'adoperare" (Giovanni Boccaccio, *Decameron*, in *Tutte le opere di Giovanni Boccaccio*, vol. 4, ed. Vittore Branca [Milan: Mondadori, 1976], 13, secs. 23–4).

39 See the Italian edition of the *Pistola*, 84v 13–24, and English translation. Also see *Decameron*, 10: "One citizen avoided the next, there was scarcely a man who would take care of his neighbour, kinsmen would seldom if ever call on each other, and even then would keep their distance – but this was not all: men and women alike possessed by such a visceral terror of this scourge that a man would desert his own brother, uncle would forsake his nephew, sister her brother, and often the wife her husband. What is more, believe it or not, mothers and fathers would avoid visiting and tending their children, they would virtually disown them." The Italian original is "E lasciamo stare che l'uno cittadino l'altro schifasse e quasi niuno vicino avesse dell'altro cura e i parenti insieme rade volte o non mai si visitassero e di lontano; era con sì fatto spavento questa tribulazione entrata ne' petti degli uomini e delle donne, che l'un fratello e spesse volte la donna il suo marito; e, che maggio cosa è e quasi non credibile, li padri e le madri il figliuoli, quasi loro non fossero, di visitare e di servire schifavano" (*Decameron* [1976], 14, secs. 27–8).

40 This brief passage on "the thing imagined" compared with "the truth of that which is itself imagined" bears a striking resemblance to a passage in chapter 15 of *Il Principe*. Compare: "But since my intention is to say something that will prove of practical use to the inquirer, I have thought it proper to represent things as they are in truth, rather than as they are imagined." (*The Prince,* trans. George Bull [London: Penguin Group, 1995], 48). The original reads "Ma, sendo l'intendo mio scrivere cosa utile a chi la intende, mi è parso piu conveniente andare drieto alla verità effettuale dalla cosa, che alla immaginazione di essa" (Machiavelli, *Il Principe* in *Opere*, ed. Corrado Vivanti [Rome: Einaudi, 1997], 159).

than my own life: therefore I will describe my life to you, so that by it you might measure all the rest.[41]

Having set the scene and declared that the *Pistola* was autobiographical, Strozzi began to develop the plot of his treatise, a plot that focused on one day in his life. That single day saw him meander from his home to the hilltop church of San Miniato and eventually back to San Lorenzo in the city centre on a wide-ranging tour of Florence's most famous public and religious spaces: from his house, the Palazzo Strozzi, to San Miniato al Monte, to Mercato Nuovo, Santa Reparata (the Duomo), the piazza (likely della Signoria), the piazza, basilica, and cloister of Santa Croce, the first widow's home, Santo Spirito, Via Maggio (the sole street name Strozzi provides), Santa Trínita, the Spini Bench, Santa Maria Novella, San Lorenzo, his new wife's home (address unspecified), and finally returning to the Palazzo Strozzi.

Everywhere he found terrified Florentine citizens, priests, widows, and nobles, all of whom he comforted or took the time to listen to. Amidst an outbreak of plague, in these recounted conversations with others he remained a gentleman, though the asides he directed at the *Pistola*'s recipient, and particularly his descriptions of the young women he encountered, are at times risqué. This sort of double life – public decorum and private perversion – is indicative of Renaissance self-fashioning, but interestingly, Strozzi allows the reader of his *Pistola* to see behind the veneer of his public persona to the real self. It is as if he is letting his reader in on a secret. The "real" Lorenzo Strozzi enjoyed life, he enjoyed women, he loved his city, and in literature he created a place where he was able to partake in all of those things without tipping over the *barca* of his public, gentlemanly life. Here is where self-fashioning and the "strains of isolation" intersect. For, outside of the literary world that he and Machiavelli concocted in the *Pistola*, Strozzi could never have acted in such a roguish manner in the streets of Florence. Like Paolo Sarpi, Strozzi had to play the chameleon to survive in the real world of Florentine politics.[42] Machiavelli by contrast, unwilling or perhaps unable to wear the necessary masks, was forced to the extremities of Florentine society and exiled. In the *Pistola*, then, he and Strozzi were able to adopt each other's perspective, see through each other's eyes. These ideas play out more fully in an analysis of Strozzi's walking tour of Florence made desolate by the plague.

41 See the Italian edition of the *Pistola*, 85r 17–21, and English translation.

42 See chapter 2.

Strozzi began his tour at his home. He does not mention the family palazzo by name, but one can assume he began there, for he had called the Palazzo Strozzi home since 1503.[43] Before leaving, he took a number of antidotes that he claimed to have faith in,[44] but no sooner had he left his house than he came across a group of grave diggers – not brigands who buried those infected with the plague, but the "usual" sort – who were terribly depressed because the source of their livelihood was drying up too soon. In other words, they wanted people to die, just not all at once.

Strolling further, Lorenzo eventually found himself outside the city proper at the ancient church of San Miniato, which he described as empty and silent. He noted that the markets, the wool beaters, and the traders that used to be found on the way to the church were gone. From San Miniato Strozzi wound his way back into the city, eventually ending up in the Mercato Nuovo, where he found no signs of business but did encounter the "horseman of the pestilence" for the first time.[45] He had not previously seen any dead, infected, and dying people; however, in the Mercato he saw a white horse bearing a litter containing a dead noble, whose body was attended by nurses from Santa Maria Nuova. That was enough to put him off the market; he fled to the Duomo, where things only got worse, and more perversely comedic.

In Florence's great church, Strozzi found only nine people: three priests, one of whom was chained to the wall to stop him from fleeing; three old, "lame" women; and three old men who hobbled around the cathedral's choir winking and making advances at the three old women. The world had turned upside down. Realizing that such a scene sounded outlandish, beyond belief, Strozzi promised his reader that everything that he described had in fact happened. Even given this promise, the sights he describes strain credulity. Nonetheless, by this point in the *Pistola*, the reader has been drawn in to the bizarre world that Strozzi and Machiavelli created; one's imagination has been engaged.[46] One can picture the places that Strozzi described and almost believe them real.

---

43 See chapter 1.

44 Strozzi noted of his antidotes that the "distinguished Mingo" would have little faith in them. This "Mingo" was Mengo Bianchelli, a famous plague doctor and physician who died in the early 1520s. For more on Bianchelli, see appendix 3.

45 See the Italian edition of the *Pistola*, 85v 4, and English translation.

46 In the *Pistola*, Strozzi's manner of delivery is almost like what later literary critics, in particular Wayne C. Booth, refer to as the "unreliable narrator." Strozzi's "unreliability," though, must be balanced with the "reality" and the accurate

From the Duomo, Strozzi meandered down to the "piazza." He did not identify this piazza by name, but it is most likely that he strolled from the Duomo to the Piazza della Signoria not only because of its proximity to the Duomo but also because it is the only piazza large enough to contain the scene that he describes. (If that is the path Lorenzo took, he might have been thinking of the route taken by the Carnival float that he and his brother, Filippo, sponsored, the "death float" designed by Piero di Cosimo.) Since the date was the first of May, a "welcome to spring" feast day in Florence, he expected to find a horse race and a throng of party-goers and onlookers in the piazza. He did find a crowd, but not the sort he had hoped for: he encountered piles of corpses, as well as coffins, stretchers, and that vile type of grave digger who was only too happy to expose himself to the plague for profit. The joys of the Calends of May were warped into a dirge.

The Florentine *calendimaggio* or "May Day" was often accompanied by feasting and burlesque Carnival songs.[47] If Strozzi did in fact write the *Pistola* for May Day, which is likely considering that both Strozzi and Machiavelli wrote numerous Canival songs,[48] then the *Pistola* might usefully be viewed as a prose version of the Florentine Carnival song.[49] Along with viewing the *Pistola* as informed by the themes of "self-fashioning" and the "strains of isolation," it might also be interpreted as a literary exercise di-

---

descriptions of place in the *Pistola*. Although there is more recent work on the concept of the unreliable narrator, Booth's *The Rhetoric of Fiction* (Chicago: University of Chicago Press, 1961) remains insightful and useful.

47 Francesco Adorno, *The World of Renaissance Florence*, trans. Walter Darwell (Florence: Giunti Gruppo Editoriale, 1999), 307.

48 For a detailed discussion of Strozzi's Carnival songs, see Pio Ferrieri, "Lorenzo di Filippo Strozzi e un codice Ashburnhamiano," in *Studi di storia e critica letteraria* (Milan: E. Trevisini, 1892). For Machiavelli's six Carnival songs see Machiavelli, *Opere*, vol. 3, ed. Corrado Vivanti (Rome: Einaudi, 1997), 23–39.

49 "In Italia dell'antico Calendimaggio sopravvive qualche frammento, come il Cantarmaggio a Firenzuola in provincia di Firenze: le sera del 30 aprile gruppi di giovani se ne vanno per le case del paese a cantare l'arrivo della bella stagione e nello stesso tempo la gloria della Madonna" (Alfredo Cattabiani, *Calendario: Le feste, i miti, le leggende e riti dell'anno* [Milan: Rusconi, 1991], 218). Cattabiani noted at least one type of "*calendimaggio*" tradition from Firenzuola, a small town located in within the "province" of Florence. See also p. 215 for the historical importance of the first day of May in the "pagan" and Christian eras: "Il 1° maggio segnava l'inizio del trionfo della luce sulle tenebre e continuo a essere celebrato anche dopo la cristianizzazione, tant'è vero che dall feste celtiche è derivato il Calendimaggio medievale." For recent critical analysis of "Carnival laughter" and the inherent sensuality of some Carnival and May Day performances and rituals, see Peter Stallybrass and Allon White, *The Politics and Poetics of Transgression* (London: Methuen, 1986).

rectly related to May Day. This tripartite complexity is astonishing given the relative brevity of the Strozzi-Machiavelli project. But the *Pistola* has a great deal more to reveal about their relationship.

As Strozzi described the scene in the piazza, he noted that "Barlachi," the town crier, was on hand to announce the entrance of the city's dignitaries.[50] The "Barlachi" to whom Strozzi referred was most likely Domenico Barlacchi or Barlacchia, a man equally famous for good humour and lung capacity.[51] Strozzi was in fact a friend of Barlacchi, and he may have inserted his friend within the horrific scene that he described.[52] But he might instead, in an inside joke, have inserted Machiavelli within the *Pistola*: Machiavelli, as noted in chapter 1, may have adopted the *nom de plume* "Barlachia" when he signed his autograph of Strozzi's *Commedia in versi*. Whatever the case, that day Barlachi, unable to find a sufficient number of citizens, was forced to gather the grave diggers to attend to the *Signoria*'s entry into the piazza. Strozzi fled from that pathetic and plague-infested spectacle to the Piazza of Santa Croce, where he was met with a more appalling scene.

It was the Florentine custom on May Day for young girls and women to gather in the city's piazzas to sing songs with lines like those Strozzi had written – *Ben venga il maggio* (Hearty welcome, May) – and to dance.[53] Traditionally, *calendimaggio* songs celebrated the coming of the planting season, budding flowers, and amorous flirtations. Lorenzo hoped that he would find a gathering of that sort outside of Santa Croce, but once again,

50 "Barlachi" is manuscript A's reading. The B ms reads "Barlachio." See the Italian edition of the *Pistola*, 86r 3, and English translation.

51 For Machiavelli's use of "Barlachia" see chapter 1.

52 Anthony M. Cummings, *Maecenas and the Madrigalist* (Philadelphia: American Philosophical Society, 2004), 249–50n30.

53 Here is an example of one of the most famous *calendimaggio* songs: "Eccolo maggio pian pian pian piano / con l'acqua in grembo e lle mezzine in mano / e ben venga maggio, e maggio ll'è venuto. / Eccolo maggio, fa fiorì l'ortica / se c'è bambini in casa che Iddio li benedica / e ben venga maggio, e maggio ll'è venuto. / Eccolo maggio, fa fiorì lle zucche, / date marito alla bella datelo anche alle brute / e ben venga maggio, e maggio ll'è venuto. / Eccolo maggio, fa fiorì lle pere / a voi Capoccia vi si chiede da bere / e ben venga maggio, e maggio ll'è venuto. / E piano piano mi volgio avvicinare, / quei giovin belli li volgio salutare; / e piano e piano avvicinar mi voglio, / quei giovin belli salutar li voglio. / Fiore di maggio, fiore di gaggia / sete i più belli che nella festa sia; / fiore di maggio gli è fiorito i rosi / unguanno dami ed un altr'anno sposi; / fiore di maggio gli è fiorì gli ontani / e prego Iddio che vi tenga tutti sani; / e ben venga maggio, e maggio ll'è venuto" (Cattabaniani, *Calendario*, 217). There are other versions of the song that begin with these lines: "Eccolo Maggio chioccola di pepe, si canta Maggio signori se volete." The Italian singer Ginevra di Marco frequently sings this Florentine/Tuscan song during live performances.

instead of the sights that ought to have greeted him, he found dancing and singing grave diggers who repeated the twisted refrain *Ben venga, ben uenga il morbo* (Hearty welcome, hearty welcome plague).[54] The world that Strozzi and Machiavelli created in the *Pistola* was an inversion of the real one, a world that offers the exact opposite of what one might expect. Only in such a concocted world could the gentleman and the former exile be truly free, as we will see below.

Fleeing the grave diggers, Strozzi entered Santa Croce itself. There, he offered his "usual devotions," without a single witness. A shriek drew him out to the cloister, where he found a beautiful young woman lying amongst the fresh graves screaming, crying, beating herself, and rending her mourning weeds. As she was obviously weeping over a loved one who had succumbed to the plague, Lorenzo was terrified to get too close her, but her beauty and his pity for her forced him to draw near. Having coaxed her into uncovering her face, Strozzi tells his reader that he recognized her; unfortunately, he does not divulge her name.

Whoever she was, Strozzi was able to tease from her intimate confessions about her love for, and sex life with, her deceased lover, such as the following:

> With what delight I gazed into his beautiful and shining eyes! Oh what pleasure when I pressed my longing lips to his fragrant mouth! Oh with such great contentment I united and squeezed my burning breasts to his warm and pure and youthful chest! Oh wretched me! So frequently and with such bliss we came to that final amorous joy, simultaneously slaking our desires![55]

Although he drew forth these confessions by acting like a gentleman and providing her with sound advice, it seems likely that he was in fact taking rather wicked pleasure in the tortured young woman's secrets and passions. Not long after the above declaration, the young woman fainted. Strozzi thought her dead, but he checked her breathing and her pulse and found both to be weak but present. Then, with "carnal" affection, he untied her dress in front – using a *double entendre*, he noted that she was not very tightly laced – and massaged her body until she recovered. This entire scene took place in a cloister full of fresh graves and on top of her own lover's grave; one cannot help but find Strozzi's actions appalling. There were no witnesses, so

54 See the Italian edition of the *Pistola*, 86r 11, and English translation. The text above is transcribed as rendered by Strozzi in ms A, including the lowercase *v* in the first "venga" and the *u* at the start of the second "uenga".

55 See the Italian edition of the *Pistola*, 86v 17–23, and English translation.

he did not need to worry about his reputation, yet he went into great detail about the manner in which he revived her, in language that was sensual despite the gravity of the situation. That language itself leads to a useful point about Machiavelli's and Strozzi's collaborative writing process.

Surely, as Machiavelli transcribed Strozzi's words, he was able to share in Lorenzo's passionate and terrifying moment with the beautiful young Florentine woman. At that moment, patron and client would have been united in a shared experience; the gentleman and the exile would have seen the world in consonant ways.[56] Here Lorenzo let Machiavelli into his mind. Of course, this applies to almost the entirety of the *Pistola,* for Machiavelli transcribed nearly all of it for Lorenzo; but moments such as the one Lorenzo shared with a beautiful, heart-broken stranger would have been of absorbing interest to Niccolò. Machiavelli was of course familiar with such writing, but I am not aware of his sharing in another's life and literary output in a similar manner. The intimacy of the connection seems striking, and likely to bring patron and client close together, albeit in a dark vision.

Having shared in such a torrid, almost voyeuristic literary exercise, Strozzi and Machiavelli brought this act of the *Pistola* to a close with Strozzi chastising the young woman for having ruined her reputation by her affair and by her public lamentations on the grave of her dead lover. He commanded her to return to her home where she might restore her tarnished reputation.

> "Sin certainly is a human thing: but enough good sometimes comes of it to amend one's ways. So that, if you will behave properly, you will see that immediately (immediately I say to you) it will be said that you have been unjustly slandered." In this manner persuading her, I led her to her own house.[57]

---

56 Machiavelli, by transcribing Strozzi's work, may have been able to share in Strozzi's warped vision of Florence He might have been able to "see" with Strozzi's literary eyes, or put another way, could perceive Florence through Strozzi's anamorphotic vision. For more on the theme of the "anamorphic eye" in the Renaissance, see Stuart Clark, *Vanities of the Eyes: Vision in Early Modern European Culture* (Oxford: Oxford University Press, 2007), 78ff. Dr Michael Templeton has pointed out to me that the sexual nature of Strozzi's "curious" or "distorted" vision in some ways resonates with Slavoj Žižek's recent and contemporary social theory. For one example, see Žižek, *Looking Awry: An Introduction to Jacques Lacan through Popular Culture* (Cambridge, MA: MIT Press, 1992), 107ff. For an examination of the "anamorphic eye" in northern European painting, see Hanneke Grootenboer, *The Rhetoric of Perspective: Realism and Illusionism in Seventeenth-Century Dutch Still-Life Painting* (Chicago: University of Chicago Press, 2005), 110ff.

57 See the Italian edition of the *Pistola*, 87r 17–21, and English translation.

From the district of Santa Croce, Strozzi crossed the Arno once again, visiting the "*nuovo tempio*" or "new temple" of Santo Spirito.[58] The church is one of the most harmonious and beautiful religious spaces in Florence, which makes Strozzi's experience there seem all the more bizarre.

Strozzi arrived at Santo Spirito at a time when the Augustinian brothers who ministered to the church and presided over the mass ought to have been preparing for the service. The brothers, however, were not thinking about the mass, but rather about survival. Strozzi seized the opportunity to indulge in a good bout of priest bashing – a favourite pastime in Renaissance Florence and one that Machiavelli had mastered years before. Despite the depravity of its subject, this portion of the *Pistola* is really quite funny.

The few brothers who remained in the church were starving to death, as they were not allowed to leave the confines of Santo Spirito for fear they would not return. Starvation and plague had already carried off the majority of the priests. Those who remained paced the central aisle of the nave from the entrance to the high altar doing nothing but swearing and cursing God. Strozzi recalled that the priests were swearing so profusely that their curses caused the candles in the church to light themselves. Shocked, he ran from the church as fast as he could. His frantic steps led him into the Via Maggio.

Obviously, Strozzi chose to cross the Arno using the Via Maggio because it was close to Santo Spirito; but he may have had a literary motive as well, one that was firmly rooted in the Carnival song tradition of double meanings. He need not have specified the path he took in fleeing from the cursing priests, yet he specified that he fled down the Via Maggio, "May Street," presumably because it was the *calendimaggio*. (He would have known that there was no real correlation between the Via Maggio and the month of May, for "Via Maggio," in the Florentine dialect, meant "Broadway" as in "Via Maggio[re].")[59] Strozzi and Machiavelli seem to have enjoyed playing word games as well as sexualizing the plague outbreak and demeaning the clergy.

58 Strozzi could properly refer to it as new because its architect, Filippo Brunelleschi, was commissioned to build the church in 1434 and its cornerstone was set in 1436. It was finally consecrated in 1482, the year of Lorenzo's birth and some eighteen years after Brunelleschi's death. See Peter Murray, *The Architecture of the Italian Renaissance*, revised ed. (New York: Schocken, 1986), 47–50 for a concise description of Santo Spirito.

59 See Rudolph Altrocchi, "Trinità or Trínita?" *Italica* 26, no. 1 (1949), 60–1 for particular references to the Via Maggio. See also the Italian edition of the *Pistola*, 87r 34, and English translation.

The Via Maggio led Strozzi to the middle of Ponte Santa Trinità, where he found a dead body. The scene, he claimed, looked nothing "like May to me."[60] He hurried past the corpse and took refuge in Santa Trinità itself. Inside the venerable old church Strozzi met an unnamed but "well-born" man of some distinction. When he inquired as to why the man chose to remain in Florence, the gentleman replied: "For love of my native city, which every one of her little-loving citizens has shunned."[61]

To Strozzi, this answer showed not patriotism or even bravery, but stupidity. He replied: "He errs much less who seeks to preserve himself for his native city so that he might be able to serve it at a later time than those who, feigning to serve it, exposed themselves to the danger of leaving it forever."[62] Why did Strozzi not follow his own advice? Why did he choose to remain in the city? Perhaps there is more to be gleaned from this conversation, which highlights the differences between the gentleman (Strozzi) and the exile (Machiavelli). The exile risked everything for love of country and the gamble failed, while the gentleman approached service to the *patria* in a pragmatic and patient fashion that endangered neither his standing with the Medici princes nor the welfare of his family. Where Strozzi may have included Machiavelli as "Barlachi" earlier in the *Pistola*, here perhaps he inserted Machiavelli as the hypocritical patriot who refused to leave Florence out of love for his native city but who, when pressed, admitted, as the gentleman in the *Pistola* does, that he stayed in Florence because he loved a woman there. In other words, Strozzi might have been poking fun at Machiavelli's outspoken patriotism.

Returning to the text of the *Pistola,* the ramifications of this exchange are somewhat less serious; indeed they are intentionally comedic. Strozzi condemns the unknown gentleman, who confesses that he remained in the city not out of patriotism but for love and then carries on about the depth of his passion. Lorenzo, in an aside, delivers the opinion that such hot-bloodedness is unbecoming in a man of mature years. The older man then tells Lorenzo that he ought to fall in love himself because love is the best means of avoiding the plague. Strozzi dismisses such talk as rubbish and goes so far as to suggest that love is a greater plague, one much more deadly than the pestilence currently ravaging Florence. Once again, Strozzi made a rushed exit, but he did not make it very far: he only crossed the street to the Spini bench.

---

60 See the Italian edition of the *Pistola*, 87r 34–5, and English translation.

61 Ibid., 87v 4–5.

62 Ibid., 87v 5–8.

Most Renaissance palaces, including Strozzi's own, had seats – of either stone or wood – appended to their facades. The Palazzo Spini (which houses Ferragamo in today's Florence) was no different. Public seats like the Spini bench were an essential part of daily life in Renaissance Florence. They were places for gathering, doing business, and relaxing, and they also provided shady spots where Florentines might escape the heat of the Tuscan sun.[63] Strozzi found, on the "nowadays deserted"[64] Spini bench, an extraordinary thing: one man attended by a throng of women.

Sitting on the bench, hearing the confessions of those women, Strozzi found Fra Alessio (Strozzi),[65] a member of the Franciscan order at Santa Maria Novella. He had been ordered away from the church because he liked the women a bit too much, and, Strozzi implied, the "charitable brothers" there wanted the women for themselves.[66] Alessio had simply opened up shop at the Spini bench, and the women followed. Strozzi asked Fra Alessio to accompany him to Santa Maria Novella and, after a brief exchange, both men made their way to "the perfectly proportioned and venerable church."[67] (Strozzi would have been familiar with Leon Battista Alberti's façade, which was praised for its harmony and proportion.) Fra Alessio saluted the altar and left the church because, Lorenzo pointed out, "he was never known for his piety."[68]

Finding himself in the church as the evening prayers and songs were supposed to begin, Strozzi hoped to mingle with a number of noblewomen

---

63 Yvonne Elet, "Seats of Power: The Outdoor Benches of Early Modern Florence," *Journal of the Society of Architectural Historians* 61, no. 4 (2002): 444–69.

64 See the Italian edition of the *Pistola*, 87v 23–4, and English translation.

65 This is likely the same Fra Alessio who Benvenuto Cellini claimed helped him to escape Florence after he had committed a murder: "I went off in the direction of Santa Maria Novella, and stumbling up against Fra Alessio Strozzi, whom by the way I did not know, I entreated this good friar for the love of God to save my life, since I had committed a great fault. He told me to have no fear; for had I done every sin in the world, I was yet in perfect safety in his little cell." (Cellini *The Autobiography of Benvenuto Cellini*, trans. J. Addington Symonds [New York: P.F. Collier and Son, 1910], 33). The original reads "Io me ne andai alla volta di santa Maria Novella, e subito percossomi in frate Alesso Strozzi, il quale io non conosceva, a questo buon frate io per l'amor de Dio mi raccomandai, che mi salvassi la vita, perché grande errore avevo fatto. Il buon frate mi disse che io non avessi paura di nulla, ché, tutti e' mali del mondo che io avessi fatti, in quella cameruccia sua ero sicurissimo" (Cellini, *Vita di Benvenuto Cellini Scritta da Lui Medesimo*, ed. Brunone Bianchi [Florence: Adriano Salani, Editore Viale Militare, 1903], 27–8).

66 See the Italian edition of the *Pistola*, 87v 29, and English translation.

67 Ibid., 87v 26–7.

68 Ibid., 88r 4.

and noblemen who often came to the church not out of devotion but for amorous liaisons. Finding the church almost empty, Strozzi nevertheless stayed because he wanted to hear the brothers sing the evening mass. When he realized that the brothers were not going to sing or to perform any other religious duties, he was tempted to leave, until a beautiful young widow who was reclining on the steps near the high altar caught his eye. The location where Strozzi first encountered the widow is important. He wrote that she was reclining near the "Cappella Maggiore," which is most likely a reference to the chapel that is located just behind the high altar.[69] When one faces that chapel and looks to the smaller chapel just to the right of the high altar, one looks directly at the Strozzi Chapel.

Given the plague-related theme of Strozzi's *Pistola*, one cannot help but recall that Boccaccio's *Decameron* began in just that spot. The young ladies whom Boccaccio introduced to the reader had, just like the widow Strozzi found in the church, gone there to hear the "Divine Office," and they had gathered near the altar.[70] So, at this point in the *Pistola*, Strozzi followed Boccaccio almost exactly. That is, until he introduced himself to the young widow.

Hers is an insightful and blunt character, acting as a foil to Strozzi's own smooth gentlemanly persona. For example, when Strozzi asked her if he could be of assistance to her, the beautiful widow replied: "My needs are such that even a lesser man than you could be useful to me."[71] Without her husband, she continued, she would be defenseless in the city, so she begrudgingly admitted that she needed a man, even an "old" one, to look after her. This was probably a swipe at Strozzi's virility. The young woman must have been an exceptional beauty, for Strozzi refused to leave her side. Here Strozzi's story is very effective, for it reads as though he is recounting an actual conversation. And though he is obviously mimicking Boccaccio, he came close to recreating the tense though hauntingly casual atmosphere of the *Decameron*'s introduction. Having just set the scene, and met the

69 Ibid., 88r 18–19.

70 *Decameron* (1998), 14.

71 See the Italian edition of the *Pistola*, 89r 8–9, and English translation. This is a difficult passage, which was translated by C.H. Clarke as "a man of much inferior position to yours could be of service to me." See the translation of the *Pistola*, incorrectly attributed to Machiavelli, in Johannes Nohl, *The Black Death: A Chronicle of the Plague*, trans. C.H. Clarke (Yardley, PA: Westholme, 2006; repr. of 1926 Unwin ed.), 225. Given that the text quickly mentions their age difference, it would seem more likely that Strozzi intended to reference his age in the passage cited above – "a younger man than you."

young widow, Strozzi swerves from the *Decameron*'s early realism to a jolting proclamation of love: minutes after meeting the widow, he asked for her hand in marriage, to which the woman replied: "With you men, ever were the promises great and the faith but small, if I have a good memory of things past."[72] Strozzi responded: "One who knows how to choose prudently does not have to put his faith in the truthfulness of others and therefore never has to repent of what he has done."[73]

Attempting to deflect the woman's accusation that he was simply making promises to get her into his bed, Strozzi turned the argument in his favour by suggesting the woman should follow her prudent instincts. But Strozzi had just described to his reader every detail of the woman's physical beauty in lurid detail, suggesting that she might indeed have been wise to judge him based on her previous experience with men rather than his appearance and polite courtesies. Even as he presented himself to the unnamed woman as a gentleman, his mind likely remained focused on sex. Lorenzo Strozzi might have been born a "gentleman," but he was far grittier, far more sensual than his polished public image leads us to believe, which is why the "asides" in the *Pistola* are so interesting and important. Here is how he described the young woman:

> She was of an agreeable size and proportionate stature for a finely formed woman. So that even from here one could conclude that all the parts of such a body were so well shaped, that if stripped of her mourning raiment, they would present a wondrous beauty to my eyes. But leaving this part free for you to gaze upon in your imagination, I will describe the part that is made manifest.[74]

After describing all of her visible attributes, Lorenzo could not restrain himself. He was compelled to describe what he was unable to see:

> Her envious clothes did not give me leave to gaze on the creamy, beautiful and finely sculpted chest, adorned with two little fresh and sweet smelling apples, which I believe were grown in the famous orchards of the Hesperides. But, by the manner in which they refused to yield to her dress, they demonstrated their beauty and firmness; and between them flashes a way, at the end of which, the wanderer might reach the ultimate bliss.[75]

72 See the Italian edition of the *Pistola*, 89r 22–3, and English translation.
73 Ibid., 89r 24–5.
74 Ibid., 88r 21–6.
75 Ibid., 88v 22–8.

Lorenzo, however, never said anything untoward to the woman in question or to the other woman whom he accosted on her dead lover's grave. (Where the latter woman is concerned, in Manuscript B of the *Pistola* Strozzi, through Machiavelli, referred to the woman using familiar forms of address: "tua" and "tuoi." But in Manuscript A, Strozzi cancelled out those familiar forms of address and replaced them with "uostra" and "uostri").[76] His lusty descriptions were directed only at his reader, who was supposed to imagine the beauty of her body in his mind. This is not gentlemanly behaviour: he ought to have kept his thoughts to himself, but he could not resist sharing them. It is here, one is tempted to suspect, that Machiavelli exerted some influence on his gentleman patron.

There are passages in Niccolò's *L'Asino* that are nearly identical in content.[77] These are covered in much greater detail in the complete translation that follows; one example will suffice here. Compare Strozzi's description of the young woman above with Machiavelli's description of the servant of Circe:

> I continued to pass my eyes over all her various parts as low as her breast, at the splendour of which I [am still] kindled, but seeing farther was refused me by a rich and shining coverlet with which that little bed was covered.[78]

Machiavelli's *L'Asino* is of course a poem, which means that his use of words was more economical, but the similarities are striking. One can gather that both men were terribly fond of women. Given that *L'Asino* was written in 1517, Strozzi could easily have had some familiarity with it. That familiarity is yet more discernible when one considers that in the *Pistola* Strozzi commented on the young woman's eyes, her eyebrows, her neck, her cheeks, her nose, and her hands – Machiavelli described each part of the woman who restored his "*virtù*" in *L'Asino* in almost identical terms.

76 Ibid., 87r 6–8, and the variations included at the foot of the page.

77 Gian Mario Anselmi and Paolo Fazion's *Machiavelli, L'Asino e le Bestie* (Bologna: CLEUB, 1984) is a good starting point for investigations into Machiavelli's poem.

78 Niccolò Machiavelli, "The Ass," in *The Chief Works and Others*, vol. 3, trans. Alan Gilbert (Durham: Duke University Press, 1965), 750–72. See p. 759, "Fourth Chapter," ll. 88–93. The Italian original is "Io venni ben con l'occhio discorrendo / Tutte le parti sue infino al petto, / A lo splendor del quale ancor m'accendo; / Ma più oltre veder mi fu disdetto / Da una ricca e candida coperta, / Con la qual coperto era il picciol letto" ("L'Asino," in *Opere*, vol. 3, ed. Corrado Vivanti [Rome: Einaudi, 2005], 51–78 [hereafter abbreviated as "L'Asino"]. Refer to 'Capitolo Quarto' on 63, ll. 88–93).

Strozzi clearly shared Machiavelli's vision of feminine beauty; otherwise he would not have co-opted it so exhaustively. The *Pistola* brought these two men, from such different backgrounds, together in a unique way, allowing each to see through the other's eyes – or to empathize imaginatively with each other.[79] Lorenzo Strozzi seems to have longed for the unrestrained freedom of his exiled counterpart, while Machiavelli would certainly have been comfortable with Strozzi's wealth and status, though it is doubtful that he could have showed the sort of public restraint that made Lorenzo so successful. The only place such an exchange was possible was within the pages of the *Pistola*.

Back in Santa Maria Novella, Strozzi and the widow who was now his fiancée were waylaid by a priest who had his eye on the latter. He offered her "assistance" of the amorous sort. Strozzi jumped in, exclaiming that the young woman did not need the kind of assistance being offered. This caused the priest to grumble and shuffle off, putting his "serpent" back in his cloak: in not-so-subtle terms, Strozzi insinuated that the priest had been exposing himself. This grotesquerie moved Strozzi to escort his bride-to-be back to her home. From there, he craved further stimulation, so he made his way to San Lorenzo, where he hoped to find young nobles and friends from his youth with whom he could converse and while away the day. But he was overcome with jealousy: he wrote that he constantly imagined his young bride being seduced by the lecherous priest from Santa Maria Novella. Bothered by that vision, he returned to his home and began to prepare for his wedding. At the end of the *Pistola* he writes:

> Well, that is what, my dearest friend, the first day of May offered to my eyes. Of that which will follow, you will learn about after the wedding; because before that I am not able to think of anything else.[80]

The problem here is that Strozzi was already married to Lucrezia Rucellai and had been since 1503. Both he and Machiavelli were "trapped" in marriage. The *Pistola* briefly allowed them both to escape the real world in exchange for a literary world where they could refashion themselves and throw off the bonds and obligations of their lives. In the pages of the *Pistola*, Machiavelli was able to experience the life of a gentleman through

79 For a discussion of "imaginative empathy" see Northrop Frye, *Northrop Frye's Notebooks on Renaissance Literature*, vol. 20, ed. Michael Dolzani (Toronto: University of Toronto Press, 2006), xlii.

80 See the Italian edition of the *Pistola*, 89v 26–28, and English translation.

Lorenzo Strozzi – a life free from constraints – and Lorenzo could live in his literary world as a completely unrestrained gentleman.[81]

Conclusion

In the foregoing I hope to have rendered plausible the suggestions that the *Pistola* might be read, at least in part, as "autobiographical," where by this term I mean that Lorenzo wrote about the life he might have wished was his. That fantasy life was one that Machiavelli, Lorenzo's client, was able to share in as he transcribed Strozzi's tract. As I have mentioned above, such a reading is influenced tremendously by Stephen Greenblatt's compelling "self-fashioning" approach, on which I have overlaid the suggestion that the *Pistola* is part of the farcical *calendimaggio* tradition.

This interdisciplinary method helps to explain why Lorenzo Strozzi renamed the *Epistola*, choosing instead to call it the *Pistola*. (The latter bears a phonetic resemblance to the rude *fistola*.)[82] The *Pistola*'s title is likely rooted in jest and wordplay. Similiarly, the upside-down world that it constructs – which culminates in a marriage rather than a funeral and focuses on love found rather than love lost – fits squarely within the comedic *calendimaggio* style, and in the types of literature that Greenblatt suggested could be interpreted through the lens of self-fashioning. Lending further credence to the notion that the *Pistola* is more complex than previously recognized, there is an important though often neglected farce written by Machiavelli that resonates with this proposed reading of the *Pistola*.

That work, Machiavelli's *Capitoli per una campagnia di piacere,* is located in the same Banco Rari codex (29) as his transcription of the *Pistola.*[83]

81 In the real world both men were united by the common thread of being trapped in loveless marriages – Lorenzo to a "deformed" Rucellai and Machiavelli to a frequently angry Marietta Corsini. It is no wonder then that both men sought pleasure from women other than their wives. Maurizio Viroli has suggested that Machiavelli's wife may not have known of his affairs and that even if she did, we do not know if she cared. She was angry because Niccolò was so rarely with her at their home. See *Niccolò's Smile*, trans. Antony Shugaar (New York: Farrar, Straus and Giroux, 2000), 49–50.

82 "Fistola," from the Latin "fistula," in this sense connotes an abnormality of the rectum. I am again indebted to Professor Massimo Ciavolella for this suggestion. The titles of the manuscripts are noted above and are discussed in more detail in the Italian edition of the *Pistola*.

83 *Capitoli per una compagnia di piacere*, Banco Rari 29, 20r–23v, Biblioteca Nazionale Centrale di Firenze.

It is a send-up of genteel confraternity culture[84] whose bizarre qualities resonate strikingly with the *Pistola*'s literary sensibilities, so much so that it might be read as an interpretive bridge between Castiglione's perfect courtier, Machiavelli's own political vision, and the autobiographical nature of the *Pistola* itself. Machiavelli wrote:

> No one is ever to show by external signs the thoughts in his mind; rather the contrary shall be done, and he who best knows how to pretend [*fingere*] or to tell lies [*bugie*] merits most commendation.[85]

In an otherwise comedic portrayal of high society, gender relations, and religious observance, these lines are telling. Everyone, according to Machiavelli, ought to cloak their intentions, their motives. This brief, tragically realistic quotation summarizes Lorenzo Strozzi's life – the life of the Renaissance gentleman. While one could argue that Carnival buffoonery provided an outlet, private literature allowed for escape from this formal and rigid system of social interaction. There, and only there, could men like Strozzi avoid "plagues" upon their houses when they chose to violate social expectations so thoroughly.

The theme of plague, as depicted in Strozzi's *Pistola*, is heavily indebted to the *Decameron*'s opening description of the plague and to the bawdy tales told by that work's narrators. The *Pistola* is, in fact, part of a lengthy plague tract and *novella* tradition that can be traced to Thucydides, Lucretius, Boccaccio, and Marsilio Ficino, to name only a few famous Mediterranean

---

84 Antonio Negri, *Insurgencies: Constituent Power and the Modern State* (Minneapolis: University of Minnesota Press, 1999). Negri writes that the *Capitoli* was "certainly composed at San Casciano after 1514"; see p. 345n97. Franco Ferrucci cited Machiavelli's *Capitoli per una compagnia di piacere*, particularly the quotation from the work on the next page of this book, in relation to mask wearing and similar injunctions in Shakespeare's plays. See Ferrucci's *Il teatro della fortuna: potere e destino in Machiavelli e Shakespeare* (Rome: Fazi, 2004), 84. Maurizio Viroli noted that the *Capitoli* is important because it helps to illustrate, in part at least, Machiavelli's ideas concerning "confession." See Viroli's *Il Dio di Machiavelli e il problema morale dell' Italia* (Rome: Laterza, 2005).

85 Niccolò Machiavelli, "Articles for a Pleasure Company," in *Machiavelli: The Chief Works and Others*, vol. 2, trans. Allan H. Gilbert (Durham: Duke University Press, 1989), 865–8; for quotation see p. 868. The original reads "Che non si debba mai mostrare con segni di fuora lo animo suo di drento, anzi fare tutto il contrario, e quello che sa meglio fingere o dire le bugie più commendazione" ("Capitoli per una compagnia di piacere," in Niccolò Machiavelli, *Opere*, vol. 3, ed. Corrado Vivanti [Rome: Einaudi, 2005], 243–7, and p. 246 for quotation).

commentators.[86] Furthermore, Machiavelli's interest in the *novella* genre has been widely studied. His *Belfagore*, while not plague literature, is one of the finest examples of its sort. The *Pistola*'s brief format and rapid plot development were likely of interest to Machiavelli.[87] Or one could examine Strozzi's almost Petrarchesque obsession in the *Pistola* with feminine beauty.[88] The many ways in which the *Pistola* might be read are further evidence of its complexity and thus of its neglected importance.

I have traced how the complicated process of patronage and what seems also to be collaboration produced an absorbing and, since the early twentieth century, largely overlooked treatise on the plague and love in early sixteenth-century Florence. Of equal importance, that process illustrates just how closely Strozzi and Machiavelli worked with one another. The fruits of that relationship were twofold for Machiavelli.

First, he was able, through association with Lorenzo Strozzi, to gain some footing in Medici-controlled Florence. Without Strozzi's patronage it is not obvious how Machiavelli would have won the commission to write the *Istorie fiorentine*. Finally, Machiavelli, through the writing process that led to the completion of the *Pistola*, was able to imaginatively view Florence through the eyes of a younger, handsome aristocrat What was the price of all of this? Collaboration on a piece of "learned pornography,"[89] which, given Machiavelli's well-known credentials in the art of titillation, might not have been a steep price to pay, though he may have found the *Pistola*'s lack of originality stifling.

Strozzi might also have benefitted from his association with Machiavelli. Those benefits were perhaps less tangible, but nevertheless important: consider what a resource Machiavelli would have been, sharing his political views and his literary talents. Strozzi, the gentleman, would have been able to see, briefly, through the eyes of the older, somewhat bitter, brilliant Renaissance writer. Through their patron-client relationship, Strozzi and Machiavelli were, for a time at least, able to overcome the "strains of isolation."

---

86 See n. 1 above for authors cited.

87 For one of the best recent studies of Machiavelli's *Belfagor*, see Filippo Grazzini, *Machiavelli narratore. Morfologia e ideologia della novella di Belfagor con il testo della "Favola"* (Rome: Laterza, 1990).

88 See Lisa Rabin, "Speaking to Silent Ladies: Images of Beauty and Politics in Poetic Portraits of Women from Petrarch to Sor Juana Ines de la Cruz," *Modern Language Notes* 112, no. 2 (1997): 147–65. Petrarch's descriptions of feminine beauty are often very similar to Strozzi's in the *Pistola*.

89 See the Foreword of this study.

Why was the *Pistola* not published as a work by Strozzi? A survey of the *Pistola* publication history reveals that it has not been published since the middle years of the nineteenth century, and all of those editions were published under Machiavelli's name. Now that it has been established that a patron-client relationship developed between Strozzi and Machiavelli in the years following 1520, and that the *Pistola* resulted from that relationship, surely that work deserves to be properly edited and translated. I have undertaken to do so: following the concluding chapter of this study, the reader will find the first, complete English translation of the *Pistola* and the first Italian critical treatment of the Strozzi-Machiavelli project.

Conclusion: *Pistola*, Patron, Client, and the Proposed Strozzi Marriage of 1525

Strozzi and Machiavelli: 1520–1522 Patron and Client

The text and context of the *Pistola fatta per la peste* take us to the heart of the relationship between Niccolò Machiavelli and Lorenzo di Filippo Strozzi – even in the absence of personal letters.[1] Strozzi's *Pistola* allows its reader to see into the private thoughts of its author. By the same token it might have allowed Machiavelli, the work's original transcriber, to share in the literary "self-fashioning" processes of his patron.[2]

In the pages of the *Pistola*, Lorenzo and Machiavelli were able to live as they could only have dreamt of living in the real and very harsh world of Florentine politics. If either had conducted their real lives as Lorenzo lived in the *Pistola*, Lorenzo would have committed political suicide and Machiavelli,

1 "I, nevertheless, want you to be able to understand the matter in greater depth, because the thing imagined compared with the truth of that which one imagines never measures up" (Italian edition of the *Pistola*, 85r 16–18, and corresponding English translation on facing page). Machiavelli used very similar terminology in *Il Principe*: "But since my intention is to say something that will prove of practical use to the inquirer, I have thought it proper to represent things as they are in truth, rather than as they are imagined" (*The Prince*, trans. George Bull [London: Penguin, 1995], 48). The original reads "Ma, sendo l'intendo mio scrivere cosa utile a chi la intende, mi è parso piu conveniente andare drieto alla verità effettuale dalla cosa, che alla immaginazione di essa" (*Il Principe*, in *Opere*, ed. Corrado Vivanti [Rome: Einaudi, 1997], 159).

2 The theme of rewriting and "sharing" with the original writer through the re-writing process, particularly as practised by Machiavelli, has been discussed at length by Barbara J. Godorecci, *After Machiavelli: "Re-Writing" and the "Hermeneutic Attitude"* (West Lafayette: Purdue University Press, 1993). For an explanation of Godorecci's methods and interpretations see 9ff.

who was only partially rehabilitated in 1522, would have lost the remaining shreds of his credibility – neither could afford to live like Benvenuto Cellini.[3]

However much one might be tempted to view the patron-client relationship that developed between Strozzi and Machiavelli as something more than that – a friendship perhaps – the surviving evidence does not allow that leap. The limited number of artefacts that we are left to sift through indicate that the "founder of modern political science," the advisor to princes, was not only Strozzi's client but was manipulated by Strozzi on a number of occasions.[4] Before focusing on this latter point, we must ask how and why the proposed Strozzi-Machiavelli relationship developed.[5]

Lorenzo Strozzi, as we have seen, was responsible for "conducting" Machiavelli into the good graces of Cardinal Giulio de' Medici. We are led to this conclusion by Filippo Strozzi's March 1520 letter to his elder brother Lorenzo, in which Filippo expressed his support for Lorenzo's efforts to help "Machiavello."[6] As a result of Lorenzo's aid, Machiavelli was awarded a contract to write the *Istorie fiorentine* in the autumn of 1520. Soon thereafter, in 1521, Machiavelli dedicated his *Arte della guerra* to Strozzi in gratitude for the latter's recent favours. The "*benefizi*" to which Machiavelli

3 For a nice summary of the mood of the *Pistola* that complements those already presented in this book, see Raymond Crawfurd, *Plague and Pestilence in Literature and Art* (Oxford: Clarendon, 1914); referring to the *Pistola* (which he incorrectly concluded was written by Machiavelli), he wrote: "In it we find no vivid picture of the awful catastrophe that was overwhelming Florence, but in place of that a cold-blooded cynical record of the trivial doings of a loafer sauntering idly through the streets of the plague-stricken city … he passes on to describe his own daily mode of living, from which his correspondent is invited to infer that of the general body of citizens. The *liaisons* of licentious monks, the vile ribaldry of infamous buriers, the vain recourse to preservatives against the plague, these are the things that are uppermost in his mind, as he depicts his own amorous intrigues against the dark background of the place, with the fidelity of a Pepys and the light-hearted insouciance of Guy de Maupassant" (154). For an interesting reading of Cellini's autobiography that in some ways corresponds with my reading of the *Pistola*, see Margaret A. Gallucci, *Benvenuto Cellini: Sexuality, Masculinity and Artistic Identity in Renaissance Italy* (London: Palgrave Macmillan, 2005).

4 De Lamar Jensen, ed., *Machiavelli, Cynic, Patriot or Political Scientist?* (Boston: D.C. Heath, 1960). This is an interesting collection of essays and extracts that deals with these aspects of Machiavelli's posthumous persona.

5 See Guy Fitch Lytle's "Friendship and Patronage in Renaissance Florence," in *Patronage, Art and Society in Renaissance Florence*, ed. F.W. Kent and Patricia Simons (Oxford: Oxford University Press, 2002). Lytle suggests that the relationship between patrons and clients might sometimes be categorized as the antithesis of friendship.

6 This letter is quoted and discussed at length in chapter 2.

referred were almost certainly linked with Lorenzo Strozzi's handling of the Medici family and the subsequent contract for the *Istorie*.[7] Moreover, the *Arte*'s carefully constructed dedication is couched in the formalized language that a client would reserve for his social superior, his magnanimous patron.

This evidence suggests that in March 1520 Lorenzo Strozzi became Machiavelli's patron. It also suggests that Strozzi's patronage led Machiavelli into a second patron-client relationship with Cardinal de' Medici, who saw to it that Machiavelli received a commission from the Florentine Studio for the *Istorie fiorentine*. In 1520, therefore, Machiavelli found himself entangled in two potentially troubling patron-client relationships: the one with Giulio de' Medici led him to write the *Istorie*, but his relationship with Strozzi seems to have produced stranger fruits.

One of those fruits ripened in the spring of 1522. Earlier in that year (and well into May), Giulio de' Medici solicited advice from Florentine republicans concerning the future of Florence's government. In April 1522 Machiavelli jumped at the chance to take part in the proposed reforms. Brashly, he submitted his *Minuta di provvisione* in the form of a decree penned by the cardinal himself.[8] It is quite likely that Machiavelli felt emboldened to take this approach as a result if his recent success with the Medici, though that success would have been impossible without Lorenzo Strozzi's patronage.

This patronage seems to have left an imprint in the *Minuta*'s oligarchic tendencies, which reflect Strozzi's influence more than they mirror Machiavelli's fashioned persona as Giulio de' Medici. Bolstering this conclusion, Strozzi's sixteenth-century biographer, Francesco Zeffi, noted that Lorenzo Strozzi was, as late as 1523, still trying to convince Giulio de' Medici to adopt a republic at Florence that was strikingly like Machiavelli's vision of Florence in the *Minuta*. It is possible that Strozzi was influenced by Machiavelli's emerging "oligarchic" tendencies. However, that scenario

7 I quoted a portion of the *Arte*'s dedication in chapter 2. Here is the full quotation: "You, Lorenzo, ought therefore to consider the qualities of these efforts of mine and give them, with your judgment, the censure or the praise which they will seem to have merited. These I present to you (being customary to honour with similar works those who shine in their nobility, wealth, ingenuity and liberality,) to demonstrate my gratefulness for the favours [*benefizi*] that I have received from you, even though my ability does not measure up; I know that where wealth and nobility are concerned you do not have many equals, few in genius and none in liberality." See chapter 2 for Italian original and bibliographica details.

8 See appendix 4 of this study for the full text of the *Minuta*.

is highly unlikely, particularly when one recalls that Machiavelli's earlier call for the reform of the Florentine government, written after the death of Lorenzo de' Medici and Giulio's rise to power in Florence, was intensely "popular" and deeply republican.[9] After 1520, and particularly during April 1522, perhaps Lorenzo Strozzi began to guide Niccolò's republicanism towards something resembling a *governo stretto*.[10]

It is also probable that Lorenzo's influence got Niccolò into very serious trouble and then extricated him from it. A month after Machiavelli submitted his *Minuta di provvisione* to Giulio, a republican conspiracy to assassinate the cardinal was brought to light and a round-up of the conspirators commenced. Troublingly for Machiavelli, several of the chief conspirators were former students of his at the Orti Oricellari. The conspirators might have misinterpreted Machiavelli's discourse on necessary political assassinations, but they nevertheless used his theories to justify their actions.[11] The prominent sixteenth-century Florentine historians Jacopo Nardi and Paolo Giovio, who knew Machiavelli and many of the conspirators, noted that Florence was buzzing with speculation about Machiavelli's involvement in the conspiracy. We cannot dismiss Nardi and Giovio out of hand.[12]

---

9 "Discursus Florentinarum Rerum Post Mortem Iunioris Laurentii Medices," in *Opere*, vol. 1, ed. Corrado Vivanti (Rome: Einaudi, 1997): 733–45.

10 For a discussion of the probable influence of Venetian republicanism and Strozzi, see chapter 1. For a classic discussion of republican political vocabulary in Florence and Venice, see J.G.A. Pocock, *The Machiavellian Moment: Florentine Political Thought and the Atlantic Republican Tradition* (Princeton: Princeton University Press, 1975), 118 ff. For more on the *governo stretto* and the last Florentine republic, see Felix Gilbert, "Florentine Political Assumptions in the Period of Savonarola and Soderini," *Journal of the Warburg and Courtauld Institutes* 20, nos. 3–4 (1957): 188.

11 Patricia J. Osmond, "Conspiracy of 1522 against Cardinal Giulio de Medici: Machiavelli and "*gli esempli delli antiqui,*" in *The Pontificate of Clement VII: History, Politics, Culture*, ed. Kenneth Gouwens and Sheryl E Reiss (Aldershot: Ashgate, 2005): 55–72. Osmond argues that the young, radical Florentines who plotted to murder Giulio de' Medici took Machiavelli's advice on conspiracy and assassination, included in his *Discorsi*, out of context. In other words, Osmond suggests that Machiavelli would not have supported the assassination of Cardinal Giulio.

12 "Per il che detto Niccolò [Machiavelli] era amato grandemente da loro, e anche per cortesia sovvenuto, come seppi io, di qualche emolumento: e della sua conversazione si dilettavano maravigliosamente, tenendo in prezzo grandissimo tutte l'opere sue, in tanto che de' pensamenti e azioni di questi giovani anche Niccolò non fu senza imputazione" (Jacopo Nardi, *Istorie della città di Firenze*, ed. Agenore Gelli, vol. 2 [Florence: Le Monnier, 1888], 77). Filippo de' Nerli wrote that the conspirators, who might have relied on Machiavelli's *Discorsi* as a blueprint for a properly ordered conspiracy, missed the point of Niccolò's text: "che se bene lo avessero considerato, o non l' avrebbero fatto, o se pure fatto l' avessero, almeno più proceduti sarebbono"

Nardi wrote that Florentines were suspicious of Machiavelli's associations with conspirators, but Giovio went further, intimating that Niccolò might have had a hand in planning the conspiracy itself. Machiavelli's own correspondence tells us nothing about his participation in or thoughts about the conspiracy or conspirators. In fact, in 1522 Machiavelli wrote only one inconsequential letter – or only one that survived.[13]

If Florentine observers and, one might imagine, the Medici were suspicious about Machiavelli's involvement in the conspiracy to murder Giulio, then how did he escape the executioner's axe? Machiavelli needed a protector to shield him from Medici fury – and Lorenzo di Filippo Strozzi might have filled that role after March 1520, and perhaps again in 1522, when Machiavelli faced a real threat to his life. Chronological and intertextual evidence bolster this conclusion.

There is a striking correspondence between the language used to describe the time of year in the *Minuta di provvisione* and in the *Pistola*. Both refer to the "*calendimaggio*" season: the *Minuta* refers to the upcoming "*calendimaggio*" and the *Pistola* refers to the recently passed "*maggio le calendi.*" Both works appear to have originated within two months of one another (the *Minuta* in April and the *Pistola* in late May or early June). Added to this, there was an outbreak of plague in 1522, further linking the *Pistola* to that year. This evidence is tantalizing, and it has been completely overlooked until now.

(Nerli, *Commentari de' fatti civili occorsi dentro la città di Firenze dall'anno 1512 al 1537,* vol. 2 [Trieste: Colombo Coen Tip. Editore, 1859], 12). This passage from Nerli was quoted by Patricia J. Osmond in "Conspiracy of 1522," 57n8. On p. 66n42 she also quoted Paolo Giovio, who was even more specific regarding Machiavelli's role in the conspiracy: "Tuttavia, poichè nei suoi scritti egli aveva continuato a esaltare Bruto e Cassio, si era sospettato che egli fosse stato architetto della congiura antimedicea in cui avevano trovato la morte Alammani e il Diacceto" (Cited by G. Procacci, *Studi sulla fortuna del Machiavelli* [Rome: Instituto storico italiano per l'età moderna e contemporanea, 1965], 266).

13 Machiavelli's own grandsons, Giuliano de' Ricci and Niccolò Machiavelli the Younger, were given the dubious task of "correcting" their grandfather's *opere complete*. Thankfully, they did not have the heart to finish their task, thereby saving and transmitting the majority of Machiavelli's works for posterity. However, Ricci did destroy at least one early play, *Le Maschere* (1504), because of its slanderous content. If he found letters implicating Machiavelli in the conspiracy, or letters that expressed concern over the outcome of the conspiracy, it is entirely possible that Ricci destroyed them. For more details on Ricci, Machiavelli, and *Le Maschere*, see Peter Godman, *From Poliziano to Machiavelli: Florentine Humanism in the High Renaissance* (Princeton: Princeton University Press, 1998), 241. For the unpublished ms of Ricci's work, see Giuliano de' Ricci, *Priorista*, MS Palatino E.B. 14.1. in the Biblioteca Nazionale Centrale di Firenze.

Machiavelli's probable struggles in 1522, the language adopted in the *Minuta di provvisione,* and the strikingly similar vocabulary used in the *Pistola* converge – linking Machiavelli and Strozzi in the former's "lost year." Perhaps Strozzi influenced the *Minuta*'s content and then, when Machiavelli needed the protection of a well-connected patron, he stepped in, keeping the usually loquacious Niccolò quiet and putting him to work transcribing the *Pistola fatta per la peste.*

Strozzi and Machiavelli: 1522–1526
The End of the Line?

It is important to emphasize that we do not have a single letter between our two protagonists, which makes it difficult to reconstruct their relationship. However, at the fringes of Renaissance historiography, we find two of Lorenzo di Filippo Strozzi's literary works that are extant as Machiavelli autographs. The fact that the *Commedia in versi* and the *Pistola fatta per la peste* survive in Machiavelli's hand signifies that the two men were probably more closely connected than the absence of personal letters between them indicates.[14] However, it is unlikely that their relationship was ever one of friendship. Rather, all of the surviving evidence suggests that Strozzi and Machiavelli were patron and client.

Between 1522 and 1525, there is nothing whatsoever to link Strozzi and Machiavelli. This complete lack of evidence is telling. While arguments *ex silentio* are dangerous, the absence of sources could indicate that the patron-client relationship between Strozzi and Machiavelli broke down in 1522. Even if it did go on after 1522 (and there is nothing to support that assertion), it could not have continued after 1524. For in 1524, when Machiavelli found himself in an awkward situation regarding his "history"

14 Andrea Gareffi has already examined the *Commedia* in his *Commedie: Commedia in versi, La Pisana, La Violante* (Ravenna: Longo, 1981), 36–40. Additionally, Pasquale Villari suggested that Machiavelli copied two of Lorenzo Strozzi's works (the *Pistola* and the *Commedia in Versi*) because he wished to have both works in his personal library. On the surface this perhaps makes sense, but upon closer inspection of the manuscripts, particularly the *Pistola*, Villari's theory falls short, for it does not explain why Strozzi edited the Machiavelli autograph of the *Pistola*, nor does it explain why Strozzi incorporated most of the changes that he made to the Machiavelli autograph in his own later autograph of the *Pistola*.

of the Medici family, he looked to his friend Francesco Guicciardini for guidance, not to Strozzi.

In August of 1524 Machiavelli wrote a very brief letter to Guicciardini expressing concern over the nature of his *Istorie fiorentine*. He was worried that he might offend Cardinal Giulio with "certain details" that he felt compelled to include in his history of Florence:

> Here in the country I have been applying myself, and continue to do so, to writing the history, and I would pay ten scudi – but no more – to have you by my side so that I might show you where I am, because, since I am about to come to certain details, I would need to learn from you whether or not I am being too offensive in my exaggerating or understating of the fact. Nevertheless, I shall continue to seek advice from myself, and I shall try to do my best to arrange it so that – still telling the truth – no one will have anything to complain about.[15]

This letter's language indicates that Machiavelli was clearly troubled about the "facts." While he claimed that he wanted to "tell the truth," he wanted to do so in such a way as to avoid insult to Giulio de' Medici. Machiavelli did not want to remind Giulio of the bad old days of 1522: it was only two years after the attempt to murder the cardinal, and presumably suspicion still hung over Niccolò's head.

Recall that at the height of Machiavelli's troubles of 1522, Strozzi probably provided Machiavelli with shelter from Giulio's anti-conspiratorial tempest. Yet in 1524 Lorenzo Strozzi was nowhere to be found (at least in Machiavelli's personal correspondence). Machiavelli still needed a well-connected sounding board, so he turned to Guicciardini. This significant piece of evidence suggests that the Strozzi-Machiavelli relationship broke down no later than 1524. In Machiavelli's later personal correspondence, Lorenzo Strozzi does makes two appearances, one in 1525 and one in 1526,

---

15 Machiavelli, *Machiavelli and His Friends: Their Personal Correspondence*, trans. and ed. James B. Atkinson and David Sices (Dekalb: Northern Illinois University Press, 1996), 351, letter 285, 30 August 1524. The Italian original reads "Ho atteso et attendo in villa a scrivere la istoria, e pagherei dieci soldi, non voglio dir più, che voi fosse in lato che io vi potessi mostrare dove io sono, perché, avendo a venire a certi particulari, arei bisogno di intendere da voi se offendo troppo o con lo esaltare o con lo abbassare le cose; pure io mi verrò consigliando, et ingegnerommi di fare in modo che, dicendo il vero, nessuno si possa dolere" (Machiavelli, *Opere, Volume Terzo: Lettere*, ed. Franco Gaeta [Turin: Unione Tipografico Editrice Torinese, 1984], 539, letter 285, 30 August 1524).

and those letters tell us something about Machiavelli's post-1522 relationship with Strozzi. Therein, we find Machiavelli out and about in Florence, writing profusely about his experiences. He was constantly meddling in the affairs of those who were far above his station – particularly Francesco Guicciardini[16] and Lorenzo Strozzi. It is entirely possible that since Machiavelli moved in their rarified social circles he thought he could act as a marriage broker to the Florentine elite; he began to advise Guicciardini on the marriage of his daughter, whom Niccolò wanted to marry Strozzi's son Giambattista.

In a letter dated 17 August 1525, Machiavelli described for Guicciardini a recent encounter that he had with "my friend."[17] Machiavelli's tone is one of heavy irony. He does not even bother to mention who his supposed "friend" was; only through careful analysis of the context does the reader discover that it was Lorenzo Strozzi. Recounting their conversation about the marriage proposal, Machiavelli claimed that Lorenzo spoke the following words: "I think I can figure out on whose behalf you are speaking to me because I know where you have been and this topic has been brought up through another intermediary."[18] In other words, where Machiavelli thought that he was helping to arrange the marriage between the Guicciardini and Strozzi families, and that Lorenzo knew nothing of the affair, Lorenzo knew the whole story. Families such as his had ways of finding out information; and Machiavelli was made to look like a fool. He tried to recover from Strozzi's jabs with the following:

> And, since we had reached the Church of the Servites during the course of our discussion, I stopped in front of its portal and said, "I should like to say these final words to you in a memorable setting so that you will remember them: 'May God grant that you will have nothing to regret about this and that your son will not have little to be grateful to you for.'" So he said, "In God's name, this is the first time we have discussed this topic: we need to speak about it daily." To which I replied that I would never say anything to him about it

16 Felix Gilbert, *Machiavelli and Guicciardini: Politics and History in Sixteenth-Century Florence* (New York: Norton, 1984). For a nicely edited Italian compilation of the letters shared by Machiavelli, Guicciardini, and Vettori, see Machiavelli, *Lettere a Francesco Vettori e a Francesco Guicciardini*, ed. Giorgio Inglese (Milan: Libri e Grandi Opere S.p.A., 1996).

17 Machiavelli, *Personal Correspondence,* letter 296, 17 August 1525, 364. For the Italian edition, see Machiavelli, *Opere, Volume Terzo*, letter 296, 17 August 1525, 558.

18 Machiavelli, *Personal Correspondence*, 364. The original reads "Io mi crederrei apporre per che conto tu mi parli, perché io so dove tu sei stato" (*Lettere*, 558).

> again because it was sufficient that I had settled my debt. This is how I turned my lance; there was no way to conceal what I knew he would discover. Now I shall wait for him to act and not let slip by any opportunity for driving this point home with general and specific discussions.[19]

Knowing what we now know about how Lorenzo Strozzi operated, one could easily argue that he was simply manipulating Machiavelli for sport. If this is the case, then his feigned surprise at the content and cleverness of Machiavelli's conversation appears cruel. However, it had the desired effect: Machiavelli thought that he was outmanoeuvring Lorenzo Strozzi when in fact he was being dexterously outmanoeuvred. Consider the implications of this outcome: Machiavelli, the adviser to princes, was clearly taken to school by Strozzi, the gentleman and courtier. Both were well versed in the wiles of simulation and dissimulation, but the courtier's easy *sprezzatura* gave him the clear edge when the two met, *tête-à-tête*. In other words, Machiavelli the cynical realist was neither as cynical nor as realistic as the courtier.

This conclusion is clearly illustrated in a letter that Machiavelli wrote to Guicciardini on 2 June 1526 in which he described another conversation he had with "L S" (Machiavelli did not even use Strozzi's full name). He was still trying to arrange a marriage between Guicciardini's daughter and Lorenzo's son, but Lorenzo had been delaying the marriage talks for a number of reasons: First, he reminded Machiavelli that his wife's health had been bad for a long time and that she was only then recovering. Second, he claimed that his son had been wasting his time and his substance for the past year and that only recently had he begun to associate with people who possessed an acceptable, educated background. Finally, Machiavelli learned that Lorenzo had also been working on a marriage for his daughter that had taken up most of his time and money. All of these things might have been true; but since Lorenzo's son Giambattista was married

19 Machiavelli, *Personal Correspondence*, 364. The original reads: "E perché noi andavamo in su questo ragionamento a Servi, io mi fermai su la porta, e gli dissi: 'Io vi voglio dire questa ultima parola in luogo memorabile, acciò che voi ve ne ricordiate: Iddio volgia che voi non ve ne abbiate a pentire, et il figliolo vostro non abbia averne poco obbligo con voi'; tanto che disse: 'Al nome di Iddio, questa è la prima volta che noi ne abbiamo ragionato; noi ci abbiamo a parlare ogni dì.' A che io dissi, che non ero mai più er dirgliene nulla, perché mi bastava avere pagato il debito mio. Io ho vòlto questa lancia in questo modo, né si è potuto celare quello che io ero certo che si aveva a scoprire. Sono bene ora per aspettare lui e non mancare di ogni occasione, e con ragionamenti generali e particulari battere a questo segno" (*Lettere*, 558).

to Maria di Bindo Altoviti not long after Machiavelli's attempts to unite the Guicciardini and Strozzi families, Niccolò was caught between the noble yet benign Guicciardini and Strozzi's callous amusements.[20] While Guicciardini's role in the matter seems to have been genuine, Strozzi allowed Niccolò to think that the latter was running the negotiations when in fact he was once again being manipulated by Strozzi, in a rather cruel game. If, somehow, Strozzi and Machiavelli remained linked post-1522, or even as late as 1524, by 1525–26 the patron-client relationship between the two men had run its course.

Final Thoughts on Strozzi, Machiavelli, and the *Pistola fatta per la peste*

The bizarre union between Strozzi and Machiavelli produced the *Pistola*, and so it is no wonder that the *Pistola*'s form and content are twisted. They reflect the strained identities and the relationship and environment of its authors. Yet the *Pistola* is more than that. For a brief moment, in the imagined world of the text, both men set aside their masks, their fashioned public images, and embraced the fleeting freedom of a literary experiment that allowed each to overcome intense political isolation. The *Pistola* allows us to understand Strozzi, Machiavelli, and Renaissance Florence on a different level.

One is left with a rather interesting *dénouement*. Machiavelli, who is properly revered as a political genius, understood the real-world machinations of Florence's aristocratic families, but not necessarily how they would affect his own life if he did not tailor his behavior to ingratiate himself with them.[21] Representative of those families, Lorenzo di Filippo Strozzi's abilities to navigate the turbulence of Florence's and Italy's political climate almost untouched speaks to his mastery of *sprezzatura* and of his ability to

20 John Najemy, *Between Friends: Discourses of Power and Desire in the Machiavelli-Vettori Letters of 1513–1515* (Princeton: Princeton University Press, 1993), letter 311, 389.

21 If he completely understood the *grandi*, would Machiavelli have written, under Cardinal Giulio de' Medici's name, a suggestion for the republican reform of Florence in 1522? This "revision" of Machiavelli as imperfectly aware of his often dangerous surroundings was forcefully set out in Peter Godman, *From Poliziano to Machiavelli* (Princeton: Princeton University Press, 1998). For some of Machiavelli's missteps, see esp. chap. 5, "The Prince and the Plant." For an analysis of Machiavelli's literary/political treatment of the Florentine aristocracy, see Alfredo Bonadeo, "The Role of the 'Grandi' in the Political World of Machiavelli," *Studies in the Renaissance* 16 (1969): 9–30.

"stage-manage" those in his circle. Even when Lorenzo was finally allowed, perhaps forced, to show his true republican self during the final days of the last Florentine republic, he did so without losing his status or reputation upon the Medici restoration. Courtiers and survivors such as Strozzi, men who shaped their image to fit any situation and were willing to sacrifice their own patriotic, republican interests for the survival of their family, were simultaneously bound together and at odds with idealists like Machiavelli. One might argue, as Guicciardini did, that tensions between courts and republics, personified in the relationship between Strozzi and Machiavelli, writ large in Florentine history and larger still between the Italian city-states themselves, birthed the flourishing of the Italian cities that we now call the Renaissance.[22]

But by 1527, the year that Machiavelli died and the year that Rome was put to the sack, "the Machiavellian moment" so famously described by J.G.A. Pocock dissolved into the epoch of Lorenzo Strozzi, *sprezzatura,* and the triumph of the Italian courts over republicanism. Caught in purgatory, the courtier's hall of mirrors and shifting identities, Machiavelli's legacy – his idealism, his genius, and his romanticism *avant la lettre* – was persecuted and reviled. This picture is a sad combination of the irony that was a hallmark of Machiavelli's style and the tragedy of his lack of contemporary recognition. Perhaps the reconciliation of his irony and his tragedy in this short study may give Machiavelli's perturbed spirit a little rest. More certainly, Lorenzo di Filippo Strozzi is now restored to his proper place in Florentine history.

22 For Guicciardini's reflections on Machiavelli's *Discourses* I.12, see Guicciardini, "Considerations of the *Discourses* of Niccolò Machiavelli," in *The Sweetness of Power: Machiavelli's* Discourses *and Guicciardini's* Considerations, trans. James B. Atkinson and David Sices (Dekalb: Northern Illinois University Press, 2002), 404–5.

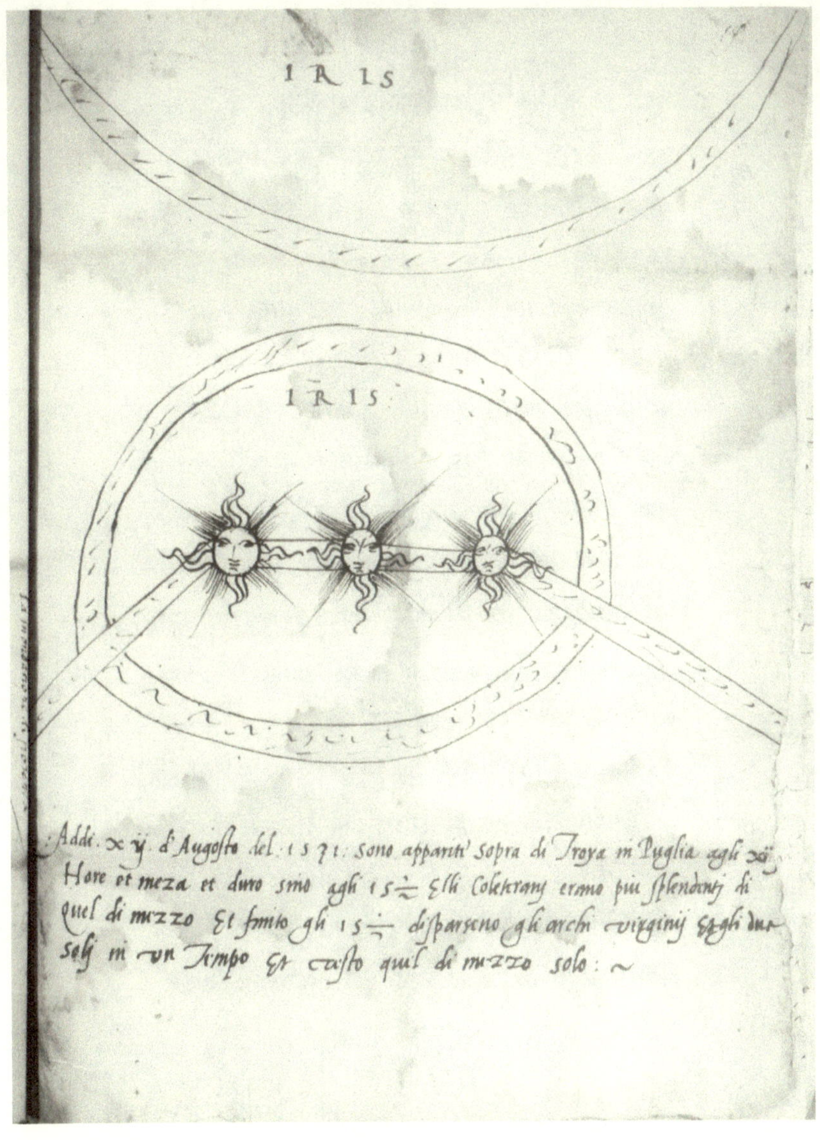

Figure 1. Florence, Biblioteca Nazionale Centrale, MS. Fondo Nazionale II.IV. 197, 19r. With the permission of the Ministero per i Beni e le Attività Culturali della Repubblica Italiana/Biblioteca Nazionale Centrale di Firenze.

Allo Excellentissimo Sig.re Cosimo
De' Medici Duca di Firenze.
Lorenzo Strozzi

Considerando io Ill.mo Duca; come quasi tutti gli
Scrittori indirizano l'opere loro à quelle perso=
ne, che per vertu, nobiltà, gloria, ò amicitia, piu
degne ne paiono loro; ò ueramente à quelle, da cui
hano riceuto, ò sperano di riceuere, honore ò utile;
& uolendo fare io il medesimo, certo nò uedeua à
chi questi miei scritti della Patienza piu meritamẽte
si conuenissero, ne cò chi io hauessi maggiore obligo,
ò chi mi potesse piu benificare, che la Ecc.tia vra;
Nò dimeno mi riteneua da si fatto proponimẽto il
nò giudicare io, quegli essere tali, che meritassero ue=
nire in luce, nò che nel cospetto di cosi raro, et glo=
rioso Principe; parendomi (et ragioneuolmẽte) potere
essere ripreso di prosuntione, ogni uolta che io mi

Figure 2. Florence, Biblioteca Nazionale Centrale, MS. Magl., XXXV, 32. Lorenzo di Filippo Strozzi, *Trattato della Patienza*, 1r. With the permission of the Ministero per i Beni e le Attività Culturali della Repubblica Italiana/Biblioteca Nazionale Centrale di Firenze.

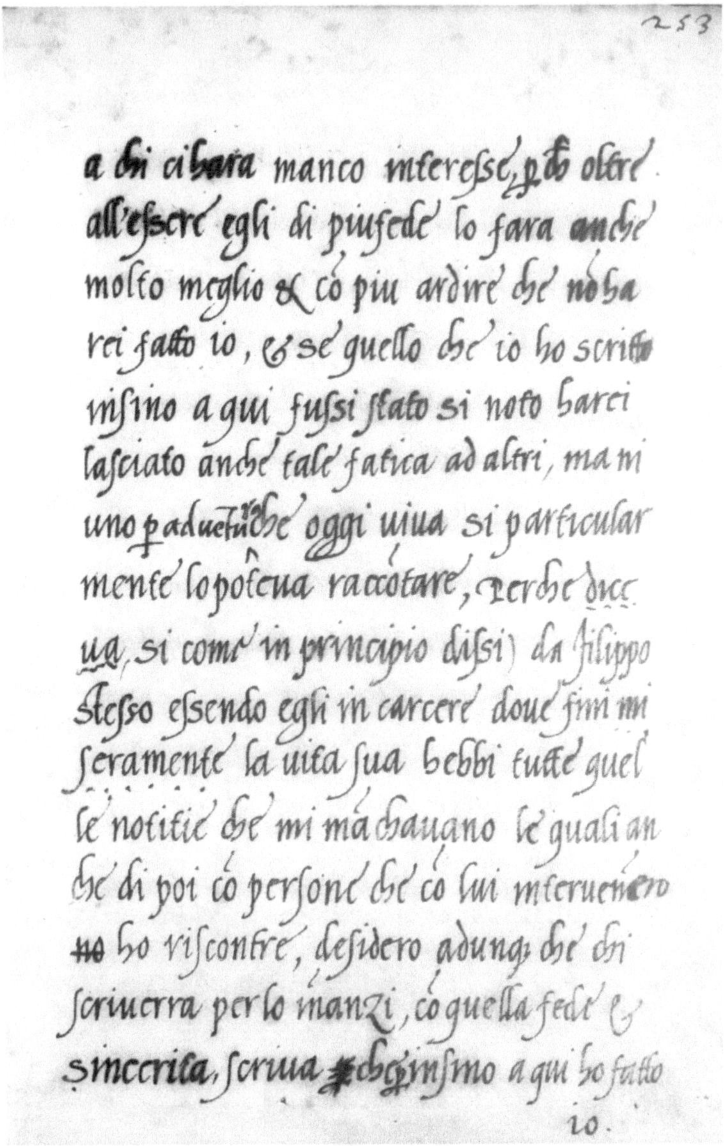

253

a chi ci harà manco interesse, però oltre
all'essere egli di piu fede lo farà anche
molto meglio & cō piu ardire che nō ha
rei fatto io, & se quello che io ho scritto
insino a qui fussi stato si noto harei
lasciato anche tale fatica ad altri, ma mi
uno paduetu che oggi uiua si particular
mente lo potena raccōtare, perche dice
ua, si come in principio dissi) da filippo
stesso essendo egli in carcere doue fini mi
seramente la uita sua hebbi tutte quel
le notitie che mi mācauano le quali an
che di poi cō persone che cō lui interuenero
no ho riscontre, desidero adunq. che chi
scriuerrà per lo inanzi, cō quella fede &
sincerità, scriua che insino a qui ho fatto
io.

Figure 3. Florence, Biblioteca Nazionale Centrale, MS. Gino Capponi, Lorenzo di Filippo Strozzi, *Vite di personaggi di casa Strozzi*, 253r. With the permission of the Ministero per i Beni e le Attività Culturali della Repubblica Italiana/Biblioteca Nazionale Centrale di Firenze.

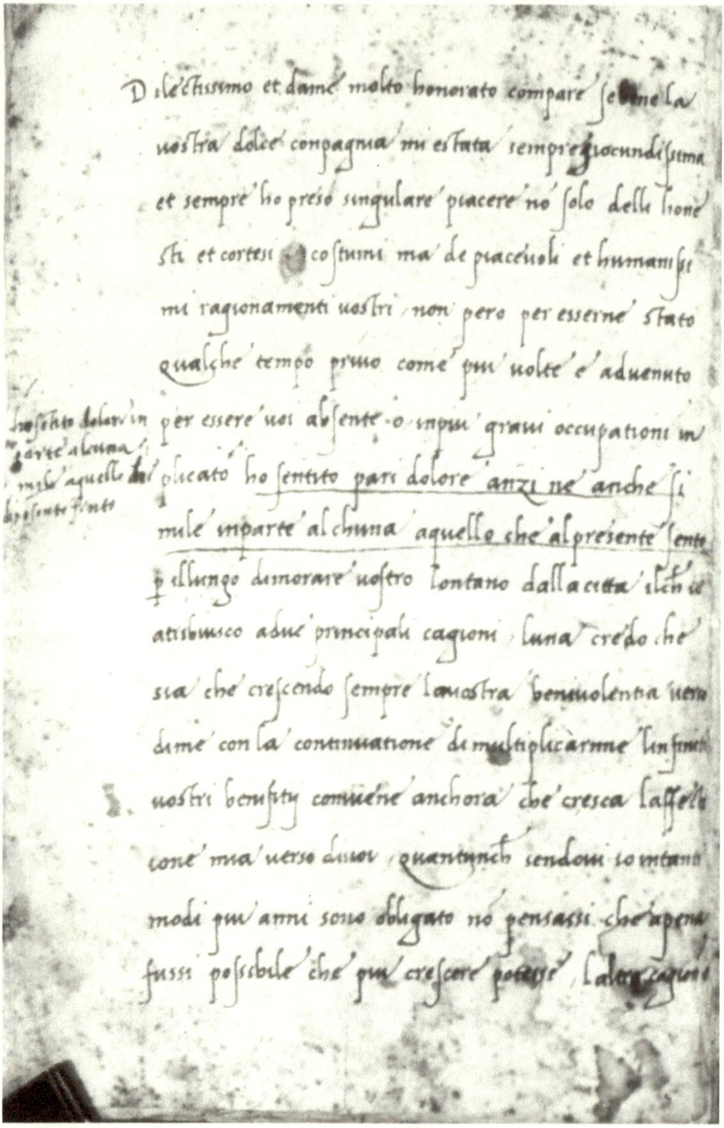

Figure 4. Florence, Biblioteca Nazionale Centrale, MS. Banco Rari 29, Lorenzo di Filippo Strozzi, *Epistola fatta per la peste*, 3v. With the permission of the Ministero per i Beni e le Attività Culturali della Repubblica Italiana/Biblioteca Nazionale Centrale di Firenze.

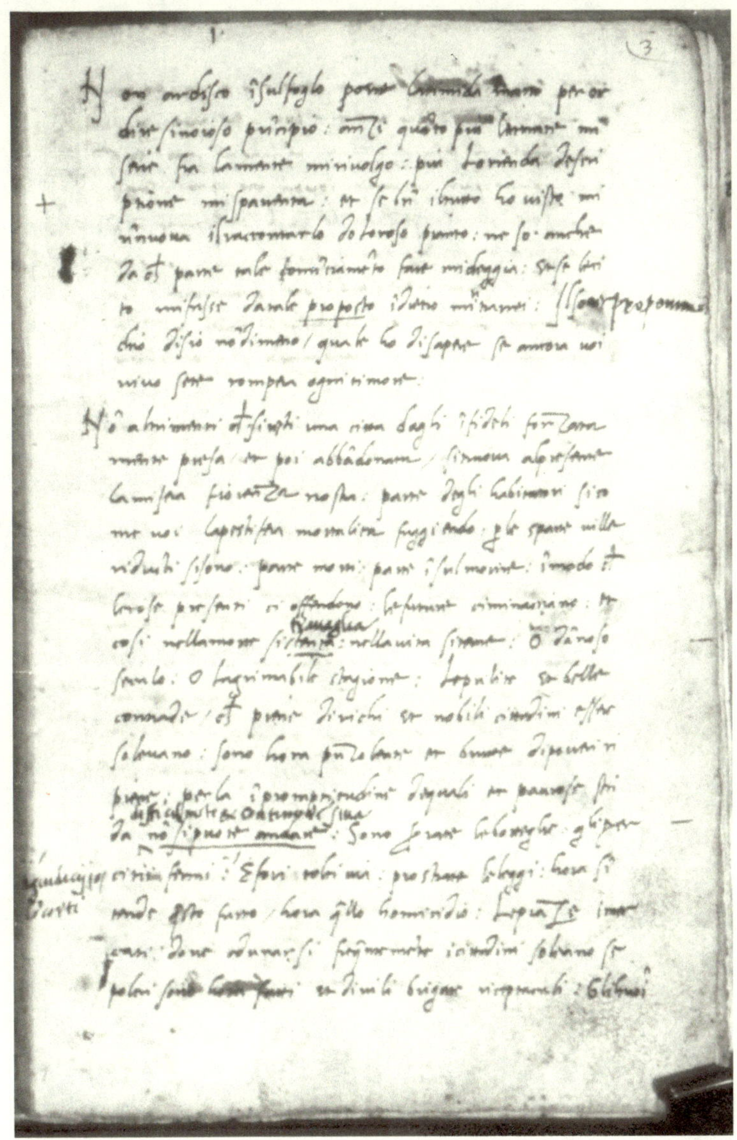

Figure 5. Florence, Biblioteca Nazionale Centrale, MS. Banco Rari 29, Lorenzo di Filippo Strozzi, *Epistola fatta per la peste*, 9r. With the permission of the Ministero per i Beni e le Attività Culturali della Repubblica Italiana/Biblioteca Nazionale Centrale di Firenze.

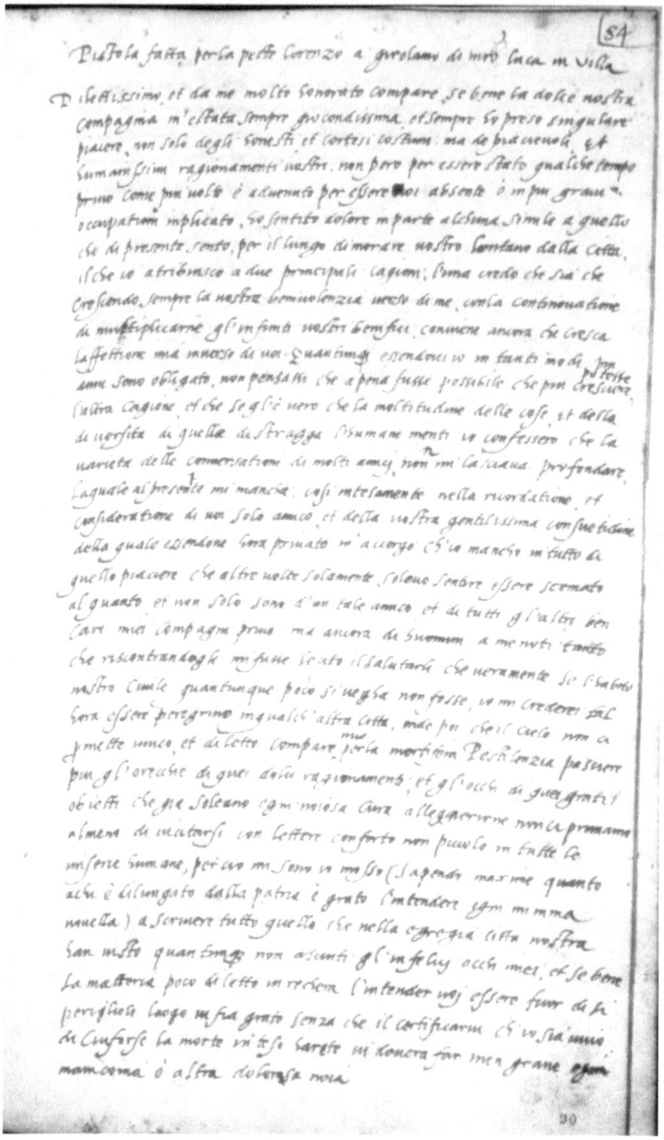

84

Pistola fatta per la peste Lorenzo a girolamo di mess. luca in villa

Dilectissimo et da me molto honorato compare, se bene la dolce nostra compagnia m'è stata sempre giocondissima et sempre ne preso singulare piacere, non solo degli honesti et cortesi costumi ma de piacevoli et humanissimi ragionamenti vostri, non però per essere stato qualche tempo privo come più volte è advenuto per esser voi absente o in più grave occupationi implicato, ho sentito dolore in parte alchuna simile a questo che di presente sento, per il lungo dimorare nostro lontano dalla città, il che io atribuisco a due principali cagioni; l'una credo che sia che crescendo sempre la vostra benivolenzia verso di me, con la continuatione di multiplicarne gl'infiniti vostri benefici, conviene ancora che cresca l'affectione mia inverso di voi.

Figure 6. Florence, Biblioteca Medicea Laurenziana, MS. Ashb., 606, Lorenzo di Filippo Strozzi, *Pistola fatta per la peste*, 84r. With the permission of the Ministero per i Beni e le Attività Culturali E' vietata ogni ulteriore riproduzione con qualsiasi mezzo. (Additional reproductions of this figure by any other means are prohibited.)

Lorenzo di Filippo Strozzi's *Pistola fatta per la peste*: An Italian Edition and an English Translation

Editor's Foreword

Concentrated thought, several false starts, and excellent advice from a number of scholars, including Professor Brian Richardson, my friends Dr Simone Testa and Dr William Gartig, and a very fine and patient philologist at the University of Toronto, led me to construct a reading text of the *Pistola*, primarily because a reading text will be the most useful for the largest number of readers. Because I wanted to increase this edition's accessibility, I also produced an English translation that is found on the facing pages of the Italian reading text. I confess that I had some misgivings about producing a reading text that aimed to reconstruct Strozzi's intended text of the *Pistola*,[1] misgivings that resulted from my own conservative approach to editing: I harbour theoretical reservations about imposing my own editorial judgments on Strozzi's texts, and a general wariness of modernized texts. But producing diplomatic transcriptions of Manuscript B (Banco Rari 29) and Manuscript A (Ashburnham 606), which I initially undertook as a part of a genetic reconstruction of the *Pistola*'s development, proved to be an unnecessarily complex treatment given the *Pistola*'s brevity, and at odds with my goals in producing this edition in the first place. Simply put, I wanted to construct an edition of the *Pistola* that was accurate, readable, easy to navigate, and uncluttered. However, working

1 G. Thomas Tanselle's many essays on the theory and practice of editing historical documents, and on producing edited works derived from multiple manuscript sources, have been a source of inspiration, especially his "Texts of Documents and Texts of Works," in *Textual Criticism and Scholarly Editing*, ed. G. Thomas Tanselle (Charlottesville: University of Virginia Press, 1990), 5–23.

through that initial, since jettisoned, genetic edition did clarify my editorial vision for this present one.

Overview

I chose Manuscript A as my base text for this edition. After all, it is Strozzi's personal copy of the *Pistola*, it incorporates nearly all of the changes that he made to Manuscript B (the majority of which is in Machiavelli's hand), and it includes the name of the work's intended recipient, an important detail not found in Manuscript B. Of fundamental importance, using Manuscript A as the base text also helps to illustrate one of the central themes of this book: that the relationship between Strozzi and Machiavelli was strained. When Machiavelli undertook the menial task of transcribing the *Pistola* for Strozzi, his immense intellect must have groaned under its mediocrity, even as he delighted in Strozzi's perverse vision of Florence. Highlighting this strained relationship, on several occasions the Machiavelli autograph portion of Manuscript B provides better readings than Manuscript A's.

What might this tell us about how Strozzi viewed his *Pistola*, and by extension his relationship with Machiavelli? It seems likely that Strozzi did not take the project all that seriously. For him, this was escapist literature that allowed him to imaginatively live the life of a fun-loving and carefree rogue. And time spent with Machiavelli would undoubtedly have been stimulating. We might also hypothesize that Machiavelli's republicanism influenced Strozzi's own political sentiment, since in 1522, when the *Pistola* was probably written, Strozzi's turn toward open republicanism was just beginning. Ironically, it is probable that in turn Strozzi's oligarchic republican tendencies influenced Machiavelli as he wrote the *Minuta*, circa 1522 (discussed at length in chapter 2 and in appendix 4). More concretely, it is possible to conclude that Machiavelli's intellectual seriousness demonstrably affected Strozzi.

This is illustrated by examining Strozzi's autograph portion of Manuscript B. The *Pistola*'s introductory epistle, for example, is written in Strozzi's beautiful, unhurried, and chancellor-esque hand, one that is also occasionally more accurate than his textual renderings in Manuscript A, his authorial copy of the *Pistola*. Machiavelli's autograph portion of Manuscript B possesses his usual precision; he seems to have fully invested himself in the project and in his obligations to Lorenzo Strozzi.

When we turn to Strozzi's authorial copy of the *Pistola,* we see that it was more carelessly produced than Manuscript B; it seems plausible that, absent the involvement of Machiavelli, Strozzi's dedication lessened. In fact, when both manuscripts are considered, Machiavelli's portion of Manuscript B seems to be the more important witness to the intended text of the *Pistola* than Strozzi's own copy of it. If so, one might reasonably wonder: why was Manuscript A chosen as the base text for this edition of the *Pistola*?

My reasons are practical as well as scholarly: Manuscript B had already been edited, albeit without much critical treatment, by a number of excellent nineteenth-century scholars, including Filippo-Luigi Polidori.[2] More importantly, the editors of the *Edizione Nazionale delle Opere di Niccolò Machiavelli* are presently preparing an edition of Machiavelli's autograph works, which is sure to include the Banco Rari 29 text of the *Pistola*. If I had chosen to use Manuscript B as my base text simply to beat the National Edition to press, the benefits and usefulness of my edition would probably be short lived. But I do not want to give the impression that I turned to Manuscript A out of some fatalistic sentiment. Far from it: my decision was based on scholarly goals.

One of my scholarly considerations was that Strozzi's personal copy of the *Pistola* has never been edited or published. This edition of the *Pistola* will therefore bring to light a "new" early sixteenth-century manuscript with a critical apparatus that allows the reader to compare Manuscript A with Manuscript B. Manuscript A is of course a copy of Manuscript B; and as is sometimes the case with copies, it not only introduces a number of variant readings, transcription errors, and inferior readings of the material found in Manuscript B, but it also includes important emendations that were not included in the earlier manuscript. When the two manuscripts are considered together, then, both seem to fall short of Strozzi's "intended" text. And it is the intended text that interests me; hence, with the unpublished Manuscript A acting as my base text, I turned to Manuscript B when its readings proved superior to those found in A. This method helped me to reconstruct what I believe to be Strozzi's intended text of the *Pistola*. The method allows one to trace the textual interaction between Strozzi and Machiavelli by recording orthographic as well as substantive variants in

2 See Niccolò Machiavelli, *Opere minori di Niccolò Machiavelli: Rivedute sulle migliori edizioni, con note filologiche e critiche di F-L Polidori* (Florence: Le Monnier, 1852), 415–28. Polidori's edition influenced my own. He sensitively introduced paragraphs and punctuation that helped me to reconstruct the intended text of the *Pistola*. See notes below for further comments.

the critical apparatus. And as noted, it also sheds light on the relationship between Strozzi and Machiavelli.

The principle that most guided me, that gave me the editorial conviction necessary to use Manuscript A as my base text, was articulated by Paul Oskar Kristeller. He once wrote that minor texts, and Strozzi's own copy of the *Pistola* qualifies as a lesser text than Manuscript B, can "be of great interest for the relations of their authors with greater contemporaries."[3] Lorenzo di Filippo Strozzi was a fascinating and important Florentine, whose contributions to politics and literature have remained relatively obscure. His *Pistola* is not a great piece of literature; its greatness derives from Machiavelli's involvement in its production. This study of the *Pistola* gives us some new insights into Strozzi's life, but it also helps us to plumb the depths to which Machiavelli's "ferocious genius" had sunk by 1522, perhaps giving us a clearer understanding of Machiavelli's life in the early 1520s.

The Details

As I noted above, during preparation of this edition of the *Pistola* I had to confront my own conservative editorial inclinations, which did not serve the goals of this edition well.[4] In the end, I made a number of editorial decisions that I hope the reader will find sound, reasonable, and useful. These decisions, or concessions, which balance some conservative aspects of textual reconstruction with a modernizing approach, were undertaken in order to make the reading text just that – readable.

3 Paul Oskar Kristeller, *Studies in Renaissance Thought and Letters*, ol. 4 (Rome: Edizioni di Storia e Letteratura, 1996), 458.

4 Along with Tanselle's scholarship, cited above, Pierre-Marc de Biasi's methodological essays on genetic criticism proved fascinating, though his methods were not really suitable for this reading edition. For a good introduction to de Biasi's vision of the "genetic text," see "Toward a Science of Literature: Manuscript Analysis and the Genesis of the Work," in *Genetic Criticism: Texts and Avant-textes*, ed. Jed Deppman, Daniel Ferrer, and Michael Groden (Philadelphia: University of Pennsylvania Press, 2004): 36–68. Giorgio Inglese's recent text *Come si legge un'edizione critica* (Rome: Carocci, 2000) was also very helpful on a number of points.

Lineation and Numeration

The left-hand margin of the reading text contains line numbers. These were introduced as I reconstructed the text and are not keyed to the A manuscript's lineation. However, it seemed best to preserve both manuscripts' foliation, so I have inserted, in the place of line "1", Manuscript A's folio number. Retaining original foliation allowed me to signify the first and last words of each folio in my edition. Additionally, in the body of the text I inserted Manuscript B's folio numbers. The word immediately following these numbers is the first word of that particular folio, and the word immediately preceding the next folio number is the last word of that particular folio. This method assists the reader who wishes to consult the original manuscripts, and it does so without cluttering the text.

Spelling, Capitalization, Word Spacing, and Paragraphs

Strozzi's and Machiavelli's original spelling is retained throughout in order to highlight the many differences in their orthography. This seemed to be the best way to record the textual interaction between the two Florentines. The letter forms "u/v" and "j/i" have been recorded as they appear in the manuscripts. On a few occasions this conservative approach introduced unsightly transcriptions, but these minor sacrifices were necessary to preserve the orthographic and phonetic texture of Strozzi's and Machiavelli's language.[5] Similarly, I chose to record accents as they are presented in the manuscripts without modernizing them.[6]

While this conservative approach does introduce numerous seemingly inconsequential variations, it helps to illustrate how very differently both

5 This policy introduced transcriptions such as "glj" (89v 4) and "cjedendo" (88v 25) into the edition.

6 Given that I chose to modernize a number of elements in the *Pistola*, Some might question why I elected not to modernize accents and apostrophes. I find that Strozzi's and Machiavelli's use of those components is so closely related to their orthography that adding (or removing) accents or apostrophes would essentially entail modernization and homogenization of their spelling, something I was not willing to do. My decision to add punctuation admittedly reveals the strains between the conservative approach that I favour and the modernizing concessions I made when editing the *Pistola*. But, to put it bluntly, it was necessary to draw the line regarding modernization in a way that allowed me to reconstruct what I suggest is the intended text of the *Pistola*, while leaving the minutiae – accents, apostrophes, distinctions between *u/v* and *j/i*, and all of the other orthographical differences exhibited in the manuscripts – unmolested.

men wrote: Machiavelli's spelling is more consistent, perhaps reflecting his chancellor's training, while Strozzi's varies widely, frequently from one line to the next. Even in this tedious chore, Machiavelli approached his scribal duties with seriousness where Strozzi, in Manuscript A at least, appears to have taken very little care. Modernizing their written language would have weakened this important point of comparison. But it proved very helpful to balance out this conservative editorial practice with a number of modernizing concessions, three of which I will mention here.[7] First, I standardized Strozzi's and Machiavelli's use of capitalization, which follows modern usage. Second, I chose to introduce modern word spacing in the reading text and in the critical apparatus, making the edition much more accessible. Finally, I introduced paragraph divisions to aid readability.[8]

Abbreviations

Initially, I had planned to preserve Strozzi's and Machiavelli's abbreviations by signifying them with parentheses, such as "no(n)". However, this method produced a page that resembled a paleographical exercise rather than a reading text; it was rejected in favour of silent expansion.[9] I recognize that this method might seem to contradict my policy regarding original spelling; in its favour, Strozzi and Machiavelli used abbreviations in almost exactly the same manner, and so nothing, or very little, is lost by silently expanding their abbreviations. It is, however, useful to discuss Strozzi's and Machiavelli's use of the ampersand (&),which is both more complex and apparently more random than their usage of other abbreviations.

7 If my edition sought only to reproduce the manuscript witnesses of the *Pistola*, modernization of all forms would have been rejected. Since this edition, though based on Manuscript A, also strives to reconstruct the intended text of the work, some deviation from the original manuscripts was deemed necessary and appropriate.

8 While I followed Manuscript A's paragraphs, I supplemented the text's original paragraph divisions with those inserted by Filippo Luigi Polidori in his 1852 edition of the *Pistola*. Though his edition only had recourse to Manuscript B of the *Pistola*, he retained the paragraphs present in that manuscript (which appear identically in Manuscript A) while adding just enough of his own to aid the reader. As is the case with his added punctuation, Polidori very sensitively modernized these two elements of the text.

9 I thank Professor Brian Richardson for his advice on the treatment of abbreviations in this edition.

In Manuscript B, to give one example, Machiavelli almost exclusively used an ampersand as an abbreviation for both the verb *è* and the conjunction *et*. Contextual analysis and comparisons with Manuscript A allowed me to determine which word, *è* or *et*, Strozzi, through his scribe, intended to use, and to transcribe it as such. In Strozzi's autograph portion of Manuscript B, however, he used the ampersand as an abbreviation for *et* but always wrote out the verb *è* (though never with the accent), making it easy to distinguish his intentions. Manuscript A presents a still less complicated picture: therein, Strozzi always spelled out the conjunction *et* and the verb *è* (always with the accent), making it much easier to interpret his intentions.

It seems that the complexities presented by Manuscript B caused Strozzi to introduce an error into Manuscript A: there is one instance in Manuscript B where Strozzi included *è* (unabbreviated and without an accent) but at the corresponding point in Manuscript A he instead recorded *et* (unabbreviated).[10] This difference affected the meaning of both manuscripts. The reading provided by Manuscript B was superior to that of A, and was therefore incorporated in the text of my edition. This and all other textual changes that I made to the base text are recorded in the edition's critical apparatus.[11]

Punctuation

I chose to follow Manuscript A's punctuation, which is very close to B's, and to key Manuscript B's to Manuscript A's.[12] As one would expect from an early *cinquecento* text, however, Strozzi's punctuation in Manuscript A is sparse at best, and so I have also silently added punctuation to make the

---

10 Examples such as this drive home Tanselle's point that "an authorial fair-copy … cannot be assumed to represent the author's intention in every respect (it may well introduce unintended slips, for example)." See "Texts and Documents," 16.

11 See 84r 14 in the edition that follows.

12 Therefore, differences in punctuation are not included in the critical apparatus. In Manuscript A, Strozzi used apostrophes, commas, colons, round brackets, periods, question marks, and semicolons. In Manuscript B, Machiavelli used the very same punctuation marks in the body of the text (far more than usual) and Strozzi used forward slashes and round brackets in B's introductory epistle and in his textual emendations. For more background on Machiavelli's use of punctuation signs, see Paolo Ghiglieri, *La Grafia del Machiavelli: Studiata negli Autografi* (Florence: Leo S. Olschki, 1969), 314–25.

text more readily comprehensible.[13] These additions, combined with modernized word spacing, silently expanded abbreviations, and standardized capitalization, created recognizable sentence and paragraph structures that helped to expose what I suggest is the intended text of the *Pistola*. The translation of the *Pistola* that is included on the facing pages of the Italian reading edition reflects modern punctuation usage.

Text, Apparatus, and the Translation

I used the presentational systems above, and the editorial methods outlined below, to reach what I believe is Lorenzo di Filippo Strozzi's intended text of the *Pistola*. In order to reconstruct the intended text, I relied on Strozzi's authorial copy, Manuscript A, but I altered that text using two criteria. First, when I encountered therein obvious errors of transcription, or omission of material that was present in Manuscript B, I opted for the reading provided by the latter. (As an example of such transcription errors, Manuscript A's *alieno* was rendered correctly as *al remo* by Machiavelli in Manuscript B. By "errors" I do not mean different use of prepositions such as *a* and *ad*, or *e* and *et*, among other possible examples; these are treated as orthographical variations, not errors.)[14] Second, I opted for the best possible reading. If both manuscripts provided suitable readings but Manuscript B's was superior, I chose the latter. (For example, Manuscript A contained *essere* in one passage of the *Pistola*, which, based on the context, is grammatically acceptable. Manuscript B, however, contained *esserne*, which is contextually superior.)[15] All of these editorial decisions are clearly noted for the reader in the critical apparatus, which is found at the foot of the page, below the Italian edition of the *Pistola*.

In that critical apparatus the reader will also find textual variations (orthographic and substantive) presented in the traditional format: lemma] variant, such as "**84r 2** Dilettissimo] Dilectissimo". "84r" refers to the folio

13 As with the paragraph divisions that I inserted, the additional punctuation I inserted follows, though not exactly, Filippo Luigi Polidori's 1852 edition of the *Pistola*.

14 *Al remo* and *alieno* provide one example of a transcription error. In other cases, Manuscript A contains verbs that lack reflexive pronouns, which are present in Manuscript B; or the verb tense in Manuscript B is superior to that of Manuscript A. In such cases I relied on B's reading. Orthographical differences between the manuscripts are noted in the critical apparatus.

15 See 84r 6 of this edition.

number of Manuscript A, "2" is the line number in the edition, "Dilettissimo" is the lemma from Manuscript A, and "Dilectissimo" is the variant reading provided by Manuscript B. If the reading found in Manuscript B is superior, the reader will find the following format employed: lemma] *A* variant, where the italicized siglum "A" refers to Manuscript A.

In an effort to present variations and textual comments in an uncluttered format, I have kept editorial symbols to a minimum. I chose to use only four: square brackets, which are employed to separate the lemma from its variant; curly brackets, used around hypothetical transcriptions; single quotation marks, placed around letters to signify where Strozzi and Machiavelli emended them or where ink splashes obscure them; and vertical lines, which act as separators between textual variants. Textual comments that are associated only with Manuscript A are not prefaced with the italicized siglum "A", whereas textual comments associated only with Manuscript B are always prefaced with "B" in italics. And as we are only dealing with two hands, Strozzi's and Machiavelli's, rather than assigning Greek sigla to them I distinguish them by using "L. Strozzi" and "Machiavelli."[16] As all of Manuscript A is in Strozzi's hand, there was no need to reference his identity when he emended the text. Where Manuscript B, which survives in Machiavelli's and Strozzi's hands, is concerned, I noted in a brief prose commentary the identity, and activity, of the hand in question.

Intertextual commentary and definitions of rare, particularly Florentine words are found below the English translation that faces the Italian edition. This commentary is keyed to the lineation and numeration of the Italian edition. Keying the English translation to the edition's numeration proved impractical because Strozzi's original sentence structure had to be reordered, making a literal translation impossible. Therefore, the English translation is presented without numeration or lineation, though it is still quite easy to move from the Italian edition to the English translation and vice versa.

One of the problems with placing the translation on the verso, or left-hand, page facing the Italian edition is that sometimes the translated text could not be made to fit on that verso. This was unavoidable. Conversely,

16 Here, I recognize that a genetic edition might have been useful, particularly if the stages of Manuscript B's development were assigned numerical signifiers, such as B1 for Strozzi's epilogue (3v–4v), B2 for Machiavelli's autograph portion of the text (9r–17r), B3 for Machiavelli's emendations, and B4 for Strozzi's. However, for ease of access, I use Manuscript A as my base text and to provide very brief prose descriptions of Machiavelli's and Strozzi's emendations to the *Pistola* manuscripts.

as intertextual commentary was not required for every page of the translation, some pages contain blank space at their foot. Other pages of the translation required lengthy intertextual references; these are presented in a smaller font to fit them on the appropriate page. These are all problems of small import, but worth noting briefly here.

Descriptions of the Witnesses

Manuscript B

Epistola fatta per la peste, Florence, Biblioteca Nazionale Centrale, MS Banco Rari 29 (formerly Magliabechiano classe VIII, 1451 bis, formerly Fondo Strozzi, 4^0, n. 366), (214 x 144 mm), 3v–4v, 9r–17r, is written on paper from the first quarter of the sixteenth century.

After examining numerous Strozzi autographs, I suggest that the dedicatory epistle (3v–4v) that precedes the body of the *Pistola*, in Manuscript B, ought to be re-categorized as a Lorenzo di Filippo Strozzi autograph even though nineteenth-century scholars suggested that the hand was unknown.[17] The body of the *Pistola*, probably written after the dedicatory epistle, survives almost entirely in Machiavelli's hand (9r–17r), though Strozzi emended the text on numerous occasions.[18] These emendations are noted in the edition's critical apparatus, as are the few instances where Machiavelli emended the text.

Strozzi and Machiavelli adhered to similar methods when they emended the text of Manuscript B. Interlinear and marginal additions are

---

17 Filippo Luigi Polidori concluded that the hand was unknown, but it was possible that the hand that produced the introductory epistle might have been the same hand that provided correction to Machiavelli's portion of the text; see *Opere Minori,* 417n, for Polidori's comments. A comment on a Lorenzo Strozzi autograph in Caroline Elam's well-known work on the Piazza Strozzi clarified my conclusions. She paid particular attention to the manner in which the final *e* in Strozzi's handwriting ended with a unique ascending flourish. The *Pistola*'s introductory letter writer's hand contains the same *e* and many other similarities that strongly indicate it is an autograph. See p. 126n15 in Elam's "Piazza Strozzi: Two Drawings by Baccio d'Agnolo and the Problems of a Private Renaissance Square," *I Tatti Studies* 1 (1985): 105–35, 274–86

18 I realize it is possible that the body of the B manuscript predated the dedicatory epistle, but the evidence at hand suggests the development of the manuscript as detailed above.

accompanied by carets, or the symbol "%", both of which indicate where such additions are to be placed in the body of the text. Deletions are either underlined or struck through. Deletions that are to be replaced by additions combine these editorial methods and symbols. The emendations made to the text of Manuscript B by Strozzi and Machiavelli are unambiguous, presenting me with very few difficulties other than deciphering deleted passages in Machiavelli's script. Strozzi's handwriting (including his emendations) is, as mentioned previously, elegant and unhurried. Machiavelli's hand, as those who have encountered it know, requires a certain amount of patience to decipher.

The remaining manuscript folios, 1r–3r and 5r–8v, probably added after the dedicatory epistle and the body of the *Pistola* were written, are not technically a part of the *Pistola*'s text. But, as they provide important contextual information about the production and reception of the text, the reader will find them transcribed in the appendix to this edition.

Manuscript A

Pistola fatta per la peste Lorenzo a' Girolamo di Maestro Luca in Villa, Florence, Biblioteca Medicea Laurenziana, MS Ashburnham 606, (330 x 235 mm), 84r–89v, is a Lorenzo Strozzi autograph, written on paper from the first quarter of the sixteenth century. The Ashburnham codex contains numerous works by Lorenzo di Filippo Strozzi, most of which are autographs.[19]

The editorial methods Strozzi adopted for the production of Manuscript A are identical to those he and Machiavelli used in Manuscript B. While Manuscript A's emendations are usually straightforward, there is one notable exception: folio 87v of Manuscript A records multiple readings of a passage. It remains unclear which reading Strozzi preferred, and so I chose Manuscript B's superior reading. I note, however, that Manuscript B's reading was also emended by Strozzi, although in this instance his intentions were readily discernible. In order to explain fully my decisions regarding the treatment of this passage (see 87v 23–25 in the edition), it is necessary to examine the passage in question in both manuscripts.

19 The most comprehensive study of the Ashburnham 606 is Pio Ferrieri, "Lorenzo di Filippo Strozzi e un codice Ashburnhamiano," in *Studi di storia e critica letteraria* (Milan: E. Trevisini, 1892): 221–32.

Manuscript B's original reading of the passage in question, found on 13v–14r of Banco Rari 29, reads:

> il uenerabile padre frate Alexo, che forse quiui per confessare fuori di chiesa qualche sua diuota attendeua, ritrouai: et da lui inteso, etc.

In the left margin of folio 13v, Strozzi added, "che per fuggire forse la peste s'era uscito della Regola" with a caret indicating that the addition was to be inserted after "Alexo", producing the following reading:

> il uenerabile padre frate Alexo, che per fuggire forse la peste s'era uscito della Regola; che forse quiui per confessare fuori di chiesa qualche sua diuota attendeua, ritrouai: et da lui inteso, etc.

87v of Manuscript A presents a different picture. Originally, it read:

> il uenerabile padre frate Alexo, che forse et per auentura quiui per confessare fuori di chiesa qualche sua diuota attendeua ritrouai: et da lui inteso, etc.

"[C]he forse ... ritrouai" is underlined for deletion. In the left margin one finds the same marginal addition that was incorporated into Manuscript B's reading of this passage: "che per ... Regola". However, in Manuscript A, Strozzi deleted this marginal addition and added another reading at the foot of the folio:

> che forse per usare meglio la carita del confessare hor questa hor quella Donna fuora di chiesa s'era uscita della Regola et per auuentura et da lui inteso, etc.

The emended reading produced by this addition is:

> il uenerabile padre frate Alexo, che forse per usare meglio la carita del confessare hor questa hor quella Donna fuora di chiesa s'era uscita della Regola et per auuentura et da lui inteso, etc.

Somewhat problematically, "et da lui inteso" was not deleted from the body of the text, but it was added again at the foot of the page. It is possible that Strozzi simply intended for the repetion to be deleted. However, he went on to underline, presumably for deletion and apparently very carelessly, the addition at the foot of the page, even though one finds a caret at the start of the addition, and a caret after "Alexo" indicating where the deleted passage was to be inserted.[20] The probable uncertainty exhibited in this passage of Manuascript A suggests that Strozzi was still revising his text. But as his revisions were so tentative, and since Manuscript B provided a fine reading, I opted for Manuscript B's reading over Manuscript A's. All of Strozzi's changes to Manuscripts A and B are discussed in detail in the critical apparatus below.

20 The reason that I suggest Strozzi underlined the addition in question "carelessly" is that his uneven underlining struck through portions of the addition. The words that were struck through, if deleted, make the revised text nonsensical.

THE ITALIAN EDITION OF THE *PISTOLA*

Pistola fatta per la peste
Lorenzo a' Girolamo di Maestro Luca in Villa [84r]

[3v] Dilettissimo et da me molto honorato compare. Se bene la dolce uostra compagnia m'e stata sempre giocondissima; et sempre ho preso singulare piacere, non solo degli honesti et cortesi costumi, ma de piacieuoli et humanissimi ragionamenti uostri; non pero, per esserne stato qualche tempo priuo, come piu uolte è aduenuto per essere uoi absente, ò in piu graui occupationi inplicato, ho sentito dolore in parte alchuna simile a quello che di presente sento, per il lungo dimorare uostro lontano dalla citta. Il che io atribuisco a due principali cagioni. L'una credo che sia che crescendo sempre la uostra beniuolenzia uerso di me, con la continuatione di multiplicarne gl'infiniti uostri benefici, conuiene ancora che cresca laffettione mia inuerso di uoi; quantunque, essendoui io in tanti modi piu anni sono obligato, non pensassi che apena fusse possibile che piu crescere potesse. L'altra cagione e, **[4r]** che, segl'è uero che la moltitudine delle cose, et la diuersita di quelle distragga l'humane menti, io confessero che la uarieta delle conuersationi di molti amicj, la quale al presente mi mancha, non mi lassaua profondare, cosi intesamente nella ricordatione, et consideratione di uoi solo amico, et della uostra gentilissima consuetidine; della quale, essendone hora priuato, m'accorgo ch'io mancho in tutto di quello

---

84r 1–2 Pistola … Villa] *B Omit* **3** Dilettissimo] Dilectissimo **3–4** dolce uostra compagnia] uostra dolce conpagnia **4** m'e stata] mi <e stata | *B* giocundissima • 'g' *added by L. Strozzi* **5** degli] delli | piacieuoli] piaceuoli **6** esserne] *A* essere **7** è] e | uoi • 'u' *obscured by spreading ink* | ò] o | graui • *followed by indecipherable erasure* **8** alchuna] alcuna **8–9** *B* ho…sento • *marginal addition by L. Strozzi with % sign indicating insertion of text, and deletion of the following underlined linear text:* ho sentito pari dolore anzi ne anche si male in parte alchuna a quello che al presente; *also in L. Strozzi's hand* **10** L'una] Luna **10** beniuolenzia] beniuolentia **11** multiplicarne • *first* 'l' *written over* 't' | multiplicarne] multiplicarnne | gl'infiniti] linfiniti | benefici] benefitij | ancora] anchora | laffettione] laffectione **12** inuerso] uerso | quantunque] quantunche **12–13** essendoui] sendoui **13** fusse] fussi **14** potesse • *interlinear addition with caret indicating placement* | **14** L'altra] Laltra | *B* e • *written as* e, *but better read as* è *following Strozzi's usage of* "e" *in B* | e] *A* et (*sic*) • *conjunction as recorded by Strozzi* | segl'è uero] segli e uero **15** la diuersita] *A* della diuersita | l'humane] lhumane **16** amicj] amici • 'ci' *trimmed* **16–17** la quale … mancha, non … profondare • *phrases originally written in reverse order; emended with interlinear Arabic numbers: 2 over* non … profondare, *and 1 over* la quale …mancha | *B* profondare • *first* 'o' *trimmed* **17** ricordatione] recordatione **19** essendone] sendone | m'accorgo ch'io mancho] maccorgo che io manco

THE ENGLISH TRANSLATION OF THE *PISTOLA*

An Epistle Written Concerning the Plague to Girolamo di Maestro Luca at His Villa

To my most beloved and highly honoured friend: although your sweet companionship has always kept me truly happy, and I have always taken singular pleasure, not only from your honest and courteous manners, but also from your pleasant and exceptionally humane reasoning: I am not happy, however, when I am deprived of it for some time, as it often happens that you are absent, or involved in graver activities. I have felt sorrow in part somewhat similar to that which I feel at present, due to the length of time that you remain far away from your city. I attribute this present sadness to two principle causes. The first I believe is, that since you are always increasing your benevolence towards me, with the continual multiplication of your infinite favors, it follows yet again that my affection towards you increases; although having been indebted to you for many years in various ways, I did not think that it was possible that my affection for you might possibly grow even more. The second reason is, that if it is true that the multitude of earthly things, and their diversity distract the human mind, then I will confess that the variety of conversations with my many friends, which at present I miss, was not allowing me to absorb (or immerse) myself as intensely in the recollection and consideration of you, truest friend, and of your most gentlemanly customs, of which, since at present I am deprived, I notice that I lack completely

---

84r 3 "compare" *or* "friend" • though "compare" implies an even deeper level of familiarity, friendship, and companionship than "amico" or "friend" in English. Francesco Vettori frequently referred to Machiavelli as his "compare." See Niccolò Machiavelli, *Opere di Niccolò Machiavelli: Volume Terzo: Lettere*, ed. Franco Gaeta (Turin: Unione Tipografico Editrice Torinese 1984), Letter 205, dated 15 March 1513, where Vettori refers to Machiavelli as "Compare mio caro." "Compare" can also be used as a sign of respect, and was sometimes used by clients when they addressed patrons, or students when they addressed teachers, which is probably the case here. Strozzi dedicated the *Pistola* to his childhood teacher, Girolamo di Maestro Luca. See chap. 3 for more background on Maestro Luca.

84r 13–14 "quantunque ... potesse" *or* "although ... more" • is a very difficult passage to translate. In the original, one finds "sono" in this sentence, but it is nearly impossible to make sense of Strozzi's phrase when "sono" is included. I chose to render the gerund as "having" and intentionally overlooked "sono."

piaciere che altre uolte solamente soleuo sentire essere scemato alquanto. Et non solo sono d'un tale amico, et di tutti gl'altri ben cari miei compagni priuo, ma ancora di huomini a me noti, tanto che, riscontrandogli, mi fusse lecito il salutarli: che ueramente se l'habito nostro ciuile, quantunque pocò si uegha, non fosse, io mi crederei tal hora essere peregrino in qualch'altra citta. Onde, poi che il cielo non ci permette, unico et diletto compare mio, **[4v]** per la mortifera pestilenzia pasciere piu gl'orecchie di quei dolci ragionamenti, et gl'occhi di quei grati obietti, che gia soleano ogni noiosa cura alleggierirne, non ci priuiamo almeno di uisitarci con lettere, conforto non piccolo in tutte le miserie humane. Per cio mi sono io mosso (sapendo maxime quanto a chi è dilungato dalla patria è grato l'intendere ogni minima nouella) a scriuere tutto quello che nella egregia citta nostra han uisto, quantunque non asciuti, gl'infelicj occhi miei; et se bene la matteria poco diletto ui rechera, l'intender uoj essere fuor di si periglioso luogo ui fia grato senza che, il certificarui ch'io sia uiuo, di cui forse la morte inteso harete, ui douera far men graue ogni maniconia ò altra dolorosa noia.

84r 20 piaciere] piacere | *B* sentire • 'n' *trimmed* **21** d'un] dun | gl'altri] gli altri **21–2** compagni] conpagni • 'ni' *trimmed* | ancora] anchora **23** mi fusse] mi fussi • *interlinear addition by L. Strozzi with caret indicating placement; replaces underlined, linear* mi sia | salutarli] salutargli | se l'habito] se lhabito **23–4** nostro … quantunque] nostro … quantunche • nostro *is a marginal addition by L. Strozzi with % sign indicating insertion before the interlinear addition* ciuile, *also by L. Strozzi. Emended phrase replaces the original linear text, also by L. Strozzi,* delle nostriale ueste quantunche • delle nostriali *underlined for deletion and* ueste *expunged by ink splash* **24** crederei] crederrei **25** qualch'altra] qualche altra **25–6** diletto] dilecto **26** mio • *interlinear addition by L. Strozzi, with caret indicating placement; not in B* | pestilenzia] pestilentia | pasciere] pascere | gl'orecchie] le orecchie **27** gl'occhi] gli occhi | obietti] obiecti **28** uisitarcci] *A* uisitarsi **30–1** *B* (sapendo …nouella) • *corrected by L. Strozzi from* /sapendo …nouella/ **30** è] e | è] e **31** l'intendere] lintendere **32** quantunque] quantunche | asciuti, gl'infelicj] asciutti, glinfelici **33** bene] ben | poco diletto] pöco dilecto **33–4** l'intender uoj … fuor] lintender uoi … fuori • *original linear text reads,* c l' essere uoi fuori • c l' *struck through by L. Strozzi* • lintender uoi • *interlinear addition by L. Stozzi with caret indicating placement* • uoi *after* essere *struck through, producing above reading* **34** luogo] loco | ch'io] che io **35** douera] douerra | far] fare **36** dolorosa • *third* 'o' *obscured by spreading ink.*

that pleasure, when on other occasions I merely used to listen to you to be satiated somewhat. And I am not only of such a friend, and of all of my other dear companions deprived, but also of the men known to me, so that, corresponding with them, I was able to greet them. Truly if our civic dress, although one seldom sees it, no longer existed, I would sometimes think myself to have wandered into some other city. Wherefore, since Heaven does not permit us, my only and beloved friend, by the deadly pestilence, to nourish our ears with more of those sweet discussions, and our eyes with those gracious subjects, which once used to lighten every tedious care, let us not deprive ourselves of visiting one another with letters; no little comfort in all of these human miseries. Therefore I am stirred (knowing how much one who is away from the fatherland is grateful to receive even the smallest piece of news) to write about all that I have seen in our distinguished city, with my wet and unfortunate eyes; and even though the matter will bring you little pleasure, hearing that you are out of so perilous a place should make you grateful. Furthermore, while it proves to you that I (of whose death perhaps you have heard) might yet live, it also will oblige you to make less grave every melancholy or other painful nuisance.

84r 30 "patria" *or* "fatherland" • for one of Machiavelli's most detailed definitions of *patria*, assuming that he wrote the work, see the opening lines of his *Discourse or Dialogue Concerning our Language*, 130–31 for English translation and 167–8 for Italian original in my *Politics, Patriotism and Language: Niccolò Machiavelli's* "Secular Patria" *and the Creation of an Italian National Identity* (New York: Peter Lang, 2005). It is quite likely that Machiavelli's concept of *patria* influenced Strozzi's use of the term in the *Pistola*. In this instance, I rendered *patria* as "fatherland"; below, I rendered it as "native city."

[9r] Non ardisco in sul foglio porre la timida mano per ordire si noioso principio; anzi, quanto piu le tante miserie per la mente mi riuolgo, piu l'horrenda descriptione mi spauenta: et se bene il tutto ho uisto, mi rinuoua il raccontarlo doloroso pianto; ne so anche da che parte tale comminciamento fare mi deggia: et se lecito mi fusse, da tale proponimento indrieto mi ritrarrej. Il souerchio desio, nondimeno, il quale ho di sapere se ancora uoi uiuo sete, rompera ogni timore. [84v]

Non altrimenti che si resti una citta dalli infedeli forzatamente presa et poi abandonata, si truoua al presente la misera Fiorenza nostra. Parte degli habitatorj, si come uoi, la pestifera mortalita fuggiendo, per le sparte uille ridutti si sono, parte morti, parte in sul morire: in modo che le cose presenti ci offendano, le future ci minacciono; et cosi nella morte si trauaglia, nella uita si teme. Ò dannoso seculo! ò lagrimabile stagione! Le pulite et belle contrade, che piene di richi et nobilj cittadini essere soleuano, sono hora puzolente et brute, di poueri ripiene; per la impromptitudine de quali et paurose strida, dificilmente, et con timore si ua. Sono serrate le botteghe, gli exercizii fermi, i giudici, ò le corti, et i fori, tolti uia, prostrate le leggi. Hora si intende questo furto, hora quello homicidio: le piazze, i mercatj, doue adunarsi frequentemente i cittadini soleuano, sepolchri sono hora fatti, et di

---

84v 2 per] far **3** l'horrenda] lorrenda **3–4** rinuoua] rinnuoua **4–5** comminciamento] cominciamento **5** *B* proponimento • *marginal addition in Machiavelli's hand, probably to replace the underlined, linear* proposto **6** indrieto] indietro | ritrarrej] ritrarrei • 'ri' *interlinear addition in Machiavelli's hand* **8** dalli] dagli **9** abandonata] abbandonata | degli] *A* dagli **10** habitatorj] habitatori **12** offendano] offendono | *B* trauaglia • *interlinear addition by L. Strozzi, probably to replace the linear* stenta, *in Machiavelli's hand* **13** ò] o | ò] o **14** nobilj] nobili **15** brute] brutte | impromptitudine] inpromtitudine **16** dificilmente … ua] difficilmente … ua • *interlinear addition, with caret indicating placement, by L. Strozzi; replaces the deleted, barely legible linear text* {non si puo ne andare}; *hypothetical transcription of text in Machiavelli's hand* | serrate] serate **17** exercizii] esercitii | i giudici ò *underlined, possibly for deletion, though retained in reading above* | *B* i giudici /o/ le corti • *marginal addition with % sign indicating placement* | et i fori] e fori | prostrate • *second* 'r' *interlinear addition with caret indicating placement* **18** si intende] sintende | furto • *interlinear addition to replace underlined* fruto (*sic*) | piazze] piaze | mercatj] mercati **19** soleuano, sepolchri] soleano, seplocri

I hardly dare to place my timid hand to the page to trace so troublesome a beginning; so that the more I mull over such miseries in the midst of the mind, the more I do recoil from the horrendous description of them: and although I have seen it all, to recount it renews painful tears; nor do I know where I ought to make a start; and if it were permitted me, from this weak undertaking, I would withdraw myself. But, the overwhelming desire that I have, to know if you are still alive, will overcome every fear.

One finds that our miserable Florence, at the present, resembles a city that has been sacked by the infidels and afterwards abandoned. Some of the inhabitants, such as yourself, have retired to country villas to escape the deadly plague; some are dead and others are approaching death; so that the while present circumstances offend us, the future threatens us; so as one struggles with death, one fears for one's life. Oh injurious age! Oh lamentable season! The neat and beautiful streets, which used to be bursting with rich and noble citizens, are now stinking, ugly and swarming with the poor. One passes by their impudent and fearful shrieks with difficulty and trepidation. The shops are locked, the businesses closed, the courts and the lawyers dragged away, prostrating the laws. Now one hears of this theft, now of that murder: the piazzas and markets, where the citizens used to be in the habit of gathering frequently, are now made into communal graves, and vile dens of thieves. Men go about alone, and in exchange for friends,

84v 10 "ville" *or* "villas" • for a nearly identical passage concerning attempts by Florentine aristocracy to escape the plague, see Giovanni Boccaccio, *The Decameron*, trans. Guido Waldman, ed. Jonathan Usher (Oxford: Oxford University Press, 1998), 8 (hereafter *Decameron* [1998]). For Italian original see Giovanni Boccaccio, *Decameron*, in *Tutte le opere di Giovanni Boccaccio*, vol. 4, ed. Vittore Branca (Milan: Mondadori, 1976), 12, secs. 19–20 (hereafter *Decameron* [1976]).

84v 8–20 "Non … riceptacoli" *or* "One finds … den of thieves" • very closely mirrors Boccaccio's description of Florence during the first plague outbreak of 1347–48. See *Decameron* (1998), 9 for English translation and *Decameron* (1976) 13, secs. 23–4 for Italian original.

uile brighate riceptacoli. Gli huomini **[9v]** uanno solj, et in cambio di amicj, gente di questo pestifero morto infesta si riscontra. L'uno parente se pure l'altro truoua, ò frattello il fratello, ò la moglie il marito, ciaschuno ua largo: et che piu? schifano i padri et le madrj i proprij loro figliuoli, et gl'abbandonono. Chi fiori, chi odorifere herbe, chi spugne, chi anpolle, chi palle di diuerse spezerie composte in man porta, ò, per meglio dire, al naso sempre tiene: et questi sono i prouedimentj. Sonci certe canoue anchora, oue si distribuisce pane; anzi per ricorre ghauoccioli si semina.

I ragionamenti ch'essere soleuano in piazza honoreuoli et in mercato [85r] utilj, in cose miserabili et meste si conuertano. Chi dice: il tale è morto, quell altro è malato, chi fuggito, chi in chasa serrato, chi allo spedale, chi in guardia, chi non si truoua: et simigliantj nuoue, atte con la sola immaginatione a fare Eschulapio, non ch'altri, amorbare. Molti uanno ricerchando la cagione del male; et alchuni dicono: gl'astrologi ci minacciono; alchuni: i profetti l'hanno predetto. Chi si ricorda di qualche prodigio; chi la qualita del tempo et la dispositione dellaria atta ad peste ne in colpa, et che tale fu nel mille trecento quarant'otto; et mille quattrocento settánt'otto et altre di tale maniera cose: in modo che daccordo tutti concludono, che non solo questa, ma infinti altri mali c'hanno a rouinare adosso. Questi sono i piacieuoliragionamenti che a ogn'hora si sentono. Et benche con una sola parola dinanzi a gl'occhi della mente questa nostra miserabile patria porre ui potessi, dicendouj che di uederla tutta dissimile, et diuersa da quella che

---

84v 20 brighate riceptacoli] brigate riceptaculi | solj] soli | amicj] amici **21** gente] *A* genti | morto] morbo | L'uno] Luno **22** ò] /o/ | ò] /o/ | ciaschuno] ciascuno **23** madrj] madri | proprij] proprii | figliuoli] figluoli **24** gl'abbandonono] gli abbandonano **25** spezerie] spezierie | ò] /o/ | meglio] meglo **26** prouedimentj] prouuedimenti • 'dimenti' *added by Machiavelli over erasure* **27** oue • *corrected from* doue | ghauoccioli] gauaccioli **85r 1** ch'essere] che essere | piazza] piaza **2** utilj] utili **3** serrato • *interlinear addition to replace deleted* fuggito | serrato] confitto **4** guardia • *final* 'a' *added above* 'i' *at extreme right of folio margin* | simigliantj • 'j' *corrected from* 'e' | con la sola • *interlinear addition to replace underlined, linear text* alle | con la sola] colla sola **5** Eschulapio] Esculapio | ch'altri] che altri | amorbare] ammorbare | ricerchando] ricercando **6** *B* et • *followed by indecipherable erasure* | alchuni] acluni | gl'astrologi] gli astrologi | alchuni] alcuni **7** l'hanno] lhanno | *B* Chi si ricorda chi si ricorda • *repetition deleted by Machiavelli* | prodigio • *emended from* prodigo **8** dispositione] *A* indispotizione | dellaria atta] *A* dell'aria alta **9** mille trecento … settánt'otto] 1348 et 1478 **11** c'hanno a … adosso] ci hanno ad … addosso **12** a ogn'hora] ad ogni hora **13** a gl'occhi] ad gli ochi **14** dicendouj] dicendoui | dissimile • *second* 's' *added linearly.*

one meets people infected with this deadly plague. Even if one parent finds the other, or a brother finds his brother, or a wife her husband, each one keeps a safe distance from their relations: and what is worse? Fathers and mothers spurn their own children, abandoning them. One holds blossoms, another odoriferous herbs, a third sponges, a fourth glass vials, and one carries in his hand (or it is far better to say, always held to his nose) small balls composed of diverse aromatic spices; and these are the precautions against the plague. I am certain that few shops, where bread is distributed, are still open; but there, the shop-goers infect each other and take home buboes.

The conversations which used to be honorable in the piazzas and profitable in the markets change to miserable and sorrowful themes: for example, one says: "such a one is dead, that other is sick, another fled, another is confined at home, such a one is in hospital, another is on the lookout, and yet another has disappeared"; and similar recent tidings, which by imagination alone would suffice to make none other than Aesculapius sick. Many go searching for the causes of the disease, and some say: "The astrologers threaten us with it"; others, "The prophets have predicted it." One recalls some marvel; one blames the quality of the weather, and the heavy air which swarms with plague, saying that it was the same in 1348 and 1478; and still more say similar things. There is such unanimous agreement that everyone concludes, that not only this, but infinite other sicknesses have laid us to ruin. These are the pleasant topics which are heard continually. And though I might be able to place our miserable native city before your mind's eye with only a single word, by saying that you might imagine it altogether different and completely unlike that which

---

84v 21–4 "L'uno ... gl'abbandonono" *or* "Even if one parent ... abandoning them" • once again, mirrors the *Decameron* almost exactly. See *Decameron* (1998), 10 for English translation, and *Decameron* (1976), 13–14, secs. 24–25 for Italian original.
84v 24–6 "Chi fiori ... i prouedimentj" *or* "One holds blossoms ... against the plague" • is lifted almost directly from the *Decameron*. See *Decameron* (1998), 9 for English translation and *Decameron* (1976), 13–14, sec. 24–5 for Italian original.
84v 26 "canoue" *or* "shops" • is a Florentine/Tuscan term.
84v 27 "ghauoccioli" *or* "buboes" • are swellings in the lymphatic system, which usually presented in the groin, armpits, and neck. This sympton of bubonic plague was famously described by Boccaccio in the *Decameron*. For English translation, see *Decameron* (1998), 7; for Italian version, see *Decameron* (1976), 10–11, secs. 10–12.
85r 5 "Eschulapio" *or* "Aesculapius" • is mentioned in the *Decameron* (1998), 14 and *Decameron* (1976), 19, sec. 48 for Italian original.
85r 9 "mille trecento quarant'otto" *or* "1348" • is highlighted in the *Decameron* (1998), 6 and *Decameron* (1976), 9–10, sec. 8.

uedere soleui gia, u'immaginassi che niuna cosa meglio che tale comparazione in uoi medesimo fatta dimostarlaui **[10r]** potrebbe; uolgio nondimeno, che considerare piu particularmente la possiate, perche la cosa inmaginata alla uerita di quello che si inmagina al tutto mai non aggiugne. Ne mi pare da poteruela dipigniere con migliore exempio che con il mio:percio io ui descriuero la uita mia, accio da essa possiate tutta quella di qualunque altro misurare.

Sappiate, adunque, che ne giorni di lauoro, partendomi io di casa in su quella hora che i terresti uapori tutti dal sole sono risoluti, per andare al mio solito exercizio; fatti prima alchuni rimedi, et presi contra alla uenenosa infermita certi antidoti, ne quali (quantunque l'egregio Mingho medico dica che sono coraze di carte), ho fede certamente, et non piciola; non sono molti passi da quella lungi, ch'ogn'altro pensiero conuiene, benche graue et da cose importanti, et necesarie la testa sgombri: perche il primo riscontro che si offerisce dinanzi a gl'occhi miei, per mio buono agurio, sono i becchini non quegli degl'amorbati, ma i consueti: i quali, come gia de pochi, hora de molti morti si dolgano, perche pare a quegli che tanta abondanza generi loro carestia. Et chi harebbe mai creduto che uenissi tempo, nel quale eglino la sanita di qualunque infermo desiderassero, come ueramente di desiderare giurauono? Io facilmente lo credo, perche morendo in altro tempo et d'altro male, ne potranno all'usato

---

85r 15 u'immaginassi • *emended from* non u'inmaginassi • non *underlined, probably for deletion* | u'immaginassi] ui immaginassi | niuna] *A* nunia (*sic*) | meglio] meglo **15–16** comparazione] comparatione | uolgio] uolgo **17** considerare • 'ar' *added over indecipherable erasure* | *B* considerare piu • *added over indecipherable erasure by Machiavelli* **18** inmaginata] imaginata | inmagina] immagina **19** exempio] exemplo **23** terresti] terrestri | dal] da il | risoluti] resoluti **24** exercizio] exercitio | alchuni] alcuni | rimedi] remedii | contra] contro **25** infermita] infirmita **25–6** (quantunque … carte)] quantunque … carte **25** mingho] mingo **26** medico • *interlinear addition with caret indicating placement; B Omit* | et • *interlinear addition* **26–7** piciola] piccola | ch'ogn'altro] ch ogn altro **28** *B* et da cose importanti, et necesarie da quella la testa • *interlinear addition in L. Strozzi's hand with caret indicating placement* • quella *struck through for deletion* | la testa] da la testa **29** dinanzi a gl'occhi] ad gli ochi **30** agurio] augurio | becchini] bechini | degl'amorbati] degli ammorbati | *B* consueti {i quali crudelmente si dolgano che in tanta mortalita alcuno per loro non noiosa}: i quali • 'i quali … noiosa' *hypothetical transcription of line struck through for deletion in ink used by Machiavelli; A Omit* **31** a] ad | abondanza] abbondanza **33–4** desiderassero] desiderassino | d'altro | daltro **35** all'usato] allo usato

you used to see (as nothing demonstrates for you better than such a comparison) I, nevertheless, want you to be able to understand the matter in greater depth, because the thing imagined compared with the truth of that which one imagines never adds up. Nor am I able, it seems to me, to illustrate this with a finer example than my own life: therefore I will describe my life to you, so that by it you might measure all the rest.

You know then that on work days, I leave my house before that hour in which all the terrestrial vapors are evaporated by the sun, to go about my usual business; having first taken some antidotes against the venomous infirmity, in which (although the distinguished doctor Mingo said that they are breastplates of paper), I certainly have faith, and not a little; I am not many steps away from home, when every other remaining thought that gathers in my mind, although grave and of things important and necessary, clears from my head, because the first things that present themselves to my eyes, by my good luck, are gravediggers. Not those gravediggers of the infected, but the usual type: who, at one time by the few, but now by the many, dead are grieved, because it seems to them that such an abundance begets their future famine. Whoever would have believed that the time would come, in which they might have wished for the good health of all of the ill, as they swear truly to yearn? I think easily, because if those dying of the plague died in another time and of another disease, they would make their usual profit. And so passing by San Miniato between the towers, where I was at one time nearly deafened by the din of the wool beaters, and the whistles and rough conversations of the wool traders, I found an all-pervasive and unwanted silence. Continuing on my journey, in the vicinity

---

85r 17–18 "la cosa … non aggiugne" *or* "the thing … never adds up" • resonates with Machiavelli's *Il Principe*, chap. 15. "But since my intention is to say something that will prove of practical use to the inquirer, I have thought it proper to represent things as they are in truth, rather than as they are imagined" (Machiavelli, *The Prince*, trans. George Bull [London: Penguin, 1995], 48). The Italian original is "Ma, sendo l'intendo mio scrivere cosa utile a chi la intende, mi è parso piu conveniente andare drieto alla verità effettuale dalla cosa, che alla immaginazione di essa" (Machiavelli, 'Il Principe,' in *Opere*, vol. 1, ed. Corrado Vivanti [Rome: Einaudi, 1997], 159).
85r 22 "partendomi io di casa" *or* "I am not … from home" • it seems very likely that Strozzi began his "tour" of Florence at the family palace, the Palazzo Strozzi, where he had lived since 1503. See chapter 1 for more detail.
85r 25 "Mingho" • a reference to Mingo/Mengo Bianchelli/o also known as Mingo/Mengo da Faenza. For more on Bianchelli, see appendix 3.

guadagnare. Et cosi passando da Samminiato infra le torre, doue per lo [85v] strepido de camati, et fischi, et ragionamenti ciompeschi assordare quasi solea, trouo grande, et non molto desiderato silenzio. Segui il mio uiaggio, et uicino a Mercato Nuouo incontrai a cauallo la morria: di che ingannato per la prima uolta **[10v]** ne rimasi; imperoche, ueggiendo da lungi da bianchi caualli, quantunque come neue non fussero, portata una lettica, che fusse qualche gentil donna ò persona di gran lignaggio, ch'andasse a suo diporto, mi pensai. Ma ueggiendoli di poi attorno, in uece di seruitori, seruigiali di Santa Maria Nuoua, non fu mestiero che d'altro domandassi. Non mi bastando questo, et per poterui del tutto piu amplia notizia dare, la mattina del lieto principio di maggio, entrai nella admirabile, et ueneranda chiesa di Santa Reparata; doue tre sarcedoti soli erano: l'uno la messa cantando diceua; l'altro per coro et organo seruiua; il terzo per confessare in una sedia, quasi di mura cinta, nel mezzo della prima naue si posaua, tenendo i ferri in gamba nondimeno, et alle braccia le manette: che cosi dal uicario ordinato stato gl'era, accio potessi le canoniche tentationj meglio in tanta solitudine schifare. Le diuote della messa erano tre donne in gamurrino, uecchie scrigniute, et forse zoppe; et ciaschuna separatamente nella sua tribuna si

---

85v 1 *B* cosi • *interlinear addition in L. Strozzi's hand with caret indicating placement* | Samminiato] Saminiato | torre] torri **2** strepido] strepito | quasi • 'si' *covered by different, probably later ink* **3** silenzio] silentio | *B* Seguito • 'to' *expunged by Machiavelli* | *B* il mio • *writtenby Machiavelli over indecipherable erasure* **4** a cauallo] ad cauallo | morria] moria **5** ueggiendo] ueggendo | *B* imperoche ueggendo • *written over indecipherable erasure by Machiavelli* **6** caualli] cauagli | *B* neue • *written over indecipherable erasure by Machiavelli* **7** gentil] gentile | ò] /o/ | ch'andasse] che andasse **8** ueggiendoli] ueggendogli | seruitori] seruidori **9** d'altro] daltro **9–10** bastando • 'st' *obscurred by ink splash* | amplia notizia] ampla notitia **12** Santa Reparata • *emended from* Santa Maria Reparata • Maria *underlined, probably for deletion* | sarcedoti] sacerdoti | l'uno] luno **13** l'altro] laltro | *B* per coro ... seruiua • *interlinear addition in L. Strozzi's hand; to replace the underlined* in maneria da se stesso alzando: gli organi seruiua, *in Machiavelli's hand* **14** *B* quasi • *marginal addition, with caret indicating placement, in L. Strozzi's hand* | mezzo] mezo | tenendo • 'endo' *added over indecipherable erasure* **16** gl'era] gli era | potessi] potesse | tentationj] tentationi **17** gamurrino] gammurrino **17–18** scrigniute • 'te' *added over indecipherable erasure* | scrigniute] scrignute | **18** *B* forse • *interlinear addition, with caret indicating placement, in L. Strozzi's hand* | *B* si • *interlinear addition, with caret indicating placement, in L. Strozzi's hand.*

of the Mercato Nuovo, I encountered the horseman of the pestilence: by whom being deceived for the first time I remained there; because, seeing from afar white horses (although they weren't of snow-whiteness) bearing a litter, which I thought to myself might contain some noble woman or person of ancient lineage, who rode about for his amusement. But seeing around them then, instead of servants, nurses from Santa Maria Nuova, there was no need to inquire further concerning the person's heritage or occupation. This not being enough for me, and in order to give you all the more extended news of the morning of the joyous beginning of May, I entered the admirable and venerable Church of Santa Reparata; where there were only three priests: the one was singing Mass; the second serves as the choir and organ; the third hears confessions in a chair surrounded by the wall, in the middle of the first nave. Nevertheless, he wore irons on his ankles, and handcuffs on his wrists: because he was ordered to be thus by the Vicar, so that he might be able better to escape temptations in canonical solitude. The pious attendants of the Mass included three women in ragged cloaks – old bent and perhaps lame women; each separately in her own pew

---

85v 1 "Samminiato" or "San Miniato" • is an ancient church (the facade dates from c. 1090) located in the Oltr'Arno, outside of the city's walls, on a hill overlooking the entirety of Florence (Peter Murray, *The Architecture of the Italian Renaissance* [New York: Schocken, 1986]: 16, 17). If Strozzi began his walk through Florence at the Palazzo Strozzi, his *casa*, then he must have crossed the Arno on his way to San Miniato, but he did not mention how, or by which bridge, he crossed to the Oltr'Arno.

85v 2 "camati" *or* "wool beaters" • is probably a Florentine dialectical form derived from "scamati," the sticks used to beat and prepare raw wool.

85v 4 "Mercato Nuovo" • is known today for its famous Loggia (c. 1547) and its bronze boar, both of which have become synonymous with the Mercato Nuovo (La Loggia del Porcellino). Neither of these were present when Strozzi wrote the *Pistola*, c. 1522. Once again, Strozzi fails to mention where he crossed the Arno on his journey from San Miniato to the Mercano Nuovo.

85v 9 "Santa Maria Nuoua" • For more detail on the history of the Hospital of Santa Maria Nuova, see K. Park and J. Henderson, "'The First Hospital among Christians': The Ospedale di Santa Maria Nuova in Early Sixteenth-Century Florence," *Medical History* 35 (1991): 164–88.

85v 12 "Santa Reparata" • here Strozzi refers to the Duomo, Santa Maria del Fiore, using the name of the cathedral that predated it. Visitors to the Duomo may still see the foundations of Santa Reparata, which are partially intact under the Duomo, by descending a set of steps found on the right-hand side of the nave as one faces the high altar of the cathedral. The present facade of the Duomo was added in the nineteenth century. During Strozzi's life, the facade of the Duomo resembled the red brick façade of San Lorenzo, which is a short walk from the Duomo. For more on the Duomo, see Murray, *Architecture*, 24, 26, 27, 28, 31, 32, 36, 38, 41, 47, 55, 100, 137.

staua; fra le quali solo dell'auolo mio la nutrice mi parue riconoscere. Erano tre similmente gli deuoti, i quali, senza mai uedersi, ad gruccie uolgeano il coro, dando taluolta d'occhio alle tre amorose: cose ueramente da non le potere credere se non chi uiste l'hauesse. Ond'io, a guisa, di chi uede quello che uedendolo apena il crede, rimasi stupefatto; et dubitando che il popolo no fusse, come in si celebre mattina solito era, dietro alli armeggiatori ridotto in piazza, la con tale speranza mi conduxi: doue armeggiare uidi, in cambio di **[11r]** huomini et caualli, croce, bare cataletti et tauole, sopra le quali [86r] diuersi morti si uedeuono portati da bechini: i quali, per necesita furono dal Barlachi per malleuadori degli eccelsi Signori chiamati, che in quell'hora la cirimonia faceuono della entrata loro. Et credo, per auentura, che non bastando il numero de uiui, si seruisse del nome d'alcuno de morti, secondo il costume chiamandogli; benche ad niuno come a Lazero aduenisse.

Non mi parendo questo spettacolo degno ò sicuro, molta dimora non ui feci; et non potendo credere che in qualche parte della citta non fusse maggior frequenzia di nobilj ristretta, uerso la famosissima piazza di Santa Crocie i miei passi riuolsi: la doue uiddi un grandissimo ballo tondo di becchini, che ad alta uoce ben venga, ben uenga il morbo diceuano. Questo era il lieto loro ben uenga maggio. L'aspetto de quali, insieme con il tuono della canzona, et le parole di quella, al tanto di dispiacere alli miei occhi,

---

85v 19 fra] tra | dell'auolo] dello auolo | *B* mi parue riconoscere • *interlinear addition, with caret indicating placement, in L. Strozzi's hand, to replace the underlined* ricognobbi, *in Machiavelli's hand* **20** uedersi • *followed by five equally spaced periods* | ad gruccie] *A omit* | uolgeano] uolgeuono **21** d'occhio] dochio **22** Ond'io, a] Onde io, ad **23** apena] appena | no • *either Florentine variant spelling of* non, *or Strozzi failed to include a tilde to indicate abbreviated form of* non | no] non **24** alli] ad gli **25** in piazza] impiaza
86r 1 caualli] cauagli **2** uedeuono] uedeuano | necesita] necessita **3** Barlachi] Barlachio | eccelsi] exelsi | quell'hora] quella hora **4** cirimonia] ceremonia | entrata • *interlinear addition, probably to replace the underlined* tornata | *B* entrata • 'ent' *illegible due to ink splash* | auentura] aduentura **5** d'alcuno] dalcuno **6** a Lazero] ad Lazaro **7** ò] /o/ | molta] molto **8** feci] fei **8–9** maggior frequenzia] maggiore frequenti **9** nobilj] nobili **10** Crocie] Croce | *B* riuolsi • 'ri' *interlinear addition in L. Strozzi's hand with caret indicating placement* | uiddi un] uidi uno | grandissimo • 'o' *emended from* 'i' **11** uoce] boce | *first* venga • *begins with small* v | ben venga … il morbo] ben uenga il morbo • *emended from* ben uenga il borbo morbo • 'borbo' (*sic*) *struck through for deletion by Machiavelli* **12** L'aspetto] Lo aspetto | con] *A* col **13** *B* dispiacere • 'dis' *interlinear addition with caret indicating placement in L. Strozzi's hand* | occhi] ochi

kneeling; among them only one, my grandfather's nurse, seemed to recognize me. There were three similarly devoted old men, who, without ever seeing one another, shuffled about the choir on crutches, at times giving the eye to the three lovelies. Truly, one could not believe such things if one had not seen them in person. Therefore I, in the manner of one who witnessed that spectacle (seeing it hardly makes one to believe it) remained stupefied. Doubting that the people would not, as they usually did, swarm behind the equestrians into the piazza (as is usual on so celebrated a morning); with such hope I partook there. Where, bustling about I saw, in exchange for men and horses, crosses, coffins, stretchers and tables, on which those diverse dead persons were carried by grave diggers. They (the grave diggers) were summoned by Barlacchi out of necessity, as supporters of the lofty Signori, who made their ceremonial entrance at that moment. And I believe, per adventure, that if the number of the living was not sufficient, he would have read out the names of some of the dead, calling them out according to the custom; even though nothing like the resurrection of Lazarus would happen.

As this spectacle seemed neither worthy nor very safe to me, I did not stay long; and as I was not able to believe that any other part of the city was, with greater frequency, filled with nobles, I directed by steps toward the most famous piazza of Santa Croce. There, I saw a tremendous number gravediggers dancing in a circle and singing loudly, "Hearty welcome, plague; hearty welcome, plague." This was their merry "Hearty welcome, May." Their appearance, together with the thunder of their song, and its words, offered as much

---

85v 24–5 "armeggiatori" *or* "equestrians" • For more detail, see Richard Trexler, *Public Life in Renaissance Florence* (Ithaca: Cornell University Press), 306–12. In that passage, Trexler discussed one role of the "armeggiatori." They were horsemen and banner bearers. It seems that Strozzi is referring to "equestrians" who usually led the feast day procession and the accompanying crowd into the piazza • the "piazza" referenced here was almost certainly the Piazza della Signoria, where Strozzi would have walked by the Palazzo Vecchio.

86r 3 "Barlachi" *or* Barlacchi • a reference to Domenico Barlacchi or Barlacchia. He was "herald of the Florentine Signoria." See Judith Bryce "The Theatrical Activities of Palla di Lorenzo Strozzi in Lyon in the 1540's," in *The Theater of the English and Italian Renaissance*, ed. J.R. Mulryne and Margaret Shewring (New York: St. Martin's, 1991), 55–69. See 61–2, 67n29 for more details. Also see the famous study by F. Pintor, "Ego Barlachia recensui," in G.S.L. 1, vol. 39 (1902), 103. "Barlachia" was a pseudonym sometimes adopted by Machiavelli himself.

86r 9–10 "piazza di Santa Croce" "*piazza* of Santa Croce" • was and remains a grand public space, surrounded by wonderful examples of Florentine Renaissance mercantile and domestic architecture. The jewel of the piazza is the Church of Santa Croce, which during Strozzi's time, like the Duomo, lacked a marble façade.

86r 11 "becchini" *or* "gravediggers" • for more detail on these characters see *Decameron* (1998), 15–16, and *Decameron* (1976) 21, secs. 57–9.

et orechi porsono, quanto gia l'honeste fanciuille con la loro lieta canzone a quelli di piaciere porgeano: tal che, senza dimora, in chiesa mi fuggi. Doue, faciendo le consuete mie deuotioni, ne ueggiendoui pure un testimonio, senti, benche lontana, una affannata et spauenteuole uoce; alla cui aduicinandomi, alle sepulture del chiustro uiddi in terra distesa in ueste negra una pallida et trauagliata giouane, la ciu effigie piu morta che uiua mi pareua, rigando le sue belle guancie d'amare lagrime, hora l'auree sue belle sparse trecie stracciandosi, hora il petto hora il uolto con le proprie mani, battendosi da muouere a pieta uno marmo: **[11v]** di che io oltre modo spauento, et dolore presi. Al lei, nondimeno, cautamente appressandomi, le dissi: Deh perche si fattamente ti lamenti? Ond'ella, perch'io non la conosciessi, subito con il lembo della ueste il capo si coperse. L'atto, come è natural cosa, mi fe cresciere di conoscerla il desio: la paura, dall'altro canto, che della

[86v] pestifera contagione machiate fusse, i passi ritardaua; dicendole nondimeno, che di me non temesse, perche quiui ero per darle et consiglio et aiuto, trouandosi ella da si grauosi affanni oppressa: et tacendo ella, soggiunsi, che non mi partirei se prima lei partire non uedesse. Prese, benche alquanto stesse, pur poi, come donna dassai et animosa, partito di scoprirsi, dicendo: Quanto sono stolta! se nel cospetto d'uno popolo non ho temuto, hora d'un huomo solo, quale alli miei bisogni sobuenire cerca, temero? Era, per l'habito, et per la smisurata passione transfigurata, si che per la uoce piu che per la effigie la riconobbi. Et dimandandole di

---

86r 14 l'honeste] le honeste **15** quelli] quegli | porgeano] porgeuono **16** faciendo] facendo | mie deuotioni • *emended from* mie orationj deuotioni • orationj *underlined for deletion* | ueggiendoui] ueggendoui **16–17** testimonio] testimone **18** *B* alle sepulture del chiustro uidi • *interlinear addition with caret indicating placement in L. Strozzi's hand* • uidi *underlined* | uiddi] uidi | distesa in] distesa uidi in • uidi *underlined, probably to be replaced by interlinear* uidi *cited in previous note* **19** *B* piu --- morta • *large ink splash; probably an intentional deletion following* piu **20** guancie] guance | d'amare] di amare | l'auree] lauree **21** trecie] trecce **22–3** oltre modo] a modo **24** Ond'ella perch'io] Onde ella perche io **25** conosciessi] cognoscessi | L'atto] Lo atto **26** cresciere] crescere | conoscerla] cognoscerla | desio] disio **26–7** dall'altro] dallaltro
86v 5 partito] *A omit* **6** Quanto] *A* Quando | cospetto d'uno] conspetto duno **7** d'un] duno **8** l'habito] lo habito **9** uoce] boce | riconobbi] ricognobbi

displeasure to my eyes and ears, as formerly the happy songs of the honorable young maidens used to bring me pleasure; so that without hesitating, I escaped into the church, where I offered my usual devotions, without a single witness, when I heard from a long way off, a worried and fearful voice. To which drawing myself, I saw laying on the ground, near the fresh graves in the cloister, in black raiment, a pale and afflicted maiden, whose face appeared more that of a corpse than a living woman. (She had) bitter tears streaming down her beautiful cheeks, (and she was) tearing out strands of her beautiful tousled hair, (and) beating her breast and then her face with her own hands. Seeing such a thing would move a block of marble to pity her. Thus, I was stricken with pain, though exceedingly frightened of her. Nevertheless, I cautiously approached her and asked: "Oh why do you lament so grievously?" She immediately covered her face with the hem of her dress, so I would not be able to recognize her. This act, as is natural, increased my desire to know her. However, the fear, of the other song which those spotted with the plague contagion sang, slowed my steps; but, I told her, that she should not be frightened of me, because I was, finding her oppressed by such severe anxieties, here to give her council and help. Calming her, I added, that I would not leave until I could see her face. She turned, hesitating somewhat, then presently, like a spirited and courageous woman, took to uncovering herself saying: "Am I so foolish, that I was not anxious in the presence of the multitude, but will now be terrified of only a single man, who certainly seeks to attend to my needs?" She was so transfigured by her garb and by her immeasurable passion, that I recognized her more by her voice than by her form. When I asked her the cause of such affliction; she exclaimed "Woe unto me! I do not know how to

---

86r 15 "in chiesa mi fuggi" *or* "I escaped into the church" • the church (or basilica) in question is the Santa Croce. For more on the history of this famous Franciscan edifice, see Murray, *Architecture*, 24, 26, 27, 28, 39, 42, 44, 237. It is interesting to note that the church's marble facade, like the Duomo's, was not added until the nineteenth century.
86r 18 "chiustro" *or* "cloister" • could be a reference to the "Primo Chiostro," where the visitor will also find the Pazzi Chapel, designed by Filippo Brunellischi, or the "Secondo Chiostro," also designed by Brunelleschi.

tanta afflitione la causa: Hei misera à me! dis'ella; non saperla fingere. Duolmi et poi mi duole ch'ogni mia contentezza ho persa, quale, sebene mill'anni uiuesse, non sono per ricoperare. Et quello che piu m'afflige, è, ch'ancora io morire non posso. Ne mi dolgo della pestilenziosa stagione, ma della trista mia fortuna, che fe che l'indissolubile amoroso nodo, da me con tanta arte, et diligenzia fabbricato, non tenne il fermo; da cui la comune nostro rouina nacque, donde uersono hora sopra il sepolchro **[12r]** dello infelice, et fido amante mio le amare lagrime. Ò con che diletto lo hebbi io piu uolte in queste gia felice, et hora infelice braccia! Con che uaghezza contemplano i suoi begli, et lucenti occhi! Ò con qual piaciere l'auide labbia mie alla sua odorifera bocha acostai! Ò con quanto contento unii et strinsi il mio infiammato al suo non freddo candido, et giouinil petto! Hei mie lassa! Con che dolcezza uenimo noi piu uolte all'ultima amorosa felicita, unitamente sadisfacendo a nostri desiderj! Ne appena hebbe queste parole dette, ch'ella subito in terra in guisa tale si distese, che tutti mi si arriciarono i peli adosso, temendo che morta

---

86v 10 à] ad | dis'ella] dixe ella **11** ch'ogni] che ogni | contentezza] contenteza **12** mill'anni] mlle anni | ricoperare] recuperare | m'afflige] mi affligge **12–13** ch'ancora] che anchora **13** pestilenziosa] pestilentiosa **14** *B* fe • *added by L. Strozzi over indecipherable erasure* | l'indissolubile] lindissolubile • 'disso' *added by Machiavelli over indeciperhable erasure* **15** diligenzia] diligenza | comune] commune **16** sepolchro] sepulcro **17** Ò] O | Ò con … io • *emended from* Ò co con che diletto ui hebbi io • co *struck through for deletion;* ui *struck through for deletion* **18** uaghezza] uagheza **19** occhi] ochi | *B* Ò] *Omit. Written in B as /O/ by Machiavelli. Rendered as* Ò *in reading text, following Strozzi's usual accent placement* | con qual piaciere] con qual lieto con qual piacere • con qual lieto *struck through for deletion by Machiavelli* | l'auide] le auide **20** acostai!] accostai! • *interlinear addition in L. Strozzi's hand with caret indicating placement* | Ò] O | et strinsi] *A* et *Omit* • et *followed by blank space* | infiammato] infammato **21** et giouinil] *A* et non giouenil • non *struck through for deletion* | mie] me | dolcezza] dolceza **22** all'ultima] alla ultima | sadisfacendo] sodisfacendo | a] ai **23** desiderj] desiderii | Ne • *interlinear addition, probably to replace underlined* et | ch'ella] che ella **24** si arriciarono] *A* saricorono

hide it. I grieve and afterwards it grieves me more that I have lost all my contentment, which, even though I might live for 1,000 years, I am not going to recover. And that which pains me even more is that I am still unable to die. I do not complain about this pestilential season, but rather about my unhappy fortune – that the indissoluble lovers' knot, which so much of my artistry and diligence fabricated, cannot remain tied; from this our common ruin was born and from thence my loving tears are now poured upon the grave of my ill-fated, faithful lover. Oh with whom I had delighted so many times in these once joyful and now miserable arms! With what delight I gazed into his beautiful and shining eyes! Oh what pleasure when I pressed my longing lips to his fragrant mouth! Oh with such great contentment I united and squeezed my burning breasts to his warm and pure and youthful chest! Oh wretched me! So frequently and with such bliss we came to that final amorous joy, simultaneously slaking our desires!" She had no sooner said these words, than she immediately collapsed upon the ground in such a way, that all of my hair stood on end, fearing that she might be dead.

non fusse; perche gl'occhi haueua chuisi, i labbri smorti, il uiso piu che lauanti pallido, et quasi senza senso: solo pareua che il moto del del suo affannoso petto alquanto di uita dimostrasse. Ond'io con quella carnale affettione che si richiede, leggiermente pare cominciai a stropricarla; allargandola dinanzi, per benche molta stretta da se stessa
non fusse; hora di drieto, hora dinanzi riuolgendola; cosi usai seco tutti [87r]
quei rimedi che gli smarriti spiriti fare sogliono risentire: feci si finalmente, ch'ella gl'agrauati occhi suoi riaperse, et si caldo sospiro **[12v]** mando fuora, che se di cera io fusse stato, liquefatto mi saria. All'hora io, confortandola, dixi: Ò semplice et suenturata donna, ad che qui piu dimorite? Se dagli parenti uostri ò da uicini ò da quegli che uostra conoscienza hanno, si soletta fusse trouata, che si dir'ebb'egli? Doue è la uostra prudenzia e la uostra honesta? Ah misera à me! Diss'ella: che l'una non hebbi mai, l'altra ho insieme con quel soaue sguardo de begl'occhi perduta; de quali, non altrimenti che dell'aqua i pesci si nutriscono, mi nutria. A cui risposi: se i consigli miei, donna, appo uoi sono di ualore alcuno, priegoui che meco, non per amore di me, che indegno ne sono: ma per l'honore uostro uogliate

---

86v 25 gl'occhi] gli ochi **26** lauanti] lo auanti | pallido] inpallidito | *B* et quasi senza senso • *marginal addition in L. Strozzi's hand, with caret and % sign indicating placement; replaces the underlined* i polsi tutti smarriti *in Machiavelli's hand* **27** Ond'io] Onde io **28** leggiermente] leggermente | pare • *interlinear addition lacks carets to indicate placement, though it is written above and between* leggiermente *and* cominciai, *producing the reading above* | a stropricarla] ad stropicciarla

87r 1 drieto] dietro **2** quei] quegli | rimedi] rimedii | sogliono] soglono **3** ch'ella] che ella | gl'agrauati] gli aggrauati | occhi] ochi **4** All'hora] Alhora **5** Ò] /O/ | dimorite • 'te' *is an interlinear addition harmonizing this emended plural, formal word with the emendations to personal pronouns that follow* | dimorite] dimori **6** uostri • *emended by L. Strozzi from* tuoi *with interlinear addition* | uostri] tuoi | ò] /o/ | ò] /o/ | uostra • *emended by L. Strozzi from* tua *with interlinear addition* | uostra] tua | conoscienza] conoscenza **7** dir'ebb'egli] direbbe egli | uostra • *emended by L. Strozzi from* tua *with interlinear addition* | uostra] tua | prudenzia] prudenza **8** uostra • *emended by L. Strozzi from* tua *with interlinear addition* | uostra] tua **8** à] a | Diss'ella] Dixella | l'una] luna | l'altra] laltra **9** quel] quello | soaue] suaue | *B* sguardo • 's' *added by Machiavelli over indecipherable erasure* | begl'occhi] begli ochi **10** dell'aqua] della acqua | nutriscono] nutriscano **12** l'honore] lo honore **12–13** *B* uogliate uenire • *emended by Machiavelli from* uenire uogliate *with interlinear Roman numerals; I over* uogliate *and II over* uenire.

Because, her eyes had closed, her lips had gone pale, and her face even paler than it was before and only semi-conscious: only the movement of her grief-stricken breast showed a little life left in her. Where I, with that carnal affection that requires it, lightly began to caress her body; unlacing her (dress) in front, although she was not very tightly laced; now laying her on one side, and now turning her (to the other); and so I used on her all those remedies that the lost spirits are made accustomed to resent. Finally, as I did so, she opened her troubled eyes again, and she exhaled so warm a sigh, that if I had been made of wax, I would have melted. Then comforting her, I said: "Oh simple and unfortunate woman, will you continue to stay here? If your parents, your neighbors, or acquaintances, found you here all alone, what might they have said? Where are your prudence and your respectability?" "Oh my misery!" she said, "I never had the former and the latter, I have lost together with that sweet look of his beautiful eyes; a gaze which nourished me as the water which nourishes fishes." To that I responded: "if my councils, Lady, are of some worth to you then you appreciate that I want you, not for love of me, for I am unworthy of it, to come with me; for the sake of your honor, which, will soon be entirely restored; even though it is somewhat obscured at present, more by the malignity of other people's wicked tongues, than fault of your own. Because, I know many women who fled from their husbands, sheltering with others

uenire; il quale, se malignita delle altrui maluagie lingue, che per colpa uostra in breue interamente recupererete. Perche, quante ne conosch'io che da mariti loro fuggitesi, sono da altri che da parenti racolte state? Quante da i uicinj et loro congiunti in piu graui errori scoperte, che hoggi sono et le belle et le buone tenute? Humana cosa è certamente il pechare: basta bene tal'hora il rauedersi. Si che, se per l'auuenire farete portamenti buoni, uedrete che tosto, tosto ui dico, si dira che stata ingiustamente infiamata siete. In questa maniera persuadendola **[13r]** alla sua propria casa la condussi.

Era gia il sole si in cima del cielo salito, che l'ombre apparieno minorj; quand'io solingo, si come stato era sempre, a prendere il desiato cibo me ne tornai; et riposato alquanto, di nuouo ad ricerchare la citta mi ricondussj, dirizando il mio cammino uerso il nuouo tempio dello Spirito Santo; doue non era quantunque l'hora fusse, alchuna preparatione del diuino officio. Li frati per la chiesa, benche pochi rimasi uene fussero, passeggiauono a capo alto; et che buono numero di loro erano morti, m'affermorono; et piu ancora ne morrebbe, perche uscire di quiui non poteuano, et prouisti da uiuere non erano. Et non ui dico se delle candele per la chiesa accendeuono, credo forse perche i loro morti al buio non andassero: tale ch'io mi parti ben tosto, cacciato piu dal timore del cielo che del morbo tante erano de frati le spesse beneditionj. Et tornandomene per uia Maggio, essendo di maggio le calendi, non uidi pure un segno che mi rappresentassi il

87r 13 *B* delle altrui • altrui *underlined by L. Strozzi, probably for deletion, though above reading is retained as it is superior to A* | delle altrui] *A* dellaltre | *B* maluagie • *marginal addition by L. Strozzi* | maluagie] *A* maluagia **13–14** che … recupererete] *A* che … ricuperere • *interlinear addition with caret indicating placement* | *B* interamente • 'ter' *obscurred by spreading ink* **14** conosch'io] cognosco io **15** racolte] raccolte **16** uicinj et] uicini e **17** pechare] peccare **18** tal'hora] talhora | rauedersi] raduedersi | l'auuenire] lo aduenire **19** ui dico, si dira] *A* si dira ui dico | infiamata] infamata **20** siete] siate **22** l'ombre] lombre • 'e' *emended from* 'a' *by Machiavelli* | minorj • 'j' *emended from* 'e' *by L. Strozzi* | minorj] minori **23** quand'io] quando io | prendere] prehendere | desiato] disiato **24** ricerchare] ricercare | condussi] ricondussj **25** *B* dirizando • *marginal addition by L. Strozzi, probably to replace underlined* et, *and* dirizai *noted in next textual comment* | *B* Santo; dirizai doue • dirizai *underlined for deletion* **26** l'hora] lhora | alchuna] alcuna | officio] ofitio **27–8** passeggiauono a capo alto] a capo alto passeggiauano • a capo alto *marginal addition by L. Strozzi with % sign indicating placement* **28** m'affermorono] mi affermorono **29** ancora] anchora | poteuano] poteuono **30** ui dico] ui diro • 'iro' *written over indecipherable erasure; Machiavelli's hand* **31** ch'io] che io **32** ben] bene | dal] da il | morbo tante] morbo et tante • et *interlinear addition by L. Strozzi with caret indicating placement* **33** beneditionj] beneditioni | essendo] sendo **34** un] uno

than their parents. How many have been uncovered in much graver errors by their neighbors and relatives, who today are held to be the beautiful and the good? Sin certainly is a human thing: but enough good sometimes comes of it to amend one's ways. So that, if you will behave properly, you will see that immediately (immediately I say to you) it will be said that you have been unjustly slandered." In this manner persuading her, I led her to her own house.

The sun had already climbed to the top of the sky, so that the shadows appeared smaller, when I found myself alone, as I always was. So, I sat a while, desiring to take my food. I rested a little and set out once again to wander the city, directing my steps toward the new temple of the Holy Spirit (Santo Spirito); where there was no sign of preparation for the divine service evident, even though it was the proper time. The friars in the church (I stayed there although they were few) were furiously pacing to the high altar and back. They declared to me that a good many of them were dead; and that yet more were sure to die, because they were not allowed to leave, and did not have any provisions to keep them alive. And I need not tell you how they light up the candles of the church with their profanities, I believe perhaps so their dead would not have to find their way out in the dark. Thus, I was driven away, more by the fear of Heaven than plague, the friars were repeating the same benedictions so frequently. And turning into the Via Maggio, since it was the Calends of May, however I did not see anything that looked like

---

87r 24 "di nuouo … ricondussj" *or* "I rested a little … to wander the city" • the next portion of Strozzi's walk took him back across the Arno to the Santo Spirito quarter.
87r 25 "nuouo tempio dello Spirito Santo" *or* "the new temple of The Holy Spirit" • a reference to the basilica that was designed by Filippo Brunelleschi. The basilica, located in the Oltr'Arno, was not completed until decades after Brunelleschi's death in 1482.
87r 33 "uia Maggio" *or* "Via Maggio" • Here Strozzi is making an obvious wordplay, taking the "Via Maggio" because it was the first of May (*maggio*). It is likely that the "Via Maggio" received its name following Dante's use of *maggio* as "Broadway" or the "Broadest Way". These interesting ideas, as they pertain to the Tuscan dialect and place/street names in Florence, were developed by Rudolph Altrocchi in 'Trinità or Trínita?' *Italica* 26, no. 1 (1949): 57–61. For particular references to the "Via Maggio," see 60–1. Strozzi made his way from the Oltr'Arno by the "Via Maggio" and the "Santa Trinita" bridge, to the city centre and the Church of Santa Trinità. The "Via Maggio" and the "Ponte Santa Trinità" were constructed as a part of an urban renewal campaign by the Florentine comune in the late thirteenth century. See Roger J. Crum and John T. Paoletti, eds., *Renaissance Florence: A Social History* (Cambridge: Cambridge University Press, 2006), 198.
87r 34 "maggio le calendi" *or* "Calends of May" • see chapter 2, nnote 5 of this study for coverage of Machiavelli's *Minuta*, c. 1522, which references this exact period.

maggio;

anzi, sopra il mezzo del ponte trouai un morto, a cui non ardiua apressarsi [87v alchuno: et entrando nella anticha chiesa di Santa Trinita, un sol huomo, ma bene qualificato, ui trouai. Et domandandolo io, quale cagione nella citta in tanto periglio il ritenessi, mi rispose: lo amore della patria, la quale da tutti i suoi poco amoreuoli cittadini era abbandonata. A cui io dissi: che molto meno erraua chi **[13v]** cerchaua alla patria mantenersi, da quella per qualche mese dilungandosi per poterli altra uolta giouare, che quegli che non gli giouando, in pericolo d'abbandonarla sempre si metteuano. All'hora egli: se il uero ho a dire a chi sello conosce, non la patria, ma quella sconsolata che tu uedi si diuotamente genuflexa, per lo cui amore disposto sono mettere la uita, qui mi ritiene. Paruemi ch'alla eta sua matura tanta caldezza non si richiedesse; et percio gli dissi, che in questi si fortuneuolj casi, il padre il figliuolo, la moglie il marito addandonaua. Et egli: tale è il mio amore che ogni grado di sanguinita auanza; et che, se a schifare la peste lo stare lieto è ottimo rimedio, in presenzia della dama amata era essa letizia, et fuora di lei tanto duolo gl'auerebbe, che per quello solo di uita amaramente uscirebbe; et che come quiui solo trouato l'haueua, solo ancora et unico intra gl'altri amori era l'amore suo: et essendo innamorato, et uiuere uolendo, uicino stessi alla amata; non essendo, da il suo essempio mosso, mi innamorassi, se schifare la pestifera mortalita uoleuo: et che ancora io ero a tempo. Io, a cui simili ragionamenti non piacquero, giudicando l'amore una peste tanto piu perniziosa quanto piu lunga, senza altro dirgli, mi parti. Et sopra il solitario in questi tempi pancone degli

---

87v 1 mezzo] mezo | un] uno **2** alchuno] alcuno | anticha] antica | di Santa • 'di' *emended to* della *with interlinear addition, though* 'di' *is the better reading* | Santa *is underlined, probably to be replaced by the interlinear* diuina, *though* Santa *is the better reading* | di Santa Trinita] della diuina Trinita | un sol] uno solo **4** periglio] periglo **5** A] Ad **6** cerchaua] cercaua **7** poterli] potergli **8** d'abbandonarla] di abbandonarla **9** All'hora] Alhora | a chi sello conosce] a chi se lo conosce • *marginal addition, in L. Strozzi's hand, with caret indicating placement* **10** diuotamente] deuotamente | lo] il **11** ch'alla] che alla **11-12** matura] *A Omit* **12** dissi] dixi **12–13** fortuneuolj] fortuneuoli **13** moglie] mogle **14** a] ad **15** presenzia] presentia | della dama amata • amata *is interlinear addition above and to the right of* dama | della dama amata] della amata **16** letizia] letitia | gl'auerebbe] gli aduerrebbe **17** l'haueua] lo haueua **18** gl'altri] gli altri | l'amore] lo amore **19** stessi] *A* stesse | essendo] sendo | da il] dal **20** essempio] exemplo | mi innamorassi] minnamorassi | uoleuo] *A* uolendo **21** ero] *A* era **22** l'amore] lo amore | perniziosa] pernitiosa **23** in] *A* a

May to me; in fact, I found a dead man in the middle of the bridge, who no one dared approach: and entering the ancient church of Santa Trinità I found only one seemingly well-born man there. I asked him for what reason he remained in a city faced with such danger and he answered me: "For love of my native city, which every one of her little-loving citizens has shunned." To whom I said, "he errs much less who seeks to preserve himself for his native city so that he might be able to serve it at a later time than those who, feigning to serve it, exposed themselves to the danger of leaving it forever." To which he replied: "if I must tell the truth to one who knows it already, it is not our native city that keeps me here, but it is that disconsolate lady who you saw so devotedly genuflecting - for whose love I am prepared to lay down my life." It seemed to me that such burning passion was not befitting of one of his mature age so therefore I said to him, "that even in the luckiest of houses that the father abandons his son and the wife her husband." And he responded: "Such is the degree of my love, that it surpasses every type of blood relation." He carried on like this: if to avoid the plague to be happy is an excellent remedy, then to be in the presence of her love was tremendous joy, and away from her love such grief that it alone would cause him to depart this life bitterly and alone as he was found here; so unique, he argued, was his love among the various types of love; and he concluded by saying that being in love, and wishing to live, that I should remain close to my lover. Not being so yet, but moved by his example, he urged me to fall in love to escape the deadly plague; and told me that I still had time. I was not persuaded by those arguments, judging love a much more dangerous and longer lasting pestilence. Without saying anything else to him I left. And on the nowadays deserted Spini bench

---

87v 2 "chiesa di Santa Trinita" *or* "the church of Santa Trinità" • is a fine and beautiful church, which is famous primarily because it was probably designed by Nicola Pisano. For more background, see Murray, *Architecture*, 24. The frescos of the Sassetti Chapel, located in Santa Trinità, are very helpful, however, when attempting to visualize Florence's urban landscape, and especially the locations of Santa Trinità and the Ponte Santa Trinità. This fresco by Domenico Ghirlandaio is discussed below.

87v 5 "poco amoreuoli cittadini" or "little loving citizens" • Machiavelli used this "cittadini amorevoli" on only two occasions: in his *Minuta*, c. 1522, and in his *Istorie fiorentine*. I suggested in chapter 2 that Strozzi's vocabulary here might have influenced Machiavelli's, as the *Minuta* and the *Istorie* were written at roughly the same time as the *Pistola*. See appendix 4, *Minuta*, 26.24–5. I used the vocabulary and word usage search functions at "Intratext.com" to gather this information.

Spini, il uenerabile padre frate Alexo, che per fuggire forse la peste s'era uscito della Regola: che forse quiui per confessare fuori di chiesa qualche sua diuota attendeua, ritrouai: et da lui inteso, **[14r]** come nella bene proportionata, et ueneranda chiesa di Santa Maria Nouella, dond'egli per li suoi buoni portamenti stato era rimosso, si adunauono per li amorosi amaestramenti degli festiui et caritatiuj frati, piu donne che in ogni altra qual si uoglia, chiesa; meco, benche non molto secondo la sua uoglia, il menai, perche [88r] temeua il fratticello di quello che certo, se senza me gito ui fosse, aduenuto gli saria. Nondimeno, fermandosi poco, anzi apena salutato l'altare maggiore, perche molto diuoto non era, si parti, et credo ch'al suo pancone per fornire l'opera si ritornasse. Io mi restai per udire la lieta compieta de fratti; doue se ben non uidi, quale solea, il gran numero delle gentili donne, et nobili huomini admiranti gl'angelichi uolti, et i diuini portamenti de richi, et ben

---

87v 24–6 *B followed here:* frate Alexo … ritrouai | *A* Alexo che • che *underlined, probably for deletion* **24–5** *B* che per … Regola • *marginal addition by L. Strozzi with caret indicating placement* • *A* che per … Regola • *marginal addition struck through for deletion, though probably initially intended to replace the linear text* che forse et per auentura quiui per confessare fuori di chiesa qualche sua diuota attendeua ritrouai,
also underlined, probably for deletion. At the foot of the folio is another underlined passage with a caret indicating placement after Alexo • che forse per usare meglio la carita del confessare hor questa hor quella Donna fuora di chiesa s'era uscita della Regola et per auuentura et da lui inteso. *Reading(s) provided by A too uncertain to rely on, therefore B followed here.* **26** da] dal **27** dond'egli] donde egli | li] gli **27–8** suoi buoni] *A* buoni suoi **28** adunauono] adunauano | li] gli | amaestramenti] admaestramenti **29** caritatiuj] caritatiui | qual si uoglia] quale si uolga
88r 1 chiesa; meco • *emended from* chiesa il menai meco • il menai *underlined, probably for deletion* | secondo • *interlinear addition with caret indicating placement* | uoglia] uolga **2** temeua] temea | fratticello] fraticello | ui • *written over indecipherable word* | fosse] fusse **3** apena] appena | l'altare] laltare **4** diuoto] deuoto | ch'al] che al **5** l'opera] lopera | doue • *interlinear addition to replace underlined, linear* donde **6** ben] bene **7** gl'angelichi] gli angelici | i diuini] diuini | ben] bene

I came upon the venerable father Alessio, who perhaps to flee the plague remained away from the monastery: perchance he was waiting there to confess one of his penitents outside the church; I learned from him that in the perfectly proportioned and venerable church of Santa Maria Novella, from where he, for his good behavior, was excluded, more ladies than one could wish for were assembled there (perhaps owing to the amorous instruction of the festive and charitable brothers) than in any other church. Although against his wishes, I took him with me, because the good friar feared what would certainly have happened to him if he had gone there without me. Nevertheless, staying only briefly, in fact scarcely having saluted the high altar, because he was never known for his piety, he left; so, I believe, that he could return to work at his bench. I remained to hear the friars' delightful Compline. There, even though I did not, as usual, see the great number of gentlewomen or noblemen admiring the ladies' angelic faces and the divine allure of their rich and well designed dresses, which together with the sweet music, invite souls to play

---

87v 23–4 "pancone degli Spini" *or* "Spini Bench" • is referenced by Machiavelli in his *Mandragola*. See act 4, scene 2, where he wrote of the "Pancone delli Spini," in Pasquale Stoppelli, *La Mandragola: Storia e filologia, con l'edizione critica del testo secondo il Laurenziano Redi 129* (Rome: Bulzoni, 2005), 223. The Spini Bench no longer exists. In fact, the palace to which it was once attached is now the Salvatore Ferragamo factory and store. Formerly the Palazzo Spini, then the Spini Feroni, and now the Palazzo Spini Ferragamo, it has been radically transformed from its late medieval, early Renaissance beginnings. In order to see the "pancone degli Spini" as it probably looked when Strozzi knew it, enter the church of Santa Trinità, proceed to the high altar, and look to the back right-hand corner of the church. There, in the Sassetti Chapel, are Domenico Ghirlandaio's frescos from the life of St Francis. The central fresco, on the back wall of the chapel, depicting St Francis resurrecting a young boy, clearly shows the piazza outside the church, the Palazzo Spini, the Ponte Santa Trinità, and the "pancone degli Spini." This bench also hosted the famous quarrel between Leonardo da Vinci and Michelangelo Buonarotti. For more on this episode, see Ridolfo Mazzucconi, *Leonardo da Vinci* (Florence: Vallecchi, 1943), 308.

87v 24 "frate Alexo" *or* "Father Alessio" • was a Dominican friar associated with Santa Maria Novella. This same "Father Alessio" plays a small part in saving the life of Benvenuto Cellini. See Cellini's *The Autobiography of Benvenuto Cellini*, trans. J. Addington Symonds (New York: P.F. Collier and Son, 1910), 33. For Italian original see Benvenuto Cellini, *Vita di Benvenuto Cellini Scritta da Lui Medesimo* (Florence: Adriano Salani, Editore Viale Militare, 1903), 27–8.

87v 27 "Santa Maria Novella" • one of Florence's most important churches, associated with the Dominican Order, where Santa Croce was associated with the Franciscan Order. The architect of the church is unknown, though tradition ascribed authorship to two unnamed Dominican friars. The church's façade was designed by Leon Battista Alberti in 1458. See Murray, *Architecture*, 56–8 for further detail.

intesi habiti, insieme con le dolci musiche, gl'animi di qualunque piu all'amoroso giuocho che alle celesti cogitationi inuitanti, ui trouai nondimeno men solitudine che in niuno altro luogo; onde conobbi quanto tal chiesa fauorita et fortunata infra l'altre chiamare si potesse: percio pensai di dimorarui in fino all'ultima hora. Doue rimasse ancora, benche gia sera fusse, per udire forse, com'io, la compieta, solo una bella giouane in habito uedouile; della cui bellezza se appena confidassi parlare potere, conoscho ch'io mi ingannerei: pure, per sodisfare in parte, con silenzio non la passero; et uoi quello piu che manchare conoscerete alla narratione mia, ui ci inmaginerete.

Ella era prima, benche sedendo sopra gli marmorei gradi alla **[14v]** cappella maggiore uicinj, in sul sinistro fiancho aguisa d'affannata persona si posassi, con il candido braccio la alquanto inpallideta faccia sostenendo, d'una conueneuole grandezza alla statura d'una poporionata et ben composta donna: si che quinci cognoscere si poteua, che le parti tutte di quel corpo talmente insieme erano conformi, che se di uestrij funebri non fossero ricoperte, di mirabile bellezza agl'occhi miei sarieno apparse. Ma lasciando questa parte libera da comtemplarsi alla uostra inmaginatione, quello solo che palese mi fu desriuero. Candido auorio sembrauono le fresche sue et dilicate carni, et si gentili et morbide,
da riseruare d'ogni quantunque leggiero toccamento forma, non meno [88v]
che d'un uerde prato la tenera et rugiadosa herbetta gli sospesi uestigi de leggieri animaletti facci. Gl'occhi, di cui meglio sarebbe il tacere che dirne

88r 8 gl'animi] gli animi **8–9** all'amoroso giuocho] allo amoroso gioco **10** *A* solitudine • 'i' *emended from* 'e' | luogo] loco | *A* conobbi *emended from* conobi | conobbi] cognobbi **11** l'altre] laltre **12** all'ultima] allultima | rimasse] rimase **13** udire] udir | com'io] come io **14** bellezza] belleza | conoscho] cognosco **15** ch'io] che io | mi ingannerei] mingannerei | silenzio] silentio **16** conoscerete] cognoscerete **17** inmaginerete] immaginerete **19** maggiore • *interlinear addition with caret indicating placement* | uicinj • 'j' *emended from* 'a' | uicinj] uicini | fiancho] fianco | aguisa] agguisa | d'affannata] daffannata **21** d'una] duna | conueneuole • *marginal addition by L. Strozzi probably to replace the underlined, linear* comunale | grandezza] grandeza | d'una] di una | ben] bene **22** poteua] potea **23** quel] quello | uestrij] uestiti **24** fossero] fussero | bellezza agl'occhi] belleza ad gli ochi **25–6** inmaginatione] immaginatione **26–7** sembrauono] sembrauano **27** dilicate] delicate

88v 1 *B* da • 'a' *added by L. Strozzi over indecipherable erasure* | riseruare d'ogni] riserbare dogni **2** d'un] dun | uestigi] uestigii **3** Gl'occhi] Gli occhi | meglio] meglo

love games so much more than to heavenly meditations. I found there less solitude than in any other place; as a result I knew how this church might be able to call itself the most favored and highly blessed than any other. Therefore I decided to stay there until the very last. Where remained, although it was already evening, perhaps, like me, to hear the Compline, only one beautiful young woman in widow's clothes; whose beauty, and I know that I delude myself, I scarcely have the power to describe to you in words. However, to satisfy you at least in part, I will not proceed in silence; but, by imagining us there, you will supply that which my narration lacks.

At first she was (although now sitting on the marble steps near to the *cappella maggiore*) reposing on her left side in the manner of an anxious person, supporting her somewhat pale face with a snow-white arm. She was of an agreeable size and proportionate stature for a finely formed woman. So that even from here one could conclude that all the parts of such a body were so well shaped, that if stripped of her mourning raiment, they would present a wondrous beauty to my eyes. But leaving this part free for you to gaze upon in your imagination, I will describe the part that is made manifest. Her smooth and tender skin resembles spotless ivory yet so soft and delicate as to preserve the traces of even the lightest touch, no less th an the fine grass of a green and dewy meadow preserves the prints made by dainty little animals. Her eyes, concerning which it might be better to say nothing at all than say only a little, seem to be two shining stars which, from time to time, she lifted with such grace, that one saw paradise opened. Her delightful brow, the length of which ends in for her splendid and beautiful eyes; about which it appears that Love jests and always flits about, shooting his arrows and wounding this, or that loving

---

88r 15–89r 2 "pure, per sodisfare … risentirebbe" *or* "However, to satisfy … might have been aroused by them" • closely resembles Machiavelli's description of the "servant of Circe" who restores Machiavell's flaccid "virtù" in his *L'Asino*. All English references to Machiavelli's *L'Asino* are from "The Golden Ass," in *The Chief Works and Others*, vol. 3, trans., Alan Gilbert (Durham: Duke University Press, 1965), 750–72 (hereafter *The Ass*); all references to the Italian original are from "L'Asino," in *Opere*, vol. 3, ed. Corrado Vivanti (Rome: Einaudi, 2005), 51–78 (hereafter *L'Asino*).

88r 18–19 "cappella maggiore" • commissioned by Giovanni Tornabuoni, and executed by Domenico Ghirlandaio and his workshop. See P. Simons, 'Patronage in the Tornaquinci Chapel, Santa Maria Novella, Florence," in *Patronage, Art and Society in Renaissance Italy*, ed. F.W. Kent and P. Simons (Oxford: Clarendon, 1987), 221–51 (cited by Paola Tinagli, *Women in Renaissance Art: Gender, Representation, Identity* [Manchester: Manchester University Press, 1997], 81n12.

88v 3–4 "Gl'occhi … Stelle parieno" *or* "Her eyes … shining stars" • "Each eye appeared a little flame, so shining, so clear and so / lively that all vision however acute was lost in it" (*The Ass*, 759, ll. 58–9). And "Ciascuno occhio pareva una fiammella, / Tanto lucente, si spegne in quella" (*L'Asino*, 62, ll. 58–9).

poco, due accese stelle parieno; quali si a tempo et con tale leggiadria grazia alzaua,che il paradiso aperto si uedeua. La lieta fronte, di cui lo spazio con giustissima misura terminaua, si chiara et rilucente, che spechiandosi in quella il semplice Narcisso, non manco di se stesso che nel limpido fonte in uaghito si sarebbe: sotto la quale l'arcate, sottilissime, ben profilate, et negre ciglia ad gli splendidi begl'occhi facieno coperchio; intorno a quei pare che scherzi et uoli sempre Amore, et indi sue suelte scharchi, hor questo hor quell'amoroso cuore ferendo. L'**[15r]**orecchie, per quello ch'apparire ne potea, erano piciole, rotunde, et tali ch'ogni perito phisionomo essere di somma prudenzia segno giudichate l'harebbe. Ma che diro io della melliflua, et delichata boccha? Tra due piaggie di rose uestite et di ligustri posta, la quale in tanta mestizia pareua che d'uno celeste riso, non so come, splendesse. Basti ch'io mi credo che da quella pigli natura essempio, quando alchuna bellissima di nuouo produre al mondo ne intende. Le rosate labbia sopra gli eburnei et candidi denti, accesi rubini parieno et perle orientali insieme miste. Haueua da Junone del suauemente exteso naso la forma tolto:cosi come a Uenere delle candide et distese guancie.

Non lasciero la bellezza della sua suelte, biancha, et uezosa gola, degna certamente d'essere di pertiose gieme ornata. Le inuidiose ueste comtemplare non mi lasciauono il lacteo, uenusto et ben raccolto petto, da duoi picioli, freschi, et odoriferi pomi adorno, com'io mi credo, colti nello horto famoso,

---

88v 4 a] al | et] *A Omit* | leggiadria grazia] legiadra gratia • legiadra, *is a marginal addition by L. Strozzi with a % sign indicating placement*; gratia *is underlined with series of dots* **5** uedeua] uedea | spazio] spatio **7** nel limpido] *A* nell'impido **9** ciglia] cigla | begl'occhi] begli ochi | a] ad **10** scharchi] scarchi **11** quell'amoroso] quello amoroso | cuore] core | L'orecchie] Le orechie **11–12** ch'apparire] che apparire **12** piciole] piccole | ch'ogni] che ogni | phisionomo] phisioniomo • *second* 'o', *an interlinear addition by L. Strozzi* **13** prudenzia] prudenza | giudichate l'harebbe] giudicate le harebbe | io • *not in B* **14** delichata boccha] delicata bocca **15** mestizia pareua] mestitia parea | d'uno] duno **16** ch'io] che io | essempio] exemplo | **17** alchuna] alcuna | produre] produrre **18** labbia] labbra **19** Junone • 'J' *emended to capital, over lower case* 'i' | Junone] iunone | *B* suauemente • *written as* sua[indecipherable erasure]uemente | *B* naso • *replaces* nastro • *struck through by Machiavelli* **21** lasciero] lascero | bellezza] belleza | biancha] bianca **22** d'essere] di essere | pertiose gieme] pretiose gemme | comtemplare • 't' *emended from* 'p' | comtemplare] contemplare **23** lasciauono] lasciauano | lacteo] latteo | picioli • *interlinear addition with caret indicating placement* | picioli] piccioli **24** com'io] come io | horto] orto

perfect measure, so bright and shining, that simple Narcissus, admiring himself in it, as in the limpid pool might have become infatuated with himself; below which the finely traced arches of her black eyebrows made a covering heart. Her ears, from what of them one is able to see, were small, round, and of such shape, that every expert physiognomist would have judged them a sign of acute prudence (or intelligence). But what can I say of the sweet and delicate mouth, situated between two cheeks adorned with delicate roses and lilies or of how, I know not, even in such sadness it seems that a celestial smile shines? But I know enough to believe that Nature will use this most beautiful one as a model when it desires to enrich the world once again. The rose colored lips upon the ivory and snow white teeth appear as fiery rubies mixed together with oriental pearls. From Juno, she has a delicately formed nose, as from Venus that of her playful and flowery cheeks.

I will not leave out the beauty of her slender, white and graceful neck, which certainly should be ornamented with precious gems. Her envious clothes did not give me leave to gaze on the creamy, beautiful and finely sculpted chest, adorned with two little fresh and sweet smelling apples,

---

88v 8 "l'arcate" *or* "brow" • "Narrow arched and black were her brows, because at the shaping / of them were all the gods, all the high and heavenly councils" (*The Ass*, 760, ll. 64–6). And "Sottili, arcati e neri erano I cigli / Perch'a plasmargli fur tutti gli Dei, / Tutti I celesti e superni consigli" (*L'Asino*, 63, ll. 64–6).

88v 14 "delichata boccha" *or* "delicate mouth" • "I do not know at all who made her mouth if Jove did not do it / with his own hand; I do not believe any other hand could have / made it" (*The Ass*, 760, ll. 70–2). And "Io non so già chi quella bocca fesse; / Se Giove con sua man non la fece egli, / Non credo ch'altra man far la potesse" (*L'Asino*, 63, ll. 70–2).

88v 14 "ligustri" *or* "lillies" • perhaps "ligustrum volgare," a flowering shrub native to many parts of the world, including the Mediterranean.

88v 18 "denti" *or* "teeth" • "Her teeth were more beautiful than ivory, and her tongue moved / like a serpent between them and her lips" (*The Ass*, 760, ll. 73–5). And "I denti più che d'avorio eran begli; / E una lingua vibrar si vedeva, / Come una serpe, infra le labbra e quegli" (*L'Asino*, 63, ll. 73–5).

88v 19 "naso" *or* "nose" • "Of that which slopes down from these [her brow] I should like to say / something that would partly correspond to the truth, but I am / silent about it because I could not describe it" (*The Ass*, 760, ll. 67–9). And "Di quel che da quei pende dir vorrei / Cosa ch'al vero alquanto rispondesse, / Ma tacciol, perchè dir non lo sparei" (*L'Asino*, 63, ll. 67–9).

88v 21 "gola" *or* "neck" • "Her neck and chin were also visible, and other beauties / enough to make happy every gloomy and unsuccessful lover" (*The Ass*, 760, ll. 79–81). And "Il collo e 'l mento ancor vedeasi, e tante / Altre bellezze, che farina felice/ Ogni meschino e infelice amante" (*L'Asino*, 63, ll. 79–81).

88v 23 "ben raccolto petto" *or* "finely sculpted chest" • "I continued to pass my eyes over all her various parts as low as / her breast, at the splendour of which I [am still] kindled, / but seeing farther was refused me by a rich and shining coverlet / with which that little bed was covered" (*The Ass,* 759, ll. 88–93). And "Io venni ben con l'occhio discorrendo / Tutte le parti sue infino al petto, / A lo splendour del quale ancor m'accendo; / Ma più oltre veder mi fu disdetto / Da una ricca e candida coperta, / Con la qual coperto era il cicciol letto" (*L'Asino*, 63, ll. 88–93)

delle Hesperide; i quali, per la saldezza loro auestimenti non cjedendo, la bellezza et tutte le loro qualita a risguardanti dimostrauono; in tra quali una uia n'appariua per la quale camminando **[15v]** alla somma beatitudine si peruerrebbe. La candida, et delicata mano, quantunque di parte della bellezza del leggiadro uiso ne priuase, col mostrare se stessa ne ristoraua; quale era lunga, sottile, espedita, et di minutissime
et lucide uene profilata, con i diti stietti et suaui, et forse di tale uertu, che [89r]
per i loro tocchamenti qualunque uecchio Priamo si risentirebbe.

Io non ueggiendo all'intorno alcuno il cui rispetto ritenere mi douessi, et ella con i pietosi occhi suoi porgendomi ardire, me gli accostai, et dissj: Graziosa donna, se il cortese domandare non u'è noioso, piacciaui dirmi qual cagione qui si lungamente ui ritiene: et s'io alli bisogni uostri porgere posso alcuno aiuto. Et ella: come uoi forse, aspettato ho de frati la compieta in uano. Li bisogni miei sono tali che, non che uoi, ogni quantunque minor persona giouare mi potria. L'habito dimostra ch'io sono del mio diletto sposo priua et quel che piu mi duole, è che egli è di peste crudelmente morto; ond'io ancora in periglio ne resto, et pero, se senza altrui giouare, a uoi stesso nuocere non uolete, state alquanto piu lontano. Le parole la uoce il modo et la cura, che mi parue che della salute mia tenesse, mi trafissero il core: si **[16r]** che nel foco entrato per lei saria, nondimeno per non le dispiaciere uie piu che per il pericolo mi ritenni, dicendole: perche si sola dimorate? Perche sola sono rimasa. L'ho hauere compagnia piaccierebbeui? Altro non desio, che honestamente acompagniata uiuere Et io, quantunque per auanti con donna accompagniarmi uolto non fusse: uistoui di si uenusto et grazioso

---

88v 25 *B* Hespedperide • 'ped' *struck through for deletion by Machiavelli* | saldezza • 's' *emended from* 'c' | saldezza] saldeza | cjedendo • 'j' *operating as* 'i', *emended from* 'r | cjendendo] cedendo **26** bellezza] belleza | a] ai | risguardanti] riguardanti | dimostrauono] dimostrauano **27** n'appariua] ne appariua **29** bellezza] belleza | priuase] priuasse **30** espedita] expedita

89r 1 uertu] uirtu **2** tocchamenti] toccamenti | qualunque uecchio • 'qualunque' *underlined* | *B* qualunque il uecchio • qualunque *is an interlinear addition by L. Strozzi;* il *is underlined, probably for deletion, producing the same reading as A* **3** all'intorno] allo intorno **4** occhi] ochi | dissj] dixi **5** Graziosa] Gratiosa | domandare] dimandare | u'è] ui è **6** lungamente] lunghamente | s'io] se io | alli] ad gli **8** miei] mia **9** l'habito] lhabito | ch'io] che io **10** egli è] *A* gl'è **11** ond'io ancora] ondio anchora | periglio] periglo | a] ad **12** modo] *A* mondo **14** dispiaciere] dispiacere **16** L'ho] Lho | piaccierebbeui] piacerebbeui **17** acompagniata] accompagnata **18** accompagniarmi] accompagnarmi | grazioso] gratioso

which I believe were grown in the famous orchard of the Hesperides. But, by the manner in which they refused to yield to her dress, they demonstrated their beauty and firmness; and between them flashes a way, at the end of which, the wanderer might reach the ultimate bliss. Her snow-white and delicate hand, although it might deprive me of part of the beauty of her elegant visage, provided its own refreshment. It was long, slender, capable and outlined with the smallest and shining veins, with the fingers straight and soft and perhaps of such virtue, that by their touches even old Priam might have been aroused by them.

I, not seeing anyone, out of respect for whom I ought to restrain myself, and she inspiring courage in me with her compassionate eyes, approached her and said: "Gracious Lady, if a courteous question is not noisome to you, might it please you to tell me for what reason you stay here for so long? And may I offer some aid to you?" To which she responded: "Like you perhaps, I have waited for the brothers' Compline in vain. My needs are such that even a lesser man than you could be useful to me. My clothes display that I am deprived of my beloved husband, and my pain is all the more for he died of the cruel plague, and thus I remain in peril. And, if therefore, you do not want to expose yourself to harm, remain at some distance." Her words, her voice, her manner, and the care that she seemed to have for my safety, pierced my heart so, that I would walk through fire for her. Nevertheless, fearing more to displease her, than the danger of the

---

88v 24-25 "horto famoso, delle Hesperide" *or* "famous orchard of the Hesperides" • the trees of this mythic orchard, tended by nymphs (the Hesperides) produced golden apples, said to offer immortality to those who ate of their flesh. Strozzi's age (roughly forty years old in 1522), the widow's apparent youth, and the beauty of her breasts (though covered by her mourning weeds), imply that Strozzi believed he would have been reinvigorated by the love and sex offered by this young woman.

89r 1 "uertu" *or* "virtue" • loss of "virtù" and "impotence" and vice versa are intertwined throughout Machiavelli's *L'Asino*. For an astutely written assessment of this topic see Michael Harvey's 'Lost in the Wilderness: Love and Longing in *L'Asino,*' in *The Comedy and Tragedy of Machiavelli: Essays on the Literary Works*, ed. Vickie B. Sullivan (New Haven: Yale University Press, 2000):120–37. Interestingly, here in the *Pistola* it is the woman's "virtue" that restores the man's.

89r 8–9 "minor persona" *or* "lesser man" • might also be rendered as a "younger man."

89r 14 "nel foco entrato" *or* "walk through fire" • on 7 April 1498, Savonarola begrudgingly allowed a representative from his own Dominican Order, Fra Domenico, and a Franciscan opponent, Fra Francesco di Puglia, to stage a "fire" walk: both priests were supposed to pass through a large fire to find out which order had God's blessing and support. In the end, Fra Francesco backed out of the challenge. As Strozzi was in Florence's great Dominican church, one wonders if he was referencing that event, though in a perverse manner. See Lauro Martines, *Fire in the City: Savonarola and the Struggle for the Soul of Renaissance Florence* (New York: Oxford University Press, 2006), 219–30 for an account of this episode.

aspetto, in cui bene misse natura ogni suo sforzo, et mosso a compassione de uostri affanni: con uoi sono disposto accompagnarmi; et se ben non molto è l'eta conueneuole, le faculta, et l'altre cose mie sono tali, che ui potro forse contentare. Di uoi huomini, diss'ella, sempre furano le promesse lunge, et la fede corta, se io ho a memoria bene molte cose passate. Risposile: chi sa prudentemente eleggiere, d'altri non si fida che di chi ragioneuolmente fidare si deue: et pero non s'ha mai di se stessa apentere. Et ella: poi che il cielo, dattore di tutti i beni, innanzi mi u'ha porto (quantunque piu uisto non u'habbi) che di me non habbi cura particulare credere non posso: et percio se di me ui contentate, mi parrebbe oltre modo errare se et io di uoi non mi contentassi. Apena queste parole hebbe dette, che uno otioso frate, a testa ritta, atto piu al remo ch'al sagrificio, il nome di cui tacere **[16v]** mi uolgio per poterne meglio senza rispetto parlare, come un falcone che dell'aria, uisto la preda, al terra piombi, inanzi s'auento [89v] a si leggiadra, et delicata donna: et come se mille uolte parlato gl'hauesse: molto domesticamente, com'è il costume loro, le domando, se niente di bisogno l'occorreua di sua opera. Io glj risposi, ch'ella hora mai de bisogni suoi fornita s'era, et che non c'haueua luogo la fratescha sua carita.

Il ribaldone, che di gia spiritaua, et per fare forse un'altro parentado piu a gusto suo harebbe guasto il nostro: quantunque per gl'occhi sfauillassi et ne panni non capessi, storciessissi come all'incanto biscia, et uisto che da lei duramente accomiatato, et da me non amicheuolmente accarezzato era,

---

89r 20 ben] bene **21** l'eta] la eta | l'altre] laltre **22** potro forse] *A* potranno | diss'ella] dixella | furano] furono **23** lunge] lunghe | molte cose • *interlinear addition, probably to replace the underlined, linear* 'alchuna delle' | molte cose] alcuna delle | passate • *emended from* passate historie • historie *underlined, probably for deletion* | passate] passate historie **24** Risposile • *emended from* Risposile: è lecito a chi scriue dire quello che egli uuole • 'è … uuole' *underlined, probably for deletion* | Risposile] Risposile: è lecito a chi scriue dire quello che uuole | chi • *emended from* ma chi • ma *underlined, probably for deletion* | chi] ma chi | eleggiere, d'altri] eleggire, daltri **25** s'ha] si ha **26** i beni] beni | u'ha] ui ha **27** u'habbi] ui habbi **28** modo] a modo **29** Apena] Appena **30** al remo] *A* alieno (*sic*) | ch'al] che al **31** uolgio] uolgo | poterne] *A* potere | meglio] meglo
89v 1 dell'aria] della aria | inanzi] innanzi | s'auento] si aduento **2** gl'hauesse] gli hauesse **3** com'è] come è **4** l'occorreua] le occorreua • le *emended from* gli *by L. Strozzi* | glj • *emended from* le, glj] gli | ch'ella] che ella **5** s'era] se era | c'haueua] ci haueua | fratescha] fratesca **6** un'altro] un altro **7** harebbe] haurebbe | gl'occhi] gli ochi **8** capessi] *A* caprissi | storciessissi] storcessi si | all'incanto] allo incanto **9** 'acc' • *struck through at line's end, and rewritten at the start of the next line,* accarezzato] accarezato

plague, I stopped short of her and asked: "Why do you stay here so alone?" [She replied] "Because I alone am spared [must] I have to have a husband in order to please you? I wish for nothing more than to live married honestly." [I replied] "And I, who before this moment never wished to marry a woman, now see your beautiful and gracious form, upon whom Nature bestowed its bounty, and moved to compassion by your afflictions, am resolved to marry you. Even though our age difference is not ideal, my means and other circumstances are such that I will perhaps be able to please you." She replied "With you men, ever were the promises great and the faith but small, if I have a good memory of things past." I responded to her: "One who knows how to choose prudently does not have to put his faith in the truthfulness of others and therefore never has to repent of what he has done." And she rejoined: "As Heaven, giver of all that is good, has brought you to me, I cannot doubt that you will show special care for me even though I have never seen you before; and consequently since you are pleased with me, it would be exceedingly wrong if I were not content with you." It was just after she spoke those words, that a lazy friar, head held high – an act suitable for rowing rather than sacrificing; whose name I will keep to myself so as to be able better to speak of him without any hesitation – as a falcon that sees its prey from the air swoops to earth, pounced on this elegant and delicate Lady; and, as if he had spoken with her a thousand times, with great familiarity as is these friars' custom, he asked if she lacked anything or if she needed his assistance. I told him, that she was never in need of his support, as she would never have a place for his brotherly love.

ristringiendosi ne suoi panni, non so che borbottando, se n'ando in mal'hora. Ne crediate pero ch'io subito cosi soletta la lasciassi; anzi, drietole sempre, infino a casa sua l'accompagnai nella quale se, insieme con il mio core, in un tratto rinchiuse. Ond'io rimaso solo di si lieta et a me diletteuole compagnia, per non deuiare dal cominciato mio ordine affrettando i passi nell'egregio et lieto tempio di Santo Lorenzo mi condussi la doue uedere consueto era chi degl'anni miei il fiore s'haueua goduto. Ma fu la nuoua inpressione tanto possente, che come quegli che del fiume Lethe gustono, d'ogni altra benche leggiadra donna **[17r]** mi dimentichai. Erano tutti i pensieri miei rimasi in quegli negri panni a uolti, attorno ai quali l'importuno et hipocrito frate uedere ad ogni hora mi pareua: tale gelosia in maniera mi tenea occupati gli spiriti, ch'altro considerare ò uedere non potea. Percio, parendomi in uano il tempo spendere, et desiando, come composto m'era, la desiata consorte riuedere, ben tosto a casa mi tornai; et ponendo alla tragicha consideratione dell'horrenda peste fine, al piaciere d'una futura comedia per la uicina sera m'apparechio.

Questo è quello dilettissimo compare mio ch'el primo di di maggio agl'occhi miei s'offerse. Quello che seguira di poi fatte le nozze intenderete che non sono prima per uolere ne per potere pensare ad altro.

Finis

89v 10 ristringiendosi] ristringendosi | n'ando] ne ando **10–11** mal'hora] mala hora **11** ch'io] che io | drietole] dietrole **12** l'accompagnai] laccompagnai | con • *emended from* col **13** Ond'io] Onde io **15** nell'egregio] nello egregio | et lieto • *interlinear addition with caret indicating placement* | Santo Lorenzo] San Lorenzo **16** degl'anni] degli anni | s'haueua] si haueua **17** Lethe] Lhete **18** d'ogni] di ogni | dimentichai] dimenticai **19–20** l'importuno] limportuno **21** ch'altro] che altro | ò] /o/ **23** m'era] mi era | a] ad **24** tragicha] tragica | dell'horrenda] della horrenda | piaciere] piacere | d'una] duna **25** comedia] commedia | m'apparechio] mi apparechio **26** ch'el] chel | di di • *second* di *is an interlinear addition with a caret indicating placement* **27** agl'occhi] alli ochi | s'offerse] sofferse | Quello che] Quelche | nozze] noze **29** finis] *Omit*

The scoundrel, acting as one already possessed, perhaps to fashion another relationship more to his taste, would fain have disturbed ours. Although he had such sparkling eyes, if he were undressed, he might have wriggled like an enchanted serpent, but when he saw that he was harshly dismissed by her, and not heartily greeted by me, he wrapped himself in his clothes again, jabbering about I know not what, and went off to some other misfortune. You must not believe that I left her there alone straight away, but rather, just behind her, I accompanied her to her house, in which, together with my heart, she locked herself. From whence I departed alone, so happy and intensely delighted by my sweet wife. So as not to deviate from the planned order of things, hastening my steps, I went to the distinguished and cheerful temple of San Lorenzo, where I hoped to see those who delighted with me in the flower of my youthful years. But it was a new emotion that overpowered me, and, as those who taste of the river Lethe, I forgot every other woman, however lovely. All of my thoughts remained wrapped in those black mourning clothes, which I constantly seemed to see about that importune and hypocritical friar; such tremendous jealousy overtook my spirits that I was not able to think on or see anything else. Therefore, to waste time here seemed vain, and as full of desire as I was, to see my longed-for wife again, at once I returned to my house; and putting an ending to this tragic consideration of the horrendous plague, I prepare myself for the pleasure of a future comedy for the following evening.

Well, that is what, my dearest friend, the first day of May offered to my eyes. Of that which will follow, you will learn about after the wedding; because before that I am not able to think of anything else.

End

89v 15 "tempio di Santo Lorenzo" *or* "temple of San Lorenzo" • is a basilica commissioned by Giovanni di Bicci de' Medici c. 1419 (St Lawrence was the patron saint of the Medici family). Giovanni provided the funding to tear down the ancient Romaneque church that stood where San Lorenzo does now, and he hired Filippo Brunelleschi to design the new building. Donatello and Michelangelo, along with other, lesser architects, had a hand in the building's final iteration. The monastic complex of which the basilica is the largest part also houses the Biblioteca Medicea Laurenziana, designed by Michelangelo and begun around 1525, and the Medici Chapel. Manuscript B of the *Pistola* is held in the Laurentian Library's collections.

89v 23 "a casa mi tornai" *or* "I returned to my house" • over the course of a single momentous though fictitious day, Lorenzo di Filippo Strozzi visited nearly all of Florence's major churches, he crossed the Arno four times, and he returned home ready to marry a beautiful widow. None of this is probable. In particular, the *Pistola* was most likely written in 1522; Strozzi was married then, and remained married until his wife died in 1527. Thereafter he remained a widower, and one who was serious about his faith and the preservation of his family.

Appendix 1: Banco Rari 29 Supplemental Transcriptions Related to, but Not Part of, the *Pistola fatta per la peste*

The transcriptions included in this appendix are important to the provenance of the *Pistola*, for they clearly refer to Lorenzo di Filippo Strozzi as the author of the *Pistola* – but they are not a part of the *Pistola*'s text. They are included here as a supplement to this new edition of Lorenzo di Filippo Strozzi's *Pistola fatta per la peste*.

The originals of the transcriptions below are found on ff. 1r–3r, 5r–8v, and at the foot of 17r of Banco Rari 29 (ff. 3v–4v and 9r–17r contain text from the *Pistola* itself, so those are contained and referenced in the above edition of the *Pistola*). Folio numbers are clearly indicated in the right-hand margins of my transcriptions. These are semi-diplomatic in that they present all of the text included on the pages just noted, with two concessions: abbreviations are expanded, though still signalled for the reader, and multiple manuscript folios are presented on each transcribed page of the edition. Finally, following the transcripts, the reader will find commentary on particular details concerned with the text.

N[ro] 366. 1r
Amadio Niccolucci
~~Niccolò Machiauelli~~ fragmenti originali
Di alcune sue Operette
Amadio Niccolucci

[1v blank]

EPISTola fatta per la 2r
peste

~~hanc epistolo~~
~~hec epist~~

hanc epistolam agit Laurentius Philippi
Stroci ~~qui colebat~~ ciues florentinus,
qui colebant plateam strocior(um), apud
forum et est multa plurcha ; quia
fecit illam ; Cum magnia diligentia
et studio, temporis et laboris et
ob id , Laudo illam cum amiratione
ob eligantiam illus, et doctrinam
magniam, ò rem ~~inau~~ in auditam
et amirabilem, quod est ista / Et —
testor Deum et homines bonos

[2v blank]

Che uoui tu ch'io [f L L Almag(nifi)co ch'io] 3r
Che uuoi tu chio facessi se me Palla
mi disse ch io no(n) gli dicesse nulla

[5r-v blank]

1r 1–4 Amandio … Niccolucci • *in Machiavelli's hand*
1r 3 Niccolò Machiauelli • *obscured by ink's acidity or, more likely, deliberately excised.*
1v "*patch*" *added to cover whole created by excision or previous folio.*
2r 1–15 EPISTola … bonos • *in Palla Strozzi's hand.*
2r 8 plurcha (*sic*)
2r 14 Et — • *indecipherable erasure*
3r 1–3 Che … nulla • *in Palla Strozzi's hand.*

m 6r
questa Pistola compose Laurentius
Philippi strozi ciues fiorentinus
que colebat plateam strocior(um)
apud forum et est plurca

[6v blank]

al mo 7r

per mi 7v
per mi fratell[o]
per
mi per mi
Qu[ale]

[8r-v blank]

Copiata al libro grande nero [17r] 16
di Lorenzo alla fine 9V
Et cosi mi disse

6r 1–5 m (*sic*) … plurca (*sic*) • *in Palla Strozzi hand.*
7r 1 al mo • *written upside down and backwards, in Lorenzo Strozzi's hand.*
7v *in Lorenzo Strozzi's hand.*
17r 16–18 Copiata … disse • *this text appears at the foot of the last folio of the* Pistola *text.*

Commentary:

1r 1–5 "Niccolò Machiauelli" • is obscured by what appears to be a burn that excised the majority of the text. This "burn" might have been caused by the acidity of the ink. However, it was more than likely an intentional excision. Jean-Jacques Marchand, in the national edition of the *Arte della guerra* noted that "si voleva evidentemente tranquillizzare un eventuale censore, dissimulando quello piuttosto compromettente cancellato per prudenza." (*L'Arte della guerra, Scritti politici minori. Edizione nazionale di Niccolò Machiavelli, sezione I: Opere politiche,* vol. 3, ed. Jean-Jacques Marchand [Rome: Salerno, 2001], 315).
2r 1–3r 3 For lengthier discussions on Palla Strozzi's contributions to the text above, see chapter 3.
17r 16–18 Oreste Tommasini suggested that the "libro grande nero" was probably the Ashburnham 606 Ms. This is certainly possible given that the Ashburnham ms. was produced after the Banco Rari ms. See Tommasini, *La vita e gli scritti di Niccolò Machiavelli nella loro relazione col machiavellismo*, vol. 2, pt. 2, p. 1021n4. The reference to Tommasini is found in *Edizione Nazionale di Niccolò Machiavelli*, p. 316.

Appendix 2
Francesco Zeffi's "Vita" of Lorenzo di Filippo Strozzi

As noted earlier in this study, the first and only editor of Zeffi's *Vita* of Lorenzo Strozzi, Pietro Stromboli, claimed that he transcribed it, "sebbene ci sia pervenuta mutila" ("even though it comes to us mutilated"). Stromboli did include a shelmark for the manuscript ("Ms. Strozziano-Uguccioni dell'Arch. Di Stato di Firenze, segnato di lettera M."), but given its apparently poor condition, scholars, with one exception, chose to rely on his transcription.[1] In 1951, Hamilton R. Mathes tracked down the manuscript of Zeffi's *Vita*.[2] While he did not include any comments on the state of the manuscript's preservation, he did include a modern shelfmark in the Archivio di Stato's *Carte Strozziane*, Serie Terza, n. 92, 14r-28r. On a recent visit to Florence, I visited the Archivio di Stato, expecting to find a severely damaged manuscript of Zeffi's *Vita*. What I found was a beautifully preserved manuscript, written on paper which dates from the first half of the sixteenth century. Zeffi died in 1542; and his biography of Lorenzo Strozzi covers the years 1482-1529/30, so the *Vita* must have been written after 1530 and before 1542. The entire manscript is an autograph in Zeffi's elegant hand. There are very few emendations in the text. However, it appears that Zeffi left out information (noted below), which he probably intended to add to a later version of the manuscript; but he passed away before he was able to finish his *Vita* of Lorenzo.

1 Francesco d'Antonio Zeffi da Empoli, "Un Ragionamento inedito di Francesco Zeffi sopra la Vita dell' Autore (Lorenzo di Filippo Strozzi)," in Lorenzo di Filippo Strozzi, *Le Vite degli Uomini Illustri della Casa Strozzi*, ed. Pietro Stromboli (Florence: Pei Tipi Salvadore Landi, 1892), vii.

2 Hamilton R. Mathes, "On the Date of Lorenzo's *Sacra Rappresentazione di S. Giovanni e Paolo*, Febr. 17, 1491," *Aevum* 25 (1951): 324–8.

Stromboli's 1892 edition provided two different titles for the Zeffi's *Vita* of Lorenzo (*Un Ragionamento Inedito di Francesco Zeffi Sopra la Vita Dell'Autore*, and *Di Lorenzo Strozzi Autore di Queste Vite, Ragionamento di Francesco Zeffi*), neither of which is found in the original. The actual title of the work, provided by Zeffi on the first folio of the manuscript is: *Vita di Lorenzo di Filippo Strozzi scritta / Da Maestro Francesco Zeffi.*[3] Stromboli's edition silently modernized Zeffi's spelling and his punctuation. This new edition remains tightly focused on Zeffi's original work, and it seems that the best way to achieve that goal is to present Zeffi's text in a semi-diplomatic format. In other words, I have tried to remain as close to the original presentation of the manuscript's folios as possible, but I have also made a three concessions.

Chief amongst those is that all abbreviations have been expanded; but these are included in round brackets to inform the reader that I altered Zeffi's presentational methods. For example, Zeffi frequently abbreviated Strozzi's first name as "Lor.°". I rendered this as "Lor(enz)o". Additionally, when Zeffi includes dates/years in the original manuscript, these are always presented with a line above them. It was not practical to replicate this feature of the text. Finally, the use of capital and lower case letters has been standardized, conforming to modern usage. These editorial changes should help to make Zeffi's text much easier to read.

Following standard practice, in the right hand margin of this edition, the reader will find the folio number, and in the left hand margin, line numbers, all of which are keyed exactly to the original manuscript. Zeffi's paragraphs (infrequently used), punctuation and spelling are presented as they appear in the original manuscript. His punctuation, in contrast to Strozzi's and Machavelli's is frequent and recognizable, allowing the modern reader to peruse the text without difficulty. As is the case with sixteenth-century manuscripts, Zeffi rarely made a distinction between the consonantal and vocalic "u"; but when he did, these are transcribed faithfully, and without critical comment. Finally, remarks on emendations and other features of the manuscript are found in the critical apparatus at the foot of the page.

3 The forward slash used here is not found in the ms. I inserted it to indicate a line break.

A Semi-diplomatic Transcription of Carte Strozziane, Terza Serie, n. 92, 14r–28r

Vita di Lorenzo di Filippo Strozzi scritta [14r]
Da M(aestro) Fran(ces)co Zeffi

Francesco Zéffi à Palla Strozzi, Salute.

Di tutte l'Istorie quelle sopra modo mi dilettano, che la vita, e li fatti di particolari huomini fedelm(en)te descri = uono; e mi credo ageuolm(ent)e, che tali siano non tanto dell'altre le più piaceuoli, mà ancora di più rileuata utilità; però che conoscendo ciascuno negl'altrui diffetti se stesso, desidera sommam(en)te uedere quali sieno i loro portam(en)ti, per poterne con l'esempio consolare, ò emendare la sua natura; e se Io debbo secondo il co = mune prouerbio con la mia canna misurare l'animo uostro, mi penso, che uoi non altrim(en)te giudichiate - tanto più che in uoi hò sempre conosciuto un desi - derio di mantenére il grado délla nobile uostra famiglia, tale, che più presto auanzare li uostri maggiori di uirtù, studiosam(en)te attendete, che di parere di quélli inferiore, e manco degno, specchian - doui frequentem(en)te nella memoria, e nelli uirtuosi costumi de primi huomini della Casata uostra, celebrati dalla studiosa penna di uostro padre, il quale, come sollecito dell'honore di tutti li Strozzi, hauendo con le sue uigilie l'origine della Casa, e [14v] li più eccellenti di quella compreso nella sua Istoria; io giudico, non riceuerebbe il giusto premio, se ancora la sua memoria in qualche parte non fusse con l' altre da se scritte congiunta. Onde se bene Io cono = sco, che la benigna, e grata uostra natura non haue = rebbe sopportato una tale ingratitudine ogni uolta, che dagl'altri fosse tal débito pretermesso; io hò uoluto in ciò preuenire, non tanto credendo col torui fatica, farui cosa grata, quanto, che scriuendo un' altro le lode del padre uostro, deuerrà essere più in fede, che uoi, il quale dalla naturale affettioné si potria pénsare essére stato abbagliato; oltre che,

Io non sò à chi più tal'obbligo s'appartenga, fuor di uoi, che à me; sì per gl'infiniti benefizi da lui stesso riceuuti; e si per essere Io stato per sua grazia molti anni familiare, é suo domestico. E perche io intendo più presto di quello ragionare con uoi, che déscriuere ordinatam(ent)e la sua uita, io non mi uolgio sottomettere à légge alcuna dell'Istoria, ò altra diligente narrazione; supplite uoi à tutto quello, che per me si mancasse.

[15r] Li due figli, che à Filippo uostro auolo nacquero della Seluaggia figlia di Messer Bartolomeo Gianfigliazzi, cioè Lorenzo uostro padré, e Filippo, come ne tempi loro non fù dubbio, che non fussino de primi huomini della città nostra, così non è certo qual di loro si debba all'altro preférire. Furono nel uostro zio gran parti, e doni d'animo, e di corpo rari, per li quali éra meritam(ent)e quasi per tutto il mondo celebré, con particolare fauore della fortuna.

Mà se consideriamo quale esser dee la uita del cittadino nella sua repubblica, e delle ciui = li uirtù, quali risplendono in Lorenzo, e quali in Filippo, senza dubbio ciaschedun principe desi - dererà nella sua rep(ubbli)ca hauere li suoi cittadini, che così à Lorenzo sieno simili, come à Filippo, e li padri priuatam(ent)e eleggeranno i loro figliuoli più secondo Lorenzo, che secondo il uiuere di Fi = lippo. Quésto è per confesso, che il uostro Lorenzo fù la gentilezza, e le delizie de suoi tempi, et in tutte le sue imprese honoreuole, e grandé. A' pena era nel settimo anno, ché recitando il Mag(nifi)co Lorenzo de Medici nel Uangelista una sua festa di San Giouanni, e Paulo, della quale il

14v 7 uolta • 'l' *emended from* 't'

15r 2 Gianfigliazzi • *inksplash above* 'n'

15r 3 cioè • *a 'burn', probably due to acidity of the ink, partially obscures* 'o'; *passes through the folio.*

15r 5 è • *rendered as* 'e' *in the ms.*

Messere, ò il Sig(no)re che dir uogliamo, era Giuliano figlio [15v] del detto Mag(nifi)co Lorenzo, elesse uostro padre per consiglie - re, doue non tanto per essere riccam(en)te adornato, quanto per l'attitudine, e prontezza d'ingegno in simili honorati piaceri s'acquistò àpò tutto il popolo fior(enti)no sì fatta grazia, che di poi nel 1494, entrando Carlo re di Francia in Fior(en)za, Lorenzo, benche di tenera età, fù tra li primi cittadini comandato dalla Si = gnoria à riscontrare il Cristianiss(im)o un miglio fuor della Porta. La oue essendo con due familiari di uelluto tanè à librea uestito, tanto destramente il suo giannetto atteggiaua, che ancor uiue ne cuori di molti cittadini la marauiglia: i quali al costume de uecchi raccontando tale honoreuole entrata, sempre d'auanti a'gl'occhi loro si rappre - senta questo grazioso giouinetto: non uolgio in questi ragionam(en)ti preterire, come della sua genti - lezza, egli adornaua ancora le altrui città, con no(n) minor grazia de forastieri, che de suoi cittadini; pérche celebrandosi in Ferrara le nozze del duca Alfonso, e di mad(am)a Lucrezia Borgia moglie di detto Duca, doue concorsero tutti li principi, e li nobili d'Italia; delle quali nozze no(n) si è di poi uisto il

pa=

paragone, Lorenzo benche giouine priuato insièmè [16r] con Matteo Strozzi, e Baccio organista principe mu - sico della città nostra talm(ent)e honorato, e con tal pompa andò alla Festa di tali nozze, che à compa - razione di qualunque principe no(n) appariua inferiore, massime nel comparire, e nell'essere ammésso ne i luoghi, e trà persone, che ad altri pri - uati non si concedono, con mirabil fauore di quan - te madonne ui si ritrouorono. Similmente,

15v 3 riccamente • *the 'burn' from the previous folio obscures* 'en'
15v 5 Popolo • 'l' *emended from* 'p'
15v 13 i quali • *emended from* 'il quali'

quantunque di poi qualche anno andando à Uenezia nélla sua ragione, in pochi mesi fa-cilm(ent)e acquistò tale beneuolenza con quelli gentilhuomini, quale in molt'anni rade uolte gl'altri con lor grande osseruanzà si procacciono; essendo li patrizij Ueneziani naturalm(ent)e superbi, e mal uolentieri nelli lor Collegij ammettendo li forastieri; tuttauia uedendo Lorenzo da tutti ésseré accarezzato, lo uolséro mettere nelle loro, che chiamano Compagnie di Calze, il che fu da Lorénzo honoreuolm(ent)e rifiutato, per essere d'animo di ritornarsene frà poco tempo in Fior(enz)a à riuedere li suoi, massime la moglie, che poco auanti haueua menata. Quésta era la Lucrezia [16v] figliola del nobile, e préstante cittadino Bernardo di Giouanni Rucellaio, la quale, perche Madonna Seluaggia il uedeua pupillo, e ricco, senza protet-tore, e difensoré rimasto, gl'haueua sposata auan-ti al témpo maturo con dota manco che conueni-ente, solam(ent)e per potere con l'autorità del suocero manténere le facultà sue; benche tal paréntado non satisfacesse à Piero di Lorenzo de Medici, che allora gouernaua, e non senza cagione; però che di qui nacque il principio della mutazione del 94, quando détto Piéro de Medici perdè lo Stato, essendosi facilm(ent)e alienati da lui, e Bernardo Rucellai per sdegno di tal parentado non àpprouato, e Paulo Ant(oni)o Soderini per hauér dato à Tommaso suo figlio la sorella di uostro padre, medesimam(ent)e contro la uolon-tà di tal principe; mà lasciamo andar questo, le nozze di poi ché la città fù quiétata nel 1503 si celebrarono nel palazzo grandé con tal pompa, ché per ancora à ogn'un priuato cedono. Qui lo sposo con altri sei compagni usò tre sorte di ueste à librea, di uelluto crimisi, di dommasco
tanè
tanè, e di tàffetà pauonazzo in tre diuersi conuiti, [17r] à i quali furono oltre li parenti inuitati, li più qualificati cittadini, e le più nobili, e belle donne della città, procurandosi diligentém(ent)e qualunque

sorte di uiuande, che fù possibile trouare. Era per sè tale opulenzia magnifica, ma le circus = tanzie molto più la rendeuano marauigliosa, perche qualunque uiuanda si portaua in tauo = la, sempre haueua sopra il piatto l'animale uiuo délla medesima specie accompagnato da uarij musiche in sù certi Trionfi; quelle p(er)sone, che p(er) la fréquenza non poteuano salire all'appa - rato, érano nel Cortile trattenunti, doue pubblica - mente si daua mangiare, e bere in modo che quantunque la spesa non arriuasse à pena à scudi 1500, nondimeno per il bell'ordine e uarietà, e certa leggiadria degl'apparati, furo - no giudicate dispendio molto maggiore. È sempre la città nostra ogni uolta ch'ella può réspirare, uaga di fare uarié inuenzioni di maschere con musiche alla materia accomodate, si à piè, come à cauallo; e taluolta à guisa di

[17v] Carri trionfali, delle quali se alcuna trà giouini si proponéua in quel tempo, sempre à Lorenzo toc - caua essere il principalé, aggiungendosi al potere spendere, l'ingegno accomodatissimo, e l'agilità del corpo; e l'anno credo 1506 fù inuentore, e con - duttore del carro della Morte, che delle mascherate, che mai si fecero in Fior(enz)a, fù forse la più meraui - gliosa, e per la materia pér sé stessa nuoua, et orrenda, e per essersi prudentem(ent)e condotta, non tanto con l'abbigliature che à ciò si ricercauano, q(ua)nto col tenerla segreta, siche ne da essi giouini, che alla spesa concorsero, non fù prima cognita, che quando l'usci fuora in pubblico, i quali con Filip - po suo fratello furono undici tutti à cauallo con circa 300 à piedi tutti uéstiti à uso ché le Morti si dipingono, talm(ent)e paurose, che molti nel uestirsi spauentati, uolentieri si sariano ritirati dall'im - presa, massimé, che essendo appunto la sera di car - neuale, paréua loro dalla solita letizia, ridursi

17r 20 uaga • *final* 'a' *emended from* 'h'

17v 14 furono, *through* **18r 11** esercitare *is written in much darker ink*

17v 20 use ché le morti • *emended from* uso della Morti • 'del' *deleted*; 'la' *emended to* 'le'; *and* ché *is an interlinear addition with a caret indicating placement.*

à un estremo dolore, il che molto più à gl'altri della città penetrò ne cuori, oltre à uederé la trionfanté morté, udendo trombe, e corni sordi, et ulu = ululanti, et all'ultimo la musica, con le parole [18r] secondo la materia, le quali di poi per Laude si usarono cantare. La mattina seguente il pri - mo di di Quaresima fù tale inuenzione da i predicatori molto lodata in pulpito, et no(n) pareua, che le persone si potessin saziare d'conferire l'una con l'altra quanto tale spettacolo l'ha - uessé commosse à pensare ad altro, che alle stolte, e disonéste licenzie, che in tal notte si présumono li falsi cristiani poter senza rispetto esercitare. Se questo come cosa pub = blica parue, ché superasse l'opinione delli spetta = tori e l'altre feste carneualesche; cosi delle fan = tasie uarie, che nelle nozze i giouini usano mos = trare; quelle maschere, che Lorenzo fece alle nozze di Giouan Battista de Nobili con Francesco di Giulia = no Salutati, et in compagnia di Giouan Battista Nasi à guisa di Pastori, furono le più ricche, e tenute le più belle, che in quei tempi si facessero, non tanto all' occhio, quanto all'orecchio satisfacendo; però chè trà questi regij rastori interuienne il Ceo poeta, il quale hauendo composta l'infrascritta Canzona, la cantò in sù la lira secondo il modo, che Baccio degli Organi gli haueua dato.

Non è pietra tanto dura [18v]
Che dal fuoco sia sicura, etc.

Non era però che Lorenzo non hauesse saputo da se comporre tale madrigaletto, si come in altre cose più importanti spesso dimostraua, mà la riputazione del Ceo per allora parue più à proposito à loro disegno. Che quantunque uostro padre nelli suoi teneri anni non attendesse molto à lettere, prouedendoli la madre i precettori più di costumi che di lettere ornati, del che spesse uolte egli meco, e con

---

18r 4 tale • 't' *emended from* 'f'

altri si dolse; nondimeno come egli puotè uscire di fanci = ullo, si messe à studiare sotto quelle persone, che erano tenute nelli studij più eccellenti, e massime sotto il Fon = zio, huomo di quei tempi, qual' i suoi monumenti per an = cora ci mostrano; onde accompagnata l'arte con l'in = gegno naturale, si messe à comporre trà gl'altri poemati più comedie, delle quali la prima si recitò nel Palazzo de Medici ad intanza del Mag(nifi)co Lorenzo Duca d'Vrbino, doue uoi, et il maggior' uostro fratello[1] ui portaste nel recitare la parte uostra in tal maniera, che trà li istrioni, che per tutto il Dominio si erano procacci = ati, si conobbe euidente la prontezza della pronun = zia uostra. Può essere, che altra uolta si sieno di - poi récitati, e condotti simili poemati più riccam(ent)e, mà in fino à quel tempo la memoria de nostri cit - tadini non haueua ancora uistone una Comedia si ben

condotta

[19r] condotta. Imperòcche uolendo Lorenzo non solo al Principe satisfare, quanto à tutto il popolo, prese sopra le sue spalle tutto quello, che à condurre honoreuolmente la comedia si richiedeua. E prima nella sala grande di sopra in detto Palazzo fece nelle scene apparire una prospettiua per le mani di Ridolfo del Grillandaio, à tutti nuoua, e marauigliosa riuscì. Dipoi hauendo di uarij luoghi fatta la prouuisione di diuersi strumenti, gli diuise in questo modo, che auanti la Comedia inco = minciassero li suoni grossi, come trombe, cornamuse, pifferi, che destassero gl'animi degl'auditori. Il secon = do Atto fèce introdurre tre Mori riccamente abbiglia = ti con tre liuti, che nel silenzio dilettarono soauem(en)te ciascuno. Nel térzo cantarono sù quattro uioloni uoci soprane, alzandosi secondo la Comedia. Al tumulto, che nel quarto romoreggiaua, accomodò li più acuti stru = menti di penna la ultima musica, furono quattro trom = boni, modulando artificiosam(ent)e, e con dolcezza le lor' uoci. Le quali musiche di poi sono state più uolte imitate

1 Giovan Battista Strozzi.

19r 3 à • *interlinear addition with caret indicating placement*

19r 8 diuersi • *written over indecipherable erasure*

19r 13 dilettarono • 'i' *emended from* 'e'

mà per allora non erano mai uenute in uso, ne forse in considerazione, perche rade uolte interuiéne, che un Principe, el capo di qualche impresa sia atto à tutte le circostanze, che in quella si ricercano. E Lor(enz)o non solo della poesia fù sempre studioso, mà ancora mirabilmente si dilettò della musica, e nel cantare adempiua con molta grazia la parte sua, tanto, che [19v] alcuna uolta pareua lasciuo, massime quando col suo liuto conferiua i suoi amori: à i quali, oltreche naturalmente pareua inclinato, essendo ancora dalle madame de suoi tempi prouocato, parue, che in questo trapassasse il segno, talché in certi sonetti, doue si tassauono li uizij de più nobili, à lui fù dato il titolo dell'Amore, benche da molti ne fusse in parte scusato perche egli haueua una moglie, che come di uirtù d'a(n)i(m)o, se non auanzaua, ella pareggiaua ogni altra, cosi di bellezza era forsé ad ogni sua egualé, inferiore, come pare, ché la fortuna si diletti congiugneré le più uolte nature dissimili. Mà in tutta quésta sua continenza, non fù mai persona, che ne uédesse un mal esempio; che mai si sentisse hauer'usato forza alcuna, ò che egli trascoresse ad altri illeciti piaceri. Quando di poi molt'anni (come di sotto diremo) fù creato del Magistrato degl'Otto di Balia, auuenne, che hauendo un artefice un caso importante, e sapendo quanto Lor(enz)o poteua nel Magistrato, e quanto fusse inclinato alle donne, gli condusse una sua figliuola giouane, e bella segretam(en)te di notte à casa, dandogli facultà di far tutto quello, che gli piaceua, la quale Lor(enz)o accolsé lietamente, e uoltatosi al padre, mi marauiglio, disse, di te, perche se bene mi dilettano simili piacéri, non gli uoglio conseguire p(er) questa uia;

molto

molto più mi affliggerebbé macolare la fanciulla, [20r] é la giustizia insieme, che non saria piacere di sì disonésto appetito, e cosi l'uno e l'altro uergognosi, e scontenti ne gli rimandò per la medesima uia, ch' erano uenuti. Accadégli anche fuori di Magistrato, ché una madre per auarizia gli condusse la figlia,

19v 16 di • *interlinear addition with caret indicating placement*

la quale facendo all'esser'uiolata qualche resisten = za, egli non ardi constrignerla altriménti, dicendo al - la madre, che quanto lo dilettaua l'amore per le cir - constanze amoreuoli, che ui interueniuono, tanto gli dispiaceua l'usarui uiolenza à forza; si che se ne rimenasse la figliola, e tenessila cara, perche era migliore di lei, pregandola, ché non la uolésse più uendere sì miseramente; et all'una, et all'altra data la mancia, disse alla fanciulla, che si man = tenesse in quella buona uolontà. Mà andiamo all'età più graue, et all'azioni di più importanza; e perche qual fusse ancora uerso la rep(ubblica), e gli altri priuati, sia manifesto: a' me non parue mai conoscer' huomo, che meglio et più sauiamente accomodare si sapesse à i tempi, che Lorenzo; senza adulazione, e diminuzione del grado suo. Egli naturalm(ent)e era incli = nato alla libertà della patria sua, più che ad altro stato, nel quale, forse più honoreuolm(ent)e haueria potuto all'ambizioso animo satisfare; e per conseruazioné di quella, non haueria ne à disagio alcuno, ne à roba, [20v] ne alla propria uita perdonato: mà se accidente fusse soprauenuto, che la Rep(ubblica) hauesse alterato, benche ciò con = tro al uoler suo seguisse, il sopportaua prudentem(ent)e, con dimostrarsi contento à quel, ch'Iddio, della sua pa = tria disponesse: et occorrendoli facultà di poter fare mutazione à quello, che più secondo la sua fantasia sarebbe stato, non perciò hauerebbe à tale impresa dato fauore, ne se ne sarebbe mai trauagliato, lasci = ando ad altri muoueré tali sedizioni, per potersi di poi nella pace godere il suo, e mantenere il grado della sua nobile famiglia; onde seppe la sua barca nelli tempestosi tempi della Rep(ubblica) Fior(entin)a tranquillare; siche per nissuna mutazione gli mancò il sicuro porto, ui = uendo à principi accetto, et accettissimo al popolo. Quando adunque Filippo suo fratello hebbe in pratica di sposare per sua moglie la Clarice di Piero de Medici ribello, non conferì altrimenti à Lor(enz)o tal parentado, se no(n) concluso, benche insieme unitamente uiuessero, non

---

20r 23 che • 'e' *added over indecipherable erasure*

per altro, se non che lo conosceua del tutto alieno dalle cose straordinarie: pure cosi Lor(enzo) s'ingegnò di turbare, et impedire tale coniugio per tutte quelle uie, che gli furono possibili; mà essendo Mad(on)na Seluaggia lor madre, e Bernardo Rucellai, e Filippo Buondelmenti à tal fatto congiuratisi, gli bisognò torsi dall'impresa, et cosi segui il parentado; il quale non prima scopertosi, che li

repu =

[21r] republiconi stimandola cosa per lo Stato dannouole, incominciorono ad esclamare, et incitatore Piero So = derini perpetuo Gonfaloniere; à tal, che non uoleua pri - ma restare di perseguitare Filippo, ch'egli uedesse la sua ultima rouina. A' ciò non hebbe Lor(enz)o pazienza; e poiche il parentado era concluso, reputandolo per il migliore; lasciato tutto lo sdegno, che per più mo - di era grauissimo, si uoltò con ogni suo ualore ad aiutare il suo fratello, et operò in mode | benche Al = fonso seguitasse fare il contrario | che Filippo trà po - co tempo si potétté la sua sposa godere. Et égli con tali nuoui consorti congiugnersi in strétto uincolo di beneuolenza; come di poi nel 1510 conobbe per es = perienza quando per suoi negozij transferendosi à Roma, mad(onn)a Alfonsina, suocéra di Filippo, lo costrin - sé à ritornarsi in casa sua, oue fù oltramodo hono = rato, massimamente da M(esser) Giulio Caualiere Gerosolim(ita)no, e priore di Capua, il quale di poi fù Papa Clemente 7 costui habitando allora col Cardinale de Medici, che diuenne poi Papa Leone X ogni mattina auanti che Lor(enz)o fusse leuato, si rappresantaua alla camera, as = pettandolo, finche à suo comodo uscisse, per andar fuora: e non bastandoli à costume delli antichi Romani salu = tarlo, gli teneua compagnia per tutta Roma, et ul = timamente lo riduceua alla sua stanza, pérseue = rando in tale ossequio più tosto, che offizio, tre mesi continoui, cioè tutto quel tempo, che à Lor(enz)o piacque

21r 2 incitatore • 'e' *obscured by spreading ink*
21r 3–4 prima • *large ink splash above* 'a'
21r 16 oltramodo • *a 'burn', probably due to ink acidity, covers* 'm'
21r 18 Clemente 7 • *arabic number used here*
21r 20 Leone X • *roman numeral used here*

stare in Roma: fù questo à marauiglia di ciascuno, che la [21v]
natura del detto m(esser) Giulio gli pareua conoscere; benche se al
fine delle sue azioni si riguarda, tale osseruanza non era tanto,
pérché la conuersazione di Lor(enz)o gli fusse à grado, quanto che
parendogli persona di qualità, se lo uolse guadagnare, p(er)
facilitare ogni suo fine; il che li riuscì pér quanto il
uincolo dell'amicizia si richiedeua; però che da Lor(enz)o fù
sempre amato da fratello; et all'incontro egli in ogni
suo grado ne tenne conto quanto che Lorenzo uolse.
Subito che Papa Leone fù creato, essendo il prefato M(esser) Giu =
lio in Fiorenza, et offerendoseli molti de più riputati cittadini
andare in compagnia à baciare li piedi al Papa, non uolse
altri seco, che Lor(enzo), doue mostrandoli Leone carezze straord(inari)e,
da tutti i Curiali era tenuto in palma di mano, et in continue
magnificenze, tal che questa riputazioné l'accompagnò in
fino à Napoli, doue allora si transferì per suo diporto, e
quasi solo, per uedere i luoghi ameni, doue anticamenté
li Romani haueuano li giardini, e le loro delizie rusticane.
Però che quiui aggiungendosi all'antica riputazione,
che li Strozzi haueuano in Napoli, la parentela di Leone,
non poteua à tanti signori e gentil'huomini satisfare,
che giornalmente lo conuitorno, insieme con la sua
honorata compagnia, nella quale erano lettere, musica,
e religione. Sarebbesi uoléntieri con simili huomini,
et in simili ésercizij trapassata giocondam(ent)e la sua uita,
senza trauagliarsi in modo alcuno della Republica,
massimam(ent)e uedendola nell'arbitrio d'un solo Principe
ri =

ridotta; mà simili huomini di nobiltà, ricchezze, uirtù [22r]
adornati, e non sospetti, è impossibile che finalmente
non sieno da chi regge, indotti à sostenere parte dél
pubblico péso: perche adunque Lorenzo fù da Medici,
e dal popolo in molti Magistrati eletto, dirò insieme
delli suoi honori secondo l'ordine de témpi, e delle mu =
tazioni accadute alla sua età, doue la mente di tal
huomo, come non ambiziosa, così giusta apparirà, et
intera, seruente più alli altrui comodi, che alli suoi proprij.
L'anno 1510 fù creato offiziale del Monte per la minore età:
il qual magistrato benche fusse il primo, e molto hono =

rato, non diméno il rifiutò, col pagare 300 scudi, secon = do la pena di qualunque refiutasse, prolungando quel = che torlosi non poteua. Per lo ché di poi tre anni, un' altra fiata fù del médesimo offizio honorato, collega di Lorenzo di Piero de Medici | il quale fù di poi Duca d'Vr = bino | e d'altri i più danarosi: e gli conuenne prestare al = la Rep(ublica) scudi 5000. Ne perciò fù di poi nel 1521 rispiarma = to, che bisognando di nuouo procacciar danari, la terza uol = ta eletto al medesime grado, gli conuenne sborsare la medesima quantità di danari. Mà ritorniamo indietro.

Il detto Mag(nifi)co Lor(enz)o de Medici gouérnando allora lo stato, de = liberò dare alli O(tto) di Balia più riputazione dell'ordinario, stimando tal magistrato importantissimo, e necessario; et eleggendo i primi de suoi cittadini, fece più mani di otto molto più che l'solito honorate; e benche uostro p(ad)re fusse desideroso d'esser preterito, nondimeno l'anno 1515 gli conuenne à tanta honoreuole molestia chinar [22v] le spalle prima, che di ciò ne fusse stato auertito mai, ò che altro ne sapesse: fatica grandé gli pare = ua | come si dice | entrar nel ballo, mà poi, che den = tro ui era, si dilettaua sempre d'esser'autore di qualche cosa honoreuole, e straordinaria. Non adunque prima prese il Magistrato, che con la grazia sua, et insieme con la riputazione, otten = ne dalli suoi compagni, che i loro partiti si uincessero con tutte le otto faue nere, cosa rara, e straordinaria, talche Ser Zanobi cancelliere di detto Offizio usò dire, che in 30 anni, ch'egli era stato al seruizio di tal magistrato, non s'era mai ueduta una simil concor - dia ne partiti. Ne di poi molto mandato Commessario à Pistoia, fù non solamente la diligenza sua notata da quél popolo, mà ancora un tratto della sua inte = grità, perche trouandosi un'Uenerdì mattina seco à desinare certi Fiorentini, li fù presentato un gran piatto di bellissime trote da un Pistolese, il quale,

---

22r 18 rep(ublica) • *spelled by Zeffi in two ways:* 'republica' and 'repubblica'; cf. **15r 11** repubblica; **21v 26** republica

22r 25 di • 'i' *obscured by spreading ink*

22r 27 preterito • 't' *emended from* 'f'

secondo il suo costume ricusato, e li fiorentini, à quali erano preposti cibi di minor pregio, dolendosi, Io non uoglio disse Lor(enz)o hauer mai occasione d'impe = dir la giustizia, uenghino le trote quando sarò per = sona priuata, e meco lietamente le goderete. Di poi non molti anni uenuto il gouérno della città nel R(euerendissi)mo Cardinale Giulio de Medici, Lor(en)zo pér l'antica amicizia tenne seco tanta familiarità, che non

sola =

solamente le cose importantissime e graui, mà [23r] le giocose, e li passatempi li conferiua.

Riteneua in questo tempo la città qualche specie, et apparenza di libertà, col mantenersi li medesimi offizij, e magistrati popolari, de quali, quelli che li Otto Signori con Gonfaloniere si chiamauano, era il som = mo principato: piacque adunque al Cardinale honora = re di tal degnità Lor(enz)o, benche secondo l'ordine questo si appartenesse prima ad Alfonso suo fratello, p(er) essere di età superiore. Costui si haueua prouocata la Casa de Medici in tanto nemica, che più uolte saria stato mal'arriuato, se Lor(enz)o non si fusse con la sua gra(zia) interposto, massimamente nel ritornare i Medici in Fiorenza, che ritraendo il fratello portar pericolo d(e)lla uita, gne ne conferì, consigliandolo, che prima si leuas - se di Firenze, che la fazioné contraria fusse drento; e più oltre gli tenne compagnia in fino à Lucca, e con tanto studio si messe ad aiutarlo, che al sicuro lo ridusse in Firenze con mal grado di Filippo suo fratello e di tutta la Casa de Medici: tuttauia non potette oprar tanto, che di Magistrato alcuno fusse honorato, per tanto non uo = lendo parere d'insultare al maggior fr(at)ello, quando fù de Signori creato, non uolse l'antico costume osseruare. Que = sto era, ché per le persone facultose, la prima uolta mas = sime, che fussero assunte à tal degnità di conuitaré i pri = mi cittadini del loro Quartiére, Lor(enz)o, non per altra cagione, che del fratello, uolendo mostrare all'uniuersale, essere

23r 6 chiamauano • 'n' *obscured by spreading ink*
23r 23 Signori • *followed by cancelled comma*

[23v] contro à sua uoglia, se al fratello maggiore fusse preceduto, pretermesse tale usanza; con tutto ciò Alfonso mostrò hauere molto a' sdegno l'honore del fr(at)ello.

Alla créazione di poi l'anno 1523 di Papa Clemente fù fatto uno delli Otto Ambasciatori huomini della città i principali, à congratularsi con sua Santità, e offerire la solita obedienza, nel quale collegio non fù alcuno, che più honoratamente tenésse il publico segno, che uostro padre, che solamente nelli suoi ar - nesi spese scudi 2000, benche tal cerimonia, per dir cosi, gli fusse più tosto danneuole, per uoler mante = nere il grado del buon cittadino, che altriménti, apò la ménte del Papa, la cui natura era tanto al dominare inclinata, che per quella non conosceua il ragioneuole, non che parénte, ò amico. Conuitò adunque una mattina Papa Clemente tutti li fiorentini Oratori, l' Arciuescouo de Minerbetti, Lorénzo Morelli, Alessan = dro Pucci, Roberto Acciaioli, Francesco Uettori, Palla Rucellai, Giouanni Tornabuoni, e Lorenzo Strozzi, do = ue interuenne ancora Iacopo Saluiati, e Piero di Nic = colò Ridolfi: e doppo lo splendido, e papale conuito, tutti con sua Santità, si ristrinsero in una stanza, et esclu = sa ogn'altra persona, fù da Clemente a loro proposto, che qual parésse a loro il miglior modo di gouernare la Rep(ublica) Fiorentina, quello senza rispetto alcuno, ciascuno uoles - se manifestare. Qui secondo il grado dell'età, dicendo ciascuno l'opinione sua, tutti, come quelli che così pen =

[24r] pensauano far cosa grata al Papa, si concordorono, che Ippolito nipote di sua Santità si mandasse capo, e' supe- riore di quel gouérno; eccétti Francesco di Piéro Uettori, e Lor(enz)o uostro padre, à i quali sarìa piaciuto eléggére un Gonfalonieré à uita, ò almeno per tre anni, con le me = desime condizioni, et ordini, che seruare si soleuano q(ua)n(do) si creaua la Signorìa, solo per mantenere qualche for - ma di ciuiltà, alla quale era di già gran tempo la città assuefatta. Il Papa, che li suoi grandi far uole = ua, mostrando aderire alla sentenza de più, determinò di

23v 8 honoratamente • 'ata' *emended from* 'euol'
24r 8 di ciuiltà • 'ciuiltà' *added after deleted* dignità

mandare Ippolito principe della Rep(ublica) insieme col Cardina - le di Cortona: e Francesco, e Lor(enz)o per dire quel che pare = ua più conueniente, restarono in mal concetto; e molto più Lor(enz)o, per non li potere esser messo ad ignoranza: im - peròche Filippo suo fratéllo, subornato dal Papa, haue = ua fatto ogni opera di ridurlo e disporlo al mandare Ippo - lito prima, che si uenisse à tal consulta in presenza del Papa. Tornandosene così in Firenze, non fù nelli dieci anni, che Ippolito tenne il Principato, mandato altrim(ent)j in luogo alcuno per publica commissione, ne alli stret - ti consigli richiamato. Solamente hebbe nella città al - cuno magistrato, più di certa riputazione, e di spesa, e briga, che di momento alcuno, come de Conseruadori di Legge, uno de due Proueditori dell'Arte de Mercanti, e delli Offiziali d'Abbondanza, e delli Dieci huomini della Pietà. Mà cacciati li Medici, e ritornata la città al popolare e libero gouerno, doue naturalmente li cittadini lo conosceuano più inclinato, bench à tutti [24v] li tempi, et à qualunque stato egli si sapesse acco = modare con tal misura, che mantenedosi la pub- blica grazia, era sempre rispettato. L'anno 1529 gli fù sopra gl'altri laborioso, et honoreuole. Primi - eramente nel Consiglio Grande del Popolo, doue li cit = tadini per uno stretto uaglio si cerneuano, rimase per le più faue nel numero della Pratica, grado re - putato de primi della città: imperòchè con tal Pratica de cittadini, la Signoria, et li Dieci della Guerra si con = sigliauono, né senza la deliberazione di detta Pratica, haueriano eseguito cosa alcuna importante: con tutto - ciò di poi ingelosita la città di papa Clemente, il quale per ogni modo macchinaua rimettere le reliquie di Ca - sa sua in Firenze, incominciando à pensare alla dif - esa, li Signori Dieci fecéro Lor(enz)o Commessario del Domi = nio à munire, e fortificare Prato, Pistoia, Empoli e Colle, hauendo in sua compagnia Iacomo Corso, e M(esser) Giouanb(attist)a da Messina, huomini esperti et intelligenti del mes = tiero della guerra. Non prima tornato da tali im = prese, che passando per à Genoua il r(euerendissi)mo Farnese, oggi Papa Paulo, Legato di Clemente all'Imperatore, Lorenzo insieme con Giouanni Borgherini fù eletto dalla Sig(no)ria Oratore à sua Signoria Reu(erendissi)ma; alla quale fù tanto accet =

ta, e sì li satisfece la buona grazia di Lor(enz)o, che no(n) solo dalli confini di Siena fino à Poggibonzi uolse la sua compagnia, mà per tutto il contado alli confini di Lucca

Lucca non lasciò dal suo fianco partire. Nella città [25r] medesimamente, nel medesimo anno non mancaua di pen = siero, e grande sollecitudine, per ritrouarsi offiziale di Abbondanza creato nel Consiglio Grande, perche non si potendo hauer grano di fuori, essendo di già la città asse = diata dall'Imperiale esercito subbornato da papa Clem(ent)e, col porre, e prescriuere al grano il prezzo determinato, cioè z.3.$_{\beta}$.5.[2] per ciascuno staio, dette non piccol freno alla carestia, in che la città allor si trouaua, trà molti altri incomodi, e timori, i quali, credo, che gli fussero fata = li, et ineuitabili; con tanta ostinazione se li opponeuo = no i cittadini, che in quel tempo haueuano in mano il go = uerno della città; alli buoni, e profitteuoli consigli, et ammonizioni, dissimulando non intendere quel che fus = se il uero, si come innanzi à gl'altri uostro padre ne fe = ce la proua, quando egli fù mandato insieme con Lion(ar)do Ginori oratore in campo nel 1529 di Settembre allo Ill(ustrissi)mo Principe di Orange Uice Re di Napoli, e Cap(ita)no Generale dell' Imperatore, il quale à danni nostri per il Ualdarno ue = niua, et incontrandolo al Ponte à Leuana, e da lui honora = tam(ent)e raccolto, in fino a Monte Uarchi hebbe con sua signo = ria molti ragionamenti piaceuoli. Dipoi il giorno se = guente adunati col Principe, et il Nunzio del Papa, tutti li signori, e capitani dell'esercito, animosam(ent)e Lor(enz)o espose la commissione datali da s(uoi) signori; che la città, atteso la buona mente di Cesare, uolentieri uoleua con s(ua) M(aesta) conuenire, essendo certà che così libera resterebbe. Quanto col Papa, non uoleua in modo al = [25v] cuno trauagliarsi, essendo certa, che quello non saria prima contento, che gli hauesse tolta di mano al pop(ol)o fiorentino la libertà; per la quale erano determinati

2 These symbols most likely refer to "small" silver florins and "small" silver "soldi," or three florins, five soldi. This would have been a tremendous amount of money for grain, but given the dire circumstances Florence faced, that price was certainly possible. For more on Florentine monetary abbreviations, see Anthony Molho, *Florentine Finance in the Early Renaissance: 1400–1433* (Cambridge: Harvard University Press, 1971), xiv.

non solamente la roba, e li proprij figlioli, mà ancora la propria uita spendere, quantunque non estima = uono, che Cesare desiderasse da loro, se non le cose giu - ste; pur quando altramente fusse, che si confidauono nell'onnipotente Iddio, e nella unione e concordia di tutta la città, nel uolersi mantenere al tutto in libertà. Al che non hauendo per allora, ne di poi ri = sposta, che secondo la commissione si potesse conclu = dere, attese à speculare le forze e il numero dell' esercito del nemico, trattenendo pure con qualche spe = ranza il Principe, tanto, che la città respirasse, et hauesse comodità di munire i luoghi più debili; allo - ra giudicando la spesa degl'ambasciadori esser sup(er) - flua, et alla propria poter più giouare, con riferire l'apparato del nemico, che col trattenersi in campo, ha = uendo dalla Signoria hauuto licenza di far ciò, che l'migliore gli paresse, si transferì in firenze; e di = ligentemente espose non solamente l'animo del Prin - cipe, mà la qualità, et il numero dell'esercito, secon = do la stessa uerità. Non credette Francesco Carducci, allora Gonfaloniere, con alcuni altri cittadini, che gouer - nauono, quel che non pareua gli tornasse à proposito; e con uane spéranze lattando il Popolo, fù finalm(ent)e cagione,

che

[26r]

che con gl'Imperiali non si facesse utili, et honoreuoli conuenzioni. Del che Lor(enz)o prese per il pericolo della patria tal dispiacere, e per conto suo tale sdegno, che di nuouo uolendolo la Signoria rimandar' al principe, non uolle mai acconsentire, dicendo, mandinsi pur quelli, che di più intelligenza, e di più credito sono ap = presso di quella. Quantunque Io ueggia la fortuna di Firenze camminare à manifesta rouina, non però sono per mancare alla patria, col dire quello, che à me parrà sempre il migliore. Uedendo per questo la buona parte de nobili la città hauer l'esercito di già sopra capo, et essere dalla parte de colli assediata, l' abbandonarono, ritirandosi fuor del Dominio à luoghi più sicuri: E consigliando Lor(enz)o al medesimo partito, non uolle mai acconsentire, dicendo, non uoleua ab = bandonare la patria, se ben la uita fussi p(er) lasciarui, aiutandola in quei modi, che gli erano leciti; benche più non s'ingerisse di cosa alcuna: anzi non uolse mai parlare fuori di Palazzo, de Signori, ne dello Stato; talchè essendo più uolte da cittadini uisitato a casa, e dettoli; noi sappiamo che hauéte parlato in benefizio pubblico caldamente, di che ui ringraziamo, et offeri = amouici: sempre rispose, che come usciua di Palazzo, si scordaua di quelli pensieri, e di quelli ragionamenti, che se haueua detto niente di buono, lo seguitassero, se altrimenti, se ne doleua, a che lo lasciassero. Trouandosi in tal tempo Filippo in Lucca grauemente malato, né si permettendo l'uscir di Firenze, chiese [26v] à suoi Signori licenza per uisitarlo. E dubitando la Signoria che non trouasse questa cagione p(er) uscir di Firenze, per non più tornare, come ferno molti al = tri, chiesono per sicurtà del ritorno malleuerìa di scudi 2000 la qual data, subito à Lucca si transfe = rì, e per la non pensata, uisitando il fratello, gli det - te tanto piacere, che grandissimo miglioramento ne prese. E confortandolo Filippo à dimorar seco in Lucca, egli per uederlo malato d'importanza, glie = ne de'intenzione, mà come lo uidde fuori di peri = colo, prese licenza, e se ne ritornò in Fiorenza; solamante per mantener la fede, non già per conto della malleueria delli scudi 2000 della quale non ne teneua conto, perche non erano quelli, che gouernauono in quei tempi, per potersene da lui, ne da malleuadori ualere: e perche molti cittadini fecero giudizio al suo partire, che non fusse per ri - tornar più; come di poi lo uiddero, corsono lietam(ent)e ad abbracciarlo, rallegrandosi non solamente del = la sua presenza, mà perche giudicarono, che ri = tornando egli, le cose di fuori de nemici non fussi = no tali, che potessino espugnare la città: e ciò fal = samente, perche mentre che stette di fuori, conob = be meglio il uero, e fù presto spauentato da proue = dimenti del Papa, che inanimito, né passò un mese, che ritornando Niccolò Capponi oratore della città

dell'

26r 19 stato • *followed by cancelled* di

dell'Imperatore, che à Genoua si trouaua; et amma = [27r] latosi in Castelnuouo de Lucchesi talmente, che Lor(enz)o amandolo egli molto più che cognato, ridomandò nuo = uamente licenza per irlo à uedere, et aiutare, la quale subito gli fù concessa senz'altra malleueria, giudicando, che se non era la prima uolta manca = to di fedé, che non fusse per mancare anco la secon = da. Mà prima si conducesse al detto Castelnuouo, egli intese la morte del prefato Niccolò: onde es = sendo ancora il fratello in Lucca, lo riuisitò, e quantunque li dicesse, come Firenze sarebbe di = nuouo da più bande stretta da nemici, di manie = ra, che per amore, ò per forza la pigliarebbono, confortandolo strettamente à non ritornare in se eui = dente pericolo; egli come quello, che preponeua la pa = tria alla morte e rouina sua, se ne tornaua, quan = do incontrando p(er) el cammino il suo maggior figliolo, fù da esso di nuouo feruentemente pregato, che ritornas = se indietro in Lucca, offerendosi egli stesso tornare in Firenze, per osseruare la fede sua; à cui disse, che era molto meglio, che corresse pericolo della uita un' uecchio, che pocchi di perdeua, che un giouane, e che molto maggior taglia pagherebbe per rihauere il figliolo, ché in ricuperar se stesso. Ritornato adun = que in Firenze, incominciorono li ambiziosi cittadini, e più della loro ostinazione amatori, che della patria, à conoscere, Lorenzo hauer sempre senza passione detto il bene della sua città. Talchè à di 9 d'Agosto [27v] 1529 ueggendo li Signori, et altri del gouerno, che più sostener la guerra non si poteua, per non ui essere ne danari, ne pane, croeorono quattro Ambasci = atori per andare à capitolare con gli nemici, i quali furon questi: M(esser) Bernardo Altouiti, Iacopo di Girol(am)o Morelli, Pier Francesco di Folco Portinari, e Lorenzo di Filippo Strozzi, uostro padre, i quali la mattina di San Lorenzo all'aprir della porta, andorono à trouare lo Ill(ustrissi)mo Signore Don Ferrando, Capitano Generale della Caualleria, e Gouernatore del campo Cesareo, et il Commessario Generale del Papa, Bartolomeo Ualori, con i quali dimororono tutto il giorno rinchiusi; di poi la sera tornorono à rifenire à Signori quel tanto haueua =

27v 4 croeorono (*sic*) • creorono

no ragionato. E fermo quando à loro Signorie piacesse; al che acconsentendo, la seguente mattina ragunati i Collegij, li Signori Dieci, et li O[ttant]a solennementé lo con = fermorono. La quale confermazione, perche si dou - eua stipulare in carta buona, non si potè ridurre al netto in fino à sera, e perciò l'altra mattina delli 12 di Agosto, con gran comitiua, i medesimi Amba = sciadori ritornarono in campo, et con li agenti del Pa - pa, e di Cesare, con non piccola fatica, doppo qualche disparere, e disperazione, a due hore di notte stipula - rono il contratto rogato per mano di Ser Bernardo Gam - beregli, menato da loro; e li Testimoni furono questi. Non mi pare da tacere qui, che se non era Lorenzo,

non

non si conueniua, ò la conuenzione era più uitupe = [28r] rosa, e dannosa per la città; la industria sua, e la stretta amicizia, che teneua con Bartolomeo Valori commessario del Papa, fece il tutto, di che n'hebbe poi mal grado col detto papa Clemente. Mà uedete sorte maluagia, erano le parti in sul capitolare, quando da Roma comparse quiui in Poste M(esser) Giouan - ni di M(esser) Luigi della Stufa mandato da Papa Clemente, e non gli piacendo le conuenzioni, che si trattauono in - trà loro, e la città nostra, le quali eron già comincia = te à distendersi con la penna, con sue parole fece alterare, e rompere ogni cosa, dicendo à Lor(enz)o, che Clemente uoleua più tosto la rouina di Firenzé, che quella di Roma, e che non poteua sostentar l'esserci - to con settanta mila ducati, come si ragionaua, che pagassino i fiorentini allora, hauendone di già sino à quel di con loro debito trecento mila; e molte altre parole simili hebbero insieme: a'cui Lor(enz)o rispose, che credéua sapere la mente di Clemente si bene, come

---

28r 7 quando da • *text originally read* 'da quando', *but editorial marks and the presence of an interlinear* 'da' *with caret indicating placement emended the text to the reading above.*

lui in tal caso, non p(er) altra cagione, se non p(er) la sua buo- na natura, perche Firenze era sua patria, e da lui ama = ta; ò sebene desideraua signoreggiarla, non uoleua la rouina di quella; conciossiache rouinata, non gli gio = ueria niente, oltre à che gli saria appresso Dio, et appresso gl'huomini un carico grandiss(im)o; e cosi rispon = dendo gagliardam(ent)e al prefato m(esser) Giouanni, operò in tal modo, che la capitolaz(ion)e trattatasi in prima, hebbe effetto; che se altrim(en)ti auueniua, male p(er) la città nostra —

Appendix 3
A Recipe for an Antidote against the Plague by Mengo Bianchelli

In his lifetime, Mengo Bianchelli (c. 1440–c. 1520) was a well-respected medical practitioner. His reputation, in Florence and Tuscany at least, was sufficient that Lorenzo di Filippo Strozzi mentioned him in the *Pistola*. His name was spelled in a number of ways: Mingo Bianchelli, Mingo Bianchello, Mengho Bianchelli/o and, last but not least, Maestro Mingo da Faenza. His plague antidotes were often published together with other plague tracts and medical treatises; most notably, one of his "recipes" was published in a 1523 edition of Marsilio Ficino's *Contro all peste*.[1] I examined that volume and here transcribe Bianchelli's antidote for the reader.

> Ricetta di Maestro Mingo da Faenza Medico singulare duna polvere da pigliarsi immediate che lhuomo si sentissi febbre o havessi sospetto di no(n) essere incorso nella infectione pestilentiale et no(n) potendo cosi inmediate almanco infra sei hore dipoi ti sara presa la febbre et non sendo febbre di peste non puo nuocere.
> Recipe Dittamo bianco.
> Corno di Cervio arso
> Bolo Armeno.
> Sandali rossi.
> Tormentilla.
> Camphora.

1 Ficino et al., *Contro alla peste. Il consiglio di messer Marsilio Ficino. Remedio di maestro Tommaso del Garbo. Vna ricepta duna poluere composta da maestro Mingo da Faenza. Vna ricetta facta nello studio di Bolognia: e molti altri remedij* (Impresso in Fiorenza: per ser Francesco di Hieronymo Risorboli, nel mese di marzo 1523). Bianchelli's "recipe" may be accessed through the Biblioteca Nazionale Centrale di Firenze's website. See also George Sarton, "The Scientific Literature Transmitted through Incunabula," *Osiris* 5 (1938): 41–123, 125–245; see p. 214 for brief reference to Bianchelli.

Di ciascuna per equal parte et pesta sottilme(n)te poi la de pigliare in questo modo, togli dramme due della detta polvere et tre oncie daqua Dindivia con tanta Tiriaca quanto e una fava.

Appendix 4
Niccolò Machiavelli's *Minuta di Provvisione per la Riforma dello Stato di Firenze L'Anno 1522*

To make his point concerning the reform of the Florentine government more forcefully, Machiavelli, in writing the *Minuta di Provvisione*, assumed the identity of Cardinal Giulio de' Medici. In other words, he fashioned his treatise to read as if it had been written, and was therefore condoned, by Giulio himself (which was almost certainly not the case). Machiavelli believed he was in good standing with the cardinal, but he nonetheless presumptuously overshot the boundaries of decorum and the rigid Florentine patron-client system. As well, his writing the *Minuta,* and the voice he assumed in writing it, endangered him by further associating him with the republican conspirators who sought to assassinate the cardinal. Of course the cardinal's intent to draw out those who had conspired against him were not known to Machiavelli or the other republican authors who submitted "suggestions"; he and they were duped by the more cunning cardinal. Here again, we confront the irony that Machiavelli, the author of *Il Principe*, was unable to discern what lay behind the masks of the princes whom he sought to advise. He needed the "courtier" to intervene on his behalf.

In chapter 2 of this study, I suggested that the oligarchic themes of the *Minuta* and Machiavelli's almost miraculous survival of the Medici-sponsored backlash against the conspirators were probably due to the intervention of Lorenzo di Filippo Strozzi. The brief treatise that follows is intended to shed light on Machiavelli's thinking in 1522 and perhaps also on the influence Strozzi's own political vision had on Machiavelli.

I transcribe the first edition of Machiavelli's *Minuta,* which was presented as a wedding gift at the Cavalieri-Zabba wedding of 17 October 1872.[1] That

1 *Due Scritture Inedite di Niccolò Machiavelli*, ed. Alessandro D'Ancona (Pisa: Tipografia Nistri, 1872), 17–29.

edition, edited by Alessando D'Ancona, is reliable. More recently, Guidubaldo Guidi published a philologically detailed edition of the *Minuta* (1970); more recently still, Corrado Vivanti included Machiavelli's brief treatise in his very fine edition of Machiavelli's *Opere* (2003).[2] The reader who wishes to consult the original Machiavelli autograph of the *Minuta* can find it in Florence, Biblioteca Nazionale Centrale, MS. Carte Machiavelli, I, 79.

In the transcription that follows, lineation and numeration are indicated in the right margin of the text. In place of line "1" I have used the page number from D'Ancona's edition. Page numbers are included in square brackets. D'Ancona's original footnotes are included throughout.

The Text of Machiavelli's *Minuta*

Yh̃s Maria

Considerando i nostri Magnifici et Excelsi [19] Signori come niuna legge et niuno ordine è più laudabile apresso ad gli huomini, o più accepto apresso a Dio, che quello mediante il quale si ordina una vera, unita et sancta Republica, nella quale liberamente si consigli, prudentemente si deliberi, et fedelmente si exeguisca; dove gli huomini nel deliberare delle cose sieno necessitati lasciare i commodi privati, et solo al bene universale rivolgersi; dove le amicitie de' tristi et le nimicitie de' buoni non habbino luogo; dove gli appetiti d'una falsa gloria si spenghino, et quelli de' veri et gloriosi honori si accendino; dove gli odii, le inimicitie, i dispareri, le sette, da le quali dipoi nasce morti, exilii, afflictione di buoni, exaltationi[3] di tristi non habbino chi le nutrisca, ma sieno in tutto da le leggi perseguitate et spente; dove si possa ne' pubblici [20]

2 G. Guidi, "Machiavelli e i progetti di riforme costituzionali a Firenze nel 1522," in *Machiavellismo e Antimachiavellismo nel Cinquecento: Atti del Convegno di Perugia 30.IX–1.X. 1969* (Florence: Olschki, 1970), 253–68. The critical edition of the *Provvisione* is found on pp. 263–8. This edition was clearly used in Niccolò Machiavelli, *Opere*, vol. 1, ed. Corrado Vivanti (Turin: Einaudi-Gallimard, 1997), 746–52.

3 L'autografo: "exaltioni."

consigli intendere quello che l' uomo vuole, et quello che si intende, liberamente parlare et consigliare; et havendo pensato, da l' altra parte, quante sette, quante divisioni, habbino per lo adrieto, et per tutti i tempi, perturbata, divisa et guasta la città di Firenze; desiderosi di vedere, s' egli è possibile, trovare modo per il quale, con sodisfactione del popolo et securtà di qualunque buono et honesto cittadino, la Republica di Firenze si administri et governi: ad che essendo con ogni instantia confortati et spinti da il R.mo Monsignore, signore Julio Cardinale de' Medici Ill.mo, et da il prodentissimo et amorevole consiglio suo consigliati et aiutati; invocato il nome dello omnipotente Iddio et della sua gloriosa madre sempre Vergine, et di sancto Giovanni Baptista, et di qualunque altro advocato et protectore della città di Firenze, acciò che quello che, per bene et pacifico vivere di quella si comincia, habbi mezzo et fine felicissimo, providono et ordinorono:

Che per virtù della presente provisione, s' intenda essere, et in effetto sia restituita al Consiglio, per lo addrietro chiamato il Consiglio maggiore, ogni et qualunque preheminenza, ordine et autorità, quanta mai in alcuno tempo havesse più ampla, da il mese di agosto dello anno 1512 indietro; et per il cancelliere delle Tratte, subito dopo la finale conclusione di questa, si ordinino le borse et ogn' altra cosa che sia necessario ordinare, perchè detto Consiglio [21]
possa exeguire quelle cose di che egli ha autorità, distribuendo gli honori, et creando i magistrati, ufici e consigli in quello modo et forma che per lo adietro, nel tempo predetto, soleva creare et distribuire. Et perchè detto Consiglio possa operare ne' sopradetti effecti, si provede che, subito dopo la finale conclusione di questa, gli operai del Palagio sieno obligati et debbino restituire la sala antica dove detto Consiglio si

ragunava, acciò che hora vi si possa ragunare ne' pristini et antichi ordini suoi: et quegli danari che affare questo bisognassino, sia obligato il Camarlingo del Monte pagarli a' detti operai, precedendo nondimanco prima lo stanziamento degli uficiali del Monte. Et perchè la sperienza per lo adrietro ha dimostro, come il numero di mille con disagio de' cittadini si ragunava, per facilitare il ragunarlo, dove prima non potevono essere meno di mille cittadini, si provede che bastino 800, et in oltre di poi tutti quelli che di più vi verranno, pure che sieno habili a detto Consiglio, secondo che per gli ordini della città si dispone, et netti di spechio;[4] e debbasi ragunare detto Consiglio in quegli dì, in quelli tempi, et a quel suono che, secondo lo antico costume, si ragunava.

Considerando ancora, che si è per experienza [22]
cognosciuto, come quando la città negli è stata negli antichi ordini suoi, et in quegli che più al vivere libero si confanno, uno Gonfaloniere di giustitia per duoi mesi è inutile, et uno ad vita è pericoloso; per fuggire l' uno et l' altro di questi inconvenienti si provede, che i Gonfalonieri di giustitia, i quali per lo advenire si debbano diputare, si elegghino et diputino per tre anni, da cominciare il tempo del primo Gonfaloniere a dì primo dì maggio proxime futuro, et da finire di tempo in tempo ogni tre anni, come segue. Et la electione di questo primo et proximo Gonfaloniere si faccia in questa modo: che per gli Ex..^{si} S.^{ri}, quattro dì almeno avanti a calendi maggio proximo, [si] nominino almeno tre cittadini di età di anni 45 forniti, habili al Consiglio, et netti di spechio, non obstante alcuno divieto: i quali così nominati, si debbino prima leggiere

4 Nel libro dello *Specchio* si registravano i cittadini contumaci al pagamento delle tasse, e con ciò si rendevano inabili agli uffici, finchè non si fossero rimessi in giorno: v Pagnini, *Decima*, I. 19.

tutti in detto Consiglio, et di poi andare a partito ad uno ad uno in detto Consiglio, secondo la età; et quale di loro harà più fave nere, vinto il partito per la metà delle fave nere et una più, quello sia deputato Gonfaloniere. Et quando alcuno non ne vincesse il partito la prima volta, debbino andare a partito un' altra volta; et quello che harà più fave nere, non obstante qualunque numero, quello sia il Gonfaloniere; et occorrendo che fussino duoi concorrenti, tante volte vadino a partito che l' uno avanzi l' altro. Il quale Gonfalonieri, così eletto, habbia quelle preheminenze, salarii et autorità, che per la legge che si fece [23] quando lo anno 1512 fu fatto Gonfalonieri Giovambatista Ridolfi, si dispone. Et venuto il fine de' tre anni, 15 giorni almeno avanti alla fine di essi, si debba, per quegli Signori che allora sederanno, ragunare il Consiglio maggiore, havendolo prima bandito tre giorni innanzi: dove possino ragunarsi tutti i cittadini fiorentini habili al Consiglio, non obstante lo spechio: et debbasi della borsa di detto Consiglio trarre cento electionarii, ciascuno de' quali nomini uno cittadino fiorentino per l'arte maggiore, di età di 45 anni forniti, non obstante lo spechio: et dipoi debbino in detto Consiglio andare tutti a partito, ad uno ad uno; et tucti quegli che vinceranno il partito per la metà delle fave nere et una più, debbino di nuovo andare a partito in detto Consiglio; et quello che harà più fave nere, non obstante qualunque numero, rimangha eletto Gonfaloniere per detto tempo di tre anni, et con le sopra detta conditioni; et così ogni tre anni per lo advenire di tempo in tempo si observi. Et quando nella ultima elettione vi fussero[5] con correnti, tante volte vadino a partito che l' uno avanzi l' altro; et s' egli occorressi che alcuno Gonfalonieri morisse avanti il fine del suo uficio,

5 Forse è da aggiungere "duoi" come sopra.

si faccia il successore per il resto del tempo, in quel modo che di sopra si dispone.

Intendasi, dopo la finale conclusione di questa, annullato il Consiglio del Popolo et del Comune et del Cento, che al presente veghiano; et [24] perchè la città non manchi di uno Consiglio di mezo, che provveggha a quelle cose alle quali il Consiglio grande non può provedere, si proveda che il Consiglio de' 70, il quale al presente veghia,[6] insieme con gli arroti a quello nuovamente facti, rimanga nel suo presente essere: et si chiami per lo advenire il Consiglio del Cento, et habbi tucta quella autorità, insieme con i Signori et i Collegi, che haveva per lo adietro il Consiglio degli 80; et di più che in esso si habbino a deliberare, et per finale conclusione ottenere, tutte le impositioni de' danari che per i tempi per lo advenire si faranno; et bastino ad ragunarsi 60 almeno di detti consiglieri, oltre a i detti Signori et Collegi; et per i dua terzi de' ragunati si debba qualunque deliberatione che gli sia posta davanti, ottenere. Questo non dimeno inteso, che la deputatione degli uomini che habbino a porre alcuna graveza, balzello o accatto, o a fare alcuna gratia, gravo et sgravo, si aspetti et apartenga al Consiglio maggiore, in quello modo che per la leggie sopra ciò allora fatta, sarà ordinato. Appartengasi ancora a detto Consiglio del Cento, ragunato nel modo sopra detto, deliberare, et per finale conclusione vincere ciascuno anno la riforma del Monte. Mancando alcuni di detti consiglieri del Cento, o per morte o per altra cagione, si deputi lo scambio in questa modo, che si faccia una borsa, dove si imborsino tucti gli uomini di detto Consiglio [25] del Cento, et per ogniuno che s' havessi ad rifare, si tragga di detta borsa x electio-

6 L'autografo: "vechia."

nari, i quali debbino nominare ciascuno[7] andare a partito nel Consiglio maggiore: et quello che harà più fave nere, vinto il partito per la metà delle fave nere et una più, quello rimanga di detto Consiglio; e così sempre per lo advenire si observi.

Se gli occorressi, per quale si voglia accidente, che per il Consiglio grande non si vincesse o consiglio o uficio o magistrato, si provede che i nominati in detto Consiglio, uficio o magistrato non vinto, vadino l' altra[8] tornata dipoi, in detto Consiglio grande, appartito, o tutti o parte, secondo che mancasse, per fornire il numero di quello magistrato che si havesse a fare; et per ogni huomo che si havesse ad eleggiere, se ne imborsino duoi, delle più fave nere[9] non obstante qualunque numero di fave si havessino; et dipoi si tragghino, et quello o [26] quegli tratti si intendino eletti o eletto in detti o in detto magistrato.

Debbino trovarsi presenti alle imborsationi et squittini che in detto Consiglio maggiore di tempo in tempo si faranno, quegli Signori, Collegi et Ministri di palagio, che secondo lo antico ordine di detto Consiglio si dispone.

Che dopo la finale conclusione di questa, s' intendino et sieno rinnovate tutte quelle leggi et ordini, i quali contro al parlamento per lo adietro sono stati ordinati; le quali et i quali in tutto et per tutto si debbino observare.

Desiderando ancora i Magnifici Signori che

---

7 Qui c'è mancanza. S'intende bene che non sono gli elezionari che debbono andare a partito. Per restaurare questo passo ne riferiamo un altro dello stesso paragrafo, stato poi cancellato, dove anche si parla di elezionari: "Et ciascuno di detti (elezionari) nomini uno cittadini di 40 anni forniti, habile al Consiglio, et netto di spechio.... i quali così nominati vadino ad partito," etc.

8 Nell'autogr. stava scritto originalmente: "l'altro giorno"; poi si è cancellato "giorno" e sostituitovi "tornata," senza correggere "l' altro."

9 Intenderei: due di quelli che nella precedente tornata avevano ottenute più fave nere, sebbene nessuno di loro avesse raggiunto il numero legale.

questo pacifico et popolare vivere che si ordina sia a beneficio de' cittadini, ad quiete della città, et a salute comune di ciascuno, per dare freno a quelli scandoli che in questo principio potrebbono nascere, et potere provedere a quelle cose che alla perfettione d' uno pacifico stato mancassino, le quali sanza la experienza non si possono nè vedere nè cognoscere, per conforto et consiglio di molti savi buoni et amorevoli cittadini, si provede che, subito dopo la finale conclusione di questa, i presenti nostri Excelsi Signori debbino deputare XII cittadini, habili al Consiglio, netti di spechio, di età di 45 anni forniti, x per la maggiore et duoi per le minori arti, i quali si chiamino Riformatori; et insieme con il R.^{mo} S. S.^{re} Julio Cardinale de' Medici Illmo et otto di loro, d' accordo habbino tanta autorità. [27] quanta ha tutto il popolo di Firenze, di riformare et riordinare tutto quello che giudicassino, per bene et quiete della città, che fusse necessario riformare et ordinare; et possino fare leggi, ordini, statuti, i quali vaglino et tenghino et habbino quella potestà et valore, che se fussino da tutto il popolo di Firenze fatti et ordinati. Et perchè ciascuno veggha che questa autorità così riserbata, è tutta a benificio della libertà et quieto et vero vivere libero di una repubblica, si delibera in prima:

Che fatta la deputatione di detti XII cittadini, s' intenda et sia annullata la Balìa che al presente vegghia, et diventi di nessuno valore et autorità. Oltre di questo, non duri detta autorità data a' detti Riformatori, come di sopra, et a detto Mre R.^{mo} de' Medici, più che uno anno, da cominciare a dì primo di maggio proxime futuro, et da finire come segue: dopo el quale anno, rimanghino detti XII cittadini et detto M.^{re}

R.^{mo} sanza alcuna autorità nè possino a ....[10] medesimi prorogarla, nè ad altri, per alcuna via retta o indiretta, d[arla].

Non possino detti Riformatori diminuire il numero del Consiglio maggiore, nè torgli alcuna distribuitione o elettione di ufici, consigli et magistrati; ma tutta le deputationi di consigli, ufici et magistrati si aspettino a detto Consiglio maggiore, salvo quello che di sotto si dirà.

Non possino ancora detti Riformatori nomi- [28]
natamente dare autorità ad alcuno cittadino, nè deputarlo in alcuno magistrato; ma di tutte le deputationi che de' cittadini si havessino ad fare, di ufici, consigli, magistrati, creati di nuovo o riformati da loro, se ne aspetti et appartenga la deputatione et elettione a detto Consiglio maggiore, in quel modo che da loro sarà ordinato.

Ma perchè in nel principio di questa governo, come di sopra si disse, alcuno scandoloso non possa havere occasione di potere, per sua privata passione, fare alcuno scandolo, et acciò che chi fusse di maligno animo, o per desiderio di vendetta, o per altra scandolosa cagione, habbi qualche freno che lo ritenga, tanto che questo nuovo governo habbi presa qualche autorità, et gli huomini in esso si sieno rassicurati, si provede che i Riformatori predetti, insieme con il R.^{mo} M.^{re}, habbino autorità di potere eleggere tutte quelle Signorie che sederanno da calendi maggio proxime advenire ad l'ultimo dì di ottobre del presente anno proximo advenire; che sono in tutto tre Signorie; et passato detto tempo, si aspetti la deputatione et electione de' Signori che di poi per i tempi sederanno, in tutto et per tucto, al Consiglio maggiore. Pro-

10 Qui è uno strappo. Forse "a sè medesimi." Così anche nell' ultima parola del periodo evvi strappo: "arla" è supplito.

vedesi ancora per le medesime cagioni, che la electione degli Otto di guardia et balia del popolo di Firenze, che sederanno in magistrato per tutto dicembre proxime futuro del presente anno, si appartenga a' detti Riformatori; dopo al quale tempo, la elettione di detti Otto si aspetti et ricaggia [29] a detto Consiglio maggiore in tutto et per tutto. Ancora si provede per le medesime cagioni, la electione da farsi solamenta de' prossimi futuri Gonfalonieri delle compagnie del popolo, et de' proxime futuri XII Buonihuomini si appartenga a' detti Riformatori; dopo i quali la electione de' successori et di tutti gli altri che per gli tempi si eleggieranno, s' appartenga et ricaggia al Consiglio maggiore in tutto et per tutto.

Possino detti Riformatori et Mre R.^{mo} riformare le cancellerie de' Signori et degli Octo di pratica, o vero Dieci di guerra, in quel modo che a loro parrà, et deputare in quelle cancellieri secondo che a loro parrà; i quali cancellieri debbino ciascuno anno, quelli de' Signori havere la rafferma da i Signori, et quelli de' Dieci o vero Octo di pratica, da' detti o detto magistrato.

Bibliography

MANUSCRIPT SOURCES

ARCHIVIO DI STATO
Carte Strozziane. Series 3, 92.
Carte Strozziane. Series 5, 1207.
Carte Strozziane. Series 5, 1209.

BIBLIOTECA DEL CONSERVATORIO
Basevi 2440.

BIBLIOTECA MARUCELLIANA
Scaff. C. Ms. CXXXII.

BIBLIOTECA MEDICEA LAURENZIANA
Ashburnham 579.
Ashburnham 606.
Rediano 129.

BIBLIOTECA NAZIONALE CENTRALE
Banco Rari 29.
Carte Machiavelli I, 79.
Fondo Nazionale II IV (formerly Magliabechiano VIII 1409).
Gino Capponi 94.
Magliabechiano. Cl. XXXV, 32.
Magliabechiano. Cl. XXXV, 106.
Palatino E.B. 14.1.
Palatino 173.

PRINT PRIMARY SOURCES

Ammirato, Scipione. *Istorie fiorentine*. Ed. L. Scarabelli. 7 vols. Turin: Cugini Pomba e Comp. Editori, 1853.

Bianchelli, Mengo. "Ricetta di Maestro Mingo da Faenza Medico singulare," n.p. In *Contro alla peste Il consiglio di messer Marsilio Ficino*. Florence: P. Di Giunta, 1523.

Boccaccio, Giovanni. *The Decameron*. Trans. Guido Waldman. Ed. Jonathan Usher. Oxford: Oxford University Press, 1998.

– *Decameron*. In *Tutte le opere di Giovanni Boccaccio*, vol. 4, ed. Vittore Branca. Milan: Mondadori, 1976.

Capponi, Guido. *Storia della Repubblica di Firenze*. 2 vols. Florence: G. Barbèra, 1930.

Castiglione, Baldassarre. *Book of the Courtier*. Trans. George Bull. New York: Penguin, 1976.

– *Il libro del cortegiano*. Ed. Walter Barberis. Turin: Einaudi, 1998.

Cellini, Benvenuto. *The Autobiography of Benvenuto Cellini*. Trans. J. Addington Symonds. New York: P.F. Collier and Son, 1910.

– *Vita di Benvenuto Cellini scritta da lui medesimo*. Ed. Brunone Bianchi. Florence: Adriano Salani, Editore Viale Militare, 1903.

Cerretani, Bartolomeo. *Dialogo mutatione della Firenze*. Ed. Raul Mordenti. Rome: Edizioni di storia e letteratura, 1990.

– *Ricordi*. Ed. Giuliana Berti. Florence: Leo S. Olschi, 1993.

Ferrarese, P. Giulio Negri. *Istoria degli scrittori fiorentini*. Ferrara, 1727.

Ficino, Marsilio. *Consiglio contro la pestilenza*. Ed. Enrico Musacchio and Giampaolo Moraglia. Bologna: Cappelli, 1983.

Florentino, Michaele Pocciantio. *Catalogus scriptorum florentinorum omnis generis*. Florence: Apud Iunctum, 1589.

Frye, Northrop. *Northrop Frye's Notebooks on Renaissance Literature*. Vol. 20. Ed. Michael Dolzani. Toronto: University of Toronto Press, 2006.

Giannotti, Donato. *Donato Giannotti and His* "Epistolae": *Biblioteca Universitaria Alessandrina, Rome, Ms 107*. Ed. Randolph Starn. Geneva: Droz, 1968.

– Letter to Lorenzo Strozzi dated 19 August 1532. In *Giornale Storico degli Archivi Toscani*, vol. 7, 156–7. Florence: G.P. Vieusseux, 1863.

– Letter to Lorenzo Strozzi dated 28 March 1533. In *Giornale Storico degli Archivi Toscani*, vol. 7, 157. Florence: G.P. Vieusseux, 1863.

– *Opere politiche e letterarie: Collazionate sui manoscritti da F.L. Polidori*. Vol. 2. Florence: Le Monnier, 1850.

– "Tragedia della Passione." In *Opere politiche e letterarie: Collazionate sui manoscritti da F.L. Polidori*, vol. 2, 371–9. Florence: Le Monnier, 1850.

– *Republica Fiorentina*. Geneva: Librairie Droz, 1990.

Giovio, Paolo. *Elogia virorum literis illustrium*. Basel, 1577.

– *Gli elogi degli uomini illustri (Letterati, Artisti, Uomini d'arme)*. *Opere*. Vol. 8. Ed. Renzo Meregazzi. Rome: Instituto Poligrafico dello Stato, 1972.

– Letter to Lorenzo Strozzi dated 22 May 1534. In *Opere politiche e letterarie: Collazionate sui manoscritti da F.L. Polidori*, vol. 2, 409–10. Florence: Le Monnier, 1850.

Guasti, Cesare. "Documenti della congiura fatta il cardinale Giulio de' Medici nel 1522." *GSAT* 3 (1859).

Guicciardini, Francesco. "Considerations of the *Discourses* of Niccolò Machiavelli." In *The Sweetness of Power: Machiavelli's* Discourses *and Guicciardini's* Considerations, trans. James B. Atkinson and David Sices, 381–438. Dekalb: Northern Illinois University Press, 2002.

– *The History of Italy*. Trans. Sidney Alexander. Princeton: Princeton University Press, 1984.

– *Ricordi*. Trans. and ed. Ninian Hill Thomson. New York: S.F. Vanni, 1949.

– *Ricordi, Edizione critica*. Ed. Raffaele Spongano. Florence: Sansoni, 1951.

Landucci, Luca. *Diario Fiorentino dal 1450 al 1516 di Luca Landucci: Continuato da un anonimo fino al 1542*. Ed. Iodoco del Badia. Florence: Sansoni, 1883.

Lucretius. *De rerum natura libri sex*. Berolini: Impensis G. Reimeri, 1860.

Machiavelli, Niccolò. "Ai Palleschi." In *Opere*, vol. 1, ed. Corrado Vivanti, 87–9. Turin: Einaudi-Gallimard, 1997.

– *L'Arte della guerra*. In *Opere*, ed. Mario Bonfantini. Milan: R. Ricciardi, n.d.

– *L'arte della guerra*. In *Opere*, vol. 1, ed. Corrado Vivanti, 529–705. Turin: Einaudi-Gallimard, 1997.

– *L'Arte della guerra, Scritti politici minori. Edizione nazionale di Niccolò Machiavelli, sezione I: Opere politiche.* Vol. 3. Ed. Jean-Jacques Marchand. Rome: Salerno, 2001.

– "L'Asino." In *Opere,* vol. 3, ed. Corrado Vivanti, 51–78. Rome: Einaudi, 2005.

– "L'Asino d'oro." In *Tutte le opere Storiche e Letterarie di Niccolò Machiavelli*, ed. Guido Mazzoni and Mario Casella, 817–40. Florence: G. Barbèra, 1929.

– "The Ass." In *The Chief Works and Others*, vol. 3, trans. Alan Gilbert, 750–72. Durham: Duke University Press, 1965.

– "Capitoli per una compagnia di piacere." In *Opere*, vol. 3, ed. Corrado Vivanti, 243–7. Rome: Einaudi, 2005.

– *The Chief Works and Others*. Trans. Alan Gilbert. 3 vols. Durham: Duke University Press, 1965.

– "Descrizione della peste." In *Opere di Niccolò Machiavelli, Cittadino e Segretario Fiorentino*, vol. 1, 222–39. Milan: Dalla Società Tipografica de'Classici Italiani, contrada di S. Margherita, No. 1118, 1804.

– "Descrizione della peste di Firenze dell'Anno 1527." In *Opere Complete di Niccolò Machiavelli con molte correzioni e giunte rivenute sui manoscritti originali*, ed. Alcide Parenti, 589–94. Florence: Le Monnier, 1843.
– "Descrizione delle peste di Firenze dell'Anno MDXXVII." In *Opere di Niccolò Machiavelli,* ed. Giuseppe Zirardini, 522–8. Parigi: Baudry, Liberia Europa, 1851.
– *Discorso delle cose fiorentine dopo la morte di Lorenzo.* Cited in Roberto Ridolfi, *Vita di Niccolò Machiavelli,* 2 vols. Florence: Sansoni, 1972.
– *Discourses on Livy*. Trans. Harvey C. Mansfield and Nathan Tarcov. Chicago: University of Chicago Press, 1996.
– *Discourses on the First Decade of Titus Livius*. Trans. Ninian Hill Thomson. London: Kegan Paul, Trench and Co., 1883.
– "Discursus Florentinarum Rerum Post Mortem Iunioris Laurentii Medices." In *Opere,* vol. 1, ed. Corrado Vivanti, 733–45. Rome: Einaudi, 1997.
– *Edizione Nazionale delle opere di Niccolò Machiavelli: Disorsi sopra le prima deca di Tito Livio*. Vol. 1. Ed. Francesco Bausi. Rome: Salerno Editrice, 2001.
– *Istorie fiorentine*. In *Opere*, vol. 3, ed. Corrado Vivanti, 303–732. Turin: Einaudi, 2005.
– *Lettere a Francesco Vettori e a Francesco Guicciardini*. Ed. Giorgio Inglese. Milan: Libri e Grandi Opere S.p.A., 1996.
– *Machiavelli and His Friends: Their Personal Correspondence*. Trans. and ed. James B. Atkinson and David Sices. Dekalb: Northern Illinois University Press, 1996.
– *La Mandragola*. In *La Madragola, Belfagor, Lettere*, ed. Mario Bonfantini. Milan: Mondadori, 1991.
– *La Mandragola*: *Storia e filologia, con l'edizione critica del testo secondo il Laurenziano Redi 129*. Ed. Pasquale Stoppelli. Rome: Bulzone, 2005.
– *Minuta di provvisione per la riforma dello stato di Firenzo l'anno 1522.* In *Due Scritture Inedite di Niccolò Machiavelli*, ed. Alessandro D'Ancona, 17–29. Pisa: Tipografia Nistri, 1872.
– *Minuta di provvisione per la riforma dello stato di Firenzo l'anno 1522*. In *Opere,* vol. 2, ed. C. Vivanti, 746–52. Turin: Einaudi, 1997.
– *Minuta di provvisione per la riforma dello stato di Firenze l'anno 1522*. In Guidubaldo Guidi, "Machiavelli e i progetti di riforme costituzionali a Firenze nel 1522," in *Machiavellismo e Antimachiavellismo nel Cinquecento*, 253–68. Florence: Leo S. Olschki, 1970.
– *Opere*. Ed. Corrado Vivanti. 3 vols. Rome: Einaudi, 1997–2005.
– *Opere*. Ed. Mario Bonfantini. Milan: R. Ricciardi, n.d.
– *Opere di Niccolò Machiavelli*. Ed. Rinaldo Rinaldi. Vol. 1, bk. 1, *De Principatibus, Discorsi sopra la prima deca di Tito Livio* (bks. I–II). Turin: Unione Tipografico-Editrice Torinese, 1999.

– *Opere di Niccolò Machiavelli: Segretario e Cittadino Fiorentino*. Ed. Gaetano Poggiali and Giovanni Battista Baldelli Boni. Livorno, 1797.
– *Opere Letterarie*. Ed. Luigi Blasucci. Milan: Adelphi, 1964.
– *Opere minori di Niccolò Machiavelli: Rivedute sulle migliori edizioni, con note filologiche e critiche di F-L Polidori*. Florence: Le Monnier, 1852.
– *Opere, Volume Terzo: Lettere*. Ed. Franco Gaeta. Turin: Unione Tipografico Editrice Torinese, 1984.
– *The Prince*. Ed. and trans. Angelo M. Codevilla. New Haven: Yale University Press, 1997.
– *The Prince*. Trans. George Bull. London: Penguin, 1995.
– *Il Principe*. In *Opere*, vol. 1, ed. Corrado Vivanti, 114–192. Rome: Einaudi, 1997.
– *Il Principe e Altre Opere Politiche: Introduzione di Delio Cantimori, Note di Stefano Andretta*. Milan: Garzanti Libri, 1999.
– *Tutte le opere Storiche e Letterarie di Niccolò Machiavelli*. Ed. Guido Mazzoni and Mario Casella. Florence: G. Barbèra, 1929.
– Machiavelli's contract for *Istorie fiorentine*. In Pasquale Villari, *The Life and Times of Niccolò Machiavelli*, trans. Linda Villari, vol. 3, 321. London: Kegan Paul, Trench and Co., 1883.
Martines, Lauro, and Murtha Baca, eds. and trans. *An Italian Sextet*. New York: Marilio, 1994.
Medici, Alessandro Ottaviano de'. Letter dated 6 December 1577 to Pietro Vasari In Giorgio Vasari, *Lo Zibaldone di Giorgio Vasari*, ed. Alessandro del Vita, 281–3. Rome: R. Instituto d'Archeologia e Storia dell'Arte, 1938.
Medici, Lorenzino de'. *Aridosia, Apologia, Rime e Lettere*. Ed. Federico Ravello. Turin: Unione tipografico-editrice torinese, 1921.
Nardi, Jacopo. *Istorie della città di Firenze*. Ed. Agenore Gelli. Vol. 2. Florence: Le Monnier, 1888.
– *Istorie della città di Firenze*. Ed. Lelio Arbib. 2 vols. Florence: Società editrice delle Storie del Nardi e del Varchi, 1838–41.
Nerli, Filippo de'. *Commentari de' fatti civili occorsi dentro la città di Firenze dall'anno 1512 al 1537*. 2 vols. Trieste: Colombo Coen Tip. Editore, 1859.
Nohl, Johannes, ed. *The Black Death: A Chronicle of the Plague*. Trans. C.H. Clarke. Yardley, PA: Westholme, 2006. Repr., 1926, Unwin.
Pitti, Jacopo. *Istoria fiorentina*. In *Archivio storico Italiano*, vol. 1, 1–203. Florence: Vieusseux, 1842.
Pollaiolo, Simone del, called "il Cronaca." *Tre Lettere*. Ed. Jodoco del Badia. Florence: Tipografia all'Insegna di S. Antonio, 1869.
Sanuto, Marin, Patricia H. Labalme, Laura Sanguineti White, and Linda Carroll. "How to (and How Not to) Get Married in Sixteenth-Century Venice

(Selections from the Diaries of Marin Sanuto).” *Renaissance Quarterly* 52, no. 1 (1999): 43–72.

Shakespeare, William. *Henry VI, Part III*. In *The Complete Signet Classic Shakespeare*, ed. Sylvan Barnet, 190–232. New York: Harcourt Brace Jovanovich, 1972.

Singleton, Charles S., ed. *Canti carnascialeschi del rinascimento*. Bari: G. Laterza, 1936.

Strozzi, Alessandra Macinghi. *Selected Letters of Alessandra Strozzi*. Bilingual ed. Trans. Heather Gregory. Berkeley: University of California Press, 1997.

Strozzi, Antonio. Letter to Alfonso and Lorenzo Strozzi dated 3 September 1512. In *Il sacco di Prato e il ritorno de' Medici in Firenze nel MDXII: Narrazioni in versi e in prosa*, ed. Cesare Guasti, 174–5. Romagnoli, 1880.

Strozzi, Filippo di Filippo. Letter to Lorenzo di Filippo Strozzi dated 17 March 1519. In Oreste Tommasini, *La vita e gli scritti di Niccolò Machiavelli nella loro relazione col Machiavellismo: Storia ed esame critico di Oreste Tommasini*, vol. 2, appendices, 1081. Turin: Ermano Loescher, 1883.

Strozzi, Filippo di Matteo Strozzi. *Ricordo*. In Lorenzo di Filippo Strozzi, *Filippo Strozzi: Tragedia*.

Strozzi, Lorenzo di Filippo. *Filippo Strozzi: Tragedia*. Ed. G.-B. Niccolini. Florence: Le Monnier, 1847.

– *Commedie: Commedia in versi, La Pisana, La Violante*. Ed. Andrea Gareffi. Ravenna: Longo Editore, 1980.

– *La Nutrice: A Comedy in Hendecasyllabic Blank Verse*. Ed. Virgil Milani. Master's thesis, Catholic University of America, Washington, DC, 1960.

– *Rime inedite di Lorenzo di Filippo Strozzi*. Ed. Pio Ferrieri. Pavia, 1885.

– “La Vita di Filippo Strozzi [Il Giovane].” In Lorenzo di Filippo Strozzi, *Filippo Strozzi: Tragedia*, vii–cxxiv.

– “Vita di Filippo Strozzi [Il Giovane],” n.p. In Benedetto Varchi, *Storia fiorentina*. Venezia, 1725.

– *La Vita di Filippo Strozzi il Vecchio*. Ed. Giuseppe Bini and Pietro Bigazzi. Florence: Tip. Della Casa Correzione, 1851.

– *Le Vite degli Uomini Illustri della Casa Strozzi*. Ed. Pietro Stromboli. Florence: Pei Tipi Salvadore Landi, 1892.

– *Vite di Alcuni Famiglia Strozzi descitte da Lorenzo nel secolo XVI*. Firenze: Pei Tipi di Salvatore Landi, 1890.

Thucydides. *A History of the Plague of Athens*. Trans. Charles F. Collier. London, 1857.

Vasari, Giorgio. *Lives of the Most Eminent Painters, Sculptors and Architects*. Trans. Mrs Jonathan Foster. Vol. 2. London: Bell and Daldy, 1871.

– *Vite de' più eccellenti pittori, scultori e architetti*. Vol. 7. Milan: Della Società Tipografica de' Classici Italiani, 1809.

– *Lo Zibaldone di Giorgio Vasari*. Ed. Alessandro del Vita. Rome: R. Instituto d'Archeologia e Storia dell'Arte, 1938.

Zeffi, Francesco, da Empoli. *Epistole di S. Girolamo, volgarizzate nel secolo XVI da Giovan Francesco Zeffi*. Ed. un religioso de' Servi di Maria. Florence: Manuelli, 1861.

– "Un Ragionamento inedito di Francesco Zeffi sopra la Vita dell' Autore (Lorenzo di Filippo Strozzi)." In Lorenzo di Filippo Strozzi, *Le Vite degli Uomini della Casa Strozzi*, ed. Pietro Strombli, vii–xxvi. Florence: Pei Tipi Salvadore Landi, 1892.

SECONDARY SOURCES

Adorno, Francesco. *The World of Renaissance Florence*. Trans. Walter Darwell. Florence: Giunti Gruppo Editoriale, 1999.

Agee, Richard J. "Filippo Strozzi and the Early Madrigal." *Journal of American Musicological Society* 38, no. 2 (1985): 227–37.

Albertini, Rudolph von. *Das Florentinische Staatsbewusstsein im Übergang von der Republik zum Prinzipat*. Bern: Francke, 1955.

Alfano, Barbara. "Il narrator delle 'Novelle' del Bandello e la funzione mediatrice della scrittura." *Italica* 81, no. 1 (2004): 16–23.

Altrocchi, Rudolph. "Trinità or Trínita?" *Italica* 26, no. 1 (1949): 57–61.

Anselmi, Gian Mario, and Paolo Fazion. *Machiavelli, L'Asino e le Bestie*. Bologna: CLEUB, 1984.

Atti del Convegno di Perugia 30 IX–1 X 1969; *Machiavellismo e Antimachiavellismo nel Cinquecento*. Florence: Leo S. Olschki, 1970.

Baker, Nicholas Scott. "For Reasons of State: Political Executions, Republicanism and the Medici in Florence, 1480–1560." *Renaissance Quarterly* 62 (2009): 444–78.

Baron, Hans. "Machiavelli on the Eve of the *Discourses*: The Date and Place of the *Dialogo intorno alla nostra lingua*." *Bibliothèque d'Humanisme et Renaissance* 23 (1961): 449–76.

– "The *Principe* and the Puzzle of the Date of the *Discorsi*." *Bibliotheque d'humanisme et renaissance* 18 (1956): 405–28.

Bausi, Francesco. *Machiavelli*. Rome: Salerno, 2005.

Bec, Christian. *Les Livres des Florentins: 1413–1608*. Florence: Leo S. Olschki, 1984.

Berger, Harry. *The Absence of Grace:* Sprezzatura *and Suspicion in Two Renaissance Courtesy Books*. Stanford: Stanford University Press, 2000.

Bertelli, Sergio. "Machiavelli and Soderini." *Renaissance Quarterly* 28 (1975): 1–16.

– "When Did Machiavelli Write *Mandragola*?" *Renaissance Quarterly* 24, no. 3 (1971): 317–26.

Biasi, Pierre-Marc de. "Editing Manuscripts: Towards a Typology of Recent French Genetic Editions, 1980–1995." Trans. Helene Erlichson. *Text* 12 (1999): 1–30.

– "Toward a Science of Literature: Manuscript Analysis and the Genesis of the Work." In *Genetic Criticism: Texts and Avant-textes*, ed. Jed Deppman, Daniel Ferrer, and Michael Groden, 36–68. Philadelphia: University of Pennsylvania Press, 2004.

Biraben, Jean-Noel. *Les hommes et la peste en France et dans les pays européens et méditerranéens*. 2 vols. Paris: Mouton, 1975–76.

Black, Robert. *Education and Society in Florentine Tuscany: Teachers, Pupils, Schools, c. 1250–1500*. Leiden: Brill, 2007.

Bock, Gisela, Quentin Skinner, and Maurizio Viroli, eds. *Machiavelli and Republicanism.* Cambridge: Cambridge University Press, 1990.

Bonadeo, Alfredo. "The Role of the 'Grandi' in the Political World of Machiavelli." *Studies in the Renaissance* 16 (1969): 9–30.

Booth, Wayne C. *The Rhetoric of Fiction*. Chicago: University of Chicago Press, 1961.

Borsi, Franco, et al. *Filippo Brunelleschi: La sua opera e il suo tempo*. 2 Vols. Florence: Centro Di, 1980.

Borsook, Eve. *Documenti relative alle cappelle di Lecceto e delle Selve di Filippo Strozzi*. Florence: Edam, 1970.

Bryce, Judith. "The Theatrical Activities of Palla di Lorenzo Strozzi in Lyon in the 1540's." In *The Theater of the English and Italian Renaissance*, ed. J.R. Mulryne and Margaret Shewring, 55–69. New York: St. Martin's, 1991.

Bullard, Melissa Meriam. *Filippo Strozzi and the Medici: Favor and Finance in Sixteenth-Century Florence and Rome*. Cambridge: Cambridge University Press, 1980.

– "Marriage Politics and the Family in Florence: The Strozzi-Medici Alliance of 1508." *American Historical Review* 84, no. 3 (1979): 668–87.

Butters, H.C. *Governors and Governments in Early Sixteenth-Century Florence, 1502–1519*. Oxford: Clarendon, 1985.

Byrne, Joseph P. *The Black Death*. Westport, CT: Greenwood, 2004.

– *Daily Life during the Black Death*. Westport, CT: Greenwood, 2006.

Cantimori, Delio, and Frances A. Yates. "Rhetoric and Politics in Italian Humanism." *Journal of the Warburg Institute* 1, no. 2 (1937): 83–102.

Cattabiani, Alfredo. *Calendario: Le feste, i miti, le leggende e riti dell'anno.* Milan: Rusconi, 1991.

Cavallo, JoAnn. "Joking Matters: Politics and Dissimulation in Castiglione's *Book of the Courtier*." *Renaissance Quarterly* 53, no. 2 (2000): 402–24.

Chiappelli, Fredi. *Nuovi Studi sul Linguaggio del Machiavelli*. Florence: Le Monnier, 1969.

Ciabani, Roberto. *Le Famiglie di Firenze.* Vol. 3. Florence: Casa Editrice Bonechi, 1992.

Clark, Kenneth. *Civilisation*. London: Folio Society, 1999.

Clark, Stuart. *Vanities of the Eyes: Vision in Early Modern European Culture*. Oxford: Oxford University Press, 2007.

Clemen, Wolfgang. *English Tragedy before Shakespeare: The Development of Dramatic Speech.* New York: Routledge, 1980.

Cohn, Samuel K. "The Black Death: The End of a Paradigm." *The American Historical Review* 107, no. 3 (2002): 703–38.

– *The Black Death Transformed: Disease and Culture in Early Renaissance Europe*. New York: Arnold, 2002.

– *Cultures of Plague: Medical Thinking at the End of the Renaissance*. Oxford: Oxford University Press, 2010.

Conati, Marcello. "Il Maggio drammatico nel parmense." In *Il Maggio drammatico: Una tradizione di teatro in musica*, ed. Tullia Magrini, 309–50. Bologna: Poligrafici L. Parma, 1992.

Craven, Stephen J. "Three Dates for Piero di Cosimo." *Burlington Magazine* 117, no. 870 (1975): 572, 574–6.

Crawfurd, Raymond. *Plague and Pestilence in Literature and Art*. Oxford: Clarendon, 1914.

Creighton, Mandell. *A History of the Papacy from the Great Schism to the Sack of Rome*. Vol. 6. London: Longmans, Green and Co., 1919.

Cummings, Anthony M. *Maecenas and the Madrigalist: Patrons, Patronage, and the Origins of the Italian Madrigal*. Philadelphia: American Philosophical Society, 2004.

– *MS Florence, Biblioteca Nazionale Centrale, Magl. 164–167*. Aldershot: Ashgate, 2006.

D'Accone, Frank A. "Bernardo Pisano: An Introduction to His Life and Works." *Musica Disciplina* 17 (1963): 115–35.

– "Transitional Text Settings in an Early Sixteenth-Century Florentine Manuscript." In *Words and Music – The Scholar's View: A Medley of Problems and Solutions Compiled in Honor of A. Tillman Merritt by Sundry Hands*, ed. Laurence Berman, 29–58. Cambridge, MA: Harvard University Press, 1972.

da Pozzo, Giovanni. *Storia letteraria d'Italia: Il Cinquecento, Tomo 1, 1494–1533*. Padua: PICCIN, 2007.

Dionisotti, Carlo. "Appunti sulla Mandragola." *Belfagor* 39 (1984): 621–44.

Eisenbichler, Conrad, ed., *The Cultural World of Elenora di Toledo Duchess of Florence*. Aldershot: Ashgate, 2004.

Elam, Caroline. "Piazza Strozzi: Two Drawings by Baccio d'Agnolo and the Problems of a Private Renaissance Square." *I Tatti Studies* 1 (1985): 105–35, 274–86.

Elet, Yvonne. "Seats of Power: The Outdoor Benches of Early Modern Florence." *Journal of the Society of Architectural Historians* 61, no. 4 (2002): 444–69.

Fabbri, Lorenzo. *Alleanza matrimoniale e patriziato nella Firenze del '400*. Florence: Leo S. Olschki, 1991.

Ferrieri, Pio. "Lorenzo di Filippo Strozzi e un codice Ashburnhamiano." In *Studi di storia e critica letteraria,* 221–332. Milan: E. Trevisini, 1892.

– ed. *Per le nozze: Vigo-Magenta: Rime Inedite di un Cinquecentista (da un codice Ashburnhamiano)*. Pavia, 1885.

– *Studi di storia e critica letteraria*. Milan: E. Trevisini, 1892.

Ferrucci, Franco. *Il teatro della fortuna: Potere e destino in Machiavelli e Shakespeare*. Rome: Fazi, 2004.

Fido, Franco. *Machiavelli, Guicciardini e storici minori del primo Cinquecento*. Padua: Piccin Nuova Libraria, 1994.

Frantz, David O. "Festum Voluptatis": *A Study of Renaissance Erotica*. Columbus: Ohio State University Press, 1989.

– "'Leud Priapians' and Renaissance Pornography." *Studies in English Literature 1500–1900* 12, no. 1 (1972): 157–72.

Frati, Ludovico, and Corrado Ricci, eds. *Il Sepolcro di Dante*. Bologna: Premiato Stab. Tip. Succ. Monti, 1889.

Gallucci, Margaret A. *Benvenuto Cellini: Sexuality, Masculinity and Artistic Identity in Renaissance Italy*. London: Palgrave Macmillan, 2005.

Gareffi, Andrea. *La scrittura e la festa: Teatro, festa e letteratura nella Firenze del Rinascimento*. Bologna: Il Mulino, 1991.

Geronimus, Dennis. *Piero di Cosimo: Visions Beautiful and Strange.* New Haven: Yale University Press, 2006.

Ghiglieri, Paolo. *La Grafia del Machiavelli: Studiata negli Autografi*. Florence: Leo S. Olschki, 1969.

Gilbert, Felix. "Bernardo Rucellai and the *Orti Oricellari*: A Study on the Origin of Modern Political Thought." *Journal of the Warburg and Courtauld Institutes* 12 (1949): 101–31.

– "The Composition and Structure of Machiavelli's *Discorsi*." *Journal of the History of Ideas* 14 (1953): 136–56.

– "Florentine Political Assumptions in the Period of Savonarola and Soderini." *Journal of the Warburg and Courtauld Institutes* 20, nos. 3–4 (1957): 187–214.

– *Machiavelli and Guicciardini: Politics and History in Sixteenth-Century Florence.* New York: Norton, 1984.

Gioda, Carlo. *Machiavelli e le sue opere*. Florence: G. Barbara, 1874.

Godman, Peter. *From Poliziano to Machiavelli: Florentine Humanism in the High Renaissance*. Princeton: Princeton University Press, 1998.

Godorecci, Barbara J. *After Machiavelli: "Re-Writing" and the "Hermeneutic Attitude*. West Lafayette, IN: Purdue University Press, 1993.

Goldthwaite, Richard. *The Building of Renaissance Florence: An Economic and Social History*. Baltimore: Johns Hopkins University Press, 1980.

– "The Building of the Strozzi Palace: The Construction Industry in Renaissance Florence." *Studies in Medieval and Renaissance History* 10 (1973): 97–194.

– *Private Wealth in Renaissance Florence: A Study of Four Families*. Princeton: Princeton University Press, 1968.

Gordon, D.J. "Giannotti, Michelangelo and the Cult of Brutus." In *Fritz Saxl, 1890–1948: A Volume of Memorial Essays from his Friends in England*, ed. D.J. Gordon, 281–96. London: Thomas, Nelson, 1957.

Gouwens, Kenneth, and Sheryl E. Reiss, eds. *The Pontificate of Clement VII: History, Politics, Culture*. Aldershot: Ashgate, 2005.

Grazzini, Filippo. *Machiavelli narratore. Morfologia e ideologia della novella di Belfagor con il testo della «Favola."* Rome: Laterza, 1990.

Greenblatt, Stephen. *Renaissance Self-Fashioning: From More to Shakespeare*. Chicago: University of Chicago Press, 1980.

– *Will in the World: How Shakespeare Became Shakespeare*. New York: W.W. Norton, 2004.

Gregory, Heather. "The Return of the Native: Filippo Strozzi and Medicean Politics." *Renaissance Quarterly* 38, no. 1 (1985): 1–21.

Grootenboer, Hanneke. *The Rhetoric of Perspective: Realism and Illusionism in Seventeenth-Century Dutch Still-Life Painting*. Chicago: University of Chicago Press, 2005.

Hale, John Rigby. *Florence and the Medici*. London: Phoenix, 2001.

– *Machiavelli and Renaissance Italy*. London: English University Press, 1966.

Hankins. James. *Plato in the Italian Renaissance*. 2 vols. Leiden: Brill, 1990.

Harvey, Michael. "Lost in the Wilderness: Love and Longing in *L'Asino*." In *The Comedy and Tragedy of Machiavelli: Essays on the Literary Works*, ed., Vickie B. Sullivan, 120–37. New Haven: Yale University Press, 2000.

Hillebrand, Karl. *Études historiques et litteraires.* Vol. 1, *Études Italiennes*. Paris: Librairie A. Franck, 1868.

Hornik, Heidi J. *Michele Tosini and the Ghirlandaio Workship in Cinquecento Florence*. Portland: Sussex, 2009.

Hörnqvist, Mikael. "Perché non si usa allegare i Romani: Machiavelli and the Florentine Militia of 1506." *Renaissance Quarterly* 55, no. 1 (2002): 148–91.

Hunt, Lynn., ed. *The Invention of Pornography: Obscenity and the Origins of Modernity*. Cambridge, MA: MIT Press, 1993.

Inglese, Giorgio. *Come si legge un'edizione critica*. Rome: Carocci, 2000.

Jensen, De Lamar, ed. *Machiavelli: Cynic, Patriot or Political Scientist?* Boston: D.C. Heath, 1960.

Jones, Rosemary Devonshire. *Francesco Vettori, Florentine Citizen and Medici Servant*. London: Althone Press, 1972.

Kahn, Victoria. *Machiavellian Rhetoric: From the Counter-Reformation to Milton.* Princeton: Princeton University Press, 2004.

Kent, F.W. *Household and Lineage in Renaissance Florence.* Princeton: Princeton University Press, 1977.

– "Palaces, Politics and Society in Fifteenth-Century Florence." *I Tatti Studies* 2 (1987): 41–70.

– "'Più superba de' quella de Lorenzo': Courtly and Family Interest in the Building of Filippo Strozzi's Palace." *Renaissance Quarterly* 30 (1977): 311–23.

Kristeller, Paul Oskar. *Studies in Renaissance Thought and Letters.* Vol. 4. Rome: Edizioni di Storia e Letteratura, 1996.

Landon, William J. *Politics, Patriotism and Language: Niccolò Machiavelli's* "Secular Patria" *and the Creation of an Italian National Identity.* New York: Peter Lang, 2005.

Limongelli, Luigi. *Filippo Strozzi, Primo Cittadino d' Italia.* Milan: Casa Editrice Ceschina, 1963.

Lowe, Kate. "Conspiracy and Its Prosecution in Italy, 1500–1550: Violent Responses to Violent Solutions." In *Conspiracy and Conspiracy Theory in Early Modern Europe: From the Waldensians to the French Revolution*, ed. Barry Coward and Julian Swann, 35–53. Ashgate: Aldershot, 2004.

Lytle, Guy Fitch. "Friendship and Patronage in Renaissance Florence." In *Patronage, Art and Society in Renaissance Florence.* ed. F.W. Kent and Patricia Simons, 47–62. Oxford: Oxford University Press, 2002.

Macaulay, Thomas. *The Works of Lord Macaulay, Complete, Edited by His Sister, Lady Trevelyan.* 8 vols. London: Longman, Green, 1875.

Mackenney, Richard. *Renaissances: The Cultures of Italy, c. 1300–c.1600.* New York: Palgrave Macmillan, 2005.

– *Sixteenth-Century Europe: Expansion and Conflict.* London: Macmillan, 1993.

Macy, Laura. "Speaking of Sex: Metaphor and Performance in the Italian Madrigal." *Journal of Musicology* 14, no. 1 (1996): 1–34.

Maria, Salvatore Di. "Fortune and the 'Beffa' in Bandello's Novelle." *Italica* 59, no. 4 (1982): 306–15.

Martines, Lauro. *April Blood: Florence and the Plot Against the Medici.* Oxford: Oxford University Press, 2003.

– *Fire in the City: Savonarola and the Struggle for the Soul of Renaissance Florence.* New York: Oxford University Press, 2006.

– "The Gentleman in Renaissance Italy: Strains of Isolation in the Body Politic." In *The Darker Vision of the Renaissance*, ed. Robert S. Kinsman, 77–93. Los Angeles: University of California at Los Angeles Press, 1974.

Martinez, Ronald L. "Comedian, Tragedian: Machiavelli and Traditions of Renaissance Theater." In *The Cambridge Companion to Machiavelli*, ed. John M. Najemy, 206–22. Cambridge: Cambridge University Press, 2010.

Masson, Georgina. *Courtesans of the Italian Renaissance.* New York: St. Martins, 1976.

Mathes, Hamilton R. "On the Date of Lorenzo's *Sacra Rappresentazione di S. Giovanni e Paolo*, Febr. 17, 1491." *Aevum* 25 (1951): 324–8.

Mayer, Thomas. *Thomas Starkey and the Commonwealth: Humanist Politics and Religion in the Reign of Henry VIII.* Cambridge: Cambridge University Press, 2002.

Mazzucconi, Ridolfo. *Leonardo da Vinci.* Florence: Vallecchi, 1943.

Menning, Carol Bresnahan. "The Monte's 'Monte': The Early Supporters of Florence's Monte di Pietà." *Sixteenth-Century Journal* 23, no. 4 (1992): 661–76.

Milani, Virgil I. "Boccaccio in Strozzi's *Commedia Erudita.*" *Italica* 43, no. 4 (1966): 369–74.

– "An Edition of Lorenzo di Filippo Strozzi's Comedy *La Violante* with an Introduction to the *Commedia Erudita* of the Cinquecento." Master's thesis, Catholic University of America.

– "La Nutrice: A Comedy in Hendecasyllabic Blank Verse by Lorenzo di Filippo Strozzi." Master's thesis, Catholic University of America, 1960.

– "The Origins of the Spanish Braggart in Strozzi's *Commedia Erudita.*" *Italica* 42, no. 3 (1965): 224–30.

Molho, Anthony. *Florentine Finance in the Early Renaissance: 1400–1433.* Cambridge: Harvard University Press, 1971.

Moreni, Domenico. *Bibliografia storico-ragionata della Toscana; a sia Catalogo degli scrittori che hanno illustrate la storia delle città, luoghi, e persone delle medesima.* Vol. 2. Florence: Accademia delle belle arti, 1805.

Muir, Edward. *Civic Ritual in Renaissance Venice.* Princeton: Princeton University Press, 1986.

Murray, Peter. *The Architecture of the Italian Renaissance.* Revised ed. New York: Schocken, 1986.

Najemy, John. "Baron's Machiavelli and Renaissance Republicanism." *American Historical Review* 101, no. 1 (1996): 119–29.

– *Between Friends: Discourses of Power and Desire in the Machiavelli-Vettori Letters of 1513–1515.* Princeton: Princeton University Press, 1993.

– ed. *The Cambridge Companion to Machiavelli.* Cambridge: Cambridge University Press, 2010.

– *A History of Florence: 1250–1575.* Malden, MA: Blackwell, 2006.– "Machiavelli and the Medici: The Lessons of Florentine History." *Renaissance Quarterly* 35, no. 4 (1982): 551–76.

Negri, Antonio. *Insurgencies: Constituent Power and the Modern State.* Minneapolis: University of Minnesota Press, 1999.

Olson, Robert J.M. "And They Saw Stars: Renaissance Representations of Comets and Pretelescopic Astronomy." *Art Journal* 44, no. 3 (1984): 216–24.

Osmond, Patricia J. "Conspiracy of 1522 against Cardinal Giulio de Medici: Machiavelli and '*gli esempli delli antiqui.*'" In *The Pontificate of Clement VII: History, Politics, Culture*, ed. Kenneth Gouwens and Sheryl E. Reiss, 55–72. Aldershot: Ashgate, 2005.

Pampaloni, Guido. *Palazzo Strozzi: Il restauro dell'edificio di Gino Cipriani.* Rome: Instituto Nazionale delle Assicurazioni, 1982.

Parel, Antony. *The Machiavellian Cosmos.* New Haven: Yale University Press, 1992.

Park, K., and J. Henderson. "'The First Hospital among Christians': The Ospedale di Santa Maria Nuova in Early Sixteenth-Century Florence." *Medical History* 35 (1991): 164–88.

Parronchi, Alessondro. "La prima rappresentazione della *Mandragola.*" *La Bibliofilia* 64 (1962): 37–86.

Pintor, Fortunato. "Ego Barlachia recensui." *Giornale Storico della Letteratura Italiana* 39 (1902): 103–9.

Plaza, Maria. *Persius and Juvenal.* Oxford: Oxford University Press, 2009.

Pocock, J.G.A. *The Machiavellian Moment: Florentine Political Thought and the Atlantic Republican Tradition.* Princeton: Princeton University Press, 1975.

Polizzotto, Lorenzo. *The Elect Nation: the Savonarolan Movement in Florence, 1494–1545.* Oxford: Clarendon, 1994.

Pozzo, Giovanni da. *Storia letteraria d'Italia: Il Cinquecento,* Tomo 1, *1494–1533.* Padua: PICCIN, 2007.

Prizer, William F. "Creation of a Carnival Song." In *Early Music History: Studies in Medieval and Early Modern Music,* vol. 23, ed. Iain Fenlon, 185–252. Cambridge: Cambridge University Press, 2009.

Procacci, G. *Studi sulla fortuna del Machiavelli.* Rome: Instituto storico italiano per l'età moderna e contemporanea, 1965.

Rabin, Lisa. "Speaking to Silent Ladies: Images of Beauty and Politics in Poetic Portraits of Women from Petrarch to Sor Juana Ines de la Cruz." *Modern Language Notes* 112, no. 2 (1997): 147–65.

Radicchi, Rino. "Descrizione della peste dell' anno 1527 di Niccolò Machiavelli." *Lanternino* 12 (1989): 11–16.

Rebhorn, Wayne A. *Courtly Performances: Masking and Festivity in Castiglione's* Book of the Courtier. Detroit: Wayne State University Press, 1978.

Richardson, Brian. "Evoluzione stilistica e fortuna della traduzione machiavelliana dell''Andria.'" *Lettere Italiane* 25 (1973): 319–38.

– *Manuscript Culture in Renaissance Italy*. Cambridge: Cambridge University Press, 2009.

– *Print Culture in Renaissance Italy: The Editor and the Vernacular Text, 1470–1600.* Cambridge: Cambridge University Press, 2004.

Ridolfi, Roberto. "Composizione, rappresentazione e prima edizione della Mandragola." In *Studi sulle commedie del Machiavelli,* 11–35. Pisa: Nistri-Lischi, 1968.

– "Schede per l'Epistolario del Machiavelli etc." In *G.S.L.I.* 138 (1961): 232–8.

– *Vita di Niccolò Machiavelli.* 2 vols. Florence: Sansoni, 1969.

Rosa, Alberto Asor. *Letteratura italiana: Storia e geografia.* Vol. 2. Turin: Einaudi, 1989.

Rubinstein, Nicolai. "Palazzi Pubblici e palazzi privati al tempo del Brunelleschi." In *Filippo Brunelleschi: La sua opera e il suo tempo.*Vol. 1, ed. Franco Borsi et al., 27–36. Florence: Centro Di, 1980.

Ruggiero, Guido. *Machiavelli in Love: Sex, Self and Society in the Italian Renaissance.* Baltimore: Johns Hopkins University Press, 2007.

Saccone, Eduardo. "Grazia, Sprezzatura, Affettazione." In *Castiglione: The Ideal and the Real in Renaissance Culture,* ed. Robert W. Hanning and David Rosand, 45–67. New Haven: Yale University Press, 1983.

Salza, Abd-el-kader. "Domenico Barlacchi: Araldo, attore e scapigliato fiorentino del secolo XVI." In *Rassenga bibliografica della letteratura Italiana.* Vol. 8, ed. E. Spoerri, 27–33. Pisa: Mariotti, 1901.

Sanctis, Francesco de. *Scrittori d'Italia: Storia della letteratura Italiana: Nuove edizione a cura di Benedetto Croce.* 2 vols. Bari: Laterza, 1912.

Sanuto, Marino. *Diarii.*Ttomo 27, ed. Federico Stefani et al. Venice, 1890.

Sarton, George. "The Scientific Literature Transmitted through Incunabula." *Osiris* 5 (1938): 41–123, 125–245.

Sasso, Genarro. "Intorno alla composizione dei *Discorsi* di Niccolò Machiavelli." *Giornale storico della letteratura italiana* 134 (1957): 482–534 and 135 (1958): 215–59.

Saxl, F. "The Classical Inscription in Renaissance Art and Politics: Bartholomaeus Fontius: Liber monumentorum Romanae urbis et aliorum locorum." *Journal of the Warburg and Courtauld Institutes* 4, nos. 1–2 (1940–41): 19–46.

Saxonhouse, Arlene W. "Comedy, Letters and Imaginary Republics." In *The Comedy and Tragedy of Machiavelli: Essays on the Literary Works,* ed. Vickie B. Sullivan, 57–77. New Haven: Yale University Press, 2000.

Schulz, Juergen. "Vasari at Venice." *Burlington Magazine* 103, no. 705 (1961): 500–11.

Seneca, Lucius Annaeus. Ed. and trans. Susanna Morton Braund. Oxford: Oxford University Press, 2009.

Shapiro, James. *Contested Will: Who Wrote Shakespeare?* New York: Simon and Schuster, 2010.

Shaw, Christine. *The Politics of Exile in Renaissance Italy.* Cambridge: Cambridge University Press, 2000.

Skinner, Quentin. *Foundations of Modern Political Thought.* Vol. 1, *The Renaissance.* Cambridge: Cambridge University Press, 2002.

– *Machiavelli.* Oxford: Oxford University Press, 1981.

Solerti, Angelo. La rappresentazione della Calandria a Lione nel 1548." In *Raccolta di studii critici dedicate ad Alessandro D'Ancona, festeggiandosi il XL anno del suo insegnamento,* 693–9. Florence: Barbèra, 1901.

Stallybrass, Peter, and Allon White. *The Politics and Poetics of Transgression.* London: Methuen, 1986.

Starn, Randolph. *Donato Giannotti and His* "Epistolae": *Biblioteca Universitaria Alessandrina, Rome, Ms 107.* Geneva: Droz, 1968.

Stephens, John M. *The Fall of the Florentine Republic: 1512–1530.* Oxford: Clarendon, 1983.

Stephens, J.N., and H.C. Butters. "New Light on Machiavelli." *The English Historical Review* 97, no. 382 (1982): 54–69.

Strocchia, Sharon T. *Death and Ritual in Renaissance Florence.* Baltimore: Johns Hopkins University Press, 1992.

Strozz, Beatrice Paolozzi. "La Nostra Casa Grande." In *Palazzo Strozzi: Cinque Secoli di Arte e Cultura,* 52–109. Ed. Giorgio Bonsanti. Florence: Nardi Editore, 2005.

Tanselle, G. Thomas. "Texts of Documents and Texts of Works." In *Textual Criticism and Scholarly Editing,* 5–23. Charlottesville: University of Virginia Press, 1990.

Tommasini, Oreste. *La vita e gli scritti di Niccolò Machiavelli nella loro relazione col Machiavellismo: Storia ed esame critico di Oreste Tommasini.* 2 vols. Turin: Ermano Loescher, 1883.

– *La vita e gli scritti di Niccolò Machiavelli nella loro relazione col Machiavellismo: Storia ed esame critic di Oreste Tommasini.* Vol. 2. Rome: 1911.

Toschi, Paolo. *Le origini del teatro italiano.* Vol. 1.Turin: Bollati Boringhieri, 1999.

Trexler, Richard. *Public Life in Renaissance Florence.* New York: Academic Press, 1980.

Trolloppe, T. Adolphus. *Filippo Strozzi: A History of the Last Days of Italian Liberty.* London: Chapman and Hall, 1860.

Villari, Pasquale. *The Life and Times of Niccolò Machiavelli.* Trans. Linda Villari. 3 vols. London: Kegan Paul, Trench and Co., 1883.

– *Niccolò Machiavelli e i suoi tempi.* Vol. 2. Milan: Editore-Libraio, 1895.

– *Niccolò Machiavelli e i suoi tempi.* 3 vols. Florence: Le Monnier, 1882.

Viroli, Maurizio. *Il Dio di Machiavelli e il problema morale dell'Italia.* Rome: Laterza, 2005.

– *Niccolò's Smile.* Trans. Antony Shugar. New York: Farrar, Straus and Giroux, 2000.

Weinstein, Donald. *Savonarola and Florence: Prophecy and Patriotism in the Renaissance.* Princeton: Princeton University Press, 1970.

– *Savonarola: The Rise and Fall of a Renaissance Prophet.* New Haven: Yale University Press, 2011.

Whitfield, J.H. "*Discourses* on Machiavelli VII: Gilbert, Hexter, and Baron." *Italian Studies* 13 (1958): 21-46.

Wooton, David. *Paolo Sarpi: Between Renaissance and Enlightenment.* Cambridge: Cambridge University Press, 1983.

Zagorin, Perez. *Ways of Lying: Dissimulation, Persecution and Conformity in Early Modern Europe.* Cambridge, MA: Harvard University Press, 1990.

Žižek, Slavoj. *Looking Awry: An Introduction to Jacques Lacan through Popular Culture.* Cambridge, MA: MIT Press, 1992.

Index

Page numbers in italics refer to figures.

www.ingramcontent.com/pod-product-compliance
Lightning Source LLC
LaVergne TN
LVHW041112090826
844660LV00061B/789/J

* 9 7 8 1 4 4 2 6 4 4 2 4 3 *